The Great South Sea

THE GREAT SOUTH SEA

English Voyages and Encounters 1570–1750

Glyndwr Williams

Yale University Press
New Haven & London

Set in Bembo by Best-set Typesetter Ltd, Hong Kong
Printed in Great Britain by Biddles Ltd, Guildford and Kings Lynn

Library of Congress Cataloging-in-Publication Data

Williams, Glyndwr.
   The Great South Sea: English voyages and encounters, 1570–1750/
Glyndwr Williams.
   Includes bibliographical references and index.
   ISBN 0–300–07244–9
   1. Oceania—Discovery and exploration—British.   2. Pacific Coast
(South America)—Discovery and exploration—British.   I. Title.
D20.W717   1997
995—dc21   97–18028
                                                                 CIP

A catalogue record for this book is available from the British Library.

10 9 8 7 6 5 4 3 2 1

For Sarah

Contents

Illustrations

Illustrations 1, 3–18, 20–24, 26–42 are reproduced by permission of the the British Library, London; Ill. 2 by permission of the Rex Nan Kivell Collection, National Library of Australia, Canberra; Ill. 19 by permission of the National Portrait Gallery, London; and Ill. 25 by permission of the National Maritime Musuem, Greenwich, London.

Maps

Documents: Abbreviations and Locations

Add. MSS	Additional Manuscripts, British Library
Adm	Admiralty Records, Public Record Office
AMAE	Archives du Ministère des Affaires Etrangères, Paris
AI	Archivo de Indias, Seville
BL	British Library
HBC	Archives of the Hudson's Bay Company, Winnipeg
HCA	High Court of Admiralty Records, Public Record Office
NMM	National Maritime Museum
OHS	Oregon Historical Society Library
OIOC	Oriental and India Office Collections, British Library
PRO	Public Record Office
SP	State Papers, Public Record Office
Saumarez MSS	Papers of Philip Saumarez, formerly held at Sausmarez Manor, St Martins, Guernsey
Wager MSS	Papers of Sir Charles Wager in the Vernon-Wager Collection, Library of Congress, Washington, DC

Preface

This is the story of an obsession. From the sixteenth to the eighteenth centuries many Englishmen were convinced that personal and national fortunes could be won in the distant reaches of the South Sea. For a few, the dream came true: Drake in one century and Anson in another returned home rich. For most, the voyages ended in disappointment, sometimes death. Despite the boldness of the rhetoric employed in print by armchair projectors from Richard Hakluyt to John Campbell, the English presence in the South Sea was essentially parasitic. Most English seamen venturing through the Strait of Magellan or around Cape Horn were raiders, preying on Spanish trade and treasure. This, in Defoe's words, was their 'Inexhaustible Fountain of Gold'. Some were officially authorized – privateers such as Woodes Rogers and George Shelvocke, or the naval captain George Anson – others brought their only commissions, as one buccaneer boasted, 'on the muzzle of our Guns'. For these predators, the South Sea was confined to the waters that lapped the shores of Chile, Peru and Mexico, a hunting ground stretching from Valdivia to Acapulco.

Wider visions were revealed on the maps drawn and published by the enterprising cartographers of Europe, disinclined to leave blank spaces for their rivals to fill. On maps from the late sixteenth century onwards the vast shape of Terra Australis Incognita loomed through the mists; the fabulous Islands of Solomon were marked (though rarely in the same place twice); and to the north the Strait of Anian promised a short passage between Atlantic and Pacific. No English expedition into the South Sea in our period matched the importance of the earlier Spanish and Dutch ventures as far as exploration was concerned, but the hypothetical geography of the Pacific exercised an influence on the promotion of the voyages, and sometimes on their course. Drake landed in New Albion, perhaps looking for the Strait of Anian, and Dampier found New Britain instead of Terra Australis. Satirical and utopian writers were as untrammelled as mapmakers by the constraints and dangers of actual voyaging. Their protagonists ranged across the great ocean from

Neville's Isle of Pines to Swift's Lilliput and on to Defoe's 'New Worlds and new seas, which had never been heard of before'. The encounters of my subtitle were as likely to be imaginative as physical. It was difficult to tell what was real from what was fictitious. Apocryphal voyages, rumours of discoveries, claims by cranks and liars attracted the curious and the uncritical. A study of English enterprise in the South Sea is, to some extent, a study in credulity.

If speculative cartographers and ingenious writers helped to create an image of the South Sea that was alluring and pervasive, the first-hand accounts of the voyages also played their part. They were studded with images and descriptions that took root in the English folk memory. They are there in the original books and in their various reprints, abridgments and serializations, in ballads, plays and engravings: Drake on the *Golden Hind* making the second circumnavigation after Magellan; Selkirk's exile on Juan Fernández, with only cats and goats for company; Dampier's wanderings, journal and pen never far from his hand; Anson and his depleted crew laying their ship alongside the Manila treasure galleon. Notwithstanding the popularity of the published *Voyages*, they were not always reliable guides. Few of the expeditions were without controversy, and the resultant accounts were often exercises in self-justification. I have tried here to scrape away the surface gloss of the printed narratives to reveal what lies beneath. The long Pacific voyages brought their own tensions; there were quarrels, mutinies and desertions. The language of these disputes was often that of the constitutional struggles of late Stuart and early Hanoverian England. Shipboard quarrels became a parody of conflicts at home as accusations of Jacobitism, party rule, cabals and arbitrary government flew thick and fast. At the bottom of the differences was usually some financial interest. There is something of this in the printed accounts. More is to be found in the unpublished records: the magnificent collection of buccaneer journals in the Sloane Manuscripts in the British Library; the boxes of papers in Chancery dealing with the Woodes Rogers expedition; memoranda in several government departments recording the bizarre South Sea proposals of John Welbe; documents scattered throughout public and private archives in Britain, and in France and Spain as well, relating to Anson's voyage.

This book stops in the 1750s. There are links, I argue in my final chapter, between the South Sea projects of George II's reign and Byron's expedition, the first of the surge of Pacific discovery voyages of the next reign; but they soon dissolved. By the time of Cook's voyages there were new men, new motives, almost a new methodology. The Admiralty had come to accept that oceanic exploration was a legitimate part of its operations; science was well represented on the discovery vessels; and Cook and his associates were insistent on the virtues of precise records and prompt publication. Not one of these observations can be said to apply in any general way to the South Sea voyages of the earlier period. Those voyages have their own place in the growing fascination – practical, literary and philosophical – with exotic regions; and it is a place important enough to deserve a book of its own.

In attempting to write that book I have accumulated many debts. My bibliography shows the extent to which I have relied on other scholars, but perhaps I might mention here a few whose work has been especially helpful, not least because they possess expertise in subject-areas that I would have hesitated to enter on my own: Kenneth Andrews, Peter Bradley, Philip Edwards, David Fausett, Derek Howse, Colin Jack-Hinton, Robert Markley, Günter Schilder, Oskar Spate, David Starkey, Norman Thrower and, finally, my good friend, sorely missed, the late Helen Wallis. None of these scholars should be held responsible for the use I have made of their work. I would also like to thank the staff at various libraries and archives: the Public Record Office, the British Library (Printed Books, Manuscript Collections, Map Library, Oriental and India Office Collections), the National Maritime Museum and the Guildhall Library, London; the Archives du Ministère des Affaires Etrangères, Paris; the Archivo de Indias, Seville; the Mitchell and Dixson Libraries at the State Library of New South Wales, Sydney; the Hudson's Bay Company Archives in the Provincial Archives of Manitoba, Winnipeg; the John Carter Brown Library, Providence, the Library of Congress, Washington, DC, and the Library of the Oregon Historical Society, Portland. For help in obtaining many of the illustrations in this book I am indebted to Peter Barber, Alan Frost and Roger Knight. The Department of History at Queen Mary and Westfield College made a generous contribution towards photographic costs, and Edward Oliver of the Department of Geography drew the maps. Finally, I am grateful to Alan Frost, Jonathan Lamb, Peter Marshall and David Quinn, who have read much of this in manuscript. Their comments have saved me from many errors and banalities; those that remain are, I fear, my responsibility.

G.W.
Queen Mary and Westfield College, London

El Mar del Sur: The Spanish Lake

As Europeans in the early sixteenth century became aware of the existence of a great continent across the Atlantic, so they also realized that between the unexpected new landmass and Asia lay a vast ocean. The first European approaches to the Pacific, by the Portuguese in one hemisphere and the Spaniards in another, took place within a few months of each other. In 1512 Portuguese vessels left Malacca, which had been seized by Afonso de Albuquerque only the year before, and sailed through the Java Sea to the Moluccas. When they reached the Banda Sea, the Portuguese were in the border-area between the Indian and Pacific oceans, though of the ocean stretching away to the east Albuquerque's subordinate, Antonio de Abreu, had no awareness as he sailed through the Sunda Islands before turning back.[1]

The next year, and many thousand miles away, came the celebrated sighting of the Pacific Ocean by Vasca Núñez de Balboa. The Spanish chronicler Oviedo tells the story of how in September 1513 Balboa crossed the Isthmus of Panama from the Caribbean and, 'having gone ahead of his company, climbed a hill with a bare summit, and from the top of that hill saw the South Sea . . . he fell upon his knees to the ground and gave great thanks to God for the mercy He had shown him, in allowing him to discover that sea.' Two days later Balboa, accompanied by the fittest of his men, reached the coast and, as the tide came in, waded into the water up to his knees. They were, Oviedo wrote, 'the first Christians to tread the shores of the South Sea; and they scooped up the water in their hands and tasted it, to see whether it was salt.'[2]

---

1. See C.E. Nowell, 'The Discovery of the Pacific: A Suggested Change of Approach', *Pac. Hist. Rev.*, 17 (1947), pp. 1–10.
2. J.H. Parry, ed., *The European Reconnaissance* (New York, 1968), pp. 233, 235. Balboa's 'South Sea' was so named in contradistinction to the 'North Sea' or Atlantic. In Antonio Pigafetta's narrative of Magellan's voyage of 1519–22 the name 'Pacific' appears for the first time, but the ocean 'remained for over two centuries, in fact nearly three, the South Sea not only in common speech (especially that of seamen) but very generally on maps and in academic discourse'. O.H.K. Spate, '"South Sea" to "Pacific Ocean"', *Journal of Pacific History*, XII (1977), p. 206.

It was a moment of high drama, one of many in the story of these years of the Conquista, but it posed more questions than it answered. How far Balboa's Mar del Sur, or South Sea, stretched, and what lands it held, remained to be determined. The process of discovery was a lengthy and hazardous one, but the most important single step came within a few years. In 1519 Ferdinand Magellan, a former Portuguese officer who had served with Albuquerque in the East, commanded a Spanish squadron which left Seville in quest of a southwestern entrance into the Mar del Sur and across to the Spice Islands. Such a route would challenge the hypothesis of Ptolemy, the Alexandrian scholar who in about AD 150 had visualized a southern antipodean continent that was joined to Africa and Asia. The southern oceans, as depicted on the rediscovered Ptolemaic world map that was in circulation from the 1470s onwards, were landlocked seas.

Magellan's fleet of five vessels coasted the shores of South America south of Brazil, wintering as they did so, but found no gap until lat. 53°30'S. This was the entrance to the tortuous, 350-mile-long strait which was to bear Magellan's name. To the north lay Patagonia, the land of giants, where they saw men 'so bygge, that the heade of one of ower men of a meane stature, came but to his waste'.[3] To the south loomed Tierra del Fuego, the land of fire, 'rocky . . . stark with eternal cold'. Most contemporary geographers took this to be the tip of a great landmass, soon to be displayed in all its continental glory on the world maps of the sixteenth century. In an intriguing aside the chronicler of the voyage, Antonio Pigafetta, added that possibly the rocky shores to their south were not part of a mainland but islands, because the crew thought that on some unseen coast they could hear the crashing of the surf. This attracted little attention in comparison with the description of the entry into the Pacific through the Strait, guarded by fearsome giants on one side and with flaming mountains on the other. It was evidence that Ptolemy was wrong, but also a warning that Europeans were entering a strange, alien world where their conventional standards might not apply. Almost 250 years later British and French discovery expeditions were still searching for Patagonian giants.[4]

Battling against squalls, desertions and shipwreck, Magellan got through the Strait in thirty-seven days to reach the open waters of the ocean which he (or his chronicler) named the Pacific. Picking up the South East Trades, the two remaining vessels followed a slanting route across the ocean. For fifteen weeks they sailed across trackless waters, sighting only two small, uninhabited islands on the way (the first probably in the Tuamotus, the second in the Line group). Pigafetta described the horrors of that crossing:

3. From Pigafetta's account as translated in Richard Eden, *The Decades of the Newe World . . .* (London, 1555), reprinted in Edward Arber, ed., *The First Three English Books on America* (Birmingham, 1885), p. 251.
4. See Helen Wallis, 'The Patagonian Giants', in R.E. Gallagher, ed., *Byron's Journals of his Circumnavigation 1764–1766* (Cambridge, 1964), pp. 185–96.

hauynge in this tyme consumed all theyr bysket and other vyttayles, they fell
into suche necessitie that they were inforced to eate the pouder that remayned
thereof beinge full of woormes and stynkynge lyke pysse by reason of the salte
water. Theyre freshe water was also putrifyed and became yelowe. They dyd
eate skynnes and pieces of lether which were foulded about certayne great
ropes of the shyps.[5]

Nineteen men died, and another thirty were incapacitated, before on 6 March
1521 the ships reached Guam in the North Pacific. Magellan was killed soon
after at Cebu in the Philippines, but the remaining two ships sailed south to the
Moluccas. There, at Tidore, they traded for cloves before parting company.
The *Trinidad*, hardly seaworthy, attempted to claw its way back across the
Pacific to the known coast of the Panama Isthmus; but after sailing far north
was forced back to the Moluccas. The *Victoria*, now commanded by Juan
Sebastian del Cano, continued to sail west, through the Portuguese-claimed
waters of the Indian Ocean, and round the Cape of Good Hope. It reached
Seville in September 1522, with a full cargo of spices, but with only eighteen
of those who had set off three years before left on board. In the following
months another seventeen straggled back, to make thirty-five in all who had
completed the first circumnavigation of the globe. Among the mix of
nationalities that made up Magellan's crews was a single Englishman, 'Master
Andrew' of Bristol; but he died near Guam, and was not to be followed into
the Pacific by his compatriots for more than fifty years.

'No other single voyage has ever added so much to the dimension of the
world,' Oskar Spate has written,[6] and dimension is the key word, for
revelation of distances rather than of new lands represented the true importance of Magellan's voyage. The tracks of the *Victoria* and the *Trinidad*
showed the daunting immensity of the Pacific, where a voyage of almost four
months' continuous sailing was marked by the sighting of only two uninhabited specks of land. It proved that Ptolemy's concept of a landlocked southern ocean was wrong, and raised the possibility that the underestimated
Ptolemaic proportions of the globe, so helpful to Columbus's arguments
thirty years before, might also be in error. In practical terms the importance
of the voyage was less clear. The passage through the Strait of Magellan was
a colossal achievement of skill and courage, but the route was hazardous, and
the west–east passage even more fraught because of the difficulty of finding the entrance in the rocky labyrinth of the Chilean coast. This was the
more dismaying because of the assumption that Tierra del Fuego was continental, perhaps an outlier of the great unknown southern continent, which
blocked any route farther south. Despite this, the voyage showed the two
possibilities that were now to dominate European thinking about the Pacific:
a continuous sea passage from the Atlantic into Balboa's Mar del Sur, and

5.   Arber, *First Three English Books on America*, p. 252.
6.   O.H.K. Spate, *The Pacific since Magellan*, I, *The Spanish Lake* (Canberra, 1979), p. 57.

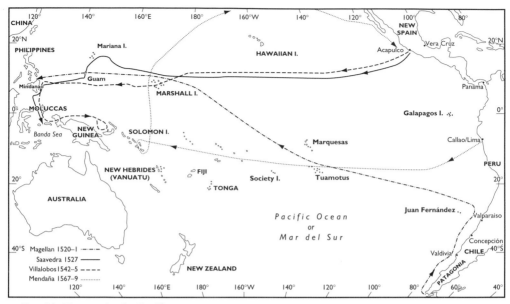

1. Spanish Voyages in the Pacific, 1520s to 1560s.

a way to the Spice Islands, though a long and difficult one, other than the route around the Cape of Good Hope. It was revealing that by far the greater part of Pigafetta's account was devoted to the expedition's adventures and misadventures in the Ladrone Islands, the Philippines and the Moluccas.

There were two further attempts in the 1520s to reach the Moluccas from the east. First was the expedition of García Jofre de Loaysa (1525–7), the successor to Magellan's, which sailed from Spain for the Moluccas by way of the Strait of Magellan; but only one vessel out of four reached the Spice Islands. Another expedition, this time prepared in New Spain, became the first to cross the Pacific from an American port, but again only one vessel got as far as the Moluccas, that of Alvaro de Saavedra. From a navigational if not commercial point of view this was an important voyage, for Saavedra by accident and good fortune sailed in the right belt of ocean (between lat. 10°N. and lat. 13°N.) and at the right season (November to January) to catch the trade winds which were essential for a good westward crossing north of the equator. He touched land at Guam and Mindanao before reaching the Moluccas in 1528, but twice failed to get back to New Spain in the face of adverse winds. To the huge problems of reaching the Moluccas from across the Pacific, either by way of the Strait of Magellan or from the new ports of Mexico's Pacific coast, were added diplomatic complications arising from uncertainty about the location of the Moluccas, and whether they fell within the Portuguese or Spanish spheres of influence as laid down by the Treaty of Tordesillas (1494). The issue was resolved when the Treaty of Zaragoza

(1529) assigned the Moluccas to Portugal. They became part of the eastern section of the Portuguese trading empire in Indonesia, and although the route around the Cape of Good Hope was long and arduous, it was soon dotted with Portuguese way-stations.[7]

Shut out from the Moluccas, Spanish attention turned north to the Philippines, which were without spices, except for some cinnamon on Mindanao, but near to China and its exotic products. The way was prospected by the voyage of López de Villalobos (1542–5) from New Spain, who gave the islands their name ('las Felipinas'), though he grossly underestimated their distance from New Spain. From the Philippines Villalobos sailed south to the Moluccas, and one of his ships reached and named New Guinea (which had probably been reached by the Portuguese in 1526). As far as the Philippines were concerned, conquest and permanent settlement had to wait for the fleet commanded by Miguel López de Legazpi (1564–5). It was two vessels from this fleet, sailing separately, which on the return voyage to Acapulco in 1565 were blown by the prevailing winds along a great semicircular track far to the north. This would soon become the regular trade route of the galleons sailing from Manila (founded in 1571) with Chinese silks and porcelain to Acapulco. There the galleons took on silver for the return voyage, which usually followed Saavedra's route three thousand miles south of the eastbound track. West or east, it was the longest unbroken trading voyage in the world, the eastbound galleons usually taking five or six months, those following the more direct westbound route nearer three months.[8]

On their eastward crossing the galleons made their landfall along the Californian coast before running south to Acapulco. This was a region claimed by Spain, but as yet hardly settled. After the conquest of Mexico by Cortes, the Spaniards had reached the Pacific coast in 1522 and expanded north towards the peninsula of Baja California and south to the Panama Isthmus. Attempts to colonize Baja California failed, and although the Cabrillo–Ferrolo expedition (1542–3) coasted north for almost a thousand miles from La Navidad and landed in modern California, they found neither riches nor any great strait that would provide a short cut through to the Atlantic. Instead, the expedition, linked with the inland explorations of Francisco Vásquez de Coronado, raised new hopes – of an easy sea route across to China or the lands adjoining. Maps of the period marked an encounter with 'Nave de Cataio' somewhere on the Californian coast, and garbled reports of Coronado's inland explorations began to reach Europe.[9]

In South America the conquest of Peru by Pizarro brought under Spanish control a region facing directly out into the Pacific, with its main lines of

7. See Spate, *Spanish Lake*, Ch. 4.
8. See W.L. Schurz, *The Manila Galleon* (New York, 1939), Pt. II.
9. See H.R. Wagner, *Spanish Voyages to the Northwest Coast* (San Francisco, 1929); M.G. Holmes, *From New Spain by Land to the Californias 1519–1668* (Glendale, CA, 1963); Dora Beale Polk, *The Island of California: A History of the Myth* (Lincoln, NB, and London, 1995).

communication centred on Callao, the port of the new capital of Lima. This was followed by expansion to the south into Chile, much of which was conquered by Pedro de Valdivia. In the 1540s municipalities were established along the coast at Santiago and Valparaíso, at Concepción in 1550 and at Valdivia in 1553. Ulloa in 1553 explored the tangled and dangerous maze of islands and straits off the southern coast of Chile, and in 1558 Ladrillero became the first seaman to sail through the Strait of Magellan from west to east. For good measure, he returned the next year, to become also the first to sail through the Strait both ways. But this was the last gasp of the Spanish thrust south. Indian resistance, particularly by the Araucanians just south of Concepción, was fierce, and Valdivia was effectively in border country. Nor did Ladrillero's experiences give much hope of using the Strait of Magellan as a regular route to and from Spain. The return passage through the Strait from the Pacific, aided by the prevailing westerlies, might be made in a few days, but time gained there could very well be lost in trying to identify the western entrance of the Strait among the many openings and inlets of a rocky coast. As Ladrillero reported, 'For a ship sailing into the Strait the mountains seem to close in so that it appears to be a dead end, and one would not venture into it without previous knowledge.'[10] Other offshore explorations revealed the Galapagos Islands and the Juan Fernández group, but they held out no promise of riches or exploitation.

More ambitious projects were also being planned, aimed at finding in the Pacific south of the equator golden prospects to match the new sphere of influence in the Philippines, and to compensate Spain for its exclusion from the Spice Islands. West from Peru and Chile lay an unexplored ocean, in whose vastness might lie the southern continent postulated by geographers from classical times onwards. The voyages of da Gama and Magellan had shown that the Indian Ocean was not enclosed by a vast landmass joined to Asia and Africa as shown in the rediscovered *Cosmography* of Ptolemy; but the modifications that geographers now made to their maps did not lead to the disappearance of an austral continent. Compelling elements in their world view required them to accept that this continent existed. There was a physical necessity for symmetry, and a religious one. The cartographer Gerard Mercator expressed the first when he wrote that, without a compensating southern landmass, the unbalanced world would fall to destruction among the stars. Juan Luis Arias elaborated the second when, seeking royal sanction for his plan to discover the southern continent and convert its inhabitants, he reminded Philip III that God's fiat had established the three geophysical levels of land, water and air, and that the purposeful symmetry of the fiat as laid down in scripture would not be satisfied unless 'in the southern hemisphere there is an uncovered surface of land correspondent, or nearly so, to that which has been discovered in the northern

10. Quoted in J.H. Parry, *The Discovery of South America* (London, 1979), p. 280.

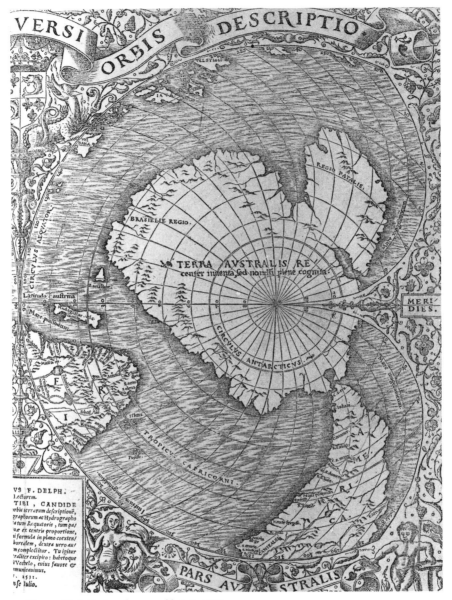

1. Oronce Finé. Section from world map, 1531.

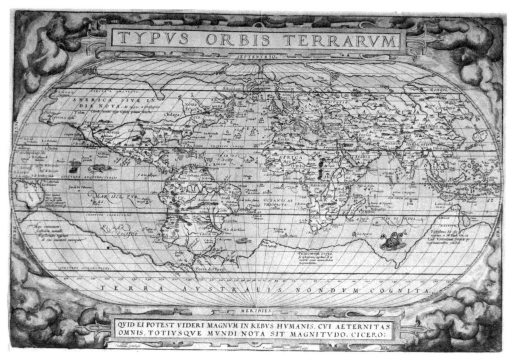

2. Abraham Ortelius. World map, 1570.

hemisphere'.[11] On Oronce Finé's world map of 1531 the continent was shown, and for the first time called 'Terra Australis' (Ill. 1). By the second half of the century many world maps featured such a continent, shown in its most exaggerated form in the maps of the most celebrated geographers of the age, Mercator and Ortelius. As they depicted it, Terra Australis ('nondum cognita', not yet known, as it was explained) occupied almost the whole of the southern hemisphere, stretching towards the equator with New Guinea marked either as a promontory or as an offshore island (Ill. 2). Legend and analogy combined to argue that in these unknown lands were regions of great wealth: Ophir, from whence King Solomon's ships brought him great quantities of gold; the fabulous and still undiscovered Beach (Lucach) of Marco Polo's travels; the islands lying west of the South American coast where, only two generations before the Spanish conquest, the fleet of Tupuc Inca Tupanqui was reported to have found gold, silver and a copper throne. In the great ocean there was room enough for a continent and for a myriad of islands, and in the end it was to be the island myth which was to be the more powerful in Europe's imagining of the

11. Quoted in J.H. Major, ed., *Early Voyages to Terra Australis, Now Called Australia* (London, 1859), pp. 11–13.

Pacific. Marco Polo had reported, rather precisely, that there were 12,700 islands in the 'Sea of India'. Balboa, before he even sighted the South Sea, stated as fact that 'in that sea are many islands where are many huge pearls in large quantity'.[12]

It is difficult to estimate how much authentic information lay behind the reports and rumours of this period. The Portuguese, working their way through the eastern seas beyond the Moluccas, may have made discoveries of which all record has now disappeared. A tantalizing question which continues to exercise scholars is whether the Portuguese might have reached Australia in the first half of the sixteenth century. Such a voyage or voyages would help to explain the mysterious Dieppe maps of the 1540s which show a huge semi-continental landmass, 'Java la Grande', roughly in the position of northern Australia.[13] In the event the Spaniards in South America were the first to undertake a sustained search for the lands thought to lie far out in the Pacific, and in 1565 a scheme was put to the Viceroy of Peru to find 'some islands, called Solomon, which lie over opposite Chile towards the Spice Islands'.[14] Two years later an expedition commanded by Alvaro de Mendaña left Callao in search of those islands. After two months sailing across the ocean the ships reached a large island which they named Santa Ysabel, and then surveyed several other large, high islands between latitudes 5°S. and 10°S. These, predictably, were named Yslas de Salomon, a representation that combined 'magical hope' with 'tactical cunning'.[15] Although Mendaña himself seems to have been convinced that these islands lay off the coast of a great continent to the south, the expedition returned home without further investigation. They did so by way of New Spain, and with so uncertain an estimation of where they had been that the Solomons were to be 'lost' for another two centuries.

Among much else, Mendaña's voyage revealed even more starkly than Magellan's the problems that faced navigators trying to establish their position in the vastnesses of the Pacific Ocean. European voyagers in the sixteenth century had no serious problems in ascertaining latitude. One or more from the seaman's astrolabe, the simple quadrant and the back-staff could be used for celestial observations (of the sun, the Pole Star, the Southern Cross or other constellations). By the first part of the eighteenth century the more sophisticated quadrant, using double reflection, which John Hadley had developed in the 1730s, offered a degree of precision in determining latitude sufficient for all practical purposes. The same could not be said of the problem of finding longitude at sea. As Lawrence C. Wroth once put it, 'the

12. Polk, *Island of California*, pp. 26, 68.
13. On this see Helen Wallis, 'Java la Grande: The Enigma of the Dieppe Maps', in Glyndwr Williams and Alan Frost, eds, *Terra Australis to Australia* (Melbourne, 1988), pp. 39–82.
14. Colin Jack-Hinton, *The Search for the Islands of Solomon 1567–1838* (Oxford, 1969), p. 31.
15. A slight adaptation of Stephen Greenblatt's words in *Marvelous Possessions: The Wonder of the New World* (Chicago, 1991), p. 178 n. 90.

story of man's efforts to determine his longitude at sea is one of the most painful in his slow progress towards the mastery of the world in which he lives.'[16] In principle the solution to the problem was known as early as the 1530s when Gemma Frisius pointed out that, if a reliable clock was carried on shipboard set to the time of the port of departure, the difference between that and local time (as determined by noon observations) would show the degrees of difference between the departure point and the ship's current position. But until the development of chronometers in the eighteenth century, and in particular John Harrison's timepieces, no clock existed that could keep accurate time during the buffetings of long sea voyages.

Instead, for all practical purposes navigators relied on keeping check of their longitude by dead reckoning: this involved a series of different estimates, a mistake in any one of which could produce significant, sometimes catastrophic, errors. As late as 1741 Anson's ships almost ran ashore on the rocks of the Chilean coast at a moment when their sailing-masters estimated that they were nearly three hundred miles out to sea.[17] In the first instance a seaman needed to know the ship's course, and how any reading of the magnetic compass was affected by variation and deviation. Neither could be judged with any confidence in the sixteenth century, for iron fittings on a ship could produce deviation, and although the concept of magnetic variation was understood and the azimuth compass had been developed to measure it (by taking a bearing on a celestial object), the operation was an awkward two-man business. That experienced navigator William Dampier gave some idea of the practical difficulties when he ran into problems near the Cape of Good Hope while in command of the *Roebuck* in 1699.

> Another Thing that stumbled me here was the Variation . . . [which] did puzzle me: Neither was I fully satisfied as to the Exactness of the taking the Variation at Sea: For in a great Sea, which we often meet with, the Compass will traverse with the Motion of the Ship; besides the Ship may and will deviate somewhat in steering, even by the best Helmsman: and then when you come to take an Azimuth, there is often some Difference between him that looks at the Compass, and the Man that takes the Altitude heighth of the Sun; and a small Error in each, if the Error of both should be one way, will make it wide of any great Exactness.[18]

Additional information that was needed before the ship's course could be plotted on a chart or simple traverse board included the amount of leeway caused by wind, the strength and set of currents, and the vessel's

16. Lawrence C. Wroth, *The Way of a Ship: An Essay on the Literature of Navigation* (Portland, ME, 1937), p. 71.
17. See p. 225 below.
18. William Dampier, *A Voyage to New-Holland, &c. In the Year 1699* (London, 1703; citation from collected edition of 1729), p. 95.

speed through the water. The effect of wind and current was almost impossible to measure precisely: much depended on the experience of the master or pilot and his knowledge of particular waters. And although by the end of the sixteenth century the log was in use to determine a ship's speed, its operation was a chancy business as the crew by glass or traditional chants tried to time the rate at which the line spun overboard. A Spaniard spoke for ocean-going seamen of all nations as he explained the difficulties when

> leagues are measured by sea, for there are obstacles that alter or impede the correct calculation of them, such as currents, tides, the ship's speed, because [of] winds, or because of heavy seas athwart the bows, or from other directions. In addition one may be deceived by the ship's burden or bulk; or by reason of the ship's bottom being cleaner or dirtier or whether it carries old or new sails, and whether they are of good or ill pattern, and wet or dry.[19]

The long ocean crossings of the Pacific, where ships might be out of sight of land for months at a time, and where the strength of the deep currents was difficult to gauge, increased the danger of cumulative errors making nonsense of navigation by dead reckoning. This lay behind the navigational problems of the Mendaña expedition of 1567–8, whose chief pilot, Hernan Gallego, underestimated the westward drift of the Pacific Ocean Current. The result was a colossal error in the placing of the Solomon Islands on the maps. Gallego calculated the run from Callao in Peru to the Roncador Reef, just off the Solomons, to be 1638 Iberian leagues (5242 nautical miles); in reality it is 2284 Iberian leagues (7309 nautical miles).[20] The error amounted to a twenty-eight-percent underestimate of the distance covered. Little wonder that the return voyage took longer than anticipated! It was the beginning of a confusion about the location, identity and even existence of the Solomons which took more than two centuries to resolve. As an English geographer grumbled in the mid-eighteenth century, 'there are in the South-Sea many Islands, which may be called Wandering-Islands'.[21]

However flawed its navigation, the first Mendaña expedition marked the beginning of a remarkable sequence of Spanish explorations in the Pacific, with hopes of discovery on a grand scale: Solomon's land of Ophir, Marco Polo's Beach, and perhaps the southern continent not far away. When Mendaña limped into port in New Spain the reaction to the discoveries of the Peruvian expedition was disparaging – no spices, gold or silver, and the inhabitants naked savages. Even so, officials went on to speculate that the islands might provide a base 'for the discovery of the

19. Jack-Hinton, *Search for the Islands of Solomon*, p. 75.
20. Ibid., pp. 71–5.
21. John Green, *Remarks in the Support of the New Chart of North and South America* (London, 1753), p. 43.

mainland, where it is reported that there is gold and silver and that the people are clothed'.[22]

Within fifty years of Magellan's voyage, the outlines of Spain's new Pacific empire were visible. Its eastern rim along the American coastline had been explored from the Strait of Magellan to the Californian coast. From Peru the silver of Potosí and other mines was being shipped along the coast from Callao to Panama on the first stage of its journey to Spain. Farther north, New Spain looked both east and west, for its precious metals went back to Europe by way of Vera Cruz, but by the 1570s it was tapping the trade of the Orient by way of Manila. Through diplomatic treaty and papal bull, buttressed by exploration, conquest and settlement, Spain claimed an ocean whose lands and waters covered one-third of the surface of the globe.

22. See Lord Amherst, ed., *The Discovery of the Solomon Islands* (London, 1901), I, p. lviii; Jack-Hinton, *Search for the Islands of Solomon*, p. 80. For the later Spanish voyages by Mendaña and his successors see pp. 55–8 below.

CHAPTER I

'The World Encompassed': Drake and his Successors

The expeditions sent west into the great ocean from Peru, the first of which was Mendaña's voyage of 1567–8, seemed to mark the next stage of expansion in what now appeared to be a Spanish lake. It was at this moment that the process was interrupted by the unexpected intrusion of another European nation – the English. From the voyage of John Cabot in 1497 onwards, English interest in Cathay, the South Sea and beyond had concentrated on the northern approaches. In common with their European counterparts, English projectors became convinced not only that North America and Asia were separate, but that there was a sea passage through or around North America that would provide a short route from Europe to the lands of the East. This route, the Northwest Passage, took a particular grip on the imagination of Englishmen, repelled by the twin obstacles of distance and Iberian power from the southern routes.

As early as 1527 Robert Thorne, a Bristol merchant resident in Seville, explained in his 'Declaration of the Indies', presented to Henry VIII, how vessels could sail into Arctic waters through the strait separating America and Asia, and so into the South Sea 'on the back side of the New Found Land'. This would soon become a standard objective for expeditions searching for a route to Cathay, but Thorne had other considerations in mind. If the ships should sail 'toward the lands and Islands situated between the Tropikes, and under the Equinoctiall, without doubt they shall finde there the richest landes and Islandes of the world of golde, precious stones, balmes, spices, and other thinges that we here esteeme most.' Thorne saw a short northern route into the Pacific as the only way in which the English, as latecomers, could challenge Spanish and Portuguese domination. 'For out of Spaine they have discovered all the Indies and Seas occidentall, and out of Portugall all the Indies and Seas Oriental: so that by this part of the Orient & Occident, they have compassed the World.'[1]

---

1. Richard Hakluyt, *The Principal Navigations Voyages Traffiques & Discoveries of the English Nation* [1598–1600] (reprint edn, Glasgow, 1902–5), Vol. II, p. 163.

In 1540 or 1541 there were further attempts to win royal support when Roger Barlow, another Bristol merchant who had lived in Seville, presented his 'Geographie' to Henry VIII. Barlow had sailed with Sebastian Cabot in 1526 on a Spanish expedition to search for the 'new spice regions' believed to lie in the South Sea. In what was to become a familiar story, the ships had not even reached the Strait of Magellan, for they were diverted to the River Plate to search for precious metals. Barlow's hope that the King would give his manuscript 'auctoritie to be put fourthe in prynte' was never realized, though his exhortations on future discovery were to anticipate the writings of Richard Eden, John Dee and the Hakluyts. The aspirations of generations of English projectors and mariners were outlined as Barlow repeated Thorne's arguments for the discovery of a Northwest Passage that would take ships 'unto the southe see on the backside of the indies occidentales' by a much shorter route than those followed by Spanish and Portuguese vessels.[2]

A year or so later, in 1542, the Dieppe hydrographer Jean Rotz presented his magnificent 'Boke of Idrography' to Henry VIII. Its charts included one of the earliest representations of Java la Grande, a landmass straddling the southern reaches of the Indian and Pacific oceans and reaching almost as far north as the equator.[3] If the King or his advisers showed any interest in this, it is not recorded, and like Barlow's 'Geographie' the spectacular decorative atlas of Rotz disappeared from contemporary view. Even so, by the 1560s the maps of the Pacific were showing the main areas of European interest in clearer form, though on most the ocean is still too narrow. As late as the 1570s Juan Lopez de Velasco was underestimating by half the distance along the galleon route between New Spain and the Philippines that had been pioneered by Urdanata in 1565. From Giacomo Gastaldi's map of 1561 onwards the strait separating Asia and America in the far north has a name – Anian. In the south the influential world maps of the Flemish cartographers Mercator (1569) and Ortelius (1570) show a huge southern continent. Both Anian and Terra Australis were to play a part in the first English venture into the Pacific.

Knowledge of Spanish overseas activities seeped back to other European countries both through the printed word and through personal contacts. Until the work of the collector and editor, Richard Hakluyt, late in the century the English lagged behind their continental neighbours in the printing of Spanish accounts. An exception was the publication in 1555 of Richard Eden's *Decades of the Newe Worlde*, which included translations of some of the most important Spanish exploration narratives. Among these was Pigafetta's account of Magellan's voyage, 'one of the greatest and most marveylous thynges that hath bynne knowen to owre tyme'. To this Eden added details of the riches of the East and of the Moluccas, and of navigation in the southern hemisphere generally. Eden's was a 'world view . . . [He]

2.   E.G.R. Taylor, ed., *A Brief Summe of Geographie* [by Roger Barlow], (London, 1932), p. 182.
3.   See Helen Wallis, ed., *The Maps and Text of the Boke of Idrography Presented by Jean Rotz to Henry VIII* (Oxford, 1981).

opened the New World, the Strait of Magellan, the East Indies, Cathay, Muscovy, and lesser regions to Englishmen's eyes.'[4]

An important, if not always reliable, channel of communication was provided by the group of English merchants resident in Spain. In 1572 the merchant Henry Hawks, who had lived both in Seville and Mexico City, gave the elder Richard Hakluyt (lawyer, and cousin of the more famous Richard Hakluyt) information, shaky in detail it is true, about Mendaña's discovery of the Solomon Islands.[5] Over the years the importance of this discovery swelled as rumour built on rumour. So in 1587 a Portuguese captured off the River Plate by the Earl of Cumberland's men told them that Mendaña had brought back forty thousand pesos of gold 'besides great stores of cloves and ginger'.[6] Hawks's friendship with Diego Gutierrez, one of the first to make the voyage from Mexico to the Philippines, enabled him to report to Hakluyt on the wealth of those 'Islands of China'. They were rich in gold, pearls and spices, Gutierrez had told him, adding for good measure that 'if there bee any Paradise upon earth, it is in that countrey . . . and as for treasure, there is abundance'.[7]

Hawks also passed on notes on New Spain which included 'a Spanish search for the North-West Passage from its supposed south-western end, and mentions that it is known in New Spain as the "Englishmen's Strait", and lies not far from China'.[8] To rely only on accounts in print would be to underestimate the amount of information available to the English. A document of the 1560s shows knowledge in England of Coronado's distant explorations north from New Spain. It claimed that he had found the western entrance of the Northwest Passage and had also encountered Chinese ships on the American coast, 'laden with merchandize, having on their flagge hanging out of the foreshippes certain birds painted, called Alcatrizae [pelicans]. The mariners also declared by signs that they came out of Cataya into the port in 30 days.'[9] Reports such as this raised English hopes of a narrow Pacific Ocean in its northern reaches, a point taken up by yet another document of the same period: 'And be yt remembered this passage at 67 degrees to Catayo is but 6000 leagues, and to pass by the straighte of Magilanus to the said Cataya is 15000 leagues.'[10]

In the 1570s, as relations with Spain worsened, plans were afoot in England for ventures into the South Sea. Behind them were those expansionist, militantly Protestant members of Court and Council who saw both material

4. See John Parker, *Books to Build an Empire* (Amsterdam, 1965), pp. 45, 48.
5. See E.G.R. Taylor, ed., *The Original Writings and Correspondence of the Two Richard Hakluyts* (London, 1935), I, p. 108.
6. Spate, *Spanish Lake*, p. 126.
7. Taylor, *Writings of the Hakluyts*, p. 110.
8. E.G.R. Taylor, *Tudor Geography 1485–1583* (London, 1930), pp. 34, 112–13.
9. Ibid., p. 266. The report had originally been printed in Gómara's *Historia General de las Indias* (1552).
10. Taylor, *Tudor Geography*, p. 267.

and spiritual profit in attacking Spain in the New World. The more cautious attitude of the Queen, supported by the Lord Treasurer, Burghley, who were both anxious to avoid open war with Spain, often made it difficult for the sponsors of the new enterprises to reveal their true objectives. By the mid-1570s two rival ventures were taking shape and bidding for official and mercantile support. One was associated with Humphrey Gilbert, who in 1565 had petitioned the Queen for a grant for the discovery of the North-west Passage. His request had been turned down because of the opposition of the Muscovy Company (founded in 1555), which held monopoly rights over ventures in northern waters. However, his lengthy 'DISCOURSE of a Discoverie for a new Passage to Cataia', written the next year, survived and was eventually printed in 1576, when it was used as supporting material for the Arctic expeditions of Martin Frobisher. Like Gilbert's earlier proposal, those ventures sought a route to the Pacific by way of the Northwest Passage (Ill. 3).

Before this, a group of West Countrymen including Richard Grenville and William Hawkins came near to obtaining the Queen's blessing for a venture that would follow a southern route. In March 1574 Grenville and his associates petitioned the Queen 'for discovery of sundry Ritche and unknownen landes'.[11] At the same time they wrote to the Earl of Lincoln, Lord High Admiral since the beginning of the reign. The letter asked him 'as the chief of the enterprise' to commend the venture to the Queen and promised him that 'the whole shalbe performed wytheoute her Majestie's chardge or adventure, or any other her Highnes' trouble, more then her gratious allowance of our good meaninge and dyrection of our proceadinges'.

Details of the venture are set out more fully in two other documents. The first is a theoretical tract on the best way to discover the Northwest Passage or Strait of Anian, which reads as a direct confutation of Gilbert's (as yet unpublished) 'Discourse'. The author allows that the northern route is much shorter in terms of distance than the proposed route by the Strait of Magellan, but points out that navigation in Arctic waters is possible for only three months of the year, and even then 'bothe daie and nighte being freesing Colde, not only men's bodies but also the very lines and tacklinge are so frozen that with very greate difficulties Maryners can handell their Sailes.' A southern route, by contrast, with ships leaving England in the summer to reach the Strait of Magellan in September or October, would see them pass into the South Sea at the most favourable season, the southern spring. They would then sail north across the equator and on to the western entrance of the Strait of Anian, reaching there in the northern summer. The vessels, in effect, would follow the sun. Whereas the lands bordering a northern route offered little of value, by following the proposed southern track

11. The relevant documents were first printed in R. Pearse Chope, 'New Light on Sir Richard Grenville', *Trans. of the Devonshire Association*, 49 (1917), pp. 210–82, from which the following quotations have been taken (pp. 221, 238, 241, 245).

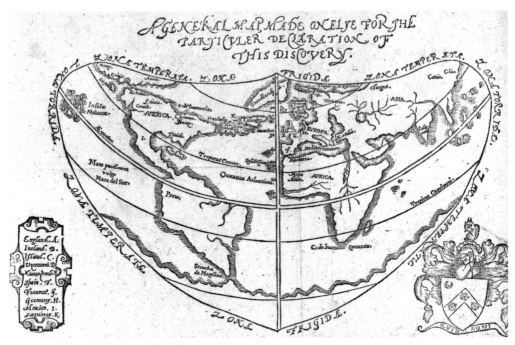

3. Humphrey Gilbert. 'A General Map', 1576.

we are assured to expecte golde, Siluer, Pearle, Spice, with grayne, and such most precious marchaundize, besides countries of most excellent temperature to be Inhabited. If we think it necessary and if we aryve to timely to enter the said straighte of *Anian*, yet have we *Cathaia* and all the *Orientall Indians* open into vs for trafique, besides the waste Occean to the Southe, which cannot but be replenished with numbers of Ilandes, The leaste wherof might abundantly suffice to furnishe our navie with the aforenamed comodoties.

The second document changed the emphasis in that there was no mention of the Strait of Anian or of Cathay; the enterprise was now seen as one exclusively to the southern hemisphere. The objectives were 'Landes Islandes and Countries southewarde beyonde the aequinoctiall or where the Pole Antartik hath anie elevation aboue the Horison', such lands not to be in the possession of 'anie Christian Prince in Europe'. This could have been a reference to the great southern continent, to the Solomons, or to those parts of the South American continent that lay outside Spanish control. That the shift was not accidental was shown by a more general exhortation: 'since the Portugall hathe atteined one parte of the newefounde worlde to the Este, the Spaniarde an other to the Weste, the Frenche the third to the Northe, nowe the fourthe to the Southe is by God's providence lefte for Englonde.'

On the practical side, the documents claimed that the promoters already had four 'Ships of our owen wel prepared', and requested in return royal consent to form a company. An undated draft seems to show that the Queen authorized Letters Patent approving the venture, which 'wee doe well like of and allow the said good mynde and entreprise of our said subjectes', and granting the adventurers 'the full and sole use' of their discoveries.[12] At this stage the process came to a halt. Our only evidence of what happened is indirect, but seems persuasive enough. It comes from John Oxenham, marauder along the Spanish Main and associate of Francis Drake, who crossed the Isthmus of Panama and in a small pinnace raided Spanish shipping in the South Sea. He was captured in 1577, and was interrogated by the Spaniards.[13] Oxenham claimed that 'Grenville bought two ships, and was about to buy two or three more, when the Queen revoked the licence, because she had learnt that beyond the Strait of Magellan there were settlements made by Spaniards.'[14] Two other members of Oxenham's crew, also under interrogation, added further details. The pilot said that he had heard that a security of £30,000 to £40,000 was demanded, 'that they would not touch lands belonging to King Philip, and on this account the expedition was frustrated.' The master pinned the blame even more firmly on the Queen, though he can only have been repeating common gossip. He is reported as telling his questioners: 'The Queen did not wish him [Grenville] to come for fear he might do harm in the possessions of her brother King Philip. Witness understands that if the Queen should die, many will come and pass through the Strait and found settlements. The Queen is the cause that no one comes.'

Instead, the first attempt was to be by the northwest, well away from the Strait of Magellan and any Spanish colonies, and it was entrusted to Martin Frobisher. The Muscovy Company had changed its attitude since its opposition to Gilbert ten years earlier, and it now granted a licence to Frobisher and his main associate, Michael Lok (the London agent of the Company). Gilbert's 'Discourse' of 1566 was published in 1576, and although some of its geographical arguments were becoming out of date, it served as a prospectus for the new venture. It stressed the commercial advantages that the discovery of a Northwest Passage would bring English merchants, who would be able to undersell their Spanish and Portuguese rivals in the South Sea and the East Indies: 'Also we may saile to divers marveilous riche Countries . . . out of both their jurisdictions, trades and traffiks, wher ther is to be found great aboundance of gold, silver, precious stones, Cloth of golde, silkes, all maner of Spices, Grocery wares, and other kindes of Merchandize.'[15] Gilbert also

---

12. Ibid., pp. 241, 245.
13. See J.A. Williamson, *The Age of Drake* (London, 1938), Ch. VIII.
14. The evidence from Oxenham and his crew is printed in Z. Nuttall, ed., *New Light on Drake* (London, 1914), pp. 5–12.
15. D.B. Quinn, ed., *The Voyages and Colonising Enterprises of Sir Humphrey Gilbert* (London, 1940), I, pp. 160, 161.

brought Coronado's supposed discoveries into the argument, this time with the suggestion, easy to make, perilously difficult to put into effect, that the English might establish a colony on the west coast of North America.[16] Given the Queen's sensitivity to settlement near Spanish areas of influence, this would perhaps have better been omitted when the manuscript was put into print.

Unlike Grenville's abortive venture, known rather than unknown lands were the objective of Frobisher's voyage of 1576. Lok made this clear:

> Neither nede I [say any] thing touching the naturall Riches and infinite T[reas]or, and the great Traffic of rich Merchandise that is in those countries of Cathay, China India and o[ther] countries thereabouts, for that every boke of history and cosmography of those parts of the world, which are to be had in every Prynters shop, does declare the same at large.[17]

The fiasco of Frobisher's voyages of 1576, 1577 and 1578, diverted from their original objective by the finding of 'gold' on the east coast of Baffin Island, has been told many times.[18] Less familiar perhaps is the disappointment in geographical terms that resulted from his failure. Again, our witness is Michael Lok, whose scathing report covers all three voyages. He described the jubilant reaction when Frobisher returned from the first voyage and claimed that he had found 'the West Sea, whereby to pass to Cathay and to the East India'. For Lok, bankrupted and imprisoned by the failure of Frobisher's next two voyages, total disillusionment followed and he complained that Frobisher's claims were false, and that no progress had been made towards the discovery of a Northwest Passage.[19]

Frobisher's quest, at least in its original form, represented one strand of English interest in the South Sea, that is, simply as part of a sea route leading to the riches of Asia, usually and vaguely termed 'Cathay'. This might be by the northwest, as Frobisher intended, or by the northeast, where the ships of the Muscovy Company had tried to batter their way through the ice of the Russian Arctic. The group of investors behind Frobisher was 'The Company of Cathay', a title which fairly represents the main objective of Frobisher's first voyage, though it is noteworthy how much more capital was invested in the gold-mining activities of the second and third voyages than in the first expedition, bound on northern discovery. A northern passage would not only provide a short route, but would keep English ships well clear of the centres of Spanish activity along the Pacific seaboard of south and central America. This was one of the main arguments of Richard

16. Ibid., p. 161.
17. R. Collinson, ed., *The Three Voyages of Martin Frobisher* . . . (London, 1867), p. 83.
18. In, for example, Samuel Eliot Morison, *The Great Explorers: The European Discovery of America* (New York, 1978), Chs IX, X.
19. Collinson, *Voyages of Frobisher*, pp. 83, 336.

Willes's enlarged and retitled 1577 edition of Eden's *Decades* of 1555. The
preface by Willes caught something of the new interest, intellectual as well
as mercantile, which had followed the voyages of da Gama and Columbus:
'Here began the studie of Geographie, that euer since Ptolomens raigne laye
troden vnder foote, & buried in dust and ashes, to spring vp agayne . . . all
Christians, Iewes, Turkes, Moores, Infidels & Barbares be this day in loue
with Geographie.'[20]

As Frobisher returned from the second of his three expeditions another was
preparing to sail, and the voyage of Francis Drake in 1577–80 showed a
different, more aggressive aspect of English interest in the Pacific. In personal
and national terms it sprang from the growing tension with Spain. The
choice of Drake as commander was significant, for his reputation was that of
a bold raider of the Spanish Main, whose narrow escape from the trap of San
Juan de Ulúa in 1568 had created in him an obsessive desire for revenge. Like
Frobisher's voyages, Drake's was privately organized. The syndicate that
financed his expedition included men close to the Queen such as Lincoln,
who had been involved with Grenville's project of 1574, the Earl of Leicester, and Sir Francis Walsingham, Secretary of State since 1573 and involved
in most of the overseas enterprises of the period. The Queen herself may
have invested in the venture. But it was not a government enterprise as such.
No royal ships were involved; there is no conclusive evidence that Drake,
despite his claims, carried a royal commission;[21] and much of the secrecy
surrounding the expedition seems to have arisen from the need to keep news
of its destination from Burghley and, presumably, from the ever-watchful
Spanish agents in London. If direct conflict with Spain in America was not
envisaged in what has survived of Drake's draft instructions, then arguably
the establishment of trade and perhaps even bases along the Chilean coast
south of the Spanish presence was very much to the fore. In terms of
objectives and promoters there were links with Grenville's earlier proposals.
Certainly, Oxenham was insistent that after the rebuff to Grenville then
Drake 'had often spoken to witness [Oxenham] saying that if the queen
would grant him the licence he would pass through the Strait of Magellan
and found settlements over here in some good country'.[22]

  For so celebrated a voyage, the motives behind Drake's expedition are
hazy and disputed. The discovery by Professor E.G.R. Taylor in 1929 of a
fire-damaged draft plan for the voyage now forms the starting point of any
discussion, but the relationship of the draft plan to Drake's final instructions
is not known, and the gaps in the draft make its interpretation a chancy
business. Professor Taylor's ingenious reconstruction of that part of the plan
dealing with the motives for the voyage runs as follows. Drake

20. [Richard Eden], *The History of Trauayle in the West and East Indies* (London, 1577), preface.
21. What evidence there is has been printed in Nuttall, *New Light*, pp. xxxix–liv.
22. Ibid., pp. 9–10.

*shall enter the Strait of Magellan*as *lying in 52 degrees of* the pole, and *having passed therefrom into* the South Sea then *he is to sail so* far to the northwards as *xxx degrees seeking* along the said coast *aforenamed like* as of the other to find out pla*ces meet* to have traffic for the vent*ing of commodities* of those her Majesty's realms. Wh*ereas at present* they are not under the obedience of *any* christian prince, so there is great hope of *gold, silver*, spices, drugs, cochineal, and *divers other* special commodities such as may *enrich her* Highness' dominions, and also *put* shipping a-work greatly. And *having* gotten up as afore said in the xxx degrees in the South Sea (if it shall be thought *meet* by the afore named Francis Drake to pro*ceed so* far), then he is to return by the same way homewards as he went out.[23]

Interpretations of this by historians have varied. Some have seen Drake's instructions, draft or otherwise, as a blind to cover the real objective of the voyage – a plundering raid along the coasts of Spanish America with the ships carrying silver from Peru to Panama as a prime target.[24] In their favour, they can point to what Drake actually did on the voyage, and its obvious link with his crossing of the Panama Isthmus in 1573 during a plundering expedition in the Caribbean. According to a later account by his nephew John, it was from a 'goodly and great high Tree' on the Isthmus that Drake, following in the steps of Balboa sixty years before, first glimpsed 'the sea of which he had heard such golden reports, hee besought Almightie God of his goodnesse to give him life and leave to sayle once in an English Ship in that sea.'[25]

Those historians who take the plan at face value fall into two schools of thought. Professor Taylor was convinced that 'the said coast *aforenamed*' was that of the great unknown southern continent, Terra Australis Incognita,[26] and there are some fragments of evidence that show that such interest was, at least, in the air at this time. These include the abortive Grenville project of 1574 with its vague reference to lands 'southewarde beyonde the *aequinoctiall'*.[27] The arcane figure of John Dee, philosopher, astrologer, magician and scholar, also seems to have been involved. Dee's main geographical interests were in the northern hemisphere, and he had acted as adviser to Frobisher; but in 1577, the year of Drake's departure, Dee was writing in

23. See E.G.R. Taylor, 'The Missing Draft Project of Drake's Voyage of 1577–80', *Geographical Journal*, 75 (1930), pp. 44–7. Professor Taylor's interpolations are shown in italics.
24. See, for example, Williamson, *Age of Drake*, pp. 172–3.
25. See I.A. Wright, ed., *Documents Concerning English Voyages to the Spanish Main, 1569–1580* (London, 1932), p. 300; Kenneth R. Andrews, *Trade, Plunder and Settlement: Maritime Enterprise and the Genesis of the British Empire, 1480–1630* (Cambridge, 1984), p. 132. The moment when Drake climbed a tree to view the Pacific was dramatized in one of the earliest operas performed on the English stage, William Davenant's *The History of Sir Francis Drake* (1659). I am grateful to Robert Shore for this reference.
26. See E.G.R. Taylor, 'Master John Dee, Drake and the Straits of Anian', *Mariner's Mirror*, 15 (1929), pp. 125–30; 'More Light on Drake', *Mariner's Mirror*, 16 (1930), pp. 134–51.
27. See above, p. 17.

terms that indicated that a voyage (presumably Drake's) was on foot to discover either Beach, Marco Polo's golden Lucach now thought to lie near New Guinea, or the Strait of Anian – or both![28]

Contemporary geographical speculation might support Dee, but it seems a slim foundation on which to fit out an expedition of five ships. A more recent interpretation of Drake's draft plan copes rather differently with 'the said coast *aforenamed*'.[29] To sail from the Strait of Magellan 'to the north-wards' as far as lat. 30°S. made little sense in the context of a search for the great southern continent. It did fit a plan to turn north once through the Strait, for the Spaniards were not thought to be on the coast south of Peru. That they had in fact established small settlements as far south as Valparaíso in lat. 40°S. by mid-century (and had moved on to the island of Chiloé in lat. 43°S. in 1567) does not necessarily invalidate this interpretation. Oxenham's evidence seems to show that the Queen was aware of Spanish settlements beyond the Strait of Magellan, but gives no clue as to whether their precise location was known. Certainly the great Ortelius map of 1570, which Drake probably had on board, showed no Spanish settlement south of lat. 33°S.[30] And in case there were any, then Drake's instructions gave him discretion – if he 'thought *meet*' – to stop short of lat. 30°S. Drake's reconnaissance of the Atlantic coast – 'the other [coast]' of the draft plan according to this interpretation – from the River Plate southwards, which he carried out before wintering in Patagonia, was to be matched by a similar excursion on the Pacific side.

Various parts of the jigsaw now fall into place: the secrecy about the voyage, and in particular the attempt to keep it from Burghley; journal entries before the Strait was reached which seemed to show that 'Peru' (a larger and vaguer stretch of territory than the modern state) was the destination; and the declaration of John Winter, one of Drake's captains who turned back in the Strait, that the expedition was 'bound for the partes of America for discoveries and other causes of trade of marchaundizes necessarie and requisite'. If this interpretation is correct, and the weight of the evidence supports Professor Andrews, then the voyage as it turned out went well beyond the outlines suggested in the draft plan. It was to be more daring, more controversial, more tragic and, in the end, more famous than could ever have been imagined at its inception. As Drake said during its course, he came 'for a greater purpose than that of seizing vessels'.[31] For both English and Spanish it was to set the tone for much that followed in the South Sea.

28. See Taylor, *Tudor Geography*, pp. 114–17; William H. Sherman, *John Dee: The Politics of Reading and Writing in the English Renaissance* (Amherst, MA, 1995), pp. 175–7.
29. See K.R. Andrews, *Drake's Voyages* (London, 1967), Ch. 3; 'The Aims of Drake's Expedition of 1577–1580', *American Historical Review*, 73 (1968), pp. 724–41; 'Beyond the Equinoctial: England and South America in the Sixteenth Century', *Journal of Imperial and Commonwealth History*, 10 (1981), pp. 4–24.
30. See Andrews, 'Beyond the Equinoctial', p. 21 n. 3.
31. Nuttall, *New Light*, pp. 10, 318.

Drake sailed from Plymouth in late 1577 with five vessels. The largest, his flagship *Pelican* (later renamed the *Golden Hind*), a new ship of about 150 tons in burthen and 70 feet in length,[32] the smallest, the *Christopher*, a mere 15 tons. For its size the *Golden Hind* was well-fitted, 'stout and strong' as the captured Portuguese pilot Nuño da Silva described her, with eighteen guns and eighty or so men. Among these were musicians, a chaplain (Francis Fletcher) who kept a good journal, and a group of gentlemen-adventurers. Her armament and large crew would make her more than a match for any Spanish vessel she was likely to meet in the South Sea; but that this was the destination, and not Alexandria, as had been given out, was kept a close secret until the ships were well out to sea. William Markham, master of the *Elizabeth*, complained in resolutely unheroic fashion that had he known of this deception 'he would have been hanged in England rather than have come on this voyage'.[33] It may have been that Markham's attitude was shared by others on board, for the *Elizabeth* was never to make the full voyage.

By the time that Drake reached the first rendezvous in the South Sea at lat. 30°S. on the coast of Chile, more than a year after leaving Plymouth, only his own vessel was left. Casualties, self-inflicted and otherwise, had affected the expedition from the moment when Drake executed Thomas Doughty, the leading gentleman-volunteer, at Port San Julian in Patagonia. This had been the scene of Magellan's mutiny almost sixty years earlier, and the gibbet where his mutineers had been hanged was still standing. Doughty, as befitted his rank, was beheaded, not hanged, after a trial where the charges were uncertain, and where only Drake's determination to rid the expedition of someone he saw as a disruptive force is clear. In Drake's view, Doughty was responsible for 'these mutinies and discords that are growne amongst us . . . Gentlemen are verye necesarye for governements sake in the voyadge,' Drake reflected, but 'I must have the gentleman to hayle and draw with the mariner, and the maryner with the gentleman.'[34]

From Port San Julian the little fleet, now consisting of only three ships, headed for the Strait of Magellan. They threaded their way through in sixteen days, compared to Magellan's thirty-seven, but it was still not an easy passage, as Fletcher stressed:

> The frete [strait] is very crooked, hauing many turnings, and as it were shuttings up, as if there were no passage at all, by meanes whereof we were often troubled with contrary windes, so that some of our ships recouering a

---

32. For a summary of the various estimates of the dimensions of the *Golden Hind* see John Sugden, *Sir Francis Drake* (New York, 1990), p. 99n.

33. Quoted in Norman Thrower, ed., *Sir Francis Drake and the Famous Voyage, 1577–1580* (Berkeley and Los Angeles, 1984), p. 4.

34. This and the following quotations are from N.M. Penzer, ed., *The World Encompassed . . . Carefully Collected out of the Notes of Master Francis Fletcher* [1628] (London, 1926), pp. 164, 28, 31, 132, 33.

cape of land, entring another reach, the rest were forced to alter their course
and come to anchor where they might.

On 6 September 1578, the *Golden Hind* sailed out of 'this labrinth' and
into open water, where it turned north. Drake's rendezvous in case of
separation – '30 deg. or thereabouts, upon the coast of Peru' – is further
evidence that the South American coast, and not the southern continent, was
Drake's first objective in the South Sea. Two days onto the new course an
'outragious & furious' storm broke over the ships and continued for fifty-six
days so that they travelled 'without the sight of sonn moon or starrs'.
Fletcher's account strained at the boundaries of language in its efforts to
convey the desperate plight of Drake's little squadron:

> The winds were such as if the bowels of the earth had set all at libertie, or as
> if all the clouds vnder heaven had been called together to lay their force vpon
> that one place. The seas, which by nature and of themselues are heavie, and
> of a weightie substance, were rouled vp from the depths, euen from the roots
> of the rockes, as if it had beene a scroll of parchment . . . Our anchors, as false
> friends in such a danger, gaue ouer their holdfast, and as if it had beene with
> the horror of the thing, did shrinke down to hide themselues in this miserable
> storme, committing the distressed ship and helplesse men to the vncertain and
> rowling seas, which tossed them, like a ball in a racquet. In this case, to let fall
> more anchors would auail us nothing: for being driuen from our first place of
> anchoring, so vnmeasurable was the depth, that 500 fathome would fetch no
> ground. So that the violent storme without intermission; the impossibility to
> come to anchor; the want of opportunitie to spread any sail; the most mad
> seas; the lee shores; the dangerous rocks; the contrary and most intollerable
> winds; the impossible passage out; the desperate tarrying there; and ineuitable
> perils on euery side, did lay before vs so small likelihood to escape present
> destruction, that if the speciall prouidence of God himselfe had not supported
> vs, we could neuer haue endured that woful state.

When the storm finally subsided, the *Golden Hind* was alone. The *Marigold*
had disappeared and was never seen again; while the *Elizabeth*, commanded
by John Winter, had turned back through the Strait. Once more, if Winter's
report is to be trusted, it was the master, Markham, who refused to accept his
captain's suggestion that they should make for the Moluccas in the hope of
meeting Drake there. Markham, it seems, was a man given to some extrava-
gance of gesture: 'the Master did utterly dislike of it, saying that he would
fling himself overboard rather than consent to any such voyage.'[35] (Winter

---

35. Richard Hakluyt, *The Principall Navigations, Voiages & Discoveries of the English Nation* [1589]:
     facsimile edn with an introduction by D.B. Quinn and R.A. Skelton and index by Alison
     Quinn (Cambridge, 1965), p. 643.

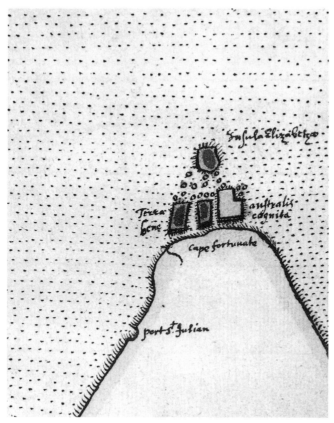

4. A section from Francis Fletcher. Sketch map of the tip of South America, 1578 (top is south).

was home by June 1579, bearing news of the events of the first part of the voyage, including Doughty's execution.) During the storm's fury the *Golden Hind* had been driven south back across the western mouth of the Strait of Magellan and into an unknown and unsuspected archipelago of islands on the far side. This was the first real evidence that the south shore of the Strait might not be the northern edge of a continental landmass. Fletcher's map of the region (Ill. 4) has the ironic notation here 'terra australis bene cognita', and his text insisted that 'We have by manifest experience put it out of doubt to be no continent of mainland but broken islands disseevered by many passages and compassed about with the sea on every side.'[36] Drake had not sailed right round Tierra del Fuego, and whether the most southerly of the islands he reached, named by him Elizabeth Island, is today's Henderson Island, or Cape Horn (Island) fifty miles to the southeast, is uncertain.[37] It

---

36. Penzer, *World Encompassed*, p. 34.
37. For the argument that Drake landed at Cape Horn see D.B. Quinn, *Drake's Circumnavigation of the Globe: A Review* (Exeter, 1981), p. 5.

was not until 1616 that the Dutch expedition of Le Maire and Schouten passed through the Strait of Le Maire and rounded Cape Horn to prove that there was another and less tortuous way into the South Sea than that through the Strait of Magellan. And although the open sea route around the Horn was later to be the one most used by shipping, for the heavily crewed sea raiders of the sixteenth and seventeenth centuries the food (especially penguins), wood and water of the Strait's shores were essential.

On Elizabeth Island, Drake took possession in the name of his sovereign, and showed that dramatic gestures were not confined to the conquistadors:

> Seeking out the Southermost part of the Island, [he] cast himselfe downe upon the uttermost poynt groveling, and so reached out his bodie over it. Presently he imbarked, and then recounted unto his people, that he had beene upon the Southermost knowne land in the world, and more further to the Southwards upon it, then any of them, yea, or any man as yet knowne.[38]

Hoping to find the other ships at the rendezvous of lat. 30°S., Drake sailed along the coast of Chile. With the help of his young cousin John he seems to have kept a careful record of the main features of the coast and its harbours. We have an intriguing glimpse of Drake at work from the captured Portuguese pilot Nuño da Silva: 'Francis Drake kept a book in which he entered his navigation and in which he delineated birds, trees and sea-lions. He is an adept in painting and has with him a boy, a relative of his, who is a great painter. When they both shut themselves up in his cabin they were always painting.'[39] Some years later two of Drake's crew remembered how 'he went to his cabin at 8 a clok and wind or rayn never stird'.[40] Francisco de Zarate, taken prisoner off the Guatemalan coast, was alarmed at the use which future marauders might make of Drake's artistic and surveying work: 'Each thing is so naturally depicted that no one who guides himself according to these paintings can possibly go astray.'[41] In addition to keeping his own records of the coast, Drake took pilots, charts and other navigational aids from captured vessels. Nuño da Silva, according to the Spaniards 'a most experienced Portuguese pilot, most skilful in the art of navigation . . . and great expert in the determination of latitude by observation',[42] was taken prisoner by Drake at the Cape Verde Islands and kept on board the *Golden Hind* for fifteen months. Drake took his chart, had it copied and translated,

38. J.A. Williamson, ed., *The Observations of Sir Richard Hawkins* [1622] (London, 1933), p. 96.
39. Nuttall, *New Light*, p. 303. Helen Wallis has pointed out that 'the name "painter" was given to a man who sailed on maritime expeditions as artist and map maker.' 'The Cartography of Drake's Voyage', in Thrower, *Drake and the Famous Voyage*, p. 124.
40. Elizabeth S. Donno, ed., *An Elizabethan in 1582: The Diary of Richard Madox* (London, 1976), pp. 237–8.
41. Nuttall, *New Light*, p. 208.
42. Ibid., pp. 101, 114.

and 'wrote down all he had learnt and had heard related concerning the routes of the Portuguese'. 'On capturing vessels', Da Silva related, 'the first things that he seized were the navigation charts, the astrolabes, compasses and needles.'[43] To exploit local knowledge of unknown coasts was a sensible and obvious expedient, but Drake's actions seem to go beyond that. They are further confirmation that the voyage was one of reconnaissance, with a view to later exploitation, as well as a plundering expedition.

So it was a matter of interest that the island of Mocha off the Chilean coast in lat. 38°S. seemed to be rich in gold and silver; that its inhabitants were hostile to the Spaniards; and that it was near gold-rich Arauco on the mainland. It was the first in a line of Chilean bases identified, but never established, by hopeful English visitors to the South Sea. As Drake raided the little settlements along the coast and seized what trading vessels he could find, the booty included enough silver and gold (valued at 447,000 *pesos*) to whet if not satisfy English appetites.[44] Despite the losses of ships, the financial success of the expedition seemed guaranteed when Drake heard at Callao that the *Nuestra Señora de la Concepción*, laden with silver, had sailed for Panama only two weeks earlier. Just north of the equator, the *Golden Hind* came up with the Spanish treasure ship, which was virtually unarmed and 'heavy and slow sailing' with twenty-six tons of silver in the hold. The Spaniards offered only token resistance, and its immensely valuable cargo, worth about 400,000 *pesos*, was transferred to the English vessel a boatload at a time. Once this was done, the whole tenor of the expedition changed. From being a lean and hungry predator, the *Golden Hind*, with its treasure on board, became vulnerable in turn. Two more prizes were taken, one laden with Chinese silks and porcelains offloaded from the Manila galleon, which had recently arrived at Acapulco, the other carrying pilots and charts for the trans-oceanic route to the Philippines followed by the galleons. One more settlement, Guatulco in lat. 15°40'N., the oldest Spanish port in Mexico, was raided. But for most of the time the *Golden Hind* kept out to sea, while Drake pondered the difficult question of the best route home.

With the coasts of Spanish America from Mexico to Chile on the alert, to return south was not an alluring prospect. Even if the *Golden Hind* could pass unscathed through those hostile waters, Drake would then be faced with the hazards of the return passage through the Strait of Magellan. Two other possibilities remained. One was to sail west across the ocean, through the Moluccas and into the Indian Ocean, and so around the Cape of Good Hope and home. Magellan's men had showed that this was practical, Drake had mentioned the possibility to Winter just before their separation,[45] and this return route would conform to that part of the draft instructions which

43. Ibid., pp. 308, 309.
44. The *peso*, or piece of eight, was the equivalent of 42.29 grams (roughly one ounce) of silver; its value in the English currency of the period was about four or five shillings.
45. Taylor, 'More Light', p. 150.

mentioned 'Great hope of . . . spices, drugs, cochineal'.[46] Also, as Nuño da
Silva pointed out, Drake was, in a sense, 'well acquainted with this route,
having learnt everything about it from all the pilots whom he captured, there
being not a single thing about which he did not inform himself'.[47] The other
possibility was the beguiling but uncertain alternative of sailing north in hope
of finding the Northwest Passage, and so by a short route passing back into
the Atlantic. The year before Drake sailed from England, Frobisher was
confident that he had found (on the southeast coast of Baffin Island) the
entrance to 'the West Sea, whereby to pass to Cathay and to the East India'.[48]
So persistent was Drake in telling his prisoners that he intended to return by
a northern strait 'of which he has relation' that the suspicion is bound to
linger that this was a ruse to hide his real intention of sailing west across the
Pacific.[49]

Of all the aspects of the voyage, the decisions and events of the summer
of 1579 are the most baffling. In the end, Drake came home by the same
route as Magellan's *Victoria*, but before that he had sailed three thousand
miles or more north. He may have been looking for the entrance of the
Northwest Passage, or, less ambitiously, for a favourable wind or current to
take him across the Pacific, or simply for a harbour where he could refit out
of reach of the Spaniards. How far Drake sailed north is uncertain; the
accounts vary between lats 42°N. and 48°N. They tell of 'extreame and
nipping cold', of natives shivering in their furs, of 'trees without leaues', and
of 'ground without greennes'[50] – so much so that some scholars have argued
that in June and July Drake's course and landing place were much further
north than generally assumed. Faced at sea with 'thicke, most stinking
fogges', Drake turned back south and found a harbour where the expedition
stayed for five weeks, in or near the great bay of San Francisco. Where
exactly Drake's landing place was has remained a matter of interminable
debate, though the 'official' site at Drake's Bay, northwest along the coast
from the Golden Gate, commands fairly general support.[51]

Relations with the local Indians (probably the Coastal Miwok of the
Drake's Bay area) appear to have been good. Here, early on, the noble

---

46. See above, p. 28.
47. Nuttall, *New Light*, p. 318.
48. See p. 19 above.
49. See, for example, the testimony of Nuño da Silva in Nuttall, *New Light*, pp. 250–2, 317–18,
    319n.
50. See Penzer, *World Encompassed*, pp. 48, 51.
51. The latest candidate for a very different site for Drake's landing place (as set out by Bob Ward)
    is Whale Cove in Oregon, five hundred miles north of the generally accepted range of locations
    in the San Francisco area. Oliver Seeler, on the other hand, argues from tree-ring evidence that
    California at the time of Drake's arrival was experiencing a period of abnormal cold, and that
    this explains the journal references to frozen rigging and the like. He advances the claims of
    Albion on the Mendocino coast of California. See the series of articles in *The Map Collector*:
    Bob Ward, 'Lost Harbour Found! The Truth about Drake and the Pacific', 45 (Winter, 1988),
    pp. 2–9; Helen Wallis *et al.*, 'Further Comments on the "Lost Harbour"', 49 (Winter, 1989),
    pp. 34–47; Oliver Seeler, 'Drake's Lost Harbour Found Again!', 54 (Spring, 1991), pp. 32–4.
    The definitive work remains Warren Hanna, *Lost Harbor* (Berkeley and Los Angeles, 1979).

primitive of the Pacific makes an appearance in the English accounts. They were 'a people of a tractable, free, and louing nature, without guile or treachery', and yet 'so strong of body, that that which 2 or 3 of our men could hardly beare, one of them would take vpon his backe, and without grudging carrie it easily away, vp hill and downe hill an English mile together'.[52] Allegedly at their initiative, Drake took possession of the country in the name of the Queen during some sort of coronation ceremony. Not for the first or last time there was a gulf of mutual incomprehension between what may have been simply the welcoming rituals of the native inhabitants and the gloss put on them by the European visitors.[53] But on the maps at least New Albion was to have a long life – a standing challenge, if only on paper, to Spanish claims of dominion over the Pacific seaboard of the Americas. Hakluyt made the point: 'The Spaniards hitherto had never bene in this part of the Countrey, neither did ever discover the land by many degrees, to the Southwards of this place.'[54]

Although New Albion held out alluring if rather wispy hopes of English enterprise sometime in the future, Drake's venture north had cast doubt on the existence of the short sea route from Europe that might make such enterprise a practical proposition. In listing the reasons for the unexpected cold as the *Golden Hind* sailed north, Fletcher reflected:

> The Chicfest of [these reasons] we conceiue to be the large spreading of the Asian and American continent, which (somewhat Northward of these parts), if they be not fully ioyned, yet seeme they to come very neere one to the other . . . And also from these reasons we coniecture, that either there is no passage at all through these Northerne coasts (which is most likely), or if there be, that yet it is vnnauigable. Adde hereunto, that though we searched the coast diligently, euuen vnto the 48 deg., yet found we not the land to trend so much as one point in any place towards the East, but rather running on continually North-West, as if it went directly to meet with Asia.[55]

In July 1579 Drake left California and sailed out into the Pacific. It was not quite into the unknown, for on board he had charts and sailing directions seized earlier in the year from a Spanish pilot about to make the voyage from Acapulco to Manila. Drake would not want, for reasons of self-preservation, to follow the galleon route to the Philippines. Rather, the Moluccas seem to have been his destination. His first landfall, after sixty-eight days at sea, was

---

52. Penzer, *World Encompassed*, pp. 61–2.
53. For more – much more – on this see Patricia Seed, *Ceremonies of Possession in Europe's Conquest of the New World, 1492–1640* (Cambridge, 1995), though, oddly, she does not deal with Drake's visit.
54. Hakluyt, *Principal Navigations*, IX, p. 326.
55. Penzer, *World Encompassed*, pp. 51, 52. It should be noted that one part of the Oregonian thesis as advanced by Bob Ward is that Drake had entered the Strait of Juan de Fuca, and although he turned back to Whale Cove to refit his ship assumed that he had found the Pacific entrance of the Northwest Passage. This view, it must be said, is not widely shared.

probably Palau.[56] Here for the first time English seamen saw and marvelled at the outrigger craft of the Pacific, in this case dugout canoes that were double-outriggered and twin-ended. The accounts struggled to describe these unfamiliar craft: 'hollow within, and cut with great arte and cunning . . . having a prowe, and a sterne of one sort . . . and on each side of them lie out two peeces of timber about a yard and a halfe long, more or lesse.'[57] Initial friendliness turned to violence, and if John Drake's later evidence is correct the encounter ended with the killing of a score of islanders by the *Golden Hind*'s guns.[58] No other account mentions this, and we have no details of what happened.

In his relations with the native peoples he met Drake was not naturally bloodthirsty. Another incident recalled by John Drake occurred at Port Desire in Patagonia when, after a minor scuffle in which Drake had his cap snatched from his head, he stopped one of his men from firing at the culprit – 'the captain told him not to kill a man for the sake of a cap'.[59] In an altogether more serious incident, when the crew were attacked by the Chilean Indians of Mocha who mistook them for Spaniards, Drake refused to retaliate after four of his men had been killed or taken prisoner, and he himself had been wounded.[60] In some ways the whole expedition was surprisingly non-violent. Despite later Spanish claims of Drake's brutality, not a single Spaniard seems to have been killed during his raids. Two were wounded, a Negro crew member of a Panama ship was hanged for concealing gold, and a youth almost frightened to death by a mock hanging.[61] Otherwise, the main casualties seem to have been churches, crucifixes and rosaries. If Drake was not personally involved in this destruction, he left his enforced guests in no doubt about his aggressively Protestant beliefs. At one prisoner on the *Golden Hind*, over-curious about the nature of divine service on shipboard, an angry Drake thrust Foxe's *Book of Martyrs*, with its engravings of Lutherans being burnt at the stake by the Inquisition. He went on to harangue the Spaniard – 'You will be saying now this man is a devil who robs by day and prays at night in public' – before throwing him into the ship's lock-up for the night. The next day he was released and set on shore with presents for himself and his family.[62]

From Palau, one of several Pacific islands to be called 'Island of Thieves' by European seamen, Drake sailed west towards Mindanao before turning south towards the Moluccas. In November he reached the spice island of

56. See William A. Lessa, *Drake's Island of Thieves: Ethnological Sleuthing* (Honolulu, 1975), and his summary, 'Drake in the South Seas', in Thrower, *Drake and the Famous Voyage*, pp. 61–6.
57. Hakluyt, *Principal Navigations*, XI, p. 124.
58. Evidence of John Drake, 1584, printed in Lady Eliott-Drake, *The Family and Heirs of Sir Francis Drake* (2 vols, London, 1911), II, p. 357.
59. Ibid., II, p. 385.
60. Penzer, *World Encompassed*, pp. 37–8.
61. For details see Nuttall, *New Light*, pp. 151, 196, 266.
62. For this episode see ibid., pp. 354–9.

Ternate, whose ruler was at odds with the Portuguese on nearby Tidore. Drake was able to trade for cloves and also negotiated some sort of treaty of friendship with the Sultan. In retrospect, this was of greater importance than all of Drake's raiding of Spanish ships and settlements and was to play its part in the establishment of the English East India Company in 1600. From Ternate the ship sailed south into the Banda Sea, and after a near escape from shipwreck coasted the southern shores of Java and so crossed into the Indian Ocean.

Six months later, in September 1580, the *Golden Hind* arrived back at Plymouth. A few crew members had been killed by Spaniards or natives, and Winter claimed that there had been some deaths from sickness before the ships reached the Strait of Magellan.[63] Even so, with fifty-six out of the original crew of eighty or so on board, the voyage was an astonishing achievement in terms of seamanship, navigation and willpower. In a curious way, to those who had not experienced the trials and tribulations of the voyage, Drake had made the circumnavigation appear almost too easy; those who blithely followed his track into the South Sea rarely had the same success.

As Drake came into home waters there was no hero's welcome for him from the government, for the air was heavy with Spanish protests. John Drake remembered how an anxious Drake

> sent a courier to the Queen . . . He also wrote to other personages of the Court, who had let him know that the Queen was angry with him, because she had heard by way of Peru and Spain of the plunder which he had taken; they had also told him that the Spanish Ambassador was at Court, and was asking for the return of what he had taken. On this he left Plymouth with his ship, and waited behind an island until the Queen sent to say that he should come to Court with some specimens of his labours and have no fear of anything. With this he went to Court by land with some horses laden with gold and silver.[64]

Despite a six-hour meeting with the Queen, during which Drake presented her with his journal and chart,[65] it took six months, and much royal calculation of financial gain, public and private, before Drake was knighted on board the *Golden Hind* in the Thames. Only then, it seems, was there a wave of popular acclaim, and 'his name and fame became admirable in all places, the people swarming daily in the streets to behold him, vowing hatred of all that durst mislike him.'[66] The *Golden Hind* itself was placed in a

63. See Taylor, 'More Light', p. 149.
64. Eliott-Drake, *Family and Heirs of Drake*, II, pp. 395–6. The value of the treasure has been estimated as more than the Queen's annual ordinary revenue. See Sugden, *Drake*, pp. 148–9.
65. This information is taken from an intercepted letter from Mendoza, the Spanish ambassador. See Thrower, *Drake and the Famous Voyage*, p. 121.
66. Quoted ibid., p. 2.

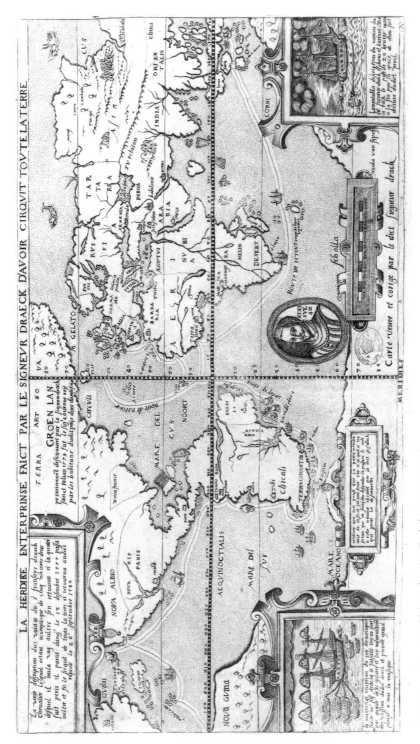

5. Nicola van Sype. World map showing Drake's voyage, c. 1583.

specially built dry dock at Deptford as a reminder of the great voyage, though not a permanent one, for by 1688 the vessel had rotted to pieces.

For an event that was to linger long in the English folk-memory, hard evidence about the circumnavigation is difficult to find. The most important primary records have disappeared. Among these were Drake's own journal, presumably illustrated with charts and those views and other depictions drawn each evening in the cabin of the *Golden Hind*. One of his charts was hung on public display in the Palace of Whitehall (though perhaps not until much later), along with some Cabot charts. Samuel Purchas saw it there, and described how, among much else, it showed that 'the South of the Magelane Straits is not a Continent, but many Ilands'.[67] That, too, disappeared, probably destroyed by fire in 1698, but its loss was not quite as grievous as that of Drake's journal, for other maps have survived which, if not exact copies, were certainly derived from Drake's chart. Among these were two engraved maps, one by Nicola van Sype, probably published at Antwerp in 1583 or later; the other the so-called Drake Broadside map by Jodocus Hondius of 1595 (though perhaps issued in England around 1590).

The van Sype map (Ill. 5) included a portrait of Drake, marked the route of the *Golden Hind* and twice showed the Royal Arms of England, just south of Tierra del Fuego and near the coast of 'Nova Albio'. This English claim to a huge area of America north of New Spain was the most striking feature of the map. Based on a single voyage and a single landing it was as grandiose a pretension to dominion as those claims of the Spaniards, which Hakluyt seemed to have in mind when he wrote: 'For the conquering of fortie or fiftie miles here and there and erecting of certaine fortresses, [they] think to be Lordes of halfe the world.'[68] Nonetheless, it was taken seriously, then and later. In 1603 Anthony Linton in his *Newes of the Complement of the Art of Navigation* criticized the 1592 world map of Plancius for omitting to show Drake's landing place in New Albion, thus 'smothering the discovery'.[69] As much as anything, New Albion represented a claim to a possible terminus of a navigable Northwest Passage, for although Frobisher's gold-seeking activities in the Arctic had come to nothing, on his final voyage in 1578 he had sailed twenty days west in a wide strait in lat. 61°N. or 62°N. He was off course for his destination in Frobisher Bay, and in the end he turned back, even though there was still 'an open Sea' before him.[70] Frobisher's 'Mistaken Straites' was Hudson Strait, leading on to the great inland sea of Hudson Bay and, later expeditions hoped, to the Northwest Passage. The three voyages of John Davis in 1585–7, which took him far to the north to Baffin Bay, as well as across the entrance of

67. Samuel Purchas, *Hakluytus Posthumus or Purchas his Pilgrimes* [1625] (Glasgow, 1906), XIII, p. 3.
68. Hakluyt, *Principal Navigations*, VI, p. 141.
69. See Günter Schilder, *Monumenta Cartographica Neerlandica*, III (Alphen aan de Rijn, Netherlands, 1990), pp. 27–8.
70. See Collinson, *Voyages of Frobisher*, p. 242.

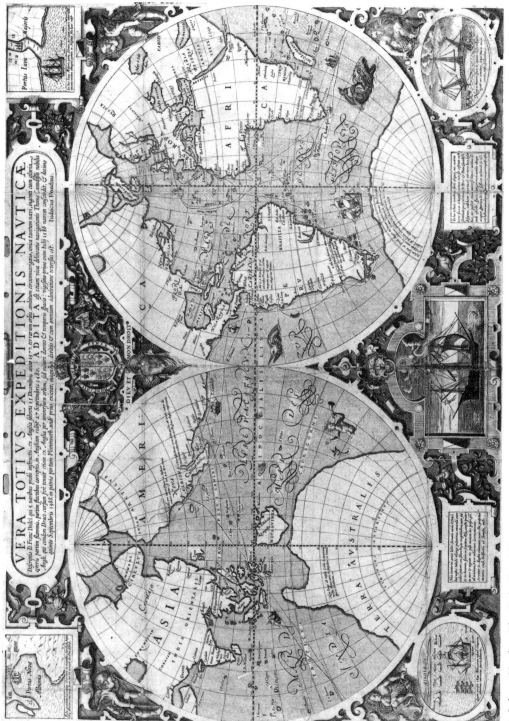

6. Jodocus Hondius. The Drake Broadside Map, c. 1595.

Hudson Strait, were further evidence of the English interest in the possibility of a passage.

In contrast to van Sype's relatively austere production, the Hondius map (Ill. 6) set Drake's route in the framework of a globe whose southern extremities were dominated by a vast 'Terra Australis', while a legend near Tierra del Fuego denied Drake's assertion that the land to the south consisted of islands. Perhaps, though, the most significant single feature of the map is the inset of Drake's 'Portus Novae Albionis', a simple sketch which has engrossed the time and energy of many devoted scholars seeking to identify Drake's harbour on the Californian coast.[71]

The voyage, despite the treasure, despite the knighting ceremony on the deck of the *Golden Hind*, did not make quite as much stir in Elizabethan England as might have been expected. A mixture of state caution and state embarrassment kept most of the details of the voyage from the public. The Queen's advisers 'are very particular not to divulge the route by which Drake returned', Mendoza complained, and for some time it was not generally known that Drake had sailed around the world – only the second expedition to do so, and the first to come back with its commander and most of its crew alive. In 1582 the well-informed diarist and sea chaplain Richard Madox noted the rumour that 'there was a sailable passage over America between 43 and 46 degree throe which . . . Sir Francis Drake came home from the Moluccas.'[72] The great Gerard Mercator, by contrast, expected Drake to return through the North*east* Passage and suspected that the expedition of Arthur Pet and Charles Jackman, sent out by the Muscovy Company in 1580 to discover that passage, was instructed to look out for Drake.[73] In 1584 the English ambassador to France, whose secretary and chaplain was Richard Hakluyt (the Younger), wrote to Walsingham, 'I find from "Mr. Haklitt" that Drake's journey is kept very secret in England, but here is in everyone's mouth.'[74] Well into the next reign confusion persisted:

> Some think it *true whilst* other some do doubt
> Whether Captaine Drake compaste the worlde about.[75]

Not until after the Armada, and then as a last-minute addition, did Richard Hakluyt include a short narrative in *The Principall Navigations* of 1589 of 'The famous voyage of Sir Francis Drake into the South Seas, and there hence about the whole Globe of the Earth'. This was based on two, possibly three, journals, but had no reference to Drake's own journal.[76] The only

71. On the maps see the authoritative analysis by Helen Wallis, 'The Cartography of Drake's Voyage', in Thrower, *Drake and the Famous Voyage*, pp. 121–63.
72. Donno, *Madox Diary*, p. 96.
73. Andrews, *Trade, Plunder and Settlement*, p. 73 n. 26.
74. Quoted in Thrower, *Drake and the Famous Voyage*, p. 139.
75. Anon., 1612, quoted ibid., p. 112.
76. Hakluyt, *Principall Navigations*, pp. 643A–643L.

other printed account of the voyage had to wait for many years after Drake's
death, when *The World Encompassed*, taken mainly from Fletcher's journal,
was published in 1628 by Drake's nephew, Francis. Reasons of state; personal
dislike of Drake, his murky past and his flamboyant behaviour; uneasiness
about his execution of Doughty: all help to explain the muted reaction. In
other ways the voyage brought a more positive message. As a feat of
navigation it had enhanced the reputation of English seafarers. It had opened
the possibility of breaking into the spice trade of the eastern seas or into the
newly revealed trade triangle between Canton, Manila and Acapulco. Above
all, it had revealed both the wealth and vulnerability of the Spanish empire
in the Pacific. Within a month of the *Golden Hind*'s return the Spanish
ambassador was informing Philip II that not only was Drake planning a new
voyage, but 'There is hardly an Englishman who is not talking of undertaking the voyage, so encouraged are they by Drake's return.'[77]

Even before Drake's return, there were suggestions for the establishment of
a more permanent English presence at the entrance to the South Sea. In
1579–80 a pamphleteer (probably the younger Hakluyt) who had talked to
members of Winter's crew advocated the taking and fortifying of the Strait
of Magellan. This was an echo of one of Grenville's proposals of 1574.[78]
Other expeditions might seize Portuguese ports in Brazil, or renew the
search for a Northeast Passage to Cathay. Such an ambitious series of thrusts
would entrench the English on the rims of both the Spanish and Portuguese
empires. In particular, the possession of the Strait of Magellan, 'the gate of
entry into the tresure of both the East and the West Indies', 'a seate
impregnable of nature', would 'make subjecte to England all the golden
mines of Peru'.[79] Proof that this part of the plan at least was unrealistic came
with the awful fate of a Spanish expedition sent under Pedro Sarmiento to
establish a fortified colony in the Strait.

The first efforts to emulate Drake were directed not so much at the South
Sea as at the East Indies, now a more open target for the English since the
union of the crowns of Spain and Portugal in 1580. Drake himself had
proposed a new voyage, as explained by Mendoza, the Spanish ambassador,
in January 1581: 'Drake is to take 10 ships to the Isles of Moluccas by the
same route as that along which he returned, which is to go almost in a
straight line to these islands from the Cape of Good Hope.'[80] Another
English expedition, reported Mendoza, was to sail to Patagonia and then into
the South Sea, yet another was headed for Cuba, and 'They are also pressing
Frobisher to renew his attempt (in spite of late unsuccess) to discover a

---

77.   *Calendar of State Papers, Spanish*, III, 1580–6 (London, 1896), p. 56.
78.   See Chope, 'New Light on Grenville', p. 234.
79.   Taylor, *Writings of the Hakluyts*, pp. 140, 142, 163.
80.   The quotations in this paragraph are from E.G.R. Taylor, ed., *The Troublesome Voyage of Captain
      Edward Fenton 1582–83* (Cambridge, 1959), pp. 5, 6.

Passage to Cathay, which Drake is of opinion must exist there.' In April, when Drake was knighted, Mendoza heard that a meeting was held between him and Walsingham, Leicester, Hawkins, Winter, Frobisher and Bingham, 'all the latter being experienced mariners'. Although the ambassador was apt to take speculative ideas or quayside gossip as hard fact, undoubtedly the circle of courtiers, merchants and seamen he had identified was actively considering further overseas projects after Drake's return. But there were problems. The Queen was still sensitive to the wider question of relations with Spain, and despite (or perhaps because of) her knighting of Drake, forbade him to leave the country.

Finally, the flurry of plans resulted in a single voyage, that of Edward Fenton of 1582 'for China and Cathay'. It was to be, as Fenton's vice-admiral remarked with some understatement, 'a troublesome voyage'. Fenton, who for reasons that remain unexplained replaced Martin Frobisher as commander of the expedition, was a soldier who had sailed with Frobisher on his second and third Arctic voyages. Some hint of the problems that led to the substitution may be found in the restrictive nature of his original instructions, which also make clear the priorities of the planned expedition. Frobisher was not to sail northeast of China, 'least perhaps he showeth some desire to searche out his formerly pretended passage NW and so hinder this voyage wch is only for trade'.[81] The main investor was the Earl of Leicester; the organizing of the voyage was in the hands of a group of merchants of the Muscovy Company; and the crews included men who had sailed with Drake, including pilots, John Drake, and others who according to Mendoza had lived in the Moluccas for some years. Rough notes made by Leicester's secretary indicate that Francis Drake was consulted, at least as to route, and had warned against the Strait of Magellan on the grounds that the Spaniards would by this time have fortified it.[82] Mendoza, on the other hand, now had information about the chart made by Drake and was convinced that his discovery that the southern shore of the Strait consisted of islands, not continent, would be exploited. He feared that while Spanish forces were guarding the main channel through the Strait the English ships would slip past well to the south, since 'there was the open sea beyond Tierra del Fuego'.[83] Fenton's instructions, approved by Burghley, were direct but perhaps not quite firm enough on this issue. Fenton was to 'goe on your course by Cape de bona Sperança, not passing by the streight of Magellan, either going or returning, except upon great occasion incident.'

In general terms, the officers were exhorted to 'deale altogether in this voiage like good and honest merchants', although the size and warlike fitting of the expedition throw some doubt on this. There were four vessels: the

81. Ibid., p. 16.
82. Donno, *Madox Diary*, p. 21.
83. This and the quotations in the next two paragraphs are from Taylor, *Troublesome Voyage*, pp. 40, 54, 60, 219, 110.

flagship *Galleon Leicester*, a new forty-gun vessel, supported by another powerful ship, the *Edward Bonaventure*, and two smaller vessels. In all, Fenton had with him about 240 men, compared to the 160 of Drake's expedition. The furore over Doughty's execution on that voyage helps to explain the lengthy and detailed instructions of 1582 on Fenton's disciplinary powers. By contrast, apart from an almost incidental reference to taking 'the right course to the Isles of Molucca', the destination of the expedition was not dwelt upon. Nor did the terms of the Queen's Broad Seal, which gave Fenton an official status denied to Drake, much clarify matters. They referred, grandly but vaguely, to a voyage 'into foreign parties to the southeastwards as well for ye discovery of Cathaia & China, as all other lands & yslandes alredy discovered, & hereafter to be discovered by Edward Fenton'.

The lateness of the departure from Southampton at the end of April 1582, and then further delays in the Channel, ruled out the possibility of a winter passage, avoiding headwinds, around the Cape of Good Hope. It may be that Fenton was already turning his thoughts towards the forbidden Strait of Magellan route, for one of the merchants on the venture wrote to Leicester in June that he thought 'owr generall wyll goo throwe the streytes of Magalan . . . for he and the pilotes sayd that the pasage that was sertayne, and contrarywyse makes the cape of Esperanza dowtefull.' The formal decision was taken in September off the West African coast, when after 'many hotte and disdainfull speaches' it was agreed, in Fenton's words, that the Straight of Magellan was 'the onlie waie'. There is no evidence that there was any suggestion, not even from those who had sailed with Drake, that the squadron should sail south of the Strait, around the islands Drake had come across in 1578. A copy of one of Drake's charts was on board the *Edward Bonaventure*, though if Richard Madox, chaplain on the voyage, is to be believed it was regarded with some scepticism (and Drake himself with some dislike):

> We examined, as it happened, the sketch of the Straits of Magellan which that golden knight of ours who had once passed through had made. Then the question arises by what art or industry he could express so vividly all the islands he had drawn there or decide for certain that they were so situated when . . . for 8 days he had been sedulously struggling with much circuitous-ness and many windings to round one single cape . . . I am convinced that that Drake of ours either found some kind of draft among the Portuguese or Spaniards and thus put forth their little commentaries as his own or I believe him to be a man who cast off all shame and dared boldly to determine things unknown and to present them to her majesty as explored and already claimed.[84]

84. Donno, *Madox Diary*, pp. 239–40. Drake's most recent biographer sees a slightly different implication here. For John Cummins, *Francis Drake: The Lives of a Hero* (London, 1995), p. 15, the incident is evidence of acknowledged Spanish and Portuguese superiority in navigation and charting – Drake's contemporaries could not believe that so detailed a chart could be English.

From Sierra Leone the three ships (the fourth had been exchanged with the local Portuguese for ivory and rice) sailed southwest across the Atlantic towards Brazil. North of the Plate estuary the capture of a Portuguese vessel brought the disturbing news that a Spanish fleet had passed on its way south to fortify the Strait of Magellan. At another of Fenton's disputatious Council meetings, held in December 1582, it was decided that the Strait route now held 'meny [and] infinite dangers', and that the expedition should give up all hopes of reaching the South Sea, and should instead head north along the coast to São Vicente where Fenton might sell his trade goods to the Portuguese.[85] But it was there, ironically, and not in distant southerly latitudes, that he encountered three of the Spanish ships heading back from the Strait of Magellan. In the fighting that followed, one of the Spanish ships was sunk. This put an end to any hope of trade with the Portuguese, and amid mutual recriminations the English ships sailed for home.

From the beginning, the voyage had been marked by conflict and confusion – over routes, objectives, tactics. Set against the merchants with their legitimate trading interests were those, notably Drake's men, who looked to a repetition of his plundering exploits in the South Sea. John Drake, indeed, had left the expedition in fury after the Council decision of December, only to be cast away and taken prisoner in the River Plate. The documents from the voyage are full of quarrels and threats; of incipient mutinies, desertions and courts-martial; of accusations of drunkenness and cowardice. At the centre of these discontents was Fenton, headstrong, bombastic, secretive. In September 1582 Madox, by now keeping his diary in cipher, gave some indication of Fenton's table-talk:

> He means to cownterfet the king of Portugals seal and flag and so to tak al as they cam to serve him . . . He seeketh both hear to rayn and to get a kingdom. He sayd he had martial law and wowld hang Draper [a steward] at the mast. He said the queen was his lov. He abhoreth merchan[t]s . . . He wold go throo the Sowth Sea to be lik Sir Fraunsis Drake.[86]

Despite the fiasco of Fenton's voyage, there is some evidence, thin but intriguing, which seems to show that a further scheme was developed to exploit, if not conquer, part of Portugal's eastern trading empire. This would be all the more tempting a target since the union of crowns in 1580 had brought it under formal Spanish rule. A document of November 1584 sets out the costs of a considerable force of eleven ships, four barks, twenty pinnaces and soldiers, called the 'Navy of ye Moluccos'. Drake, Raleigh, John and Richard Hawkins, Leicester, Hatton and the Queen herself are all listed as being involved in the enterprise. If this document was more than a pipe-dream, then it would seem to indicate a full-blown assault on the

85. Taylor, *Troublesome Voyage*, p. 247.
86. Donno, *Madox Diary*, p. 194.

Portuguese East Indies. The disappearance of the scheme from view is not surprising given the flare-up of Anglo-Spanish hostilities in the Caribbean in 1585.[87]

The Spanish ships that Fenton encountered in Brazil were part of an ill-starred venture following Drake's voyage to fortify the Strait of Magellan against further foreign incursions into the South Sea. As Drake was leaving the western Pacific in October 1579 two Spanish vessels, commanded by Pedro Sarmiento de Gamboa, sailed from Callao for the Strait. He was to intercept Drake if he returned that way and was in any case to make a detailed survey of the Strait which could be used if the Spanish government decided to fortify it. The following August Sarmiento reached Spain with his charts and report, and preparations were made for a huge fleet of twenty-three ships which was not only to fortify but also to colonize the Strait. The expedition was dogged by misfortune and ineptitude from the beginning. Six ships were lost before the fleet could get away from Spanish waters in late 1581; others were sunk or forced back en route to the Strait; two attempts to enter were beaten back by the fierce currents. Not until the beginning of 1584 was Sarmiento with five ships able to set up a base, Nombre de Jesus, inside Cape Virgenes at the Atlantic entrance of the Strait. From there settlers struggled overland, with ships in support, to establish a second township, Rey Don Felipe, well into the Strait. On his way back to Nombre de Jesus Sarmiento was driven out to sea, never to return.[88] Three years later in 1587 English ships passing through the Strait picked up a man from a forlorn group of twenty-one men and two women at the First Narrows – 'which were all that remayned of foure hundred, which were left there three yeeres before in these streights of Magellan, all the rest being dead with famine'. Further into the Strait, the English went ashore at Rey Don Felipe. The township, with its wooden forts, houses, churches and a gibbet, was still intact; but as for the settlers, men, women and children, 'they dyed like dogges in their houses, and in their clothes, wherein we found them still at our comming'. Not all were dead, however, in that charnel house, renamed Port Famine by the English, for in 1589 the Bristol ship *Delight* picked up another survivor who told his rescuers that he 'had lived in a house by himselfe a long time'.[89]

The commander of the English expedition that came across the desolate site of Rey Don Felipe in 1587 was Thomas Cavendish, a wealthy young Suffolk squire who had been involved in Ralegh's Virginia venture of 1585. Leading a squadron of three ships from his flagship *Desire* (120 tons) on this new venture into the South Sea, Cavendish was intent on emulating Drake.

87. The document is in BL: Lansdowne MS 41, ff. 9–10; for an interpretation of it see Cummins, *Drake*, p. 134.
88. For the main documents, translated into English, see C.R. Markham, ed., *Narratives of the Voyages of P.S. de G.* (London, 1895).
89. For these encounters of 1587 and 1589 see Hakluyt, *Principal Navigations*, XI, pp. 298–300, 382–3.

He took fifty days to get through the Strait, but once out 'into the Sea called by Magelan, Mare pacificum, the peaceable or the calme Sea',[90] was able to turn north without further difficulty. Like Drake, Cavendish sailed north, raiding, burning and looting, this time without any queries being raised about the legality of his actions, for England and Spain had been at war since 1585. Cavendish's depredations were more damaging to the Spaniards than profitable to the English, for he had little room on his ships for the bulk cargoes carried by the Spanish traders. Typical was the capture of two ships near Paita,

> the one laden with sugar, molasses, maiz, Cordovan-skinnes, montego de Porco, many packes of pintados, many Indian coates, and some marmalade, and 1000 hennes: and the other ship was laden with wheate-meale, and boxes of marmalade. One of these ships which had the chiefe marchandise in it, was worth twentie thousand pounds, if it had bene in England or in any other place of Christendome where wee might have solde it.[91]

As it was, Cavendish burnt the two ships and most of the merchandise. Similarly, on the shore raids he had to stop his men burdening themselves with booty in case they were attacked on the way back to the ships. The seepage of casualties was also having its effect, and at the beginning of June 1587 the smallest of the three vessels was scuttled because of the lack of crew.

Luck turned Cavendish's way when a French pilot on a ship captured off the Mexican coast gave details of the forthcoming arrival of the annual galleon from Manila, the 'nao de China' as it was called by the Spaniards. Sailing past Acapulco, the American terminus of the transpacific route from the Philippines to New Spain, the two English ships lay in wait for the galleon at Cape San Lucas, the usual landfall of the galleons. Unknown to the English, one galleon had already reached port, but on 4 November another great ship, the *Santa Ana*, between six and seven hundred tons, was sighted. It was more formidable in appearance than in reality, for it carried no cannon and its decks were encumbered with cargo. Apart from two arquebuses the only weapons available to the crew were stones picked out of the ballast. After an unsuccessful attempt to board the galleon the English simply lay off, firing into the helpless vessel, until after six hours of this ordeal the Spaniards surrendered.[92] A Spanish official later explained: 'As no other ships but ours have ever been sighted on this voyage they have always sailed with as little fear from corsairs as if they were on the river of Seville.'[93] The value of the galleon's cargo is as difficult to assess as in other seizures of this kind. The account by Francis Pretty as printed by Hakluyt claimed that there were

90.   From the account by 'N.H.' printed in Hakluyt, *Principall Navigations*, p. 810.
91.   Hakluyt, *Principal Navigations*, XI, p. 312.
92.   See W. Michael Mathes, ed., *The Capture of the Santa Ana* (Los Angeles, 1969), esp. pp. 38–47.
93.   Quoted in Schurz, *Manila Galleon*, p. 7.

122,000 *pesos* on board. Antonio de Sierra more than quadrupled this figure to 600,000 *pesos* and added that the most valuable part of the galleon's cargo lay in its 'silkes, sattens, damasks, with muske & divers other marchandize', worth perhaps two million *pesos* at Acapulco.[94] Only forty tons of merchandise could be taken on board the English ships; the rest (five hundred tons) was burnt, as well as the galleon itself. It was a heavy blow to the trade link between New Spain and the Philippines, but Cavendish saw it as a beginning rather than an end to English enterprise in the North Pacific and China Seas, and he took off the galleon all those crew members who might be useful in the future. They included three young Filipinos, 'a very good [Spanish] pilot' who knew the galleon route from New Spain to the Ladrones and the Philippines, and a Portuguese, 'who hath not onely bene in Canton and other parts of China, but also in the islands of Japon being a countrey most rich in silver mynes, and hath also bene in the Philippinas'.[95]

As the two ships left the Californian coast in mid-November 1587 they lost company, and the consort vessel, the *Content*, was never seen again. It was characteristic of Spanish nervousness about possible English discoveries in the South Sea by Drake or others that the captured Spanish pilot assumed that the vessel had headed north to return home by way of the Northwest Passage. Now on its own, the *Desire* followed the lengthy galleon route across the North Pacific to Guam. Here sixty or seventy canoes came out with plantains, coconuts and fish. These craft, unlike those seen by Drake at Palau, were single-outriggers –

> not above halfe a yard in bredth and in length some seven or eight yardes, and their heades and sternes are both alike, they are made out with raftes of canes and reedes on the starrebordside, with maste and sayle: their sayle is made of mattes of sedges, square or triangle wise: and they saile as well right against the winde, as before the winde.

The tone of Pretty's narrative changed at this point as he described how as the canoes continued to follow the ship Cavendish and some of the crew fired at them, perhaps killing some their occupants, who were seen to fall or jump into the water.

Guided by the captured Spanish pilot (soon to be hanged for trying to communicate with the shore), the *Desire* sailed west from Guam until it reached Cape Espiritu Santo, the regular landfall in the Philippines of westbound galleons. But here Cavendish turned south, away from the main centres of Spanish activity, for with a valuable cargo and a weakened crew, to engage in serious fighting would have been foolish. As he left Philippine waters he sent a truculent message to the local Spanish commander, advising

---

94. See ibid., p. 318; Mathes, *Capture of the Santa Ana*, p. 27n.
95. This and the quotations in the next three paragraphs are from Hakluyt, *Principal Navigations*, XI, pp. 327, 242, 329, 245, 341.

him 'to provide good store of gold: for he meant for to see him with his company at Manilla within fewe yeeres'.

Unlike Drake, Cavendish did not reach the Moluccas, but sailed from Gilolo to Java, where for the first time he met Portuguese traders. They were anxious to hear news from Europe, especially about Don Antonio. On being assured that he was still alive, the Portuguese told Cavendish 'that if their king Don Antonio would come unto them, they would warrant him to have all the Malucos at commandement, besides, China, Sangles, and the yles of the Philippinas, and that hee might be assured to have all the Indians & on his side that are in the countrey.' Such extravagant claims are put in perspective when it is realized that news of Cavendish's visit was transmitted, first to Goa, and then to the Spanish authorities. By this time Cavendish was home, after an arduous but uneventful voyage across the Indian Ocean, round the Cape of Good Hope and so back to Plymouth.

Cavendish arrived back on 9 September 1588, his homecoming a golden epilogue to the recent victory over the Armada. The doleful reports of Spanish agents in London quoted Armada losses on one line, the rumoured size of the booty brought back by Cavendish on the next. This varied in value from a half-million crowns to three million.[96] In an atmosphere of patriotic triumph Cavendish experienced a warmer welcome from Queen and Court than Drake had eight years earlier. Although there was to be no knighthood for Cavendish, the *Desire* anchored in the Thames in November after a triumphant procession up the Channel. A Spanish agent reported the scene:

> Thomas Cavendish's ship has been brought from the West Country, and was sailed before the Court at Greenwich. Amongst other things the Queen said, 'The king of Spain barks a good deal but does not bite. We care nothing for the Spaniards; their ships, loaded with silver and gold from the Indies, come hither after all.' Every sailor had a gold chain round his neck, and the sails of the ship were a blue damask, the standard of cloth of gold and blue silk. It was as if Cleopatra had been resuscitated. The only thing wanting was that the rigging should have been of silken rope.[97]

Within the year Hakluyt had printed an account of Cavendish's 'worthy and famous voyage . . . made round about the globe of the earth, in the space of two yeeres and lesse then two monethes', alongside Drake's earlier circumnavigation. Out of the first three circumnavigations, two were by the English, who 'to speake plainly, in compassing the vaste globe of the earth more than once have excelled all the nations and people of the earth.'[98] Though the gold from the Manila galleon was the most dramatic evidence of

96. See *Calendar of State Papers, Spanish*, IV, 1587–1603 (London, 1899), pp. 437, 473, 483, 486.
97. Ibid., pp. 491–2.
98. Hakluyt, *Principall Navigations*, p. 810, sig. 2v.

Cavendish's success, there is no doubt that he saw the opening of China to English enterprise as the next step. In his summary of the voyage for the Lord Chamberlain, dated the day of his arrival at Plymouth, Cavendish described his raids among Spanish shipping and his capture of the galleon, and then went on:

> I navigated to the Islands of the Philippinas hard upon the coast of China; of which countrey I feare to make report of, least I should not be credited; for if I had not knowen sufficiently the incomparable wealth of that countrey I should have bene as incredulous thereof, as others will be that have not had the like experience.[99]

Cavendish brought back with him a 'large map' of China, presumably taken from the galleon, and though this has not survived, some of its detail was published by Hakluyt. It was altogether appropriate that the English translation of 1588 of the account by Juan González de Mendoza, *The Historie of the Great and Mightie Kingdome of China*, was dedicated to Cavendish. As Robert Parke acknowledged, 'your worshippe in your late voyage hath first of our nation in this age discouered the famous rich Ilandes of the *Luzones*, or *Philippinas*, lying neere vnto the coast of China.'[100] Whereas Drake had picked up only scanty information about the trade between China and the Spaniards, Cavendish had identified the pivotal role of Manila: 'a very rich place of golde and many other commodities; and they have yeerely traffick from Acapulco in Nueva Espanna, and also 20 or 30 shippes from China and from the Sanguelos, which bring them many sorts of marchandize'.[101]

The two accounts (by 'N.H.' and Francis Pretty) of Cavendish's voyage, printed by Hakluyt, and the ancillary documents gave much fuller information about the venture than anything else available about Drake's voyage and pointed to future enterprise. At the end of Pretty's account, for example, came the 'rare and special notes' kept by the master on the *Desire*

> concerning the heights, soundings, lyings of lands, distances of places, the variation of the Compasse, the just length of time spent in sayling betweene divers places, and their abode in them, as also the places of their harbour and anckering, and the depths of the same, with the observation of the windes on severall coastes.[102]

Here, for example, was the information that on the *Desire*'s passage from California to the Ladrones between November and late January the winds had been from the east and east-northeast – the first reference in English to

99.   Hakluyt, *Principal Navigations*, XI, p. 377.
100. Quoted in David B. Quinn, ed., *The Last Voyage of Thomas Cavendish 1591–1592* (Chicago, 1975), p. 17 n. 30.
101. Hakluyt, *Principal Navigations*, XI, pp. 329–30.
102. Ibid., XI, p. 348.

the steady northeast trades that blow from October to April across the Pacific north of the equator. That Cavendish, unlike Drake, tortured prisoners, hanged unsatisfactory pilots and a priest, ruthlessly burnt Spanish settlements and on one occasion seems to have abandoned his sick and dying men, was not given prominence.

Clearly, Cavendish saw his circumnavigation as the preliminary to another expedition, and Spanish nerves were kept on edge as their agents in London reported preparations for further ventures.[103] As usual, there was not much correlation between projects reported and actual expeditions, and it was three years before Cavendish sailed on his follow-up voyage. It was an ambitious venture: five ships, headed by the *Galleon Leicester* of four hundred tons, 350 men and a wide range of objectives. A plundering raid along the Pacific seaboard of Spanish America would be the preliminary, but the presence on board of the Portuguese pilot and the two Japanese taken on the first voyage confirmed Cavendish's interest in the Philippines, China and perhaps Japan. The most significant figure among Cavendish's captains was the Arctic explorer John Davis, who had returned from his third Arctic voyage in 1587 claiming that he 'had bene in 73 degrees, finding the sea all open, and forty leagues betweene land and land. The passage is most probable, the execution easie.'[104] His hopes of another voyage were dashed by the diversion of resources in 1588 to meet the Armada, and then by the death in 1590 of Walsingham, patron of so many overseas ventures. Davis was sailing with Cavendish with one purpose only: once the squadron reached California, Davis intended to sail north with two vessels to find the Pacific entrance of the Northwest Passage.[105]

Cavendish's second voyage was a dismal failure. Harassed by storms, scurvy, divided counsels and continual separations, the expedition was unable to win clear of the south Atlantic. One attempt by Cavendish to get through the Strait of Magellan in early winter failed; another by Davis succeeded to the extent that he reached the Pacific, but faced with appalling winter weather and the loss of one of his ships he too turned back. Raids on Portuguese settlements and shipping brought little compensation to Cavendish, and his exhortations to his crew to try the Strait once more fell on deaf ears: 'They all with one consente affairmed plainelie they woulde never goe that waye againe.'[106] As the sole surviving ship under his command sailed for home, Cavendish, still only thirty-two years old, made his will, wrote an account of the voyage with the knowledge of his own impending death before him and was buried at sea.

A final attempt to emulate the success of Drake and Cavendish (on his first voyage) was made by Richard Hawkins in 1593. His narrative of the

---

103.   *Calendar of State Papers, Spanish*, IV, pp. 489, 504, 511, 525.
104.   Hakluyt, *Principal Navigations*, VII, p. 423.
105.   See A.H. Markham, ed., *The Voyages and Works of John Davis* (London, 1880), p. 232.
106.   Quinn, *Last Voyage*, f. 28.

expedition was not published until 1622, which probably explains the absence of any mention of raids along the coasts of Spanish America among the
expedition's objectives. Such a reference would not have been tactful in the
reign of James I. Even without this, the range of the expedition was wide
enough, as Hawkins wrote that he was bound 'for the Ilands of *Iapan*, of the
Phillippinas, and *Molucas*, the Kingdomes of *China*, and *East Indies*, by way of
the *Straites of Magelan*, and the South Sea'.[107] The expedition got through the
Strait, and after standing out to sea turned north along the coasts of Chile and
Peru in search of booty. But much had changed along the coast since Drake's
voyage: there were fortifications, armed ships, convoys, lookouts. In June
1594, after a bloody engagement in which three-quarters of his crew were
killed or wounded, Hawkins's ship the *Dainty* was taken, and with it
Hawkins and his surviving men. The rhetoric was as heroic as ever – 'Came
we into the South-sea to put out flagges of trace . . . white ragges',[108]
Hawkins appealed to his men – but it now had a tone of desperation.

  As the war with Spain drifted into stalemate and failure, marked by the
deaths of Drake and John Hawkins (father of Richard) on the unsuccessful
Caribbean expedition of 1595–6, so the South Sea lost its appeal. There were
no more easy pickings along the coasts of Spanish America, and so there was
little reason to brave the Strait of Magellan. In 1600 the incorporation of the
East India Company marked the beginning of concerted English efforts to
exploit the riches of the East, but the route would be round the Cape of
Good Hope rather than that prospected by Drake and Cavendish across the
Pacific. The sprawling and vulnerable Portuguese trading empire in the
Indian Ocean became the main target, and the Dutch the main rivals. There
were still hopes of an easier route to China and the South Sea, but these
were more than ever centred on the Northwest Passage.

In retrospect, the South Sea ventures of Elizabeth's reign fitted into the
general pattern of English overseas enterprise in that period – 'a long and
painful series of failures and disasters, only occasionally relieved by some
brilliant feat'.[109] Foremost among the latter were the circumnavigations of
Drake and Cavendish. For a long time they served as role models, with links
stretching to Anson's voyage of the mid-eighteenth century. For Hakluyt and
other publicists they provided support for the new patriotic insistence on the
skill and daring of English seamen.[110] For acquisitive contemporaries they
provided first-hand information on Spanish seaborne commerce in the Pacific: the route along which silver passed from Peru to the Isthmus, and the
galleon trade between Manila and Acapulco, with its lucrative feeder spur

107. Williamson, *Hawkins' Observations*, p. xlix.
108. Ibid., p. 144.
109. Andrews, *Trade, Plunder and Settlement*, p. 1.
110. See Richard Helgerson, *Forms of Nationhood: The Elizabethan Writing of England* (Chicago,
      1992), pp. 149–91.

stretching to Canton. There was little evidence that English interest went further than plunder, despite the references in promotional literature to the opening of new trades or the establishment of settlements. Of the Pacific as a whole there was still little grasp. The emphasis was on the margins: the coasts of Spanish America, China, the Philippines, the Moluccas. The vast spaces of Oceania remained a void and attracted little attention. The tracks of Drake and Cavendish across the North Pacific strengthened the notion of an empty ocean. The narrative of Drake's voyage covered the unbroken navigation of more than two months from California to Palau in a half-dozen words: 'wee continued without sight of land.'[111] Pretty's narrative of the crossing by Cavendish offered only slightly more detail: 'Wee were sayling . . . the rest of November, and all December, and so forth until the 3 of Januarie 1588, with a faire winde for the space 45 dayes: and we esteemed it to be between 17 and 18 hundred leagues.'[112] Except in Drake's New Albion there had been no prolonged contact with the native inhabitants. At Palau and Guam the fleeting nature of the encounters in the waters off the islands was shown by the fact that the English notes on the outrigger canoes were fuller than their descriptions of the islanders themselves. Not only did the diplomatic situation under the Stuarts rule against further hostilities with Spain, but English attention and investment were turning towards the new plantations across the Atlantic and towards the Cape of Good Hope route and the trade of the East. It would be more than seventy years after Richard Hawkins's unsuccessful venture before another English vessel entered the South Sea.

---

111. Hakluyt, *Principal Navigations*, XI, p. 123.
112. Ibid., XI, p. 238.

CHAPTER II

Geographical Enigmas and Literary Utopias

The first century of the European arrival in the Pacific had sketched in some of the main features of the ocean, but had left unresolved two major issues. In the north a sea passage from the Atlantic had still not been found, despite repeated attempts (mostly English) to discover a Northwest Passage. To the south the existence of a great continent in temperate latitudes was still an open question. As exploration during the seventeenth century seemed to narrow the options, if not provide conclusive answers to these puzzles, so a countervailing mixture of speculative geography and apocryphal narratives kept alive hopes of some dramatic discovery.

On the Northwest Passage little progress was made after the discovery of Hudson Bay and Baffin Bay in the first decades of the seventeenth century. Nine years after Frobisher in 1578 entered Hudson Strait by mistake, John Davis crossed the same 'very great gulfe', but did not enter it. It remained for Henry Hudson in 1610 to rediscover Hudson Strait and to sail on westwards into the huge bay which has since borne his name. Whatever the reality of earlier voyages into Hudson Bay, it was Hudson who established the fact and not merely the rumour of an arm of the ocean penetrating far into the northern parts of the American continent. The survivors' report of 'a spacious sea' was accepted as proof that the route to the South Sea lay open. Despite the death of Hudson himself, in England a new company was established to follow up his discovery of 'a streight or narrow sea by the which they hope and purpose to advance a trade to the great kingdoms of Tartarie, China, Japan, Solomons Islands, Chili, the Philippins and other countrys in or upon the said [South] Sea'.[1]

Financed by almost three hundred investors, 'The Governor and Company of the Merchants of London, Discoverers of the North-West Passage' sponsored the voyages of Thomas Button (1612–13) and William Baffin

---

1.   Quoted in G.M. Asher, ed., *Henry Hudson the Navigator* (London, 1860), p. 253.

(1616). Button coasted six hundred miles of the west and north shores of Hudson Bay, but found no sign of a passage. Nor did Robert Bylot, a survivor of Hudson's final voyage, who was sent out in 1615 with Baffin as his pilot. As the search shifted farther north, Baffin and Bylot in 1616 pushed through heavy ice in Davis Strait to open water. At their farthest north they were in lat. 78°N., not reached again until the nineteenth century. To the west they saw Lancaster Sound but also 'a ledge of ice', and Baffin's final verdict was that 'there is no passage nor hope of passage in the north of Davis Straights'.[2] The search was virtually over, for that century at least. In 1619 Jens Munk took a Danish expedition into Hudson Bay, but only three men survived its wintering at Churchill River. Final disillusionment came with the rival voyages to Hudson Bay of Luke Foxe and Thomas James in 1631. Their only encounter, off the shore of Hudson Bay east of Port Nelson, was marked by a rather absurd disagreement over protocol. There was a touch of black humour in Foxe's journal description of the meeting: 'I did not thinke much for his keeping out his flagg . . . To this [James] replide, that hee was going to the Emperour of Japon, with letters from his Majestie . . . "Keep it up then", quoth I, "but you are out of the way to Japon, for this is not it."'[3] There was a glimpse of hope in Foxe's report of an unusually high tide near an opening in lat. 64°N. on the northwest coast of the Bay − called Ne Ultra (No Further) by Button in 1612, the opening was optimistically renamed Roe's Welcome by Foxe − but it was not enough to tempt further discoverers. When English ships returned to Hudson Bay later in the century fur-trading rather than exploration was the priority.

So disheartening had been the repeated efforts at discovery through the ice-choked bays of the Atlantic that more thought was given to the feasibility of an approach from the Pacific. Grenville had raised the possibility in 1574, and more than a hundred years later William Dampier argued in favour of an attempt to find the western entrance of the passage.

> If I was to go on this Discovery, I would go first into the *South-Seas*, bend my course from thence along to *California*, and that way seek a Passage back into the *West-Seas* [i.e. the Atlantic]. For as others have spent the Summer, in first searching on this more known side nearer home, and so before they got through, the time of the Year obliged them to give over their Search, and provide for a long course back again, for fear of being left in the Winter; on the contrary, I would search first on the less known coast of the South-Sea-side, and then as the Year past away, I should need no retreat, for I should come farther into my Knowledge.[4]

2. C.R. Markham, ed., *The Voyages of William Baffin, 1612–1622* (London, 1881), p. 150.
3. Miller Christy, ed., *The Voyages of Captain Luke Foxe of Hull, and Captain Thomas James of Bristol* (London, 1894), II, p. 359.
4. William Dampier, *A New Voyage Round the World* ([1697]/1729), pp. 273–4.

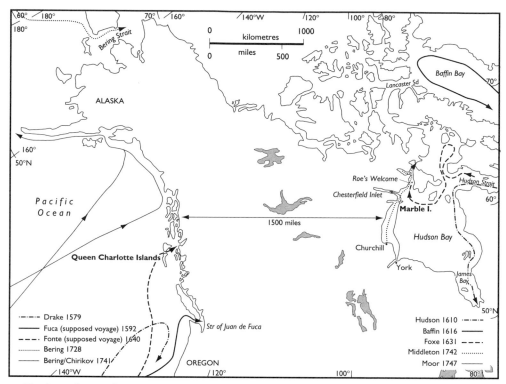

2. Northern Approaches, 1570s to 1740s.

Such thoughts were encouraged by the fact that the Strait of Anian still appeared on many of the maps of the Pacific coast of North America. Its phantom presence was given some substance by the alleged discovery of a deep inlet on that coast between lat. 47°N. and lat. 48°N. by Juan de Fuca in 1592. The affair of the Fuca voyage still presents many puzzling features, but the main outlines are clear. The account of the voyage was first printed by Samuel Purchas in 1625 in his collection of voyages, *Hakluytus Posthumus or Purchas his Pilgrimes*. It told how in 1596 Michael Lok, the English merchant and promoter much involved in Frobisher's Arctic voyages, met a veteran Greek pilot named Juan de Fuca in Venice. Fuca had served the Spaniards in the West Indies and the South Sea for forty years, and claimed to have been on the *Santa Ana* when it was captured by Cavendish off Lower California in 1587. After this misfortune, he said, the Viceroy of New Spain sent him in 1592 on an expedition to find the Strait of Anian.

With the help of 'a great Map' (which has not survived) he explained to Lok how he sailed north

> untill hee came to the Latitude of fortie seven degrees, and that there finding that the Land trended North and North-east, with a broad Inlet of Sea, between 47. and 48. degrees of Latitude: he entred thereinto, sayling therein

more then twentie dayes, and found that Land trending still sometime North-west and North-east, and North, and also East and South-eastward, and very much broader Sea then was at the said entrance . . . that he went on Land in divers places, and that he saw some people on Land, clad in Beasts skins: and that the Land is very fruitfull, and rich of gold, Silver, Pearle, and other things, like Nova Spania.[5]

Later investigations showed that a Greek pilot named Juan de Fuca had served in Mexico between 1588 and 1594, and there is nothing surprising about a Spanish attempt to explore north along the coast (as Cabrillo had done in 1542–3, and as Vizcaíno was to do in 1602–3), nor about the subsequent lack of official interest in Spain in the venture. But the fact is that there is no record of a discovery expedition in 1592, with or without Fuca on board, which sailed as far north as lat. 48°N.[6] Whether the story printed by Purchas was concocted by Lok, or whether the merchant was himself beguiled by a hard-luck story by the old pilot, who would have been aware of the keen English interest in the Northwest Passage, has never been determined. That Lok indeed met Fuca is confirmed by the *Naval Tracts* of Admiral Monson, written about 1610, but not published until 1704. Monson described how Cavendish burnt the *Santa Ana*, and then put her crew ashore to make their way as best they could to Navidad. He continued that some years later the ship's Greek pilot met Lok in Italy 'and related to him all the Particulars of his Voyage'.[7]

The Fuca story was not the only hare that Purchas set running in his 1625 *Pilgrimes*. Spanish hopes of finding a port of call north of Cape San Lucas for the eastbound galleons from Manila, together with continued anxiety about the possible existence of the Strait of Anian (both Drake and Cavendish were rumoured to have passed through it on their return to England), led to the northern expedition of Sebastián Vizcaíno in 1602–3. One of his vessels, the *Tres Reyes*, sailed as far north as lat. 43°N. to the region of Cape Blanco. After the expedition's return one of its cosmographers, Father Antonio de la Ascensión, incorporated what he claimed to be the discoveries made from the *Tres Reyes* into a series of memorials which argued that California was an island, and that it lay just south of the entrance of the Strait of Anian.[8]

In 1625 this concept was given wide circulation in a map by Henry Briggs of 'The North Part of America' which appeared in Purchas (Ill. 7). California

---

5. Samuel Purchas, *Hakluytus Posthumus or Purchas his Pilgrimes* [1625], XIV (Glasgow, 1906), pp. 416–17.
6. A critical examination of the Fuca account is included in H.R. Wagner, 'Apocryphal Voyages to the Northwest Coast of America', *Proceedings of the American Antiquarian Society*, 41 (1931), pp. 179–234; for a rather less censorious analysis see Warren L. Cook, *Flood Tide of Empire: Spain and the Pacific Northwest, 1543–1819* (New Haven, 1973), pp. 22–29.
7. Awnsham and John Churchill, *A Collection of Voyages and Travels* (London, 1704), III, p. 432.
8. For a good summary see Polk, *Island of California*, Ch. XXIV.

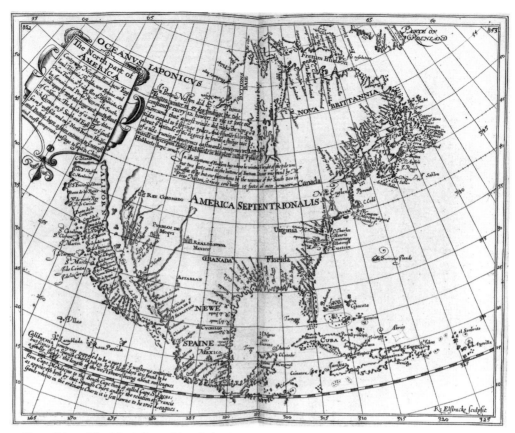

7. Henry Briggs. 'The North Part of America', 1625.

is shown as an island, with Cape Blanco as its northern tip. On the opposite
mainland the coast begins to turn, seductively, to the northeast, and towards
Hudson Bay. The legends proclaimed that the depiction of California was
based on a captured Spanish chart and linked it with those English explorations in Hudson Bay which had opened 'a faire entrance to ye nearest and
most temperate passage to Japan and China'. In the Briggs map, Spanish
speculations, Drake's unknown northern track in 1579 and the explorations
of Hudson and Baffin were brought together in a classic example of wishful
(on the Spanish side, fearful) thinking. Not all geographers accepted the idea
of an insular California, but more than a hundred maps followed Briggs's
error before Father Eusebio Francisco Kino at the turn of the century
reached the head of the Gulf of California and later drew a map that depicted
California, once again, as a peninsula. In February 1709 a paper was read at
the Royal Society, London, on 'ye discovery of California whereby it

appears not to be an island'. The Strait of Anian, however, was to take rather longer to disappear from the maps.[9]

With none of the sixteenth-century voyages producing clear evidence of a southern continent, scepticism about its existence grew. Edward Wright's world map of 1599 (Ill. 8), published by Hakluyt, showed only an unnamed fragment of coastline south of Java. Wright's map was to achieve fortuitous fame through its identification with Shakespeare's 'new map, with the augmentation of the Indies' mentioned in *Twelfth Night* (the 'augmentation' probably a reference to the prominence of the Solomon Islands on the map); but aside from this it was a fine early example of English cartography.[10] A few years later Bishop Joseph Hall asked a pertinent question in *The Discovery of a New World* (1609): 'If they know it for a Continent, and for a Southerne Continent, why then doe they call it unknowne?' Nathaniel Carpenter was equally waspish when he wrote of the 'South Continent' that 'we cannot imagine [it] to be so great in quantity, as it is printed in our ordinary Mappes: forasmuch as all places at the first discovery are commonly described greater then they are.'[11]

Other cartographers preferred to show the great continent filling most of the southern hemisphere. The Hondius Drake Broadside Map followed the Terra Australis concept, if not the precise shape of the Ortelius and Mercator maps. The explanation by Cornelis Wytfliet as to why his world map of 1597 showed a continental landmass in the southern hemisphere can stand for generations of believers:

> the south-land . . . the southernmost of all countries, extends immediately towards the Polar Circle, but also towards the countries of the east beyond the Tropic of the Capricorn and almost at the equator its confines are to be found, and in the east, separated by a narrow strait it lies in front of New Guinea, but is explored only at a few coastal places, because after one and other voyage that route has been discontinued and thence rarely sails are set except that ships are driven off by cyclones. It takes its beginnings two or three degrees under the equator and is assigned such an extension by some that it may well appear to be the fifth continent after having been discovered fully.[12]

Disagreement about the existence of a southern continent was fuelled in the early seventeenth century by the conflicting reports brought back by the

9. On this see R.V. Tooley, *California as an Island* (London, 1964).
10. See Helen Wallis, 'Edward Wright and the 1599 World Map', in D.B. Quinn, ed., *The Hakluyt Handbook* (London, 1974), I, pp. 69–73.
11. Quoted in W.T. James, 'Nostalgia for Paradise: *Terra Australis* in the Seventeenth Century', in Ian Donaldson, ed., *Australia and the European Imagination* (Canberra, 1982), pp. 65, 68.
12. Cornelis Wytfliet, *Descriptionis Ptolemaicae Augmentum* (1597), quoted in Günter Schilder, *Australia Unveiled. The Share of the Dutch Navigators in the Discovery of Australia* (Amsterdam, 1976), p. 18.

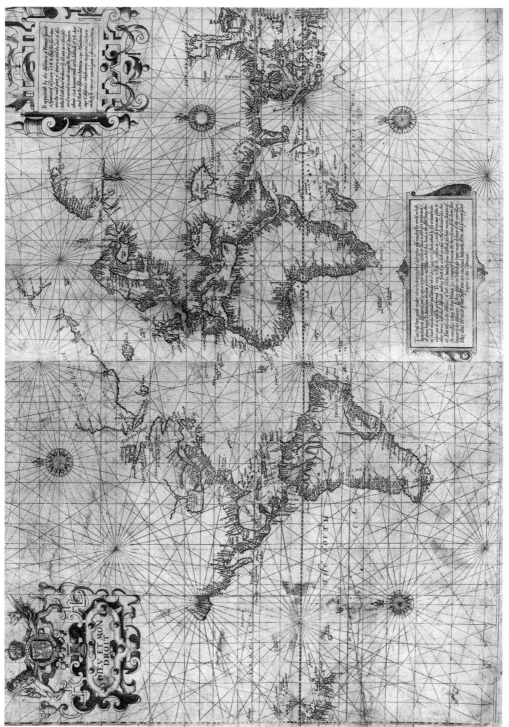

8. Edward Wright. World map, 1599.

last of the Spanish explorers of the Pacific and the first of the Dutch. The expansionist urge that had taken Spain across the Americas into the South Sea and as far west as Manila was fading in the face of the new Dutch threat, but there was enough impetus left around the turn of the century to promote a voyage whose impact on the European imagination was out of proportion to its geographical significance. It was a curious introduction to an era in which the results of Pacific exploration, mainly Dutch, seemed designed to stifle the speculative hopes of the geographers.

After his expedition of 1567–8, which reached the Solomon Islands, Mendaña was thwarted in his hopes of a quick return to the area to found a new Spanish colony. Not until 1595 did he once again sail west, in command of an expedition of four ships and four hundred people that was to become a byword for muddle, dissension and violence. The Solomon Islands were never found, though the ships touched at the Marquesas, where the slaughter of perhaps as many as two hundred of the islanders made an ominous beginning to the relationship between Europe and Polynesia. From the Marquesas the expedition kept west until it reached Ndeni or Santa Cruz Island, still more than two hundred miles short of the nearest island in the Solomon group, where again there was much indiscriminate killing and a half-hearted attempt at settlement. On the death of Mendaña, the Portuguese chief pilot, Pedro de Quiros, took the survivors to Manila in the remaining ship.

At Manila, Quiros informed the Lieutenant-Governor of the discovery of the Marquesas, but in terms that are a reminder that only two years earlier Hawkins had entered the South Sea as the latest in a series of English raiders since the dreaded Drake. Quiros himself had interrogated a prisoner from Hawkins's expedition at Lima in 1594, and he was clearly fearful of further English incursions into the South Sea. He asked the Governor to keep the existence of the Marquesas secret, for 'since the islands are situate mid-way between Peru, New Spain and here, the English could do much harm in these waters if they got to hear of them and settled there.'[13]

For every attempt by Spain to hide its explorations from the English, there would appear in England some published claim of Pacific discovery, exciting but imprecise. So in 1604 Edward Grimston's translation of José de Acosta's *Historia Natural y Moral de las Indias* put before English readers the notion that both the 'Isles of Solomon' and an austral continent might have been discovered by the Spaniards:

> In this South Sea, although they have not yet discovered the ende towards the West, yet of late they have found out the Ilands which they call Salomon, and which are many and great, distant from Peru about eight hundred leagues. And for that we find by observation, that wereas there bee many and great

13. J.S. Cummins, ed., *Sucesos de Las Islas Filipinas by Antonio de Morga* (Cambridge, 1971), pp. 104–5.

Ilandes, so there is some firm lande neere unto the Ilands of Salomon, the which doth answere unto our America on the West part, and possibly might runne by the heigth of the South, to the Straightes of Magellan.[14]

Possibly even more damaging to Spanish hopes of keeping their Pacific discoveries secret was the information that seems to have been passed on to the English by Pedro Sarmiento de Gamboa, who had sailed with Mendaña. He was captured by Raleigh's ships in 1586 as he was heading back to his imperilled colony in the Strait of Magellan and was taken to London where he was treated as an honoured guest rather than as a prisoner. Sarmiento's report for his English hosts, perhaps even a chart drawn by him, could explain the configuration of the Solomons on a number of English charts and globes at this time.[15]

Quiros meanwhile was pressing for another expedition, but the two ships (the second commanded by Luis Vaez de Torres) and a launch which finally sailed from Callao at the end of 1605 had larger objectives than simply the colonization of the Marquesas. Quiros had convinced himself that the frailty of the native craft of the islands and the direction of the prevailing winds indicated that the light-skinned islanders had come from unknown lands nearby, and before long these lands had taken shape in his mind as the great southern continent.[16] So, the aim of the expedition was to circumnavigate the world, 'returning to Spain by the East Indies, first discovering . . . the unknown lands of the south; thence proceeding via New Guinea to arrive at China, Maluco, and the two Javas, the Great and the Less, and all the other famous islands abounding in silver, gold, gems and spices.'[17]

That it was continent and not islands for which Quiros was searching was shown by his sailing southeast away from the location of Santa Cruz in search of a great land, 'Manicolo', of which the islanders at Taumako had informed him. At the beginning of May 1606 he came to the high, mountainous land of Espiritu Santo, the largest island in the group later to be named the New Hebrides (today's Vanuatu). The quest, he thought, was over as he named the new land Austrialia del Espíritu Santo – the first word not a variant of Australia, the Austral or South Land, but a tribute to Austria, of which Philip III was Archduke (though at times Quiros reverted to what seems to have been his original spelling of 'Australia'). The attempt to found 'Nueva Jerusalen' and go on to 'take possession of all these islands and lands which I have newly discovered and wish to discover as far as the Pole'[18] ended in

---

14. From *The Naturall and Morall Historie of the East and West Indies*, quoted in Jack-Hinton, *Search*, p. 83.
15. See Helen Wallis, 'The Cartography of Drake's Voyage', in Thrower, *Drake and the Famous Voyage*, pp. 151–3.
16. See Celsus Kelly, ed., *La Austrialia del Espíritu Santo* (Cambridge, 1966), I, pp. 13–14.
17. Jack-Hinton, *Search*, p. 138. 'The great' Java was a reference to the mysterious Java la Grande of the mid-sixteenth-century Dieppe maps.
18. Kelly, *La Austrialia del Espíritu Santo*, I, p. 220.

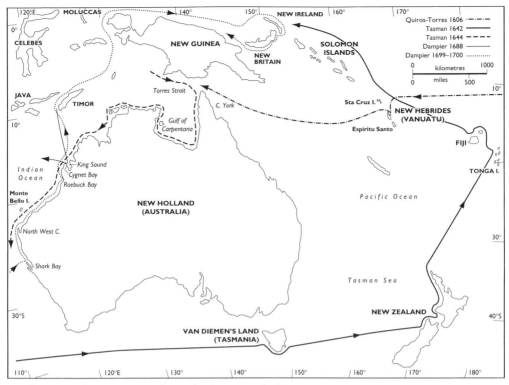

3. The Search for Terra Australis in the Seventeenth Century.

violence and the abandonment of the site. It was left to Torres to carry out further exploration, and to reach the Moluccas and then Manila by way of the strait between Australia and New Guinea which now has his name.

Memories of Torres's discovery soon dimmed, though rumours of the strait he had found persisted until James Cook repeated the passage in 1770.[19] The discovery of Espiritu Santo, by contrast, was to be inflated by Quiros to epic and mystical proportions and stamped its glittering image on generations of navigators and projectors. After a humiliating return from his voyage, Quiros begged his way from Mexico to Spain, where he bombarded the King, the Council of State and the Council of the Indies with memorials (about seventy in all) urging renewal of the quest. Although he received some encouragement, particularly from Philip III, sceptical Spanish officials were able to keep Quiros and his clamorous petitions at arm's length. He died in 1615 in Panama, but enough of his writings were published (and translated into several languages, including English) to keep alive memories of his supposed discovery. In a spiralling series of claims, Quiros insisted that

19. See Spate, *Spanish Lake*, p. 140.

the continent that awaited discovery was (in the words of the English translation of 1617 of his *Eighth Memorial*) 'as great as all *Europe & Asia* the lesse'. It was the 'fifth part of the Terrestrial Globe, and extended it selfe to such length, that in probabilitie it is twice greater in Kingdoms and Seignories, then all that which at this day doth acknowledge subiection and obedience vnto your Maiestie'. In terms of its climate and produce it was an earthly paradise, while its numerous inhabitants were only awaiting conversion. It offered spices, silver and gold; and this was confirmed in the first-hand observations of Quiros and his officers rather than merely rumoured: 'The riches which I haue seene in those parts, is Siluer and Pearle; another Captaine in his Relation, doth report that he hath seen Gold.'[20]

It seemed altogether appropriate that the contrasting view of the potential of this general area should come from the Dutch, enemies to Spain in Europe and formidable rivals to its imperialism overseas. In 1602 the governing body of the Dutch provinces consolidated existing organizations into the United East India Company or Vereenigde Oost-Indische Compagnie (VOC) and granted it a monopoly of Dutch trade in the vast region between the Cape of Good Hope and the Strait of Magellan. Once established in the East Indies, the VOC began seeking further markets, and in 1605 officials at Bantam sent the *Duyfken* 'to discover the great land Nova Guinea and other unknown east and south lands'.[21] The cartographical thinking behind this project was shown by the Plancius chart of 'Insulae Molvccae', where New Guinea appeared as a great promontory with an attached legend stating that it was probably part of the great southern continent. To the east were the Solomons, with again hints of continental shapes close by, and to the west Marco Polo's Beach. The spaces between were filled with sketches of the new objectives of Dutch enterprise: cloves, nutmeg and sandalwood.[22]

A few months before Quiros reached Espiritu Santo, the Dutch in March 1606 made their first Australian landing, in the Gulf of Carpentaria, though this was assumed to be part of New Guinea. The voyage of Willem Jansz in the *Duyfken* was the precursor to a series of reconnaissance probes by the Dutch in the first half of the century, which revealed the western outlines of Australia from Cape York in the northeast to Van Diemen's Land (Tasmania)

20. For all this, and much more, see *'Terra Australis Incognita', or A New Southerne Discoverie, Containing a Fifth Part of the World. Lately Found Out by Ferdinand De Qvir, A Spanish Captaine* (London, 1617). There is a useful collection of facsimile reprints of the various versions of the *Eighth Memorial* of Quiros printed between 1609 and 1625 in Carlos Sanz, ed., *Australia: Su Descubrimiento y Denominación* (Madrid, 1973).
21. Schilder, *Australia Unveiled*, p. 43.
22. See William Eisler, *The Furthest Shore: Images of Terra Australis from the Middle Ages to Captain Cook* (Cambridge, 1995), pp. 42–3.

in the south. But they found not the legendary South Land of untold riches, but New Holland, whose proud name flattered to deceive. The Dutch accounts portrayed the region as arid and flyblown, without exploitable resources, with only a few inhabitants, and those as backward as any people in the world. In his journal of 1623 Jan Carstenz described them as 'barbarians all much alike in build and features, pitch-black and entirely naked . . . they have no knowledge at all of gold, silver, tin, iron, lead and copper; even nutmegs, cloves and pepper which had been shown to them several times on the voyage made no impression on them.'[23] The Dutch explorations represent the first major, undisputed steps in the accurate delineation of the Australian continent. The emergence of this real geographical entity from the shadow cast by the looming but undiscovered mass of Terra Australis made cartographers more cautious as to how they showed the region southeast of Indonesia. By the late 1620s, Dutch cartographers had included the west coast of Cape York on their maps, usually connecting it to New Guinea in a rather indeterminate way. In the 1628 additions to his chart of the Malay Archipelago and the region to the south, Hessel Gerritsz marked 'the coasts of western and southern Australia from 21°S down to 35°S, with every discovery drawn separately and hypothetical coasts deliberately omitted'.[24]

One of the most important Dutch voyages of the period was not directed at Australia at all and was not fitted out by the VOC. This was the expedition of Jacob Le Maire and Isaac Schouten in 1615–16, which aimed to evade the monopoly rights of the VOC by sailing into the Pacific from the east. With the crews encouraged in the venture by a public recital in mid-Atlantic of the *Eighth Memorial* of Quiros,[25] the two ships sailed past the Atlantic entrance of the Strait of Magellan, through the strait (to be named after Le Maire) between Tierra del Fuego and Staten Island, round Cape Horn and so into the South Sea. By doing so, the voyage confirmed Drake's speculation that Tierra del Fuego was insular, and in time the passage round the Horn rather than through the Strait of Magellan became the normal route. In May 1616 the ships reached the northern fringes of the Tongan group (the first Europeans to do so), which they at first hoped might be the location of Quiros's discovery. Here, and at the Horne Islands, the Dutch recorded their first impressions of Polynesia. They had reservations about the apparent lack of religion and morals, but found much to admire and enjoy. For Schouten in particular there was enough for him to declare that he had found his own Terra Australis.[26]

23. Quoted in Günter Schilder, 'New Holland: The Dutch Discoveries', in Williams and Frost, *Terra Australis to Australia*, p. 91.
24. Ibid., p. 97.
25. See Kelly, *La Austrialia del Espíritu Santo*, I, p. 5.
26. See Eisler, *Furthest Shore*, p. 73.

Unlike many of the Dutch accounts, Schouten's was published in English, under the beguiling title *The Relation of a Wonderful Voiage* (1619), but news of the expedition reached England as early as the summer of 1617. That July Sir Dudley Carleton, English ambassador to the Hague, reported 'a new discoverie of a passage into *mare pacificum* betwixt 60 and 70 leagues beyond the straites of Magellan in the heith of 55 degrees and a few minutes. The passage being seaven Duch miles in breadth and no more in length, so as in less than a day it may be sayled through. You can appreciate what this could lead to, if it is true.'[27] There had already been attempts to interest the English East India Company in a venture to the Pacific. Sir James Lancaster tried in 1614, and on several other occasions, to persuade the Company 'to have a ship appointed to go through the Straits of Magellan to the Isles of Solomon', but to no avail.[28] The voyage of Le Maire and Schouten brought a flurry of interest in Company circles, and in 1618 Sir Thomas Ditchington met Le Maire on behalf of the East India Company. This initiative was supported by the King, James I, who expressed enthusiasm for southern discovery and 'to have the business prosecuted as soon as possible; he cares not by whom, so long as it be effected.' Here lay the problem, however, for the King seems to have granted a patent, not to the East India Company, but to Ditchington and his associates. These informed the Company that there was 'a new passage towards Mare Zur, under the tropics towards the Isle of Solomon, where the navigators [Le Maire and Schouten] passed by 300 islands, and saw ginger, cloves, and other spices in the land of the inhabitants.'[29] At this point the project disappears from view, caught, it seems, between the reluctance of the East India Company to pursue speculative discoveries and the inability of the patentees to raise capital. In 1622 the Company lost a ship, the *Trial*, and a hundred men off the northwest coast of Australia; but the vessel was in that area not through design but as the result of a gross navigational error by the master as he attempted to follow the new Dutch route in lat. 20°S. from the Cape of Good Hope to Java.[30] A final attempt to emulate the Dutch came in 1625 when Sir William Courteen, a leading London merchant and ship-owner, unsuccessfully petitioned James I for rights to 'all the lands in ye South parts of ye world called Terra Australis incognita extending Eastwards & West-wards from ye Straights of Le Maire together with all ye adjacent Islands &c. [as] are yet undiscovered or being discovered are not yet traded unto by any of your Maties subjects'.[31]

★

27. *Devonshire Manuscripts*, VI, *Papers of William Trumbull the Elder 1616–1618* (London, Historical Manuscripts Commission, 1995), p. 241.
28. Jack-Hinton, *Search*, p. 188.
29. This, and the preceding quotation, in ibid., p. 199.
30. See J.N. Green, ed., *Australia's Oldest Wreck*, British Archaeological Reports, Supplementary Series 27 (Oxford, 1977).
31. Printed in George Mackaness, ed., *Some Proposals for Establishing Colonies in the South Sea* (Sydney, 1943), pp. 6–7.

The Dutch explorations of the first thirty years of the century had not thrown much light on the question of the relationship between the Terra Australis of myth and the unpromising coastline of New Holland. Was the latter simply the bulging extremity of a huge continental landmass stretching south and east as shown on the older, more speculative maps? If so, there might yet be rich and fertile lands awaiting discovery. It was in this context that the VOC voyage of Abel Tasman in 1642–3 was of crucial importance. Tasman was an experienced explorer who had done useful survey work in the North Pacific, and in 1642 Anthony van Diemen, Governor-General of the Dutch East Indies, appointed him to the command of an expedition that was to 'sail to the partly known as well as the undiscovered South and East lands, to discover them and find some important lands'.[32] Tasman's two ships sailed from Batavia far out into the Indian Ocean before swinging back towards New Holland in southerly latitudes. Turning east towards Australia in lat. 44°S. Tasman in November 1642 sighted a coast which he named Van Diemen's Land (modern Tasmania). Ten days of cruising off the coast and a brief landing failed to reveal any inhabitants, and what evidence there was of human activity was not reassuring – distant horns and notches in trees cut so far apart that only men of huge stature could have made them. Tasman then sailed east until he reached the coast of a land he called New Zealand, where he turned north. A brief and bloody encounter with the Maori of South Island left four of his men dead at Golden Bay ('Murderers' Bay' to Tasman). From here he continued north, past the unseen opening of Cook Strait, along the coast of North Island, and across the open sea to Tonga. Here the reception was very different: gifts were exchanged, festivities held, even a musical concert put on by the Dutch. There were problems, of a sort recorded almost as routine by later visitors to Polynesia. Though friendly, 'this people is exceedingly lascivious wanton and thievish', a disapproving Tasman wrote.[33] As the ship turned northwest for Batavia they touched at New Ireland, where some amicable bartering took place, and as at Golden Bay and Tonga the artist on board, Isaac Gilsemans, was able to record his impressions of the people and their surroundings.

In June 1643 the ships arrived back at Batavia, only to receive a frosty welcome from van Diemen, who thought little of Tasman's achievement. He 'has not made many investigations regarding the situations nor form and nature of the discovered lands and peoples,' the Governor-General reported home, 'but has in principle left everything to a more inquisitive successor.'[34] Despite this, Tasman was sent out once more in 1644, this time to investigate

32. Schilder, 'New Holland: The Dutch Discoveries', in Williams and Frost, *Terra Australis to Australia*, p. 97.
33. Andrew Sharp, ed., *The Voyages of Abel Janszoon Tasman* (Oxford, 1968), p. 168.
34. Schilder, 'New Holland: The Dutch Discoveries', in Williams and Frost, *Terra Australis to Australia*, p. 100.

the northern shores of New Holland. He was to settle the question of whether there was a strait separating New Holland and New Guinea, and also whether there might be a north–south strait through New Holland to Van Diemen's Land. No log or written report survives from the voyage, but later charts showing Tasman's track make it clear that he found neither strait. Van Diemen once more expressed criticism of the handling of the voyage to the directors of the VOC. Tasman, he wrote, had come across 'nothing profitable, only poor, naked people walking along the beaches; without rice or any fruits, very poor and bad-tempered in many places'.[35]

The disappointment of van Diemen was tangible and understandable; but in terms of knowledge, if not of profit, Tasman's first voyage, in particular, was of prime importance. It set the terms of reference for the geography of the region until Cook's arrival in Australian waters in 1770. By circumnavigating, if at a distance, New Holland, Tasman showed that it could not be part of a greater southern continent. That was pushed back at least as far as the stretch of New Zealand coastline sighted in December 1642–January 1643, named 'Statenlandt' by Tasman because he thought that it might be joined to Le Maire's Staten Land or Island of 1616. Not all was negative. What had been seen of New Holland might be arid and unpromising, and New Zealand appeared to be the home of grim and menacing people; but the Tongam Islands offered a more welcoming prospect and strengthened Schouten's opinion that Quiros's vision might yet have some substance. At the very least the Spanish and Dutch discoveries seemed to point to a string of islands running southeast from the region of New Guinea across the Pacific, possibly merging into a continental landmass east of New Zealand.

The continuing curiosity of English traders about the activities of their powerful Dutch rivals led to some scraps of information about Tasman's discoveries reaching England at a surprisingly early date. The records of the East India Company include a rough sketch of part of the coast of Van Diemen's Land sent home in January 1644 by the English resident at Bantam. It was annotated, rather ambitiously, with the legend 'A Draught of the South Land lately discovered 1643'. An accompanying letter noted that it had taken 'extraordinary friendschipp' to obtain the map, and went on to state:

> The Dutch have lately made a new discovery of the South Land in latitude of 44 degrees and their longitude 169, the draught whereof is herewith sent. They relate of a gyant-like kinde of people there, very treacherouse, that tore in peeces lymbemeale their merchant, and would have done them further mischiefe, had they not betaken them to their shipps. They make mention alsoe of another sort of people about our stature, very white, and comely, and rudy, a people gentle and familiar, with whome, by their owne rellations, they have had some private conference. We are tould that the Dutch Generall

35.   Ibid., p. 103.

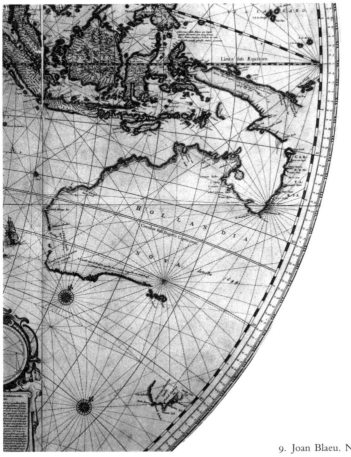

9. Joan Blaeu. New Holland, 1648.

intends to send thither againe and fortifie, having mett with something worth the looking after.[36]

Here, in a few sentences, was conflated much of the Dutch experience and the English suspicion: the contrast between Tasman's reception in New Zealand and in Tonga; the inference that valuable discoveries had been made and were being kept secret. Even so, there was no likelihood that the English company would spend any of its limited resources in vying with the Dutch in so remote a region.

Within a year or two of Tasman's return in 1644 Dutch cartographers were showing his discoveries on their maps. The first known example, Joan Blaeu's revised version in 1645–6 of the world map first produced by his

36. Schilder, *Australia Unveiled*, p. 189n.

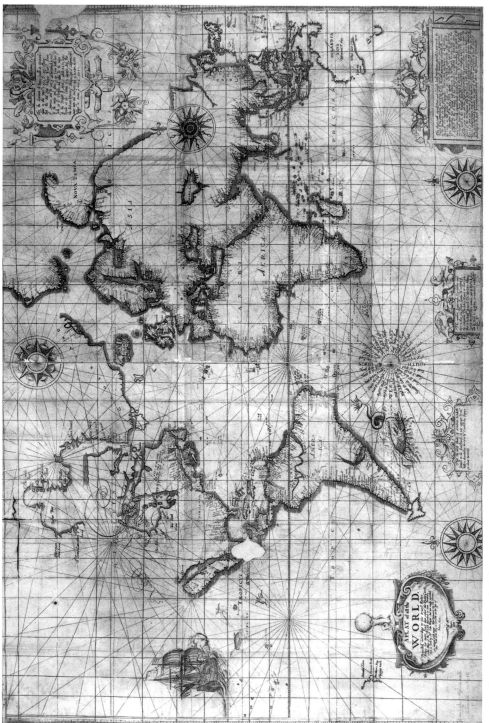

10. Joseph Moxon. 'A Plat of all the World', 1655.

father in 1619, had a symbolic significance. Blaeu removed from the original map the sweeping outlines of Terra Australis and replaced them with New Holland as charted by Tasman and the earlier VOC explorers (Ill. 9).[37] There was no particular eagerness on the Dutch company's part to publicize Tasman's explorations, nor should any be expected in this era of monopoly trade. His discoveries in southern latitudes held out little prospect of immediate commercial gain, yet any foreign incursion into those waters would be a threat to the Dutch position. As the directors noted ruefully at this time (of another region): 'It were to be wished that the said land continued still unknown and never explored, so as not to tell foreigners the way to the Company's overthrow.'[38] On the other hand, there was little of the fearful concern with secrecy that had marked many of the earlier Spanish discoveries. If there had been, Tasman's explorations would not have been shown on published maps and would hardly have been displayed on the great world map laid on the floor of the new city hall in Amsterdam in about 1650 for all to see. Nor would the superb Klencke Atlas have been presented to Charles II in 1660 with, among its maps, Joan Blaeu's 'Archipelagus Orientalis sive Asiaticus', which showed New Holland and much else. Among the first signs of recognition outside Holland of the significance of Tasman's explorations was an English world map of 1655 by Joseph Moxon (Ill. 10), whose representation and naming of 'Nova Holandia' was taken from a Dutch map, presumably one of Blaeu's. Until the publication of Thévenot's fine map of 1663, Moxon's was the best representation of Tasman's discoveries to be issued outside Holland, but located as it was in a technical treatise on navigation it made no impact on the English cartographers of the day.[39]

Printed accounts of Tasman's voyage were slow to appear, but when they did English translations soon followed. A narrative by the surgeon Hendrik Haelbos was published in Dutch in 1671, and in the same year a shortened and rather unsatisfactory English translation was printed in John Ogilby's *America*. One of the interesting aspects of the version was that the English editor linked the Tasman voyage with the Quiros discoveries of 1606, pointing out that 'no Spaniard hath since that time set Foot on the unknown South-Land. But the [Dutch] East-India Company undertaking the Design with great eagerness, sent thither two Ships.'[40] It was this inclusion of the hopeful Spanish predictions of the results from an eastern approach to the region that helped to keep alive European interest despite the unenthusiastic

---

37. For the map, and the process of revision, see ibid., pp. 102–3.
38. Quoted in J.E. Heeres, ed., *Abel Janszoon Tasman's Journal of his Discovery of Van Diemen's Land and New Zealand in 1642* (Amsterdam, 1898), p. 74.
39. The map's title is 'A Plat of all the World . . . first set forth by Mr Edw. Wright And now newly Corrected and inlarged with many New Discoveries by Jos. Moxon . . . 1655'. It is placed at the end of *Certain Errors in Navigation Detected and Corrected by Edw. Wright . . . With Many Additions . . . Printed by Joseph Moxon* (London, 1657).
40. John Ogilby, *America* (London, 1671), p. 654.

reports that accompanied the Dutch approach from the northwest. The brief
narrative was short on geographical detail, lacking any indication of the
latitude or longitude of the 'South-Land' or any map. It had more to say on
encounters with the 'Southlanders' in New Zealand, where the clash at
Tasman's 'Murderers' Bay' was described.

The second narrative of the Tasman voyage to appear in print was that of
Dirck Rembrantsz van Nierop, based in part on Tasman's own journal.
Published in Dutch in 1674, it was translated into English and printed in the
Philosophical Transactions of the Royal Society in 1682. Twelve years later it
was reprinted, with a fuller introduction, in a collection of voyages published in London. There was more detail in the van Nierop account,
though without a map the narrative must have been difficult to follow. In
his introduction Tancred Robinson again hinted at a possible connection
between the Dutch explorations and the expedition of Quiros and Torres,
which

> sailed at several times above 800 Leagues together on the Coast of a Southern
> Continent, until they came to the height of 15 degrees of South Latitude,
> where they found a very fruitful, pleasant and populous Country . . . This
> vast Tract of Land perhaps may be one side of, or may belong to, Jansen
> Tasman's Land, Van Diemen's Land, Zelandia Nova, Carpentaria, and New
> Guiney.[41]

Robinson put Tasman's voyage into perspective for English readers in a way
that seemed to invite a response: it was 'the more considerable, in that 'tis the
Discovery of a New World, not yet known to the English'. Not until the
second edition of Nicolaas Witsen's *Noord en Oost Tartarye* in 1705 was a
fuller account of Tasman's explorations available in print, together with the
illustrations from his journal; but there was no contemporary English edition
of this important work.[42]

In his introduction to the compilation of 1694 Robinson not only spelt
out the significance of the Dutch discoveries but suggested that there were
others 'which they have not yet divulg'd'. Here he was repeating a rumour
that had taken firm hold in England. William Temple, Charles II's ambassador at the Hague, reported:

> I have heard it said among the Dutch, that their East India Company have
> long since forbidden, and under the greatest penalties, any further attempts of
> discovering that continent, having already more trade in those parts than they
> can turn to account, and fearing some more populous nations in Europe might

---

41. [Anon]., *An Account of Several Late Voyages & Discoveries to the South and North* (London, 1694),
     pp. x, xxvii–xxviii.
42. See 'The Southland in the Writings of Nicolaas Witsen', in Eisler, *Furthest Shore*, pp.
     139–41.

11. Guillaume de l'Isle. 'Hémisphère Méridional', 1714.

make great establishments of trade in some of those unknown regions, which might ruin or impair what they have already in the Indies.[43]

Ironically, the determination of Dutch cartographers to replace the earlier speculative charts with more accurate productions strengthened suspicions that they were deliberately concealing important discoveries. Some of the Spanish discoveries of the Mendaña and Quiros voyages, imprecise and unconnected, were omitted from the Dutch maps. On Blaeu's great

43. Quoted in Major, *Early Voyages*, p. vii.

world map of 1648, for example, not only is there no shadowy Terra Australis Incognita, but the Solomon Islands and the eastern part of New Guinea have also disappeared. The contradiction between an interpretation that situated the Solomons close to New Guinea and one that put their location only eight hundred leagues or so from Peru was resolved by simple deletion.

French cartographers, who towards the end of the century were replacing the Dutch as the foremost mapmakers of Europe, had fewer inhibitions about linking and supplementing known discoveries with the intriguing outlines suggested by rumour and hypothesis. They showed considerable ingenuity in brightening the sombre image of New Holland promoted by the Dutch and drew on Quiros to suggest the presence of rich countries inside the great oval traced by Tasman on his voyage of 1642–3. Nicolas Sanson's 'Mappe-Monde Géo-Hydrographique' of 1691 showed New Guinea as a great island set to the northeast of the Gulf of Carpentaria, with a 'Terre de Quir' marked farther east and the elusive Solomon Islands set between the two. Farther south, 'Terra Australis Incognita' was still much in evidence. Guillaume de l'Isle, the most prestigious of the French cartographers of the period, produced an influential interpretation in his 'Hémisphère Méridional' of 1714 (Ill. 11), a map based on a polar projection that sharpened the image of the South Lands. It not only did this, but it brought to the fore those vast unexplored stretches of ocean in southern latitudes where an unknown continent might be hidden.

In England, as elsewhere, older cartographic forms retained a tenacious grip long after the publication of maps and accounts of the Dutch discoveries. For some publishers Marco Polo remained more relevant than Tasman. The first English edition of the *Cosmography and Geography* of Bernard Varen illustrates the point, containing a bizarre mixture concocted from Polo's travels and inaccurate reports of the Dutch voyages:

> The Gulph Lantchidololinum floweth from the Indian Ocean, between the Provinces of the South Country Beach and New Guiney: it stretcheth from the North to the South, and terminateth at the unknown parts of the South Continent. Another Gulph is near unto it towards the West, between Beach and the other procurrent land of the South, where is the Land called Anthonij à Diemen, which is the Name of a Dutch Master of a Ship by whom it was discovered.[44]

In 1682 the editors of an English compendium took the information in their 'Antarctique' section straight from Quiros:

> those vast Countries, which lying under the South Pole, are longly and largely extended through the cold, temperate, and torrid Zone: where not only *Peter*

---

44. [Bernard Varen], *Cosmography and Geography in Two Parts* (London, 1683), I, p. 61.

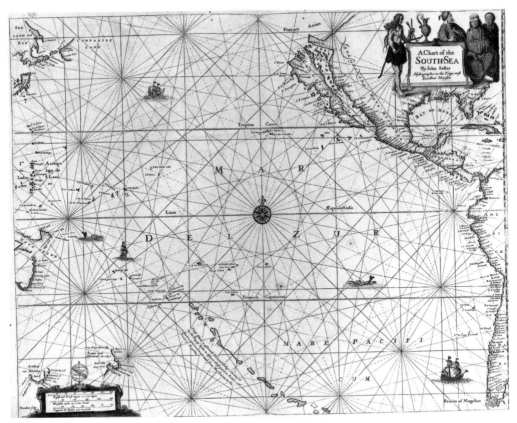

12. John Seller. 'A Chart of the South-Sea', 1675.

Ferdinand a *Spaniard* preached, but also are commendable for the constitution of the Ayre and soil; and largeness of the Countries; equalizing *Europe* and *Africa* taken both together.[45]

Where imaginative reconstructions failed, a crude environmental geography might be brought into play, so that it could be seriously argued that 'the East Side of Nova Hollandia . . . lying North and South as Peru does, and in the same lattd, I belive . . . abounds in Gold and Silver Mines.'[46]

The nearest approach to a standard representation of the South Sea in England was John Seller's 'Chart of the South-Sea' (Ill. 12), part of his *Atlas Maritimus* (1675). Although showing the Dutch discoveries, it also retained the older, fallacious interpretation in which some of the discoveries of

45. [Petavius et al.], *A Geographicall Description of the World* (London, 1682), pp. 1–2.
46. BL: Sloane MS 4044, f. 214v.

13. Joseph Hall. World map, c. 1605.

Mendaña and Gallego in 1567 were attributed to Gallego alone in a suppositious voyage of 1576. These were displayed in the form of a chain of islands running southeast from New Guinea across the ocean towards Tierra del Fuego to form 'the eroded offspring and an indication of the austral continent'.[47] It is not without significance that Seller's charts were on board an English buccaneering vessel, which by 1687 was sailing into the seas south of the Dutch East Indies.[48]

Juxtaposed with the actual discoveries, mostly disheartening, of the seventeenth-century navigators, was a continuing hope that somewhere in the unexplored vastnesses of the southern ocean lay lands of unimaginable fruitfulness and wealth. It was part of a never-ending quest, spiritual as well as material, expressed by the poet John Donne when he wrote: 'As though this

47. Jack-Hinton, *Search*, p. 220.
48. See p. 107 below.

World were too little to satisfie man, men are come to discover or imagine new worlds, severall worlds in every Planet.'[49] In his 'Hymne to God my God', Donne was more precise:

> Is the Pacific Sea my home? Or are
> The Eastern riches? Is Jerusalem?
> Anyan, and Magellan and Gibraltar
> All streits, and none but streits are wayes to them.[50]

As the Americas and the Far East became known, so speculative attention increasingly focused on the Pacific. There the Quiros fantasy shed its glow, and utopian visionaries set extraordinary lands and societies in the area they vaguely identified as Terra Australis. At the beginning of the century, before the Dutch explorations, the standard map of the southern hemisphere was dominated by a huge continental mass, and in Joseph Hall's *Mundum alter et idem* (1605) this was divided up into separate countries to provide the satirical setting for the voyage of 'Mercurius Britannicus' in the ship *Fantasie* (Ill. 13). Published in English in 1609 as *The Discovery of a New World or a Description of the South Indies Hitherto Unknown*, Hall's satire was a model for much that was to come. A dystopia, it stood at the opposite extreme from Quiros's New Jerusalem, but both could be brought into play as images of the austral regions. They were known and unknown, isolated from the rest of the world and yet within reach. As Hall wrote in a later work: 'For God Himselfe that made the Sea, was the Author of Navigation, and hath therein taught us to set up a wooden bridge, that may reach to the very Antipodes themselves.'[51] In his *Anatomy of Melancholy* (1621), Robert Burton announced:

> I will yet make an Utopia of mine own, a New Atlantis, a poetical commonwealth . . . For the site of [which] I am not fully resolved, it may be in *Terra Australis Incognita*, there is room enough (for of my knowledge neither that hungry Spaniard [Quiros], nor Mercurius Britannicus [Hall], have yet discovered half of it) or else one of these floating islands in Mare del Zur (or) perhaps under the Equator, that paradise of the world.[52]

Austral settings or references were becoming commonplace in the literature of a period torn by clashing ideologies and civil conflict. Republicanism, millennialism, utopianism, all could find expression in a world turned upside

49. See James, 'Nostalgia for Paradise', in Donaldson, *Australia and the European Imagination*, p. 69.
50. Quoted in Rodney W. Shirley, *The Mapping of the World: Early Printed World Maps 1472–1700* (London, 1993), Introduction, p. xvi.
51. Ibid., p. 63.
52. Quoted in David Fausett, *Writing the New World: Imaginary Voyages and Utopias of the Great Southern Land* (Syracuse, NY, 1993), pp. 42–3.

down.[53] Antipodal inversion seemed particularly appropriate, and among works that used a southern theme of one sort of another were Francis Bacon's 'New Atlantis' of the second decade of the century; Richard Brome's play *The Antipodes*, published in 1640 on the eve of the Civil War; Benjamin Worsley's *Profits Humbly Presented to his Kingdom*; James Harrington's *Oceana* (1656); and the 'new' *New Atlantis* (1660). Quiros's last voyage had shown how reality and fantasy could become indistinguishable; and in the second edition of his much-respected *Cosmographie* (1657), Peter Heylyn seemed to be making precisely this point. He followed Joseph Hall's satirical line as he marvelled that no further discovery had been made of a region 'so large, so free from the Incumbrances of Frosts and Ice, and endless Winters'. 'Without troubling the Vice-royes of *Peru*, and *Mexico*, or taking out *Commission* for a new Discovery,' Heylyn continued, he would try his fortune and 'make a search into this *Terra Australis* for some other Regions, which must be found either here or no where. The names of which [are] 1. *Mundus alter & idem*, 2. *Utopia*, 3. *New Atlantis*, 4. *Fairy Land*, 5. The *Painters Wives Iland*, 6. The Lands of *Chivalry*, and 7. *The New World in the Moon*.'[54]

If imaginary voyages found their way into standard reference works, so actual events of the period can be glimpsed in a new literary genre centred on voyaging, shipwreck and marooning. In 1668, the republican theorist Henry Neville published a slim booklet, *The Isle of Pines: Or a Late Discovery of a Fourth Island, in Terra Australis Incognita*. Its geographical setting was in the southern ocean somewhere between the Cape of Good Hope and the East Indies. The island's name was not a reference to trees but to the fictitious narrator, George Pine, shipwrecked there in 1569; for the result of his stranding on the island with four women was that he fathered forty-seven children and by his death boasted 1789 descendants. Its mix of erotic detail and narrative realism was so appealing that a month later a sequel appeared by the Dutch captain who, readers were told, had come across the island in 1667 and had acquired Pine's manuscript. Like other sequels, this did not have the success of the original piece, 'an overnight sensation' which was immediately translated into Dutch, French, German and Italian.[55] In seeking to explain the popularity of this little book, David Fausett has linked its appearance to the real, if rather mysterious, Dutch shipwrecks on the west coast of Australia, notably the disasters that befell the *Batavia* in 1629 and the

53. The literature is voluminous, but see in particular Christopher Hill, *The World Turned Upside Down* (London, 1972), Charles Webster, *The Great Instauration* (London, 1975), W.H.G. Armitage, *Heavens Below* (London, 1961).
54. Peter Heylyn, *Cosmographie* (2nd edn, London, 1657), pp. 1091, 1093. The last reference is a reminder that this period also produced satires featuring space flights, journeys to the centre of the earth and time travel. David Fausett comments that such works 'went further than austral travel in spatial displacement but, in doing so, lost the crucial element of realism.' *Writing the New World*, p. 76.
55. Ibid., pp. 81, 84.

Vergulde Draeck in 1656. The attempts by the VOC to conceal the detail of these shipwrecks, involving as they did murder, the collapse of authority and lost treasure, would increase interest in a story set somewhere near the coast of the South Land. In this context the initial reception of *The Isle of Pines* might have had a connection with the possibility of the return to Europe of a survivor from the 1656 shipwreck, and the lack of enthusiasm for the sequel explained by the realization that Neville's book was not, after all, a description of that event.[56] There is an odd postscript to the matter, for *The Isle of Pines* was reprinted exactly one hundred years later, in 1768, as Cook set sail on his first Pacific voyage. Set in this context, the piece is a prefiguration of the new European exploration and exploitation of the Pacific, for however benign the climate and lush the vegetation of George Pine's island, the handiwork of man was needed to control and improve nature. The country would be a paradise, 'had it the culture that skilful people might bestow on it'.[57]

Neville's piece was followed by longer works of fiction which also relied on a semi-documentary approach for credibility and impact. *History of the Sevarites* by Denis Vairasse was written by a French Huguenot, but was first published in 1675 in English.[58] It was in the form of a travel account kept by a Dutch sea-captain who had sailed for Batavia in 1655 on the VOC ship *Golden Dragon* (the *Vergulde Draeck* of the genuine maritime disaster), but had been wrecked on the coast of the South Land. Before dying in 1672, he had given the manuscript narrative of his adventures to the ship's doctor. Like Neville, Vairasse used the voyage–shipwreck–castaway sequence as a way of reaching his utopia, but through the device of the publisher's preface claimed that the setting was a real one:

> There are many, who having read *Plato's* Commonwealth, Sir *Thomas More's Utopia*, the Lord *Verulam's New Atlantis*, (which are but ideas and ingenious fancies) are apt to suspect all relations of new discoveries to be of that kind . . . Among all remote countries, there is none so vast, and so little known, as the third Continent, commonly called Terra Australis. It is true, Geographers give some small and unperfect descriptions of it, but . . . there is such a Continent; many have seen it, and even landed there, but few durst venture far in it.[59]

The next year, Gabriel de Foigny's *La Terre Australe connue* appeared, though it was not translated into English until 1693. This purported to be the narrative of Nicolas (James in the English translation) Sadeur, who after

---

56. For a fuller explanation see ibid., pp. 81–90.
57. Henry Neville, *The Isle of Pines* (London, 1668, repr. 1768), p. 11.
58. For the complicated publication history of its later parts see Fausett, *Writing the New World*, p. 113.
59. Quoted in James, 'Nostalgia for Paradise', p. 79.

being shipwrecked reached the South Land. Again, there was the insistence on authenticity, for the 'Notice to the Reader' at the beginning of the book described how Sadeur on his return had died in Italy but had left the editor a manuscript of his travels, 'much stained with sea-water'. His account contained references to earlier explorers such as Quiros, and viewed from one aspect the book was fantasy based on fantasy insofar as it appeared to elaborate and extend the claims of Quiros. The South Land had a population of 144 million inhabitants, totally uniform and homogeneous, with no variation of individual type, sex or race. 'We found a Country much more Fertile and Populous than any in Europe; that the inhabitants were much Bigger and Taller than the Europeans; and that they lived much longer than they.' Logically and prophetically, these splendid physical specimens, so superior to their European counterparts, were called, for the first time in English, 'Australians'.[60]

Like earlier utopias, these books tell us more about the Europe of the period, its hopes, tensions and problems, than about the imagined and remote setting. But there were connections with the new voyage-accounts that were beginning to appear by the late seventeenth century, and an effort to use the slowly increasing geographical knowledge of the South Land in the cause of verisimilitude. That distant region was serving two different purposes. For utopian and satirical writers, 'it was the last major notional exterior, or generator, of collective difference';[61] for geographers, merchants and navigators, it still promised to be a region of limitless wealth, another America. As far as contemporaries were concerned, the distinction was not always clear. In 1695, the compiler of *A New Body of Geography* indiscriminately grouped the southern lands, known and unknown, real and imaginary, under the twin headings of 'New Holland' and 'Terra Australis Incognita'. He insisted that the latter was 'a vast tract of Land', and in a jumble of assertions described how

the inhabitants are white, of a large Stature, strong, industrious and couragious: It is very sad to fall into their Hands, as some *Europeans* have found by unhappy Experience. Some modern Relations tell us, That in all that vast Country they have neither King nor Prince, all the People are only combin'd together in several Factions, in the Form of a Commonwealth. They chuse Governours only to make the lazy work, punish Offenders, and render Justice to every Man. They are Idolaters, and have Oratories to pray to their Idols in: They observe certain Fasts, and wash their Bodies on certain Days every Year.[62]

60. [Gabriel de Foigny], *A New Discovery of Terra Incognita Australis, or the Southern World. By James Sadeur* (London, 1693), preface.
61. Fausett, *Writing the New World*, p. 175.
62. [Thesaurus Geographicus], *A New Body of Geography* (London, 1695), pp. 497, 505–6.

Such concoctions had a longer life than they deserved, but by the 1690s general geographies of this kind were facing a rival in the shape of accounts of individual voyages whose detail was more precise and less fanciful. The appearance of William Dampier's *New Voyage Round the World* in 1697 was a landmark in this change of literary fashion, but it was more than that. It indicated a revival of English enterprise in the South Sea, as predatory as that of Elizabeth's reign, though some of its protagonists were as likely to have pen as sword in hand.

CHAPTER III

'They Were Not Come Out to Go upon Discovery': Buccaneers and Interlopers in the South Sea

After the Pacific voyages of Drake, Cavendish and Hawkins in the late sixteenth century, the western coasts of Spanish America were left unmolested by English seamen until the reign of Charles II. The hope that the precious metals which existed in such profusion in Peru and Mexico might also be found farther north had lured many English across the Atlantic to the eastern coasts of North America; but they found no Potosí in New England, no Zacatecas in Virginia. As the northern colonists forgot their early dreams of silver and gold, and instead developed a more mundane economy along the Atlantic seaboard, promoters of overseas expansion in England continued to regard with envy Spain's colonial empire. The magnificent churches and public buildings of the cities of Spanish America were visible evidence of the wealth of the region. From the plantations of the Caribbean islands to the grassy pampas of the southern regions stretched great tracts of fertile land. Exports of sugar, tobacco, cotton, hides and dye-woods swelled the value of the cargoes of precious metals shipped across the Atlantic; but it was the latter that caught the attention of Europe. In the public imagination, 'the wealth of the Indies' lay in the holds of the treasure fleets that crossed the Atlantic each year. From the mid-seventeenth century onwards, schemes were put forward to tap the silver lifeline of the Spanish empire, ironically at a time when Spain's bullion imports were in decline.

Since many of England's foreign trades ran an adverse balance, merchants found it the more frustrating that they could not gain direct access to the Spanish American market, whose demands for woollens, manufactures and dried fish were beyond the capacity of producers in Spain. English merchants could send their American-bound goods only as far as Spain, and although this trade brought in some bullion, the costs and delays associated with the bureaucracy of the Casa de la Contratación at Seville acted as a constant irritant and a strong incentive to attempt a direct trade with Spanish America.[1] Most efforts towards this were centred on the Caribbean, where

---

1. See Jean O. McLachlan, *Trade and Peace with Old Spain 1667–1750* (Cambridge, 1940), Ch. 1.

traders, privateers and smugglers sought to breach the barriers that Spanish officialdom had erected around its lucrative American trade. The Caribbean became a focal point of the struggle for trade and dominion between the maritime nations of Europe, for it was at once an area of bustling commercial activity and a bottleneck which the galleons from Portobelo and the *flota* from Vera Cruz had to negotiate before they broke clear into open sea.

The story of English ambitions and conquests in the Caribbean is a familiar one, but from the Commonwealth period onwards there were also attempts, of varying significance, to exploit Spain's American empire by way of its remote but vulnerable Pacific seaboard. A rather shadowy project surfaced in 1655 to send an expedition into the South Sea to seize bases in Chile, but then sank from sight. There was no doubting the anti-Spanish sentiments of Cromwell's government, but the Caribbean rather than the South Sea was its favoured centre of operations, as the 'Western Design' and the seizure of Jamaica showed. After the Restoration a different approach was suggested to the government of Charles II in the form of a full-scale reconnaissance of the Strait of Magellan as a preliminary to establishing a new trade route into the South Sea and on to the East Indies.[2] Again, there was no immediate response from the government, but six years later the scheme took firm shape as the ill-fated expedition of John Narborough.

Narborough, in later career to become an admiral and receive a knighthood, was a twenty-nine-year-old naval captain in 1669. Commanding the three-hundred-ton, thirty-eight-gun vessel H.M.S. *Sweepstakes*, he sailed from the Thames for the South Sea in September of that year together with a hired pink carrying stores and provisions. He had on board trade goods worth £300, a mysterious agent who went under the name of Don Carlos and claimed to have knowledge of the region, and orders from the Duke of York, Lord High Admiral, 'to make a Discovery both of the Seas and Coasts of that part of the World, and if possible to lay the foundations of a Trade there'. He was further instructed 'not to do any injury to such Spaniard as you shall meet with, or meddle with any places where they are planted'.[3] Unlike the proposed venture of the Cromwellian period, the Narborough expedition was not openly hostile to Spain; but in Spanish eyes its motives were just as suspect as if Narborough was intent on a plundering raid.

As the two ships sailed south past the River Plate and headed for the famed Strait of Magellan, so the agent's claims that he had sailed 'in a Galley' along the Atlantic coast of South America, through the Strait and as far north on the Pacific coast as Lima evaporated. 'He told me I might do what I would,' complained Narborough, 'for he did not understand the Coast, nor

2.   See Peter T. Bradley, *The Lure of Peru: Maritime Intrusions into the South Sea, 1598–1701* (London, 1989), pp. 88, 96, 98, 215 n. 4.

3.   [Anon.], *Account of Several Late Voyages & Discoveries*, p. 10.

where 'twas inhabited.'[4] To add to the expedition's troubles, the pink disappeared on the run down the coast of Patagonia and turned back for home. In Narborough's narrative, it needed all his eloquence to steady the nerves of his crew:

> The Company thought 'twoud be dangerous being a lone Ship, a stormy Sea to sail in, and unknown Coasts to search out, and if we should happen to run a-ground any where, could expect no relief; these suspicions I soon put out of their Heads, by telling them of the great Riches of the Land, and that *Captain Drake* went round the World in one Ship, when in those days there were but ordinary Navigators.[5]

Rather than risk a winter passage through the Strait, Narborough stayed at Port St Julian and Port Desire from the beginning of August until mid-October. Once within the Strait, Narborough negotiated and charted its tortuous windings with skill and care, and both his journal and that kept by the master's mate, John Wood, have considerable detail on the navigation. Wood's journal, very much that of a practical seaman, set the passage through the Strait in the context of previous voyages, Spanish and English. In addition to the natural hazards of the passage there was the disconcerting prospect of encountering giants, for rumours were still circulating that the Patagonians were of huge size. Apart from a casual reference to natives in the Strait being of 'mean stature',[6] the version of Wood's journal that was printed in 1699 is silent on this matter. In his manuscript copy, however, Wood had been more forthcoming. There he wrote that the Patagonians 'were Very Well set Men of no such Extraordinary Stature as is reported by Magellan and other Spaniards; to be 10 or 11 foot high none of these being above 6 at the most but I suppose they did imagining none would come here to disprove them.'[7] At Elizabeth Island just beyond the Second Narrows, Narborough encountered a group of Patagonians. These he engaged in an amicable but ultimately futile dumb-show: 'I laid Gold and bright Copper into the Ground, and made as if I found it there, and looked to and fro on the Earth as if I looked for such things; they looked one on another and spake to each other some words, but I could not perceive that they understood me, or what I meant.'[8]

The *Sweepstakes* emerged from the Strait and into the South Sea in November 1670, and the next month reached Valdivia. There relations with the Spaniards seemed friendly enough at first, although there was an odd and foreboding occurrence on the day of arrival when Don Carlos went ashore

---

4. Ibid., p. 19.
5. Ibid., p. 43.
6. William Hacke [Hack], ed., *A Collection of Original Voyages* (London, 1699), p. 81.
7. BL: Sloane MS 3833, f. 2v.
8. Hacke, *Collection of Original Voyages*, p. 63.

and failed to return. Narborough's officers learnt that the Spaniards knew little of the country to the south, and that they were at war with the local Indians, who were reputed to possess immense amounts of gold. They claimed that their Spanish hosts used nothing but silver utensils, even down to cooking pots and pans. With one thing and another, Narborough was convinced that 'the most gold in all the land of America is in Chile'.[9] On more mundane matters he noted that, since Valdivia lay at the far end of a long and tortuous trade route from Spain via the Isthmus and the ports of South America, European manufactures were both scarce and expensive.

On the third day after his arrival, Narborough sent eighteen of his sharpest men ashore to inspect 'the manner of the Harbour, and the Fortifications the Spaniards have, and the disposition of the People; and that it was my whole desire to have Conference with the Natives of the Country that are at Wars with the Spaniards . . . to lay the Foundation of a Trade there for the English Nation for the future.'[10] The folly of this mission was exposed when the Spaniards promptly seized four of the boat party, including Lieutenant Thomas Armiger. In a fatally nonsensical move, Narborough ensured that Armiger would not be returned by sending him an open letter after his capture. 'Lieutenant, take what notice you can of the Fortification of the Fort, and what strength they have of People in it, and whether they are able to withstand a Ship . . . I will use all my endeavours to have you off, when I understand the strength of the place . . . Burn all the Letters you receive from me.'[11]

After the Spaniards failed to respond to either pleas or threats, Narborough decided to return home. Twenty years later Grenville Collins, who had carried out hydrographic surveys on the voyage (and in 1681 was appointed 'Hydrographer to the King'), blamed everything on the desertion of the pink. He added that she had carried 'materials for building a small Sloop in the *South Sea*, being more convenient for discovery. And had not this misfortune happened, our design was to have sailed to *California*, and from thence to have searched the North Coast.'[12] Given the discretion that Narborough seems to have been given in his instructions (of which no full copy survives), such a northern voyage might well have been included among his options – though it must be said that neither as a successor of Drake nor as a forerunner of Cook does Narborough inspire confidence.

The same day that the *Sweepstakes* sailed, Don Carlos came out from hiding to give himself up to the Spaniards, insisting that he was 'director of the ship'. This was the beginning of a bizarre sequence of claims and

9.   [Anon.], *Account of Several Late Voyages & Discoveries*, p. 92.
10. Ibid., pp. 96–7.
11. Ibid., p. 104.
12. James Burney, *A Chronological History of the Discoveries in the South Sea or Pacific Ocean* (London, 1803–17), III, p. 319.

pretensions over the next twelve years by a man whose alleged identities included that of the illegitimate son of Prince Rupert of the Palatinate. Under interrogation at Lima he told his Spanish questioners what they anticipated and feared: that the English intended to establish a settlement which would command the Strait, 'take possession of Valdivia and hold it against Spanish power, and sack and destroy the port of Callao and swallow up shipping in the South Sea'.[13] As it was, Narborough's fleeting visit brought turmoil to the coast. As reports of the expedition made their way north to Lima, they were inflated by a process of Falstaffian exaggeration until the *Sweepstakes* was transformed into a fleet of twelve men-of-war that had seized all the shipping in Valdivia harbour and was thought to be on its way to attack Panama – a prospect that caused the Viceroy of Peru to halt the regular silver shipments to Panama.[14] The threat to Panama was real; however, it came not from the ineffective Narborough, but from Henry Morgan, whose men rampaged overland across the Isthmus to sack the city in January 1671.

Narborough, meanwhile, was quietly retracing his course through the Strait of Magellan and reached England in June 1671. The ill-conceived attempt to combine a trading enterprise with a reconnaissance mission had failed. Its motives were so transparent that Narborough was fortunate to withdraw his head from the Spanish noose with the loss of only four men (and the dubious Don Carlos). At home his voyage seems to have caused little stir at the time and was probably a source of embarrassment to the government since during his absence England and Spain had negotiated the Treaty of Madrid (1670), whose only concession to the shipping of either nation was that it allowed help to be given in American waters to vessels in genuine distress.[15] The voyage, as Wood remarked in the final sentence of his journal, had been 'resented' by the Spanish authorities.[16]

If Narborough had done nothing else, his return voyage had shown the fallacy of the Spanish reports that insisted that wind and current made a west–east passage of the Strait impossible. The problem, as Narborough admitted, was that for a ship sailing down the Pacific coast of Patagonia towards the entrance of the Strait 'there are many Openings and Sounds on the North-side, which seem fairer for a passage than the Streight it self doth.'[17] The answer was to sail as far as Cape Pilar, near the south side of the entrance, and then turn east. Since Narborough's journal was not published until more than twenty years later, it was his detailed chart of the Strait – 'drawn by my own hand on the place' – which was published in 1673, that proved most

---

13. Bradley, *Lure of Peru*, p. 96. For more on Don Carlos see Peter T. Bradley, 'Narborough's Don Carlos', *Mariner's Mirror*, 72 (1986), pp. 465–75.

14. These Spanish reports, dated January 1671, are now in BL: Add. MS 21,539, ff. 1–13.

15. See F.G. Davenport, ed., *European Treaties bearing on the History of the United States and its Dependencies*, II (Washington, 1929), p. 195.

16. Hacke, *Collection of Original Voyages*, p. 100.

17. [Anon.], *Account of Several Late Voyages & Discoveries*, p. 117.

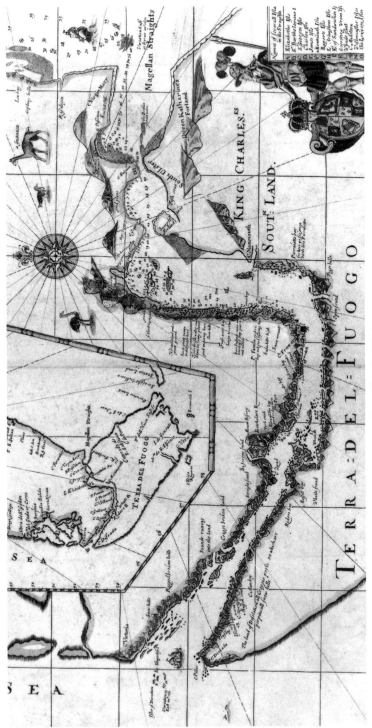

14. John Thornton/John Narborough. Section from 'A New Mapp of Magellans Straights', 1673.

useful and remained the standard authority for decades to come (Ill. 14).[18] When the journal finally found its way into print in 1694, six years after Narborough's death, readers could note his insistence that the amount of gold in Chile, the proximity of the great silver mine at Potosí and the feebleness of Spanish control over the region meant that 'the most advantageous Trade in the World might be established in those parts'.[19] But he also had to confess that the experience of his voyage in 1670 had revealed that this was practical only if the Spanish government was willing to admit foreign traders – an unlikely proposition – or if the English were prepared to use force. Unwittingly, Narborough had expressed the dilemma that was to afflict attempts to trade with Spanish America for the next hundred years.

After Narborough's unsuccessful venture, little more was heard about the South Sea in official circles. Instead, it attracted the attention of unofficial forces in the shape of those disreputable marauders, the buccaneers. By the 1670s their usual sphere of operations in the Caribbean had been worn thin by incessant raiding, sacking and plundering. Henry Morgan's descent on Panama in 1671 was the first sign of this, but although his bloody assault sent tremors along the whole of Spanish America's Pacific seaboard, it was a limited operation. Morgan had no truck with a plan by some of his men to take one of the ships captured at Panama and sail it across the Pacific to the East Indies. His force was to return across the Isthmus by the way it had come, along the Chagres River. Comprehensive and shocking though the sacking of Panama was, the financial rewards for Morgan's men were small – between £15 and £18 a head.[20] Even so, the assault set a precedent. By the end of the decade it was followed by forays that took the buccaneers across the Isthmus and onto the thinly defended coasts of Peru, Mexico and Chile.

   These were makeshift and improvised ventures which relied on seizing local vessels once the raiders reached the South Sea; but during the 1680s, buccaneer ships fitted out in Europe or the Caribbean came through the Strait of Magellan or round Cape Horn. Neither exploration nor trade featured high on the buccaneers' list of priorities. 'Gold was the bait that tempted a Pack of Merry Boys of us', one of them wrote.[21] Violent, disputatious, anarchic, they looted and burnt their way along the Pacific coasts from Valdivia to Acapulco. Some held commissions of one sort or another to give a touch of legality to their actions, for the distinction

---

18.   Ibid., p. 71. See also Helen Wallis, 'English Enterprise in the Region of the Strait of Magellan', in John Parker, ed., *Merchants and Scholars: Essays in the History of Exploration and Trade* (Minneapolis, 1965), p. 212.
19.   [Anon.], *An Account of Several Late Voyages & Discoveries*, p. 110.
20.   For the above details see Peter Earle, *The Sack of Panama* (London, 1981), pp. 241–2, 244.
21.   Philip Ayres, *The Voyages and Adventures of Captain Barth. Sharp and Others, in the South Sea* (London, 1684), preface.

between an unlicensed buccaneer or pirate and a privateer was an uncertain one in this period. The commissions of the latter were often of dubious legal validity – sometimes outdated or bought from a foreign official. One obtained to cover an expedition of five vessels fitted out in Jamaica cost only ten pieces of eight. Unfortunately it was due to run for only three months, so it was altered by the buccaneers 'to make it last for three years – for with this we were resolved to seek our fortunes'.[22] Most relied on the intimidating authority flourished before the Governor of Panama by Captain Sawkins when he warned him that the buccaneers would 'bring our Commissions on the muzzles of our Guns, at which time he should read them as plain as the flame of Gunpowder could make them'.[23]

Moving between sea and land, and when at sea switching from ship to ship, sometimes taking to boats and canoes, the buccaneers led a life of hardship and danger. Unlike in the Caribbean, where friendly harbours were usually not far distant, all ports in the South Sea were closed to them. In overcrowded and often ramshackle craft they might be at sea for months rather than weeks; food and water were often in short supply; and scurvy was an ever-present, lurking menace. They received no wages as such, but operated on the chancy basis of 'no purchase, no pay'. As an Englishman in Jamaica wrote of the buccaneers at this time, if men had no fortune of their own and were unable to amass one through legitimate activity, the only alternative to destitution was 'to make themselves a fortune upon the goods of others . . . by a course of plunder and of violence'.[24] The reality was that rich prizes were rare, and even when they occurred the share for each man could be miserably small, as in Morgan's Panama operation. 'Life was a lottery with few winning the jackpot, and injury, death or imprisonment in Spain as the loser's draw.'[25]

With elected captains whose position was safe only until the next murmuring of discontent, the activities of the buccaneers were as unpredictable as they were hazardous. Their crews were made up of many nationalities, and if Spain was the common enemy this was more often for plain commercial reasons than for political or religious motives. In England the buccaneers from Morgan onwards held a place in popular esteem that reflected admiration both for their perceived role as fighters against Spain and popery and for the 'rags to riches' aspect of their activities. Up to a point at least, they seemed men of humble origin in charge of their own destinies. An essential element in this heroizing process came from their own writings. Given the

22. [A.O. Exquemelin], *Bucaniers of America . . . Inlarged with Two Additional Relations, viz. the One of Captain Cook, and the Other of Captain Sharp* (London, 1684), I, p. 63.

23. [Basil Ringrose], *Bucaniers of America. The Second Volume Containing the Dangerous Voyage and Bold Attempts of Captain Bartholomew Sharp and Others; Performed upon the Coasts of the South Sea* (London, 1685), II, p. 38.

24. Quoted in Nuala Zahediah, '"A Frugal, Prudential and Hopeful Trade"; Privateering in Jamaica, 1655–89', *Journal of Imperial and Commonwealth History*, 18 (1990), p. 162.

25. Ibid., p. 151.

conditions under which the buccaneers operated, it is remarkable how many of them managed to keep journals that were a cut above the usual sea-log. Among their ranks were men with the instincts, if not the training, of scholars and scientists: Basil Ringrose, who had enough classical learning to negotiate with the Spaniards in Latin, and whose narrative 'Containing the Dangerous Voyage, and Bold attempts of Captain *Bartholomew Sharp*, and others', was published in 1685 as Volume II of the enlarged second English edition of Exquemelin's *Bucaniers of America*; the barber-surgeon Lionel Wafer, whose notes on the Cuna Indians of southeast Panama have remained of interest to anthropologists in the present century;[26] and William Dampier, an observer of endless curiosity who waded through the rivers of Darien with his journal secured inside a length of bamboo cane, and whose books were to become classics of travel and adventure.

Dampier, and only Dampier, has an intriguing explanation of the timing of the overland thrust that brought the buccaneers onto the South Sea coast again. During the winter of 1679–80 privateers in the Caribbean had intercepted letters from Spanish merchants which warned that the English were about 'to open a Door' into the South Sea:

> This Door they spake of we all concluded must be the Passage over Land through the Country of the *Indians* of *Darien*, who were a little before this become our Friends, and had lately fallen out with the *Spaniards* . . . And upon calling also to mind the frequent Invitations we had from those *Indians* a little before this time, to pass through their Country, and fall upon the *Spaniards* in the *South-Seas*, we from henceforward began to entertain such Thoughts in earnest.[27]

Among the leading figures in the new irruption of buccaneers across the Isthmus and onto the South Sea coasts was Bartholomew Sharp, well versed in the underworld of maritime skullduggery. At his trial for piracy in 1682 (where Narborough, now an admiral, was one of the judges), Sharp stated that he had been a buccaneer for sixteen years, but if Dampier's memory was correct he had been on the Isthmus of Panama almost thirty years earlier.[28] In April 1680 Sharp was one of a force of 330 men under the command of

26. There is a modern edition: L.E. Elliott Joyce, ed., *A New Voyage and Description of the Isthmus of America by Lionel Wafer* [1699] (Oxford, 1934).

27. William Dampier, *A New Voyage Round the World* (London, 1697/1729), pp. 180–1. The proliferation of editions of Dampier's book (right up to the present) makes for considerable problems of citation. All page references here are to the collected edition of Dampier brought out by his original publisher, Knapton, in 1729 under the title *A Collection of Voyages*; and this collection will also be cited in references to Dampier's later books. In all cases, the first publication date given is that of the first edition of the individual book.

28. See Christopher Lloyd, 'Bartholomew Sharp, Buccaneer', *Mariner's Mirror*, 42 (1956), pp. 291–301; Derek Howse and Norman J.W. Thrower, *A Buccaneer's Atlas: Basil Ringrose's South Sea Waggoner* (Berkeley and Los Angeles, 1992), pp. 27–8, 30–32; Dampier, *New Voyage*, p. 129 (though Sharpe's age was given as thirty-two at his trial).

15. [Herman Moll]. 'The Isthmus of Darien & Bay of Panama', 1697.

John Coxon who struggled on foot and in canoe across the Isthmus from the Caribbean, where they had just sacked Portobelo. Although they reached 'the fair South-Sea' and seized ships on the coast, casualties, divisions and desertions left the buccaneers too few in numbers to attack Panama. Once Coxon had turned back and his successor, Richard Sawkins, had been killed, the wilful individuality which was always present among the buccaneers came to the fore. Sharp's insistence that they should carry on with Sawkins's plan 'to remain in the South Sea and ... go home round about America, through the Strait of Magellan' split the buccaneers 'in full council', where all were present, and sixty-three left the main force at this point.[29] Sharp now had less than half the original force under his command. Among them were those assiduous reporters of events – Ringrose, Wafer, Dampier – almost an accompanying press corps. In all, five journals were published about the buccaneers' exploits of 1680–1 in the South Sea, making them among the most fully recorded of all piratical activities.

Too weak to attack the main Spanish citadels along the coast, Sharp's force pillaged smaller ports and ships before retiring to Juan Fernández at the end of 1680. With its water and goats this was 'a very refreshing Place to us',[30] and it was to become a favourite refuge of the buccaneers. In the process it gained another kind of fame as the lonely way-station of those stranded or marooned there, sometimes for years on end. A captured Spanish pilot on board Sharp's ship told Ringrose that 'many years ago a certain ship was cast away upon this Island, and only one man saved, who lived alone upon this Island five years before any ship came this way to carry him off.'[31] In their haste to get away as Spanish warships came in sight, the buccaneers were unwittingly helping to establish the tradition as they were forced to leave one of their crew, a Miskito Indian called Will, on the island.

The beginning of 1681 saw yet another change of command. Sharp was first turned out in favour of Watling and then reinstated when Watling was killed a few weeks later. Sharp singled out John Cox as the ringleader in the plot against him, but did so in terms that reflected little credit on his own judgment. Cox, he wrote, was 'a true-hearted dissembling New England Man . . . whom meerly for old Acquaintance-sake, I had taken from before the Mast, and made my Vice-Admiral; and not from any Valour or Knowledge he was possess'd of; for of that his share was but small.'[32] According to one crew member, the division was between those who had kept their gains and those who had gambled them away until they were 'scarce worth a groat'. The latter were in the majority and so 'turned *Sharp* out of his commission, pretending they could do it as being a free election'.[33] Another contender for the command was Edmund Cook, but he was put in irons on what was probably a trumped-up charge of sodomy, for it was soon replaced by an accusation that he intended to betray the crew to the Spaniards.[34]

It was such episodes that the privateer Woodes Rogers, who was to have his own problems with his crew, seems to have had in mind when he

29. [Ringrose], *Bucaniers*, II, p. 43.
30. Hacke, *Collection of Original Voyages*, p. 45. The name Juan Fernández covers three islands; the one visited by the buccaneers and their successors is Mas-a-Tierra. Lying about 360 miles off Valparaíso, it was renamed Robinson Crusoe Island by the Chilean government in 1966. See R.L. Woodward, *Robinson Crusoe's Island: A History of the Juan Fernández Islands* (Chapel Hill, NC, 1969).
31. [Ringrose], *Bucaniers*, p. 119.
32. Hacke, *Collection of Original Voyages*, pp. 45–6.
33. [Exquemelin], *Bucaniers*, p. 76.
34. BL: Sloane MS 48, f. 87; [Ringrose], *Bucaniers*, II, p. 121; B.R. Burg, *Sodomy and the Pirate Tradition* (New York, 1984), pp. 147–8.

criticized the lack of discipline and bravery among the buccaneers. He at least was not beguiled by the 'Merry Boys' of popular fancy:

There was no distinction between the Captain and Crew: for the Officers having no Commission but what the Majority gave them, they were chang'd at every Caprice . . . and for any thing I could learn, they scarce shew'd one Instance of true Courage or Conduct, though they were accounted such fighting Fellows at home.[35]

It was with a degree, but only a degree, of exaggeration that Defoe later wrote that

he once knew a buccaneering pirate vessel, whose crew were upwards of seventy men, who, in one voyage, had so often changed, set up, and pulled down their captains and other officers, that about seven-and-forty of the ship's company had, at several times, been in offices of one kind or another; and among the rest they had, in particular, had thirteen captains.[36]

The first months of 1681 were spent in further raids on Spanish ports and shipping. One estimate is that as a result of Sharp's depredations the Spaniards lost twenty-five ships, two hundred men and four million pesos.[37] A final and notable capture was that of the *Santa Rosario* off Guayaquil in July. From this ship Sharp took a rare prize – a 'great Book full of Sea-Charts and Maps'. His manuscript journal made the most of the drama and the importance of the capture:

In this prize I took a Spanish manuscript of prodigious value. It describes all the ports, roads, harbours, bayes, sands, rocks & riseing of the land & instruc- tions how to work a ship into any port or harbour between the Latt. of 17°15'N° and 57°S° Latt. They were goeing to throw it over board but by good luck I saved it. The Spaniards cried when I gott the book. (farwell South Sea now).[38]

This volume of manuscript charts and sailing directions, known as a Waggoner (after the Dutch cartographer L.J. Waghenaer who published the first such compendium in 1584), promised to open the doors of Spain's seaboard empire to the English; and Sharp's acquittal on charges of

35. Woodes Rogers, *A Cruising Voyage Round the World* (London, 1712), p. xvii.
36. [Daniel Defoe], *An Account of . . . the Late John Gow* (London, 1725), pp. 279–80. I owe this reference to Professor Jonathan Lamb. For more on this see J.S. Bromley, 'Outlaws at Sea, 1660–1720: Liberty, Equality and Fraternity among the Caribbean Freebooters', in Frederick Krantz, *History from Below: Studies in Popular Protest and Popular Ideology in Honour of George Rudé* (Montreal, 1985), pp. 301–20.
37. Bradley, *Lure of Peru*, pp. 126–7.
38. Howse and Thrower, *A Buccaneer's Atlas*, p. 22.

piracy when he returned to England probably owed much to his possession of the volume. After the trial the sailing directions were translated into English, and the whole Waggoner handed over to the Thameside chartmaker, William Hack, for copying. At least a dozen of his copies survive, including handsome presentation copies given to Charles II, ministers and courtiers.

A different manuscript version (the one that forms the basis for the superb modern edition of 1992) bears the name of Basil Ringrose. This was of particular value since it contained descriptions of the Pacific coast of California (not in any of the Hack copies), the Spanish place-names were retained and the sailing directions incorporated Ringrose's own observations as well as those taken from the captured Spanish collection. The volume's charts and views were done in colour, not only for appearance's sake but to pick out coastlines, islands, buildings, soundings and other features of interest. However, it had no lines of latitude and longitude, a common scale, or other information considered normal even by the standards of late seventeenth-century charts. In summary, the Waggoner was the sort of guide, packed with detail in a rough-and-ready way, that was used by the Spanish pilots along the coast. At the end of 1684, Dampier while off Panama noted that although the buccaneers had captured some Spanish pilots, the knowledge of their prisoners was extremely localized. However, 'we supplied that defect out of the Spanish Pilot-books, which we took in their Ships; These we found by Experience to be very good Guides.'[39] How navigators unfamiliar with the coast would have fared remains a matter for speculation, for there is no evidence that any of the English versions so painstakingly copied were ever taken to sea. Nor was the Waggoner published, for as one of Sharp's men noted after his return to England, 'the printing thereof is severely prohibited, lest other nations should get into those seas and make use thereof.'[40] The dire predictions of the Spanish crew in 1681 were never realized. If any contemporary use was made of Sharp's great prize, it was by those armchair South Sea projectors in England excited by thoughts of tapping the silver lifeline of Spanish America.

When Hack published Sharp's journal in 1699, he omitted any mention of the Waggoner, and this is not the only evidence of editorial interference. Sharp returned to the Atlantic in a captured Spanish ship, the four-hundred-ton *Trinity*, by way of Cape Horn, thereby becoming the first Englishman to round the Horn. This was not a matter of choice, for in bad weather Sharp had missed the western entrance to the Strait of Magellan and had been blown south to 'near 60 d.S.Lat and as far, if not farther, than any before me'.[41] This is followed in Hack's manuscript copy by a significant addition:

---

39. Dampier, *New Voyage*, p. 163.
40. [Exquemelin], *Bucaniers*, I, p. 81.
41. Hacke, *Collection of Original Voyages*, p. 55. An anonymous journal of the voyage puts the farthest south by observation at lat. 58°5'S. See BL: Add. MS 11,410, f. 356.

'therefore do find by experience that there is no such a tract of land as the dutch call Terra Australis incognito.'[42] A similar remark appears in the summary of the voyage in Exquemelin, where Sharp's track was produced as evidence that 'there is no such *Continent* as *Terra Australis incognita*, as is named and described in all the Ancient Maps.'[43] Not only did Hack omit Sharp's sceptical comment, but the map by Herman Moll which accompanied Hack's *Collection of Original Voyages* marked the coastline of 'Davis Land'. This was a buccaneer 'discovery' of 1687 which added fuel to the arguments for a southern continent.[44]

Among the buccaneers Sharp was outstanding for his seamanship, for with a sullen and unruly crew he took his ship on an unbroken voyage of six months (one of the longest on record) from the South Sea round the Horn to the Caribbean. Whether by accident or design, he did not pass through the Strait of Le Maire, but kept well to the east of Staten Island before turning north. This route was given pride of place in the publisher's preface to Ringrose's journal of Sharp's voyage, which was published in 1685. There it was lauded as 'the grand discovery of a new passage into the South Sea, beyond the Streights of *Ferdnando de Magellan* and *le Maire* through an open and in no wise dangerous Ocean, without those formidable perils both from Rocks, Currents, and Shoals, which hitherto have rendred the two passages aforementioned altogether inaccessible to Trading.'[45] Not all his crew were as impressed, for Ringrose reported an unsuccessful plot by some of them to kill Sharp on Christmas Day 1681 while on the homeward track. When the *Trinity* reached the West Indies the crew dispersed; the ship itself was given to those seven or eight members of the crew who had lost all their money through gaming. Among these was the keeper of a journal which noted that on the final distribution of the plunder in the South Sea each man was given 1100 pieces of eight, 'though it was some of our fortune to loose our voyage by play afterwards'.[46] This was a fitting note on which to close an account spilling over with quarrels, desertions and mutinies, of men too drunk at times to sail the ship and, sometimes, to save their own lives.

The different versions, manuscript and printed, of the journals kept by the buccaneers – John Cox, William Dick, Basil Ringrose, William Dampier, Lionel Wafer, Bartholomew Sharp – form a puzzling, sometimes contradictory, mass of evidence.[47] Deletions, additions and changes both of style and substance occur even in journals kept by the same writer. So the seizing of

42. See Edward Lynam, *The Mapmaker's Art* (London, 1953), p. 107.
43. [Exquemelin], *Bucaniers*, I, p. 83.
44. See p. 101 below.
45. [Ringrose], *Bucaniers*, II, preface.
46. BL: Add. MS 11,410, f. 354.
47. See Colin Steele, *English Interpreters of the Iberian New World from Purchas to Stevens. A Bibliographical Study 1603–1726* (Oxford, 1975), pp. 84–8, 177–8; Howse and Thrower, *A Buccaneer's Atlas, passim.*

the great Waggoner on the *Santa Rosario* on 29 July 1681 is described only
in the earliest printed account of Sharp's voyage (by William Dick in the
1684 edition of Exquemelin's *Bucaniers of America*). Otherwise the episode
disappears from view, except in two manuscript versions of Sharp's journal,
one of which was prepared for the Admiralty. The most likely explanation is
that this was an attempt to keep news of the atlas from the French; certainly
the Spaniards could be expected to know of their loss, and there is even
evidence that at one time the Spanish ambassador in London had the prized
volume in his possession.[48]

Elsewhere, Ringrose's journal shows signs of editorial additions designed
to inflate the courage and perspicacity of Sharp as a buccaneer leader.
The journal's modern editors give an example of this in connection with the
attack of 22 May 1680 on Puebla Nueva, when Sawkins was killed. The
words inside the brackets are the additions to Ringrose's rough holograph
journal (BL: Sloane 3820, f. 30) before it appeared in print in 1685 as the
second volume of the second edition of Exquemelin's *Bucaniers of America*:

> And here they kiled our Valiant Capt. Sawkings, a man as stoute as could bee
> and [likewise next unto Captain *Sharp*, the best] beloved above any that ever
> wee had amongst us and he well deserved, for wee may attribute but the
> greatest honour to him in our fighte at Panama, [with the Spanish *Armadilla*
> or Little Fleet. Especially considering that, as hath been said above, Captain
> *Sharp* was by accident absent at the time of that great and bloody fight].[49]

Further investigation shows that there was a three-stage process which
involved Ringrose's holograph journal, the copy made by Hack for the Duke
of Albemarle (BL: Sloane MS. 48) and, finally, the printed version in the
second edition of Exquemelin. A clear example of successive alterations
concerned a sickening incident in which a Spanish prisoner, an old mestizo,
was casually murdered after his interrogation about the fortifications of the
nearby port of Arica:

> Thursday Jan: 27 [1681]: this morning examining the old man and finding him
> in many lyes shott him.[50]

> Thursday Jan: ye 27th: this morning Examining ye: old man and finding him
> in many lyes shott him concerning Arica as wee supposed but our old
> commandr Capt Sharp was much troubled at such a Rash thing and tooke
> water and washed his hands and said Gentlemen – I am clear of ye Blood of
> this man (and said I will warrant you a hott day for this).[51]

---

48. See Howse and Thrower, *A Buccaneer's Atlas*, p. 27.
49. Ibid., p. 11.
50. BL: Sloane MS 3820, f. 86. The actual murder seems to have been committed by the
     quartermaster, John Duill. See BL: Add. MS 11,410, f. 348.
51. BL: Sloane MS 48, f. 83.

Thursday, January 27th. This morning on board the ship we examined one of the old men who were taken prisoners upon the island the day before. But, finding him in many lies, as we thought, concerning Arice, our Commander [John Watling] ordered him to be shot to death, which was accordingly done. Our old Commander, Captain Sharp, was much troubled in his mind and dissatisfied at this cruel and rash proceeding, whereupon he opposed it as much as he could. But, seeing he could not prevail, he took water and washed his hands, saying: *Gentlemen, I am clear of the blood of this old man; and I will warrant you a hot day for this piece of cruelty, whenever we come to fight at Arica.*[52]

The assault on Arica three days later, on 30 January 1681, was a disaster. The buccaneers' commander of the moment, John Watling, was killed, together with twenty-seven of the crew. Others were wounded or taken prisoner. The demoralized survivors turned once more to Sharp, but the circumstances of his taking up command again differ according to which account is consulted. William Dick's explanation of the matter was brief and to the point: 'Now Captain Sharp was chosen again, his conduct being thought safer than any other man's, and they having had trial of another leader.'[53] Ringrose's holograph journal (Sloane MS 3820) does not mention the leadership question, but his entries stop on 1 February when he fell sick, and this may be the explanation for his silence. Certainly Hack's copy of Ringrose has plenty to say on the matter, and this was taken over with a little more elaboration into the printed version:

Being surrounded with difficulties on all sides and in great disorder, having no head or leader to give orders for what was to be done, we were glad to turn our eyes to our good and old Commander, Captain Bartholomew Sharp, and beg of him very earnestly to commiserate our condition and carry us off. It was a great while before he would take any notice of our request in this point, so much was he displeased with the former mutiny of our people against him, all which had been occasioned by the instigation of Mr Cook. But Sharp is a man of an undaunted courage and of an excellent conduct, not fearing in the least to look an insulting enemy in the face, and a person that knows both the theory and practical parts of navigation as well as most do.[54]

William Dampier was among the crew of the *Trinity* at this time, and when eventually he returned to England in 1691 and read the Ringrose book, he felt strongly enough about what he saw as its misrepresentations to give a quite different account. According to Dampier, after Watling's death

---

52. [Ringrose], *Bucaniers*, II, p. 404.
53. [Exquemelin], *Bucaniers*, I, p. 274.
54. [Ringrose], *Bucaniers*, II, p. 408. The manuscript version of this passage is in BL: Sloane MS 48, f. 86.

so opposed were 'the abler and more experienced Men' on board to Sharp's reappointment as commander that they blocked it. For ten weeks the buccaneers were without a commander, until in mid-April 1681, off the Island of Plate, an election was held on the understanding that the winners would keep the ship, and the losers would return across the Isthmus. Sharp's party won, and Dampier, 'who had never been pleased with his Management', was one of the group of forty-four crew members who left in a long-boat and two canoes to face the perils of the Isthmus.[55] Among those who stayed on board was Ringrose.

Even the abortive mutiny on the homeward voyage takes on a different colouring if other sources than Ringrose are consulted. In Ringrose, the episode appears as further evidence of the sagacity of 'our worthy Commander, Captain Sharp', who on hearing of a plot to kill him on Christmas Day made sure that the supply of wine was exhausted long before, 'being persuaded they would scarce attempt any such thing in their sobriety'.[56] An anonymous journal gives a more circumstantial and convincing explanation of what happened. Along with his 'cabin mess' Sharp became drunk and quarrelsome, fetched his pistol from his cabin and shot one of the crew, Richard Hendricks, in the head. Luckily, the bullet only grazed Hendricks's neck (it was found the next day, embedded in the mast), and he survived. Before his escape was realized, the crew took arms and, 'had they not been soberer than others, and more discretion in them, Sharp had certainly been killed.'[57]

Ringrose's journal in its extended form, as copied (and perhaps edited) by Hack, and then published, was an exercise in rehabilitation as far as Sharp was concerned. The importance of this aspect is suggested by the anonymous journal-keeper on the *Trinity*, who wrote that as the ship came into the Atlantic from the South Sea the crew were eager to 'meet with English, Dutch or Portuguese to hear how our business was discourst of at home'.[58] Who made the decisive alterations – Ringrose, Hack or perhaps even Sharp – is not known. Ringrose was in England from March 1682 to October 1683, when he sailed once more for the South Sea with Captain Charles Swan in the *Cygnet*. There is an informative note on him by William Dick in his narrative of Sharp's voyage which appeared in the second edition of Exquemelin's *Bucaniers of America*, published in May 1684:

Mr. *Ringrose*, who was with us in all this Voyage, and being a good Scholar, and full of ingeniosity, had also very good skill in Languages. This Gentleman kept an exact and very curious Journal of all our Voyage, from our first setting

55. Dampier, *New Voyage*, p. vi.
56. [Ringrose], *Bucaniers*, II, p. 198.
57. BL: Add. MS 11,410, f. 356v.
58. Ibid.

out to the very last day, took also all the observations we made,[59] and likewise an accurate description of all the Ports, Towns and lands we came to. His Papers, or rather his *Diary*, with all his Drafts, are now in the hands of a person of my acquaintance at Wapping in *London*, and, as he telleth me, are very nigh being printed.[60]

The question of whether Ringrose or William Hack of Wapping revised the journal for publication was not mentioned by Dick, though his remarks suggest the importance of Hack's role. Sharp also was in England for much of 1682 and 1683, and in contact with Hack, though by 1684 he was away in the Caribbean, a poacher turned gamekeeper, tracking down pirates.[61] After his acquittal in June 1682, there was every reason for Sharp to appreciate the rewards of respectability, for by now his buccaneering predecessor, Henry Morgan, had acquired a knighthood and the lieutenant-governorship of Jamaica. The identity of the editor of Ringrose's narrative is perhaps less important than the realization that the buccaneers' journals of this period served more than one function, and that from Ringrose to Dampier self-justification was an important element.

By 1684 many of Sharp's old shipmates were back in the South Sea, including Dampier and Wafer. With them was a newcomer, Ambrose Cowley, tricked (so he claimed) into joining the buccaneers as their sailing master. After seizing a forty-gun Danish slave-trader, 'a lovely Shipp', as Cowley remarked in his journal, off Sierra Leone and renaming it *Batchelor's Delight*, the buccaneers under John Cook sailed for Cape Horn and the South Sea. In latitude 47°S. in the South Atlantic a new island was discovered, named after Samuel Pepys, Secretary to the Admiralty between 1686 and 1688. It had, so Cowley's journal (published in the Hack *Collection*) maintained, a harbour able to hold a thousand ships. No such place exists at that location, but a manuscript copy of Cowley's journal speculated that the island was one of the Sebald de Weert's group (the Falklands) of the Dutch maps. Cowley claimed that his efforts to investigate further were frustrated by his crew: 'they told me that they were not come out to go upon discovery.'[62] If the sighting was of the Falklands, then the gross four-degree error in latitude can only be explained by the fact that Cowley's journal up to August 1684 was written later, and from memory.

As they sailed south Dampier tried to persuade Cook to avoid the Strait of Magellan on the grounds that

59. These included frequent observations of magnetic variation, taken with the aid of 'a good Dutch Azimouth compass'. [Ringrose], *Bucaniers*, II, p. 194.
60. [Exquemelin], *Bucaniers*, I, p. 79.
61. See Howse and Thrower, *A Buccaneer's Atlas*, pp. 31–2.
62. BL: Sloane MS 54, ff. 5, 7v.

Our Men being Privateers, and so more wilful, and less under Command, would not be so ready to give a watchful Attendance in a Passage so little known. For altho' these Men were more under Command than I had ever seen any Privateers, yet I could not expect to find them at a Minute's call in coming to an Anchor, or weighing Anchor.[63]

His advice was not taken, but the westerlies made it impossible to fetch the entrance of the Strait, and it was decided to make for the Strait of Le Maire. This had its own dangers, for off its entrance the ship met 'such a short cockling Sea, as if it had been in a Race, or place where two Tides meet; for it ran every way, sometimes breaking in over our Waste, sometimes over our Poop, sometimes over our Bow, and the Ship tossed like an Egg shell, so that I never felt such uncertain Jerks in a Ship.'[64] Finally, the *Batchelor's Delight* hauled east of Staten Island and made the same open-sea passage round the Horn that Sharp's *Trinity* had made, in the opposite direction, two years earlier.

Once into the Pacific a chance meeting north of Valdivia with another buccaneer ship under the command of John Eaton led to the two ships sailing together to Juan Fernández. There Will, the Miskito Indian accidentally stranded on the island three years earlier, was found alive and well. His story, recounted in the published journals of Cowley and Dampier, formed part of the material that Daniel Defoe later drew on for his *Robinson Crusoe*. Will may have served as inspiration for Man Friday, but his resourcefulness has more than an echo of Crusoe himself. Dampier described how Will had been hunting in the woods when his ship, commanded by Captain Watling, made its hurried departure:

He had with him his Gun and a Knife, with a small Horn of Powder, and a few Shot; which being spent, he contrived a way by notching his Knife, to saw the Barrel of his Gun into small Pieces, wherewith he made Harpoons, Lances, Hooks and a long Knife, heating the pieces first in the Fire, which he struck with his Gun-flint, and a piece of the Barrel of his Gun, which he hardned; having learnt to do that among the *English*. The hot pieces of Iron he would Hammer out and bend as he pleased with Stones, and saw them with his jagged Knife; or grind them to an edge by long labour . . .

With such Instruments as he made in that manner, he got such Provision as the Island afforded; either Goats or Fish. He told us that at first he was forced to eat Seal, which is very ordinary Meat, before he had made Hooks: but afterwards he never killed any Seals but to make Lines, cutting their Skins into Thongs. He had a little House or Hut half a Mile from the Sea, which was lin'd with Goats Skin; his Couch or Barbecu of Sticks lying along about two foot distant from the Ground, was spread with the same, and was all his

63. Dampier, *New Voyage*, p. 80.
64. Ibid., p. 82.

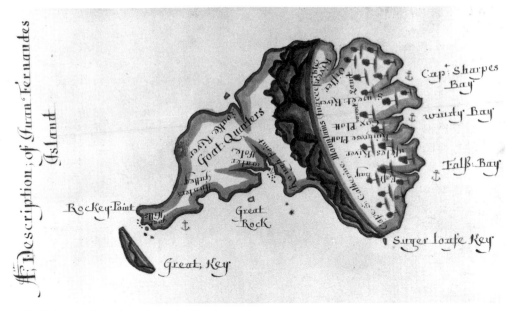

16. Bartholomew Sharp. 'Juan Fernandes Island', c. 1682.

Bedding. He had no Cloaths left, having worn out those he brought from *Watlin*'s Ship, but only a Skin about his Waste. He saw our Ship the Day before we came to an Anchor, and did believe we were *English*, and therefore kill'd three Goats in the Morning, before we came to an Anchor, and drest them with Cabbage, to treat us when we came ashore.[65]

Both goat meat and greenstuffs were welcome, for scurvy had appeared among the crew, and the ship stayed at the island for sixteen days so that the sick men could recover. As they headed for the mainland coast, the bucca-neers found that the Spanish silver ships had been warned off the sea, and they had to content themselves with taking and looting ordinary trading vessels. Rather than returning to Juan Fernández to provision and recuperate, the ship headed for the Galapagos Islands, known only through uncertain Spanish report and, according to Dampier, shown on the maps too close to the mainland.[66] In 1680 Sharp had been told by a captured Spanish officer 'that had we gone to the Islands of *Galapagos*, as we were once determined to do, we had met in that Voyage with many Calms, and such Currents, that many ships have by them been lost, and never heard of to this day.'[67] The prisoners on board the *Batchelor's Delight* also seem to have tried to discourage any attempt to reach the Galapagos. According to Cowley's manuscript

65. Ibid., pp. 84–5, 86.
66. Ibid., p. 100.
67. [Ringrose], *Bucaniers*, I, p. 64.

journal, 'the Spaniards laugh at us telling us they were Inchanted Islands . . . and that they were but Shadowes and not reall Islands'.[68] With its most easterly island five hundred miles out in the Pacific, the Galapagos group offered a plentiful food supply and security from Spanish search vessels. The giant tortoises of the Galapagos were so numerous, Dampier wrote, that '5 or 600 men might subsist on them alone for several months'.[69] Cowley's survey of the islands, complete with English names, was printed in Hack's *Collection*, and for the first time this remarkable group of islands was brought to Europe's attention. Among Cowley's names were those of Colonel Bindloss, brother-in-law of Henry Morgan, and Philip Dassigny, the translator of the Waggoner brought back by Sharp in 1682. The inclusion of these names suggests that Cowley may have had more knowledge of bucca-neering circles than he claimed at the beginning of his journal. The particular names given by Cowley also brought some criticism later by the cartographer Herman Moll, who singled him out as 'having it seems a particular fancy to christen the Places he came to'.[70]

In August 1684 Cowley made a hurried switch to Eaton's ship, the *Nicholas*, leaving his journal and most of his possessions behind. From the northern part of the coast of Peru the ship sailed across the North Pacific to Guam, a voyage of eight thousand miles which left almost every man on board suffering from scurvy. Cowley's manuscript journal again has detail that is missing from the version printed by Hack. The daily entries show that from late January 1685 food was short, and that by late February the situation was becoming desperate: 'wee having a very sickly shipp scarce one man free from the scurvy and the best halfe keeping their Cabbins not being able to come out or to eat their victualls by reason of their sore mouths and our victualls bad for sick men not else but boyled bread and Rotten peases and fishes'.[71] At last, in mid-March 1685, the ship reached Guam. There Eaton found that the islanders, the Chamorros, were in revolt against the Spaniards. Both sides seem to have vied for the support of the buccaneers, who were desperate for fresh food. The islanders came on board with potatoes, plantains and coconuts, but the Spaniards could offer hogs and much else besides. In the pages of Cowley's journal, the Chamorros emerge as an alien and grotesque people. They were of huge stature, he wrote, up to eight and a half feet tall; they never buried their dead, but used their bones for lances; and they were 'treacherous'. The published account is blunt enough, but it is Cowley's manuscript journal that is more revealing:

The Captaine [Eaton] told the Governour that the Indians had fallen upon us and that we had killed some of them, he wished that we had killed them all

68. BL: Sloane MS 54, f. 7v.
69. Dampier, *New Voyage*, pp. 101–2.
70. [Herman Moll], *A View of the Coasts, Countrys, & Islands within the Limits of the South-Sea Company* (2nd edn, London, 1711), p. 124. For more on this see p. 181 below.
71. BL: Sloane MS 54, f. 22.

and began to tell us of theire Rebellion, and how that they had cut of [out]
a Hollands Shipp that had fallen in there some Yeares agoe as we did, and gave
us a comrn. [commission] to kill and take what wee could finde upon the one
halfe of the Island that had Rebelled against him, then we made Warr's
with those Infidels and went on Shoare every day, fetching provisions,
fireing at them where ever wee saw them, that the greatest part of them left
the Island.[72]

Efforts by the islanders to negotiate with Eaton were repulsed, and the
relationship ended with a particularly unsavoury episode when four of the
'Gyants', brought on board as prisoners, were killed in the water, hands tied
behind their backs, while trying to escape. As Cowley noted laconically, it
took forty shots in the body to kill one of them, and another swam a mile
before he died.[73]

As the buccaneer vessel left, Eaton presented the Governor with a farewell
gift: small arms, swords and four barrels of gunpowder. By an ironic coincidence the Spanish commandant, Josef de Quiroga, was the officer who had
detained Narborough's four men in Valdivia in 1670. Elsewhere in the South
Sea the English, from Drake's time onwards, had made efforts to enlist the
support of the native inhabitants against their Spanish overlords. When the
buccaneers crossed the Panama Isthmus in 1680, Dampier acknowledged that
the passage had been possible only with the help of the Cuna Indians, who
the next year gave shelter to his injured companion, Lionel Wafer. Set
against this, Cowleys and his compatriots' brutality to the Chamorros was
exceptional. On the other hand, thirty years after Cowley's involvement in
the affairs of Guam, we can see Robinson Crusoe in action. 'When the
cannibals come ashore with European prisoners, Crusoe releases a bound and
exhausted white man, who says in Latin "*Christianus*" . . . The man is Spanish
and Christian, though Catholic; the English, Protestant, Crusoe, arms him,
and they join to kill some natives, who are defenceless on the beach.'[74]

After the departure from Guam, the twists and turns of the ship's course
are difficult to follow as it sailed first to Canton and then south to Borneo
and Java. The printed version of Cowley's journal gave the impression that
because the ship was foul and slow it was unable to take any prizes, but the
manuscript journal shows that an 'Indian' ship under a Greek captain was
seized in April 1685 and another in July.[75] With the crew 'Factious, and not
under Command of their Captain', the dissatisfied Cowley left and then
rejoined the ship. In Java the ship's company split into three, and Cowley,
together with the surgeon, sailed for Europe in a Dutch ship. Thirteen years
later his journal was to be printed, but it was a sanitized version of events
which omitted as much as it declared.

★

72. Ibid., f. 26.
73. Hacke, *Collection of Original Voyages*, p. 19.
74. Michael Seidel, *Robinson Crusoe: Island Myths and the Novel* (Boston, 1991), p. 44.
75. BL: Sloane MS 54, ff. 30v, 32.

Cowley had been reticent on the reasons for this venture into the North
Pacific, a voyage that was repeated the next year by Captain Charles Swan
with Dampier on board. Swan's career on the American coast showed that,
amid the havoc created by the buccaneers, the occasional expedition sent
from England in the hope of opening legitimate trade with the ports of Peru
or Chile had faint chance of success. Swan's vessel, the *Cygnet*, had arrived
at Valdivia in 1684 carrying £5000 worth of trade goods, but after being
repulsed and having several of his men killed or wounded, Swan decided that
he might as well sell his wares cheap to the nearest buccaneer and join their
number. The process was a fairly peremptory one as Swan 'got up all his
Goods on Deck, and sold to any one that would buy upon Trust: the rest
was thrown over-board into the Sea, except fine Goods.'[76]

By March 1685 the buccaneers, English and French, numbered about a
thousand men, and after deciding against an attack on Panama, lay in wait
offshore for the treasure fleet from Lima. A letter of 4 March 1685 from
Swan, trader turned buccaneer, conveys something of the nervous exhilara-
tion of the moment:

> We shall soon be 900 men in the South Seas. Assure my employers that I do
> all I can to preserve their interest, and that what I now do I could in no wise
> prevent . . . The King might make this whole Kingdom of Peru tributary to
> him in two years' time. We now await the Spanish fleet that brings money to
> Panama . . . If we have success against them we shall make a desperate alarm
> all Europe over.[77]

The buccaneers waited for their prey off Pacheca Island in the Bay of
Panama, and there on 28 May the Spanish fleet of fourteen sail came into
view. Unknown to the buccaneers, the Spaniards had already off-loaded their
treasure on the way north, and 'came purposely to fight us'. Several references in Dampier's manuscript journal (though omitted from the published
version) show that Swan was being guided by 'his astrologer',[78] but the
latter's advice seems to have been less than prescient. The contest was an
unequal one. Only two of the ten buccaneer vessels carried cannon, whereas
six of the Spanish were heavily gunned 'Ships of good force'. It was 52 guns
against 174, 960 men against 3000. After a running fight the buccaneers gave
up and turned tail. Dampier reflected: 'Thus ended this days Work, and with
it all that we had been projecting for 5 or 6 Months; when instead of making
our selves Masters of the Spanish Fleet and Treasure, we were glad to escape
them.'[79]

This fiasco prompted captains such as Eaton and Swan to seek fresh
pastures. They were wearied by their lack of spectacular pickings on the

76. Dampier, *New Voyage*, p. 137.
77. Printed in John Masefield, ed., *Dampier's Voyages* (London, 1906), I, p. 545.
78. BL: Sloane MS 3236, ff. 81, 81v, 151v.
79. Dampier, *New Voyage*, p. 209.

4. The South Sea of the Buccaneers.

American coast, where they jostled for prizes and where every Spaniard now seemed alert to their presence.[80] Panama, rebuilt and relocated since its sacking by Morgan, was no longer an easy target. Dampier noted: 'There are a great many Guns on her Walls, most of which look towards the Land. They had none at all against the Sea, when I first entered those Seas with Capt. *Sawkins*, Capt. *Coxon*, Capt. *Sharp*, and others; for till then they did not fear any Enemy by Sea: But since that they have planted Guns clear round.'[81]

By contrast, there might be rich prizes between the Philippines and China, especially the Acapulco treasure galleon which sailed each year to Manila. This was certainly the lure that Swan dangled before his crew, accompanied with references to the glorious successes of Drake and Cavendish; but Dampier's journals indicate that he and Swan had other ends in view.

80. For more on this see Bradley, *Lure of Peru*, Ch. VII.
81. Dampier, *New Voyage*, p. 179. See also Christopher Ward, *Imperial Panama: Commerce and Conflict in Isthmian America, 1550–1800* (Albuquerque, 1993), pp. 175–6.

Though Dampier was sick with dropsy, he was still intent on 'further discoverys', and together with his captain had long planned a crossing of the Pacific. The problem was, as Dampier put it, to persuade 'the untinking [sic] Rabble' of a crew, anxious about the lack of food on the ocean run ahead. 'Some thought,' Dampier continued, 'such was their Ignorance, that he would carry them out of the World; for about two thirds of our Men did not think there was any such way to be found.'[82] Such doubts were strengthened by what seemed to be the never-ending length of the crossing, and although Dampier made no reference to scurvy, he noted that when Guam was sighted after fifty days the ship was down to three days of provision. This gave him the chance to regale his readers with one of those anecdotes that helped to make the *New Voyage* a best-seller:

> I was afterwards informed, the Men had contrived, first to kill Captain *Swan* and eat him when the Victuals was gone, and after him all of us who were accessory in promoting the undertaking this Voyage. This made Capt. *Swan* say to me after our arrival at *Guam. Ah!* Dampier, *you would have made them but a poor Meal*; for I was as lean as the Captain was lusty and fleshy.[83]

The crew's fury against Swan was no doubt increased by recalling his earlier insistence that the English accounts, which put the distance at well under two thousand leagues (or six thousand miles), were more reliable than the Spanish ones. After the crossing, Dampier's own estimate was that it was 7300 miles. As he mildly remarked, 'the *South-Sea* must be of a greater breadth by 25 degrees than it's commonly reckoned by Hydrographers.' His log entries for the run from Mexico to Guam omitted any reference to magnetic variation, so essential to navigation by dead reckoning, 'for Capt. Swan who had the instruments in his Cabbin, did not seem much to regard it.'

On Guam the situation was much as it had been on the occasion of Eaton's visit the previous year. The Spaniards were weak, and nerve-wracked by the hostility of the surviving islanders. These offered their assistance to Swan to capture the island, but were turned down. Even news that the Acapulco galleon had run aground south of Guam and might still be within striking distance failed to move Swan, 'for he was now wholly averse to any Hostile action'. In his manuscript journal Dampier gave more details of the galleon: 'they had 50 great guns and but foure mounted they had 300 seamen and 500 passagers and they had 800000 Dollars of merchants money besides private Adventures very considerable.'[84] The description in Dampier's journal of the Guam islanders was cursory, but he gave a detailed and enthusiastic description of the island's products, in particular coconuts and breadfruit, and of the local outrigger proas: 'They sail the best of any Boats in the World,'

82.   BL: Sloane MS 3236, f. 175; Dampier, *New Voyage*, p. 276.
83.   This, and quotations in next two paragraphs, are from ibid., pp. 283–4, 200, 288, 303.
84.   BL: Sloane MS 3236, f. 203v.

he wrote, and he tried one out himself, estimating that it might do as much as twenty-four knots.[85]

From Guam the *Cygnet* swung across to the southern Philippines, where Dampier picked out Mindanao as a good centre for future English enterprise. There was gold to the north and spices to the south, while the island lay clear of the main areas of Spanish and Dutch power. The best route there, Dampier thought, would be around Cape Horn, touching at the Galapagos Islands for refreshment on the outward voyage and possibly at New Holland on the return. 'And to speak my Thoughts freely, I believe 'tis owing to the neglect of this easie way that all that vast Tract of Terra Australis which bounds the South-Sea is yet undiscovered: Those that cross that Sea seeming to design some Business on the Peruvian or Mexican Coast, and so leaving that at a distance.' Here Dampier interpolated Edward Davis's information that sailing south in the *Batchelor's Delight* from the Galapagos group in 1687 he saw in lat. 27°S., fifteen hundred miles off the coast of Chile, a small sandy island – 'and to the Westward of it a long Tract of pretty high Land, tending away to the North West out of sight. This might probably be the Coast of Terra Australis Incognita.'[86] Davis's report seemed to be confirmed by Lionel Wafer, who in 1698 recalled how, as the ship reached lat. 27°S., 'betweene Three or four Hundred Leagues from the main land we see Terra Australis Incognita'. By the time Wafer's account of his voyages was published the next year, the details of the sighting had changed somewhat. The location of the small island he now agreed with his captain was fifteen hundred miles out to sea, and from there

> To the Westward, about 12 leagues by Judgment, we saw a range of high Land, which we took to be Islands, for there were several Partitions in the Prospect. This Land seem'd to reach about 14 or 16 Leagues in a Range, and there came from thence great Flocks of Fowls. I, and many more of our Men would have made this Land, and gone ashore at it; but the Captain would not permit us.[87]

The identity of the small sandy island has long puzzled investigators, and although some have speculated that the long stretch of high land beyond was Easter Island, the general consensus is that it was one of those cloud banks so often mistaken for land in the Pacific.[88] Three-quarters of a century later discovery ships from France and Britain were still searching for 'Davis Land'.

After three years Davis, in command of the *Batchelor's Delight*, was on his way out of the South Sea. His departure in one of the only two buccaneer

85. Dampier, *New Voyage*, pp. 299–300. But see Richard Shell, 'The Chamorro Flying Proa', *Mariner's Mirror*, 72 (1986), pp. 135–43.
86. Both quotations from Dampier, *New Voyage*, p. 352.
87. Joyce, *Wafer's New Voyage*, pp. 125, 143.
88. See, for example, Andrew Sharp, *The Discovery of the Pacific Islands* (Oxford, 1960), pp. 88–90.

vessels large enough to make the long voyage back to the Atlantic at this
time (the *Cygnet* was the other) marked the end of an era, certainly as far as
the English buccaneers were concerned. The drying-up of the flow of
replacements was not simply a matter of the news of fewer prizes and better
Spanish precautions becoming known. In the Caribbean the disruptive
activities of the buccaneers in the South Sea were being regarded with
increasing disfavour by the English authorities. They warned that Jamaica and
the other English islands were suffering as the Spanish silver trade was
interrupted; James II issued a general proclamation against pirates; and the
Spaniards began to take retaliatory action.[89]

The alliance of England and Spain in 1689 in the war against France was
another signal that the glory days of the buccaneers in the South Sea were
over. There was a postscript to their activities, for the new Anglo–Spanish
understanding encouraged one more attempt to send an English expedition
into the South Sea with trade goods. In 1689 Captain John Strong was given
a privateer's commission (to be used only against the French) to take the 270-
ton, 38-gun *Welfare* into the South Sea. In the event, the voyage was a
disaster and made a dispiriting finale to the years of English endeavour and
ambition in the South Sea. Two manuscript journals exist: one kept by
Strong and another, fuller and more self-consciously literary, by the purser
and supercargo Richard Simson.[90] Scattered references show that he was
writing with an eye to publication;[91] but the doleful story he related, though
not without interest, was unlikely to excite a publisher in the way that the
exploits of the buccaneers had done. The expedition had two main objectives apart from its official purpose of taking French prizes. First, Strong
hoped to find the wreck of a Spanish treasure ship, supposed to have been
lost on a voyage from Lima in 1659; and second, and more dangerously, he
intended to trade with the Spaniards on the coast. Simson's journal shows
that the *Welfare* carried a whole range of trade goods: baize, arms, tools and
other iron work. This cargo, the promoters of the venture hoped, would
bring a profit of 1600 percent.[92]

The *Welfare* sailed from Plymouth on 1 November 1689. The mate, David
Innis, doubled as the expedition's 'Conjurer in Chief', and on the day of
departure 'being on a Fryday (and he said in the houre when Venus ruled),
erected an Astrological Scheme, for predicting the Success of our Voyage'.[93]
The ship took more than three months to struggle through the Strait of

89. For more on this see Bradley, *Lure of Peru*, p. 160; also Robert C. Ritchie, *Captain Kidd and
      the War against the Pirates* (Cambridge, MA, 1986).
90. Strong's journal is in BL: Sloane MS 3295, with a fair copy in Harleian MS 5101; Simson's in
      Sloane MS 86. For the Spanish reaction to the venture see Bradley, *Lure of Peru*, pp. 170–9.
91. For example, a note that a section on disease was not suitable for 'any nice or Longing Lady's'
      to read. BL: Sloane MS 86, f. 58.
92. Ibid., f. 4v.
93. BL: Sloane MS 3295, f. 47v.

Magellan in early 1690, being blown back by the westerlies time and time again. On one occasion, when it ran aground, the 'conjurer' was brought into action. 'He briskly encouraged the men, telling them that tho' he foresaw things were not like to goe well with himselfe this Voyage he was sufficiently sattisfied the Shipp would come off and return home.'[94] By the time the *Welfare* reached the South Sea in May 1690, it had lost a tenth of its crew through sickness. At Valdivia the ship was warned off the port, whose forts had been designed by Thomas Armiger, Narborough's lieutenant captured there in 1670. By the end of June, fifty of the crew of ninety were 'extraordinary sick and weak . . . not capable of any service'.[95] Another attempt to land farther north resulted in the loss of the vessel's 'linguister' or translator, who was either captured by the Spaniards or possibly deserted to them.

At sea the only vessels seen were Spanish, one of which was intercepted after a chase on the assumption that it might be a French privateer. It was perhaps just as well that it was not. An arms drill just before the engagement resulted in casualties among the *Welfare*'s crew, as 'one was so foolish as to discharge ball, and shot his Neighbour through the Breeches, others were slightly wounded with small shott.'[96] In the actual engagement no fewer than twenty-four shots fired at the chase from the 'Great Gunns' all missed. Only when Strong and the master aimed and fired a cannon themselves was a hit registered, and the prize brought to. It was bound from Guayaquil to Paita carrying timber. After an embarrassing initial meeting, relations between the officers of the two ships became amicable, or so it appeared. Gifts were exchanged, and fresh meat was sent on board the *Welfare*. Both Strong and Simson hoped that this encounter would lead to further trading opportunities, for 'It is incredible,' Simson wrote, 'what they told us of the Riches of the Country.'[97] As the purser realized later, English and Spanish assumptions about the relationship between the two groups on board the privateer were somewhat different:

> The errour lay here, to believe men that were in a State of Captivity, as those Gentlemen had reason to think themselves to be. There being Centinells wth. drawn Curlaces, at the Round house door and other two with Musketts, att the Head and Poop, all the time of their being aboard of us, besides two Files of Men for the greater Solemnity at their reception into the Shipp. If therefore they thought themselves Captives they would as such dissemble.[98]

Depressingly, Spaniards encountered two weeks later claimed that European goods coming from Cartagena to Panama and farther south were

94. Ibid.
95. Ibid., ff. 51v–52.
96. BL: Sloane MS 86, f. 23.
97. Ibid., f. 28v.
98. Ibid., f. 48.

cheaper than the goods on the *Welfare*, and that in any case to trade with foreigners was a hanging offence. They also told Strong that there were four Englishmen stranded on Juan Fernández, and for humanitarian and practical reasons the undermanned privateer headed for the island. The men had been with Davis on the *Batchelor's Delight*, homeward-bound in late 1687. Lionel Wafer was on board and described how the men lost their money gambling and, 'being unwilling to return out of these Seas as poor as they came', demanded to be left on Juan Fernández.[99]

The Englishmen, once found, did not appear to be in distress. They had four Negro boys to help them; seals, sea-lions and goats were plentiful; their only problem seemed to be occasional Spanish raids. When these occurred, the castaways retreated into the hilly interior where they had dug passages and hung ropes 'for their convenient retreat'.[100] According to Simson, they also experienced a religious conversion while on the island, and gave up swearing and blaspheming for a 'perfect and thorough reformation'. One of them promised that if they embarked on the *Welfare* 'he would Endeavour the like reformation amongst our Men.' Taking them off the island was not quite the straightforward matter that Strong had assumed, for he found himself listening to a good deal of rhetoric about the virtues of the simple life. An indignant Simson describes the negotiations:

> Our Comander had come a great deal out of his way to carry them home, believing that his kindness therein would have been gratefully accepted; but they subtilly pretended that they lived as Kings in the Island having no Law, or Superiour to Controule them, that they wanted for Nothing, Turnipp-topps, supplying their want of Bread, their food being venison, their drink Goates milk and Excellent water, for severall dayes they made a showe as if they had been of all the Men in the world, the most Content with their Condition, thinking with themselves that our Captain would allow them wages, as he did other Seamen; but they pulled off this Vizard before we sayled from thence, and declared themselves glad to have the oppertunity of seeing their owne Country once more.

The local knowledge of the men was useful in provisioning the ship, but once at sea they proved a disturbing presence among a crew whose behaviour had already caused problems. As Simson pontificated: 'A Ship is not improperly called a wooden world, various occasions shew the various tempers of men there, we had some of several Nations, humours and abillitys.' One of the castaways told Simson 'in the Old-Privateers Stile' that the Spaniards lacked both skill and courage, that their seamen were 'but bunglers', and that 'vast riches' were there for the taking by an enterprising

99.   Joyce, *Wafer's New Voyage*, p. 127. BL: Sloane MS 3295 notes that five men left the *Batchelor's Delight*, but that one had been picked up by a Spanish vessel visiting the island.
100. Quotations in this and next paragraph are from BL: Sloane MS 86, ff. 39, 42, 39v, 43v, 40.

captain. Strong, by contrast, was determined to build on the good relations he considered he had established with the Spaniards during their earlier encounters. In November the *Welfare* reached the coast just south of Concepción, and Strong sent his pinnace towards the shore with a letter for the local commander. The boat was manned by the first mate and fourteen of the ship's best seamen, including three of the men picked up at Juan Fernández. What followed makes predictable reading. Ignoring Sharp's warning not to land, or, if they did, to remain armed and watchful, the boat's crew went on shore to mingle with the welcoming Spaniards, leaving two of their number in the anchored pinnace. As the seamen and their hosts shared a meal on the beach, a squadron of sixty horsemen swept down on them. Only one Englishman regained the boat, though shot in the leg. Whether the rest were killed, wounded or captured in the fracas was not clear to the watchers on the ship. Simson feared the worst, while Strong's despairing journal entry read: 'We lost eleavon of ye lustiest men we had Aboard by ye treachery of these false hearted Spaniards.'[101] Later Spanish references to ten prisoners suggest that one man was killed on the beach. Of the rest, two of the Juan Fernández castaways were executed because of their past record, and the remaining eight sent into the interior of Chile.[102] Among the captives was the astrologer, his fate perhaps a sad reflection on his professional skill, though Simson remembered that 'before he went over the side into the boat, he lookd as if he had been bewitched, Black Clouds of Melancholy hanging on his Brow's, and Nabal like he would hardly speak to one.'[103]

Like Narborough twenty years before, Strong decided that he could do nothing to rescue his men. He drifted letters ashore in bottles asking that they be well treated, and then headed for the Strait of Magellan and home. Instead of the huge profit that the promoters of the voyage envisaged, they were faced with a £12,000 loss. Whatever the diplomatic situation in Europe, and regardless of the encouragement individual merchants or local officials in the South Sea might give of their willingness to trade, the Spanish government's policy of prohibition of the foreigner remained intact. The last word can rest with Richard Simson in the rueful prologue to his journal: 'A Traverse of near 40000 Miles might have promised more, we for a long time, and to little purpose, convers'd with Monsters of both Men and Beasts.'[104]

101. Ibid., f. 47v; BL: Sloane MS 3295, f. 83v.
102. See Bradley, *Lure of Peru*, p. 179.
103. BL: Sloane MS 86, f. 47v.
104. Ibid., f. 1v.

CHAPTER IV

'I Speak as to the Compass of my Own Knowledge': Dampier's Explorations and Writings

As disillusioned English buccaneers abandoned the Pacific coasts of Spanish America in the late 1680s, many thousand of miles to the west the *Cygnet*, now under the command of Captain Reed but with Dampier still on board, continued its wanderings. During 1687 it spent seven months in the North China Seas before sailing south through the Philippines and Dutch East Indies until by the end of the year it was south of Timor. To go farther south would take the vessel into waters totally unknown to English seamen. Like most initiatives taken on board the *Cygnet*, the decision to keep south was actually more a matter of chance (and an acknowledgment of the prevailing winds) than premeditated design. Dampier explained: 'We stood off South, intending to touch at New-Holland, a part of Terra Australis Incognita, to see what that Country would afford us. Indeed as the Winds were, we could not now keep our intended Course (which was first westerly, and then northerly) without going to New-Holland, unless we had gone back again among the Islands.'[1]

The reference to New Holland as 'part of Terra Australis Incognita' is evidence of Dampier's confusion on this matter, since Tasman's track of 1642–3 had shown that if both lands existed they must be separate. A later passage in Dampier's published account confirms the uncertainty: 'New-Holland is a very large Tract of Land. It is not yet determined whether it is an Island or a main Continent.'[2] There was no knowledge of Tasman's voyage here, nor should any be expected. Dampier had left England at the start of his journeyings in 1679, at a time when nothing had been published in English on Tasman except the cryptic Haelbos account. Although by the time his book was published in 1697 Dampier would

1. Dampier, *New Voyage*, p. 461.
2. Ibid., p. 463.

have had the opportunity to consult the fuller account of Tasman's voyage published in English in 1682 and reprinted in 1694, there is no evidence that he did so. Instead, there is a laconic admission in his Preface to the *New Voyage*: 'Nor have I given my self any great Trouble since my Return, to compare my Discoveries with those of others.' Dampier's ignorance of the waters ahead of the *Cygnet* in December 1687 should not be exaggerated, however, for he had with him a chart of the region between Timor and New Holland that was sufficiently detailed to show shoals and rocks near the Australian coast.[3]

The existence of this chart on the *Cygnet* raises the larger question of what sort of charts and other information buccaneer vessels carried on board. A selection of printed charts and maps would no doubt have been obtained before the vessel left its home port, but these would normally have been limited both in range and detail. From Drake to Anson marauders in the South Sea gave priority to seizing pilots, charts and sailing directions from captured Spanish vessels, but the *Cygnet* was well south of the Spanish sphere of activity and knowledge. Dampier's published account offers no clue to the identity of this chart, but an annotation in his own hand in a manuscript copy of his journal does: 'Wee had but one draft of the East India in our ship and not a man acquainted in these partes all the account wee had was out of Sillar his waggoner by which wee had hitherto guided our selves after we left the American coast.'[4] The reference is to John Seller's *Atlas Maritimus* of 1675, a volume or 'Waggoner' that included two charts of relevance to this part of the *Cygnet*'s voyage. The first was 'A Chart of the Eastermost part of the East Indies' (Ill. 17), which showed a shoal off the south coast of Timor and the opposite shore of New Holland. The other, which would have been the guide 'after we left the American coast', was 'A Chart of the South Sea' (Ill. 12).

The *Cygnet* sighted the Australian coast on 4 January 1688 and the next day anchored in a 'pretty deep Bay' in lat. 16°50'S. in the northwest corner of King Sound. The bay was later named after the vessel, and the outlying islands called Buccaneer Archipelago. According to Dampier's book, the vessel remained there until 12 March, but his shorter manuscript journal gives 12 February as the departure date. Internal evidence points to the correctness of the dates in the manuscript rather than the published version;[5] even so, it represents the longest known stay by Europeans on the Australian mainland. Earlier Dutch landings had been for a matter of days, if not hours.

3. Ibid., p. 462.
4. BL: Sloane MS 3236, f. 226. For more on this manuscript journal see pp. 112–14 below. For 'Sillar' [Seller] see Coolie Verner, 'John Seller and the English Chart Trade in Seventeenth-Century England', in Norman J.W. Thrower, ed., *The Compleat Plattmaker* (Berkeley and Los Angeles, 1978), pp. 127–57.
5. See the detailed evidence on this in my chapter, 'New Holland to New South Wales: The English Approaches', in Williams and Frost, *Terra Australis to Australia*, p. 157 n. 13.

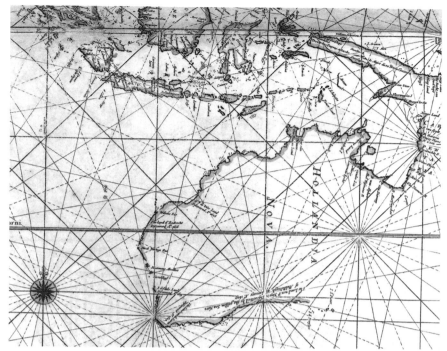

17. John Seller. Section from 'Chart of the Easternmost Part of the East Indies', 1675.

Dampier's description of the area around Cygnet Bay was as unenthusiastic
as the accounts of his Dutch predecessors elsewhere on the coast: dry, sandy
soil; no surface water; some thin grass and stunted trees; little animal
or bird life. If the place itself was unattractive, its human inhabitants
were still less alluring, and the description of the Aborigines in the *New
Voyage* was to live long in the European memory. Naked, black, without
covering or habitations,

> The Inhabitants of this Country are the miserablest People in the
> World . . . setting aside their Humane Shape, they differ but little from
> Brutes. They are tall, strait-bodied, and thin, with small long Limbs.
> They have great Heads, round Foreheads, and great Brows. Their Eyelids are
> always half closed, to keep the Flies out of their Eyes . . . They have great
> Bottle-Noses, pretty full Lips, and wide Mouths . . . They are long-visaged,
> and of a very unpleasing Aspect, having no one graceful Feature in their Faces.
> Their Hair is black, short and curl'd, like that of the Negroes; and not long
> and lank like the Common Indians. The Colour of their Skins, both of their

Faces and the rest of their Body, is Coal-black, like that of the Negroes of Guinea.[6]

They had no metal or implements; their only weapons were wooden swords and spears. They grew no crops, trapped nothing and seemed to live on the small fish stranded at low tide. Their speech was guttural and unintelligible. Their first reaction to the intruders was a distant shaking of their wooden weapons, but the beating of a drum by the buccaneers was enough to frighten them off, and subsequent contacts were peaceful enough. A few Aborigines were taken on board the ship, though they showed no curiosity about their new surroundings. Attempts were made to press them into service carrying water casks, but to no avail – 'all the signs we could make were to no purpose, for they stood like Statues, without motion, but grinn'd like so many Monkeys, staring one upon another.'[7] The description as it appeared in the *New Voyage* was to be transmitted to generations of readers, and not only to armchair readers. More than seventy years later and a continent's breadth away, James Cook and Joseph Banks on the *Endeavour* had Dampier's book to hand as in April 1770 they strained for their first sight of the inhabitants of the coast of southeast Australia. Banks wrote: 'we stood in with the land near enough to discern 5 people who appeard through our glasses to be enormously black: so far did the prejudices which we had built on Dampiers account influence us that we fancied we could see their Colour when we could scarce distinguish whether or not they were men.'[8]

Although 'Dampier's initial account of the Aborigines is an excellent first approximation',[9] the shorter description in his manuscript journal is both more accurate (for example, on the nature of the Aborigines' hair) and more dispassionate. 'They are people of good stature but very thin and leane I judge for want of food[;] they are black yet I belive their haires would be long, if it was comed out but for want of Combs it is matted up like a negroes' hair.' Dampier then went on to explain how they moved from place to place, 'for they are not troubled with household goods nor cloaths'.[10] In rather more elaborate words Cook echoed this in his later description of the Aborigines of New South Wales: 'they covet not Magnificent Houses, Household-stuff &ca, they live in a warm and fine Climate . . . so that they

---

6. Dampier, *New Voyage*, p. 464. Defoe's description of Friday seems almost deliberately antitheti-
    cal to this: 'hair long and black, not curled like wool . . . colour of his skin was not quite black
    . . . his nose small, not flat like the negroes'. *The Life and Adventures of Robinson Crusoe*
    (Harmondsworth, 1965), pp. 208–9.
7. Dampier, *New Voyage*, p. 462.
8. J.C. Beaglehole, ed., *The Endeavour Journal of Joseph Banks 1768–1771* (Sydney, 1962), II, p. 50.
    For more on this see my article, '"Far More Happier than We Europeans": Reactions to the
    Australian Aborigines on Cook's Voyage', *Historical Studies*, 19 (1981), pp. 500–2.
9. A.A. Abbie's assessment in John Kenny, *Before the First Fleet: Europeans in Australia 1606–1777*
    (Kenthurst, NSW, 1995), p. 111.
10. BL: Sloane MS 3236, ff. 222r–222v.

have very little need of Clothing.'[11] These, too, were not to appear in the published version of Cook's journal.

From New Holland the *Cygnet* sailed into the Indian Ocean to the Nicobar Islands, where Dampier was allowed to leave the vessel, after the crew had voted on the matter in yet another example of the self-willed democracy of the buccaneers. It was a sign of the strained relations between him and some at least of the crew that he believed that he had been in danger of being marooned in New Holland.[12] His adventures were far from over, as he sailed with a few companions in an outrigger canoe to Sumatra, and then on to Achin. After recovering from a serious illness there, Dampier travelled for another two years, during which he spent time in Malacca, Tonkin and Madras, as well as serving as a gunner in the East India Company fort at Bencoolen (Sumatra). At last Dampier was showing signs of travel-weariness – 'I began to long after my native Country, after so tedious a Ramble from it'[13] – and in January 1691 he set sail from Bencoolen in a Company ship and arrived home in September.

With him came an enforced visitor to England, Jeoly, 'the painted Prince' (Ill. 18). Captured from an offshore island, he was taken to Mindanao, where an English trader bought him. At Bencoolen Dampier acquired a half-share in Jeoly and agreed to take him to England, where he looked to gain 'no small Advantage to my self from my painted Prince'.[14] Once home, shortage of funds compelled Dampier to sell his interest in Jeoly, who was exhibited at side-shows before dying of smallpox. According to Dampier, Jeoly's decorative tattoos (a term that had not yet found its way into the English language) had been pricked onto his skin by one of his five wives. 'I cannot liken the drawings to any figure of animals, or the like; but they were very curious, full of great variety of lines, flourishes, chequered-work, &c. keeping a very graceful proportion.'[15] In his *New Voyage* Dampier claimed that he hoped to use the 'prince' in opening trade contacts with his homeland; his manuscript journal has more on this:

> I brought a painted Man from thence [Mindanao] whoe was Prince of a small Iland but 18 Leagues from Mindanao whoe told me that there was much Gold on his Iland and I know he could not be inform'd of the manner of gathering it unless he had known it himselfe besides he knew not the vallue of it neither have the people of his Iland any comerce with other People.[16]

11. J.C. Beaglehole, ed., *The Journals of Captain James Cook: The Voyage of the Endeavour 1768–1771* (Cambridge, 1955), p. 399.
12. BL: Sloane MS 3236, ff. 222v–223, 227.
13. Dampier, *New Voyage*, p. 519.
14. Ibid.
15. Ibid., p. 514.
16. BL: Sloane MS 3236, f. 202v.

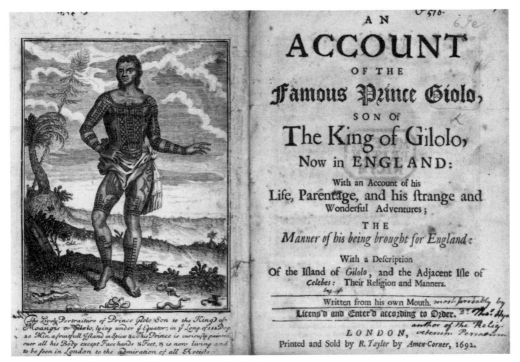

An

ACCOUNT

OF THE

𝔉𝔞𝔪𝔬𝔲𝔰 𝔓𝔯𝔦𝔫𝔠𝔢 𝔊𝔦𝔬𝔩𝔬,

SON OF

The King of Gilolo,

Now in ENGLAND:

With an Account of his
Life, Parentage, and his ſtrange and
Wonderful Adventures;

THE

Manner of his being brought for England:

With a Deſcription
Of the Iſland of *Gilolo*, and the Adjacent Iſle of
Celebes: Their Religion and Manners.

Written from his own Mouth.

Licenſ'd and Enter'd according to Order.

LONDON,
Printed and Sold by *R. Taylor* by *Amen-Corner*, 1692.

18. [Thomas Hyde]. Jeoly or Gilolo, the 'painted prince', c. 1691.

Gold or no gold, there seems to have been little serious interest in the unfortunate man. An advertisement during his stay in London notified all and sundry that 'he will be exposed to publick view every day . . . at the Blew Boars-head in Fleet Street . . . if his health will permit'; but that arrangements could be made to take him to the houses of 'Persons of Quality'.[17] Jeoly's value as a freakish exhibit was heightened by chapbook romances about his relationship with a beautiful princess. These, Dampier noted, 'were stories indeed', as were the tales circulating about the magical properties of Jeoly's bodypaint.[18] The broadsheet of 1692 about his public showing is now filed in the British Library with advertisements on the display of giants, monsters, dwarfs and hermaphrodites.[19]

New research on Dampier shows that in 1694 and 1695 he was at La Coruña involved in an abortive attempt by an English consortium to salvage Spanish wrecks in American waters and to open trade with Spanish American

17. BL: 551 d. 18 (2).
18. See [Thomas Hyde], *An Account of the Famous Prince Giolo* (London, 1692); Dampier, *New Voyage*, p. 346.
19. See BL: N TAB 2026 (25).

colonists.[20] The venture collapsed when mutineers led by Henry Every (soon to become beter known as 'Captain John Avery') sailed away on the flagship of the little fleet to embark on a spectacular career of piracy in eastern waters. Dampier does not seem to have been directly involved in the mutiny, but the episode threw a long shadow across his subsequent career. It seems likely that it was during his long stay at La Coruña that Dampier first turned his attention to the account of his earlier travels which was published in 1697 as *A New Voyage Round the World*. Clearly, he must have spent much time in the preparation of the book, and the manuscript journal with its alterations and additions gives some indication of the nature of this task. It also raises a number of questions, not of all of which are easy to answer. Of Dampier's care in writing and safeguarding his journal there can be no doubt. Slipping away from the *Cygnet* among the Nicobar Islands in May 1688, Dampier was in a native canoe which overturned, soaking 'my Journal and some Drafts of Land of my own taking, which I much prized', and which were only saved after much drying in front of 'great Fires'. Unfortunately, among the drawings that were lost was a chart of one of the *Cygnet*'s landing places in New Holland.[21] Three years later, Dampier described yet another escapade in which 'I came by stealth from Bencooly, and left all my books Drafts and Instruments Cloaths bedding [illegible] and wages behind. I only brought with me this Journall and my painted prince.'[22]

Despite the reference to 'this Journall', the manuscript journal now in the Sloane Manuscripts in the British Library is not the one kept by Dampier on the voyage. There is ample internal evidence to show that it was written after Dampier's return from the East Indies to England in 1691.[23] It is, however, a manuscript of great interest which has only recently received the attention it deserves.[24] At 471 pages it is considerably shorter than the 550 printed pages of the *New Voyage*, and the main text is not in Dampier's hand. However, in a margin so wide (it extends across a third of the width of each page) that it must have been specified in advance, Dampier has added corrections and additions, keyed to the text by letters of the alphabet, asterisks and crosses. These are integral to it, which seems to indicate that Dampier had marked up some earlier version of his journal, and then had it copied so that he could make his additions. Even with these, the composite

20. See Joel H. Baer, 'William Dampier at the Crossroads: New Light on the "Missing Years," 1691–1697', *International Journal of Maritime History*, 8 (1996), pp. 97–117.
21. For this episode see Dampier, *New Voyage*, p. 487, and BL: Sloane MS 3236, f. 221.
22. Ibid., f. 232v.
23. To take just one example, there is the reference to one of Dampier's shipmates, 'Daniel Wallis, a young man now liveing in Waymouth'. Ibid., f. 208v.
24. In Philip Edwards, *The Story of the Voyage: Sea-narratives in Eighteenth-Century England* (Cambridge, 1994), pp. 20–32. James Burney, *A Chronological History of the Voyages and Discoveries in the South Sea or Pacific Ocean*, IV (London, 1816), pp. 223, 243, seems to have been the first to note the existence of the manuscript journal and the discrepancies between it and the published account.

manuscript journal is still shorter than the published book. Both in style and substance the latter is different, adding long descriptive passages on the places Dampier visited, the customs of their inhabitants, their trading potential and, in particular, their natural history. There were then at least three stages of composition, and probably more. There was the original journal or journals kept by Dampier on the voyage. The length of time he was away argues against the existence at any time of a single journal but rather in favour of a number of separate journals and notes, in fact a miscellany. None of this material has survived. Second, there is the manuscript journal now in the British Library, made at some time after 1691 and studded with his annotations. Some at least of the material in this was taken from the journals of Dampier's sailing companions. We know, for example, that while on the *Cygnet* in 1684 he had read the journals kept by Captain Swan and the chief mate, and had included some of their entries in his own account.[25] And third, there is the book of 1697, which alone conforms to Dampier's description of his work as a 'mixt Relation of Places and Actions'.[26]

There is little disagreement that in producing a book from his journal and notes Dampier received help. Charles Hatton noted, 'He is a very good navigator, kept his journal exactly . . . but, you must imagine, had assistance in drawing up his history.'[27] Dampier himself, while claiming the main credit, later acknowledged that it was 'far from being a Diminution to one of my Education and Employment, to have, what I write, Revised and Corrected by Friends'.[28] Guesses as to the identity of these helpers have included, inevitably it seems, Swift and Defoe. There are signposts that might seem to point in their direction: the intriguing reference on the first page of *Gulliver's Travels* to 'my cousin Dampier', and Defoe's interest in the South Sea hard on the heels of the publication of the *New Voyage*.[29] But there is no direct evidence, and it seems unlikely that any will now emerge.

The matter of editorial help or intrusion cannot quite be left there. A comparison of the manuscript journal with the book shows more than a process of enlargement and literary polishing. A prime example of a change in meaning has already been given in the different entries on the Aborigines. Quite simply, what passes for Dampier's description in the *New Voyage*, the earliest first-hand account by an Englishman, is not only judgmental and derogatory in tone, but in some of those places where it differs from the manuscript version is factually wrong. Whose hand made the change, and why, is a matter of speculation. In 1773 John Hawkesworth did something rather similar to the journals of James Cook and Joseph Banks,[30] but in the

25. See BL: Sloane MS 3236, f. 46.
26. Dampier, *New Voyage*, preface.
27. Quoted in Edwards, *Story of the Voyage*, pp. 20–1.
28. William Dampier, *A Voyage to New-Holland, &c. In the Year 1699* (London, 1703/1729), preface.
29. See pp. 134, 209–10 below.
30. See Williams, ' "Far More Happier than We Europeans" ', p. 510.

1690s there would hardly seem to have been enough public, or even scholarly, interest in the Aborigines to justify the change from Dampier's rather laconic manuscript entry to the vituperation of the published account. Other changes are easier to explain, in that they tend to put a gloss on Dampier's own motives and actions and conceal some of the more artless admissions of the manuscript journal.[31]

The final folio of the journal contains an apologia by Dampier. It is a justification of his rather shadowy role on the voyages, and of his right to produce an account at all. In a sense it is an assertion of the superiority of the observer over the commander as a recorder of events, and a recognition that discoveries are only discoveries when they are properly and publicly reported:

> It may be Demanded by som why I call these voyages and discoverys myne seeing I was neither master nor mate of any of the ships; to such demands I answer that I might have been master of the first I went out in if I would have accepted it for it was known to most men that were in the seas, that I kept a Journall and all that knew me well did Ever judg my accounts were kept as Exact as any mans besides most if not all that kept Journalls Either Loozed them before they gott to Europe or Else are not yet returned nor Ever likely to com home therefore I judge that mine is the more Entire I having still persued my writing therefore I think I may most justly Challenge a right to these Discoverys than any other man yet I can plainly see that some men are not soe well pleased as if it came from any of the Commanders that was in the South Seas though most off them I think all besides Captain Swan were wholly incapable of keeping a sea journall and took no account of any actions neither did they make any observations in those partes yet such is the opinion of most men that nothing pleaseth them but what comes from the highest hand though from men of the meanest Capacityes.[32]

The fact that Dampier's *New Voyage* served as a model for many of the travel narratives of the eighteenth century should not obscure the general changes taking place in travel writing during his lifetime. By the later seventeenth century, narrators had won clear of the dependence on classical and biblical texts to explain the new worlds overseas. Even if the guides being drawn up to aid travellers in exotic regions were generally most appropriate to societies that conformed to familiar European shapes,[33] there was also recognition of the value of first-hand accounts from observers

31.   See Edwards, *Story of the Voyage*, pp. 21–5, 28–30.
32.   BL: Sloane MS 3236, f. 233.
33.   See, for example, the list of ten categories given in Bernard Varen's *Geographia generalis* of 1650, quoted in Annemarie De Waal Malefit, *Images of Man: A History of Anthropological Thought* (New York, 1974), p. 45.

outside the conventional scholarly disciplines. In England a considerable step forward came with the establishment in 1662 of the Royal Society, whose *Philosophical Transactions* became a hospitable if chaotic repository of travel accounts. Its first volume contained Robert Boyle's 'Directions for Sea-men, Bound for Far Voyages', and in 1667 Thomas Sprat expressed the hope that 'there will scarce a ship come up the Thames, that does not make some return of experiments'.[34] The Society's emphasis on the importance of observations of physical phenomena by seamen and other travellers was justification, if any were needed, for Dampier's approach. It was to the President of the Royal Society, Lord Montagu, that Dampier dedicated the *New Voyage*, but his relationship with Hans Sloane, Secretary to the Royal Society, was probably more important. At some stage Sloane acquired the clerical copy of Dampier's journal (together with the journals of many of his buccaneer contemporaries in the South Sea), and soon after the publication of the *New Voyage* arranged for Thomas Murray to paint Dampier's portrait (Ill. 19).[35]

The Society practised what it preached. In addition to the inclusion of numerous accounts by travellers in the *Philosophical Transactions*, in 1693 *A Collection of Curious Travels and Voyages*, edited by the botanist John Ray, was issued under its auspices. The next year a Fellow of the Society, Tancred Robinson, provided the Introduction to another compilation, *An Account of Several Late Voyages & Discoveries*, which included the journals of Tasman and Narborough. If Dampier saw this collection, the skeletal nature of the Tasman and Narborough logs may have encouraged him to flesh out his own journal with the voluminous notes he had made on natural history and the like. Certainly, Robinson's Introduction might be seen by Dampier as a challenge to do just that: '*The Advantages of taking judicious and accurate Journals in Voyages and Itineraries, are so great and many, as the Improvements of* Geography, Hydrography, Astronomy, Natural and Moral History, Antiquity, Merchandise, Trade, Empire, &c., *that few Books can compare with them either for Profit or Pleasure.*'[36] If Dampier needed another nudge towards publication then there was Robinson's complaint that he could not say anything about recent English voyages in the South Sea because he had not seen any journals. Ignorant of Dampier's cache of observations, notes and sketches, he finished on an even sourer note: '*Tis to be lamented, that the* English Nation *have not sent along with their* Navigators *some skilful* Painters,

---

34. *Philosophical Transactions*, 1 (8) (8 Jan. 1665/6), p. 140; Thomas Sprat, *History of the Royal Society* (London, 1667), p. 86.

35. There is evidence that Hans Sloane acquired copies of some at least of the buccaneers' journals soon after their writing. Sloane went to Jamaica in 1687 as physician to the Duke of Albemarle, governor of the colony. Albemarle died in 1688, but several of the copies of the journals in Sloane's collection are dedicated to the Duke, presumably while he was still alive. See, for example, BL: Sloane MSS 46A, 46B, 48, 49.

36. This and the next quotation are from Anon., *Account of Several Late Voyages & Discoveries*, pp. v, xxix.

19. William Dampier. Portrait by Thomas Murray, c. 1698.

Naturalists, *and* Mechanists.' Finally, in 1696 the Royal Society issued Robert Southwell's *Brief Instructions for Making Observations in All Parts of the World*, and its emphasis on climate, land forms and natural history matched Dampier's work to come.

A New Voyage Round the World was published by James Knapton, with maps by Herman Moll, in February 1697; and by the end of the year it was in its third edition. It repeated and surpassed the commercial success of Exquemelin's *Bucaniers of America*, whose first English edition in 1684 had sold so well that a second, enlarged edition which added Ringrose's journal was published within three months of the first, and was reprinted in 1695,

1699 and 1704. The title-page of Dampier's book showed the remarkable range of his travels; not a single voyage at all, but a whole series of wanderings, excursions and diversions to

> the *Isthmus* of *America*, several Coasts and islands in the *West Indies*, the Isles of *Cape Verd*, the Passage by *Terra del Fuego*, the *South Sea* Coasts of *Chili*, *Peru*, and *Mexico*; the Isle of *Guam* one of the *Ladrones*, *Mindanao*, and other *Philippine* and *East-India* Islands near *Cambodia*, *China*, *Formosa*, *Luconia*, *Celebes*, &c. *New Holland*, *Sumatra*, *Nicobar* Isles; the *Cape* of *Good Hope*, and *Santa Hellena*.

It had taken him thirteen years to complete his interrupted circumnavigation, a fact he turned to his advantage, 'as one who rambles about a Country can give usually a better account of it, than a Carrier who jogs on to his Inn, without ever going out of his Road.'[37] Dampier's book had all the narrative excitement of Ringrose, and much else besides: sections on natural history, on the customs of exotic peoples, and reflections on possible areas for English enterprise. So, while at Guam in 1686 Dampier made notes on the various uses of the coconut – drink and food; its shell used for cups and dishes, its husk turned into rope and cables – which ran to six pages of print. He concluded:

> I have been the longer on this subject, to give the Reader a particular Account of the use and profit of a Vegetable, which is possibly of all others the most generally serviceable to the Conveniences, as well as the Necessities of humane Life. Yet this Tree, that is of such great use, and esteemed so much in the *East-Indies*, is scarce regarded in the *West-Indies*, for want of the knowledge of the benefit which it may produce. And 'tis partly for the sake of my Country-men, in our *American* Plantations, that I have spoken so largely of it.[38]

It was this blend, apparently so artless, of the sensational and the practical that appealed to a wide readership. Dampier avoided the fanciful exaggerations of some earlier travel accounts, insisting, 'I speak as to the compass of my own knowledge.' Despite his heavy-handed joke about the threat posed to Captain Swan and himself by a hungry crew off Guam, Dampier was not generally inclined to titillate his readers with gory accounts of cannibalism: 'As for the common opinion of *Anthropophagi*, or Man-Eaters, I did never meet with any such people.'[39] His more reflective sections were written – as befitted a keen-eyed but untrained observer – in a straightforward prose style. It might be 'dry and jejeune' (Dampier's own, self-deprecating phrase), but

37. Dampier, *New Voyage*, preface.
38. Ibid., p. 295.
39. Ibid., p. 485.

it was intended to satisfy those who are 'more desirous of a Plain and Just Account of the true Nature and State of the Things described, than of a Polite and Rhetorical Narrative'.[40]

By 1699 the *New Voyage* was in its fourth edition, and in that year Knapton published a second volume of Dampier's *Voyages and Descriptions*, including material that had been squeezed out of the 1697 volume. It included sections on Tonkin, Achin and Malacca, as well as Dampier's earlier voyages as a youth to Campeachy. Most notably, it contained 'A Discourse on the Trade-Winds, Breezes, Storms, Seasons of the year, Tides and Currents of the Torrid Zone throughout the World'. This last added much first-hand observation, especially of the relatively unknown Pacific Ocean, to Edmond Halley's 'Historical Account of the Trade Winds', published in the *Philosphical Transactions* for 1686. Again, Dampier was at pains to stress the practical nature of his interest – 'In all my Cruisings among the Privateers, I took notice of the risings of the Tides; because by knowing it, I always knew where we might best haul ashore and clean our Ships' – but in the end he produced a work which stands as 'a classic of the pre-scientific era'.[41]

The maps included in the *New Voyage* were the work of Herman Moll, Dutch-born but soon to become one of the best-known cartographers in England, and whose particular interest was the South Sea. In his 'Map of the East Indies' (Ill. 20) the outline of New Holland loomed large, and it would seem to reflect Dampier's geographical notions at this time. It hints at continental rather than insular dimensions, and this is strengthened by the explicitness of the legend, 'New Holland or Terra Australis Incognita'. This has a bearing on Dampier's second voyage to New Holland in 1699. The publication of the *New Voyage* gave Dampier a reputation as an authority on distant regions, and in 1697 and 1698 he made several appearances before the Council of Trade and Plantations to provide information on various regions, but especially Darien, where the Scots were planning a settlement.[42] He had become a minor celebrity, dining with Pepys and Evelyn and attracting the attention of the First Lord of the Admiralty, the Earl of Orford. Letters from Dampier to Orford reveal the thinking behind a naval discovery expedition (a rarity in itself) which left England under Dampier's command in 1699, and whose fortunes he recounted in *A Voyage to New-Holland*, published in two volumes in 1703 and 1709. The detached observer who had made a virtue

40. Dampier, *Voyage to New-Holland*, preface.
41. William Dampier, *Voyages and Descriptions* (London, 1699/1729), Part III, p. 97; Joseph C. Shipman, *William Dampier: Seaman-Scientist* (Lawrence, KS, 1962), p. 8.
42. See *Calendar of State Papers Colonial: America and West Indies, 1696–7* (London, 1904), p. 525; *1697–8* (London, 1905), pp. 445, 462–3.

20. [Herman Moll]. 'A Map of the East Indies', 1697.

out of his refusal to accept a position of authority on his previous voyages was now a captain in the Royal Navy.

Despite the government's growing interest in the South Sea as the Spanish Succession issue reached crisis point, there is no hint that Dampier's voyage represented any serious thrust of national policy. A letter to Orford makes it clear that the choice of area to be explored came from Dampier, not the Admiralty, and that his motives were practical and commercial:

> Your Ldship has been pleased to order me to make a proposal of some voyage wherein I might be serviceable to my Nation. I know there are several places which might probably be visited with good Advantage: but as there is no larger Tract of Land hitherto undiscovered yn ye *Terra Australia* (if that vast space surrounding ye South Pole, and extend so far into ye warmer Climate be a continued Land, as a great deal of it is known to be) so 'tis reasonable to conceive yt so great a part of the World is not without very valluable commodities to incourage ye Discovery.[43]

There is evidence to suggest that at this time Dampier was in touch with Thomas Bowrey, a merchant with many years' experience of the East Indies, who after his return to England in 1688 became an energetic promoter of South Sea schemes. Dampier first met Bowrey in Achin in 1688, a

43. Dampier's correspondence with the Admiralty is in PRO Adm 2/1692 (no folio numbers); the main documents are printed in Masefield, *Dampier's Voyages*, II, pp. 325–30.

few months after his visit to New Holland. Bowrey was 'extraordinary kind' to Dampier, who had been ill, and at one stage hoped to take him to Persia. Even after Dampier turned down the offer Bowrey gave him money and 'treated me always with Wine and good Cheer'.[44] When Bowrey returned to England he brought with him a collection of manuscript maps (now in the British Library), one of which was a copy of a Dutch map showing Tasman's voyages of 1642–3 and 1644.[45] A version of this map (Ill. 21) seems to have been taken by Dampier on his voyage – 'Mr. Tasman's Draught', as he termed it. The correlation between place-names (many inaccurately translated or transcribed from the Dutch) on the map and in Dampier's published account, and the knowledge Dampier showed of Tasman's soundings on the northwest coast of Australia (also marked on the map), point to this conclusion. Whether Bowrey was involved in the formulation of Dampier's plans for the voyage is a matter for speculation, but it is clearly a possibility.

Although Dampier's original letter to Orford had laid heavy stress on Terra Australis, further letters shifted the emphasis as the preparations for the voyage slowly proceeded. In a note about possible routes, Dampier thought that he should sail straight from Madagascar

> to the northernmost part of *New Holland* where I would water if I had occasion, and from thence I would range towards *New Guinnia*. There are many Islands in that sea between *New Holland* and *New Guinnia* which are not frequented by any Europeans, and it is probable that we may light upon some or other that are not without *Spice*; should I meet with nothing on any of these Islands I would range along the Main of New Guinia to see what that aforded; and from thence I would cross over to the East side of the *Island Gilolo* . . . [then] range away to the Eastward of New Guinia and so direct my course southerly coasting by the land, and where I found a harbour or river I would land.[46]

The stress here is on islands, preferably unexploited spice islands, rather than on the continent. Only after touching at these would Dampier bend his course around New Guinea and head south for unknown coasts.

The westerly approach was for Dampier second best, for another letter from him reveals that originally he had hoped to leave England in the early autumn (of 1698) so that he could enter the Pacific by way of a summer rounding of Cape Horn. He would then sail between lats 35°S. and 40°S. to the east coast of Terra Australis before turning north to New Guinea. This was in line with the suggestion he had made in his *New Voyage* that the Cape Horn route was the 'easie way' to that 'vast Tract of Terra Australis which

44. Dampier, *New Voyage*, p. 504.
45. BL: Sloane MS 5222 (12).
46. Masefield, *Dampier's Voyages*, II, p. 326.

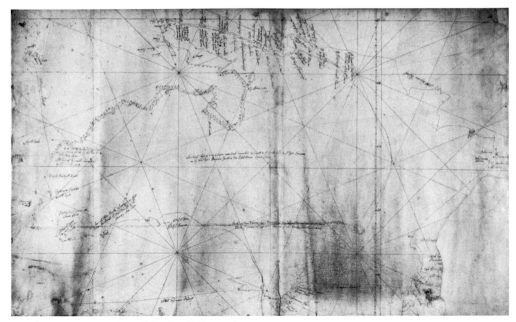

21. Thomas Bowrey. Chart of the Dutch discoveries, c. 1688.

bounds the South-Sea', and of which he thought that the 'long Tract of pretty high Land' sighted by Davis fifteen hundred miles off the coast of Chile might be part.[47] As it was, the loss of the season instead forced him to specify the Cape of Good Hope route, 'and from thence to stretch away towards New Holland, and then to New Guinea and Terra Australis'.

To construct any systematic geography from these musings is not easy. The reference in Dampier's first letter to Orford of 'a continued land' from the South Pole into warmer latitudes seems to envisage a landmass separate from New Holland. This could be reconciled with Tasman's discoveries by the assumption − which became a favoured one in the eighteenth century − that the stretch of the New Zealand coast reached by Tasman in 1642–3 was the edge of the great southern continent. From there, it could be argued, he had sailed north towards New Guinea with the mysterious east coast of New Holland lying somewhere to port, and the equally unknown shoreline of the southern continent to starboard. Amid such speculation, one thing is clear: Dampier saw New Holland as an obstacle, a barrier concealing more promising lands to the east, hence the orginal plan for an approach from Cape Horn. His letters to Orford may have concealed as much as they revealed. A trading venture to islands just outside the Dutch sphere was possibly more appealing than a risky voyage to totally unknown shores. During his earlier wanderings he had clearly been alert to the possibility of exploiting some of

47. See p. 101 above.

the regions he visited. So, in February 1687 he was busy making drafts of the
island of Luzon. As he noted in his journal: 'I made the best use of my time
to improve my knowledge in those partes that if ever it should please God
to release me from this Course of life I might be able to give a relation of
my travells to my Country men which may in time conduce to the profitt
of my nation the only thing that I aimed att.'[48] Away to the southeast, near
but not in the Moluccas, lay the home of Jeoly, the captive 'painted Prince'
who, as Dampier recorded in his manuscript journal, 'told me that there was
much Gold on his Iland'.[49]

The temptation to investigate such opportunities rather than go further
afield would be all the stronger since despite Dampier's request for two
vessels he was given only one, the 290-ton *Roebuck*, and that with a crew of
only fifty instead of the seventy he had asked for. The order in which he
mentioned his objectives in one of his letters to Orford is perhaps significant:
'ye remoter part of the *East India Islands* and the neighbouring Coast of *Terra
Australis*'.[50] An additional consideration is that Dampier, despite the modest
fame that had come his way since the publication of the *New Voyage*, would
have hoped for some financial gain from the undertaking over and above the
£100 advanced him by the Admiralty 'upon my mencioning the Lowness of
my present circumstances'.[51]

In the event, the voyage was a troubled and contentious one – 'vexatious'
was Dampier's word. As the ship crossed the equator on its run into the
South Atlantic, Dampier was already grumbling about a crew 'too lazy to
shift themselves when they were drench'd with the Rains . . . they would
however lye down in their Hammocks with their wet Cloaths.'[52] Successive
journal entries harp on the men's inadequacies: 'Ignorance', 'Obstinacy',
'Refractoriness' and 'Backwardness' are some of the terms used. So great was
'the Aversion of my Men to a long unknown Voyage' that Dampier feared
mutiny, and to avert it he called at Bahía in Brazil. There, he wrote,

> I hop'd to have the Governour's Help, if need should require, for securing my
> Ship from any such mutinous Attempt; being forced to keep my self all the
> way upon my Guard, and to lie with my Officers, such as I could trust, and
> with small Arms upon the Quarter-Deck, it scarce being safe for me to lie in
> my Cabbin, by Reasons of the Discontents among my Men.[53]

At Bahía, Dampier sent ashore his first lieutenant, George Fisher, an old navy
man who after numerous quarrels with his captain from the Downs onwards

48. BL: Sloane MS 3236, f. 203.
49. Ibid., f. 202v.
50. First letter in Dampier file, n.d. PRO: Adm 1/1692.
51. Letter of 28 Sep. 1698, ibid.
52. Dampier, *Voyage to New-Holland*, p. 29.
53. Ibid., pp. 31, 32.

had been put in irons. From there Fisher was sent back to England, where he accused Dampier of striking him with a cane on the quarter-deck, confining him to his cabin and finally putting him in irons. Dampier's case was put in a letter that accompanied Fisher home: 'He shaked his Fist att me, Grind [sic] in my Face, and told me that he cared not ———— ———— for me . . . called me Old Dog, Old Villain, and told my men Gents take care of that Old Pyrateing Dog for he designs to Run away with you and the King's Ship.'[54] Fisher's litany of complaints against Dampier, together with the death of the *Roebuck*'s boatswain, John Norwood, while confined to his quarters, formed part of the case against Dampier at the court-martial which awaited him on his return from the voyage. None of this is mentioned by Dampier in his published account of the voyage, where he simply notes that at Bahía he was able 'to allay in some Measure the ferment that had been raised among my Men'.[55] Instead, in a way familiar to readers of his *New Voyage*, he engaged in a lengthy description of Bahía, its inhabitants, trade and natural history.

From Brazil Dampier took the *Roebuck* and its reluctant crew across the South Atlantic, past the Cape of Good Hope without calling there, and into the Indian Ocean. In August 1699 the ships reached Australian waters and anchored in the bay visited by a Dutch expedition under Willem de Vlamingh only two years before.[56] Located in lat. 25°20'S., long. 113°30'E., it is still known by Dampier's name of Shark's (now Shark) Bay. A week's search failed to find water, so Dampier sailed north as far as North West Cape and then followed the coast around. In lat. 20°21'S. he was running along a chain of islands (since named Dampier Archipelago) which he suspected might extend right back to Shark Bay. Like many seamen, he was predisposed to sense straits and passages through almost any coastline: 'by the great Tides I met with a while afterwards, more to the N. East, I had a strong Suspicion that here might be a kind of Archipelago of Islands, and Passage possible to the S. of New Holland and N. Guinea into the great S. Sea Eastward; which I had thoughts also of attempting in my Return from N. Guinea.'[57] Tasman's chart on board the *Roebuck* showed, on the contrary, 'a firm, continued Land'; but Dampier suspected from his own soundings that Tasman had not approached the coast as closely in 1644 as 'the prick'd Line of his Course' indicated. It is unfortunate that Dampier published no detailed chart of his own route along the northwest shores of Australia in the *Voyage to New-Holland*, especially since Samuel Thornton's 'Draught of the Coast of New Holland' (Ill. 22), first issued in 1703, took only the inset of Shark Bay from Dampier. Possibly Dampier's general chart of this part of

54. Dampier to the Admiralty, 22 Apr. 1699. Printed in Masefield, *Dampier's Voyages*, II, p. 333.
55. Dampier, *Voyage to New-Holland*, p. 59.
56. See Günter Schilder, *Voyage to the Great South Land. Willem de Vlamingh 1696–1697* (Sydney, 1985).
57. Dampier, *Voyage to New-Holland*, pp. 93–4.

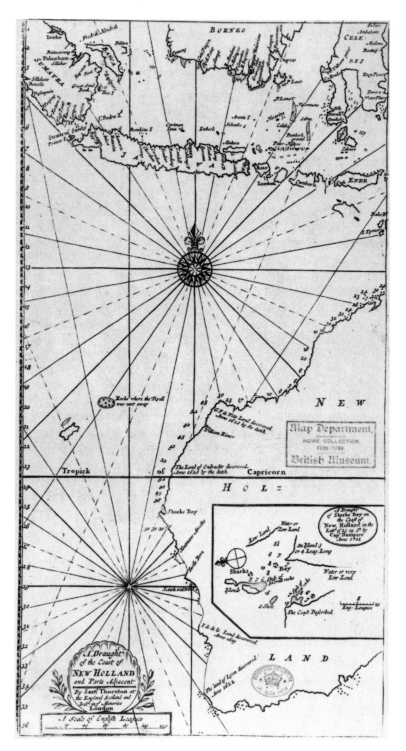

22. Samuel
Thornton. 'The
Coast of New
Holland', 1703.

his voyage was among his 'Books and Papers' lost when the *Roebuck* sank in
1701.

Still looking for water, Dampier continued in a generally northeast direction, standing on and off from the shore. At the end of August he landed
again, probably at Roebuck Bay, where the modern town of Broome now
stands. Here, digging produced some water, but so brackish that it was fit
only for boiling oatmeal. Inland, all that could be seen were sand hills and
some coarse grass. In a running skirmish with a dozen Aborigines one was
shot and wounded, while a seaman was struck in the face with a wooden
spear which at first was thought to be poisoned. In Dampier's version of
events there is little doubt but that the Aborigines were the aggressors –
'menacing and threatning of us' – until he was forced, reluctantly, to
open fire.[58] The journal of the *Roebuck*'s master, Jacob Hughes, gives an
account – presumably at second hand since normally he seems to have
remained on the vessel during the shore excursions – that differs a little in
detail and emphasis:

> Our Capt. endeavoured to speake with them but could not they being so very
> shy. Att last coming pritty nigh them one of our men Alexander Beale ran att
> them and came up with one who flung at him a stone, and having in his hand
> a wooden Lance he pusht heartly at hime so that he ran it through his Chin,
> when the said Beale saw that he struck at him with his Cutlace cleaving one
> part of his head. The Blacks running to the others assistance our Capt. being
> by shott att one of them so that he fell down.[59]

The encounter was too brief and violent for Dampier to add much to his
description of the Aborigines in his *New Voyage*. The only significant addition concerned the body markings of one of the Aborigines, 'a kind of Prince
or Captain [who] was painted (which none of the rest were at all) with a
Circle of white Paste or Pigment (a sort of Lime, as we thought) about his
Eyes, and a white streak down his Nose from his Forehead to the tip of it.
And his Breast and some part of his Arms were also made white with the
same paint.' Otherwise, Dampier contented himself with the observation that
these 'New-Hollanders' seemed similar to the ones he had met in 1688 forty
or fifty leagues to the northeast, with 'the most unplesant Looks and the
worst Features of any people that I ever saw'. He went on, in words that
seem to show that he had a copy of his *New Voyage* to hand (and not his
manuscript journal), to remind his readers that 'these were much the same
blinking Creatures . . . with the same black Skins, and Hair frizled.'[60] Here,
with scurvy affecting some of his crew and with little hope of finding food

58. Ibid., p. 100.
59. PRO Adm 52/94, 1 Sep. 1699.
60. Dampier, *Voyage to New-Holland*, p. 102.

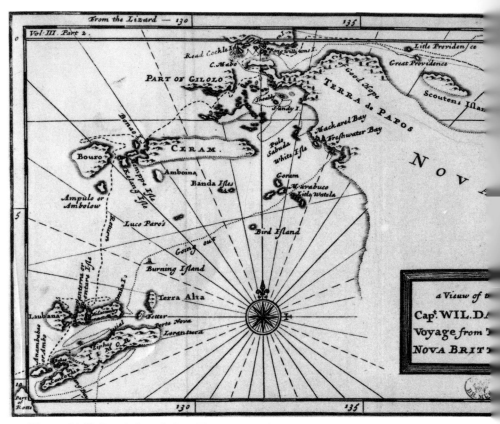

23. [Herman Moll]. Dampier's track from Timor to New Britain, 1703.

or water, Dampier bore away for Timor after a final attempt to make his 1688 landfall had been thwarted by shoals.

As he resumed his narrative of the *Roebuck* voyage in the second volume of his account, published in 1709, Dampier retraced in some detail his thinking at the time. His coasting along the shores of New Holland had been simply in search of refreshment

> for the further Discoveries I purposed to attempt on the *Terra Australis*. This large and hitherto almost unknown Tract of Land is situated so very advantageously in the richest Climates of the World, the *Torrid* and *Temperate* Zones; having in it especially all the Advantages of the Torrid Zone, as being known to reach from the *Equator* it self (within a Degree) to the *Tropick* of *Capricorn*, and beyond it; that in coasting round it, which I design'd by this Voyage, if possible: I could not but hope to meet with some fruitful Lands, Continent or Islands, or both.[61]

61. William Dampier, *A Continuation of a Voyage to New-Holland, &c. In the Year 1699* (London, 1709/1729), pp. 123–4.

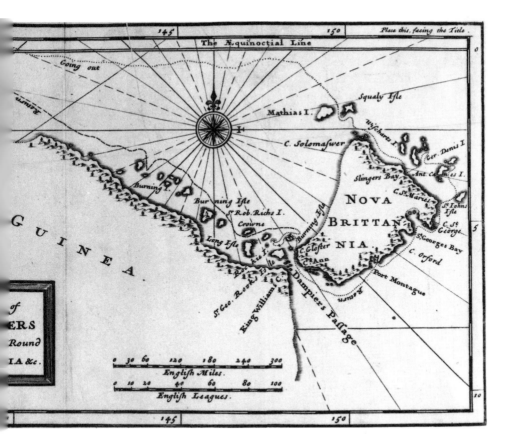

Dampier made it clear that once on the west coast of New Holland he preferred a north-about approach to the alternative, which was to 'coast it to the Southward, and that way try to get round to the East of New Holland and New Guinea'. The likelihood of severe weather and intense cold, lack of enthusiasm among the crew – 'heartless enough to the voyage at best' – and suspicion that far southerly latitudes would contain little of value were given as reasons for the northern track. All this seems an over-elaborate explanation (perhaps in response to some criticism, now lost to sight, of his lack of continental discoveries) to justify a course that was predicted by Dampier before the voyage began. His observations on what he thought was the broken nature of the northwest coast of Australia had given him another reason for a clockwise course, for he thought that he might discover a strait that would provide a short passage back from the seas to the east once he had rounded New Guinea.

From Timor Dampier worked his way around the northern coast of New Guinea, and to the east established the existence of a large island (later found to be two islands) which he named New Britain. For the first time, Dampier began to scatter the names of royalty, noble patrons and admirals across the chart: capes Anne, Gloucester and Orford; Port Montagu; islands named after Sir George Rooke and Sir Robert Rich (Ill. 23). Contact with the inhabitants was fleeting. Some trade was carried on from the ship, but landing for wood and water was a tense business, accompanied by much firing of cannon to warn off possible attackers. Attempts at Montagu Harbour to trade for pigs ended in musket fire, though if Dampier's account is to be trusted no one was killed. The encounter stands as a stereotype for many confrontations between Europeans and Melanesians in this early contact period:

> When they [Dampier's men] came to Land, the Natives in great Companies stood to resist them; shaking their Lances, and threatning them; and some were so daring, as to wade into the sea, holding a Target in one Hand and a Lance in the other. Our Men held up to them such Commodities as I had sent, and made Signs of Friendship; but to no Purpose; for the Natives waved them off. Seeing therefore they could not be prevailed upon to a friendly Commerce, my Men, being resolved to have some Provision among them, fired some Muskets to scare them away.[62]

As he bore away from New Britain, Dampier put the best face he could on matters: 'It is very probable that this Island may afford as many rich Commodities as any in the World; and the Natives may be easily brought to Commerce, though I could not pretend to it under my present Circumstances.'[63]

With Dampier in indifferent health, the crew 'very negligent, when I was not upon Deck my self', and the *Roebuck*'s pinnace badly damaged, it was time to head for home. The decision was justified when in February 1701 the *Roebuck* sprang a leak and sank at Ascension Island. In the shipwreck some of Dampier's papers were lost, but among those that survived were drawings of flora and fauna from New Holland and elsewhere (Ill. 24) and some coastal profiles, done by 'a Person skill'd in Drawing' (as Dampier rather kindly described the unknown artist).[64] It has been suggested that one artist drew the plants, and another, less expert, the birds, fishes and coastal profiles. Regardless of artist, the drawings are of historical importance as the first of Australian wildlife to be published in Europe. Even more surprisingly, considering the vicissitudes of the voyage, Dampier managed to save some plant specimens, twenty-three of which still survive in the Sherardian Herbarium, Oxford.[65]

---

62. Ibid., pp. 214–15.
63. Ibid., p. 220.
64. Dampier, *Voyage to New-Holland*, preface.
65. See Serena K. Marner, 'William Dampier and his Botanical Collections', in Howard Morphy and Elizabeth Edwards, eds, *Australia in Oxford* (Hertford, 1988). The plants are listed by A.S. George and T.E.A. Aplin in Kenney, *Before the First Fleet*, pp. 78–80.

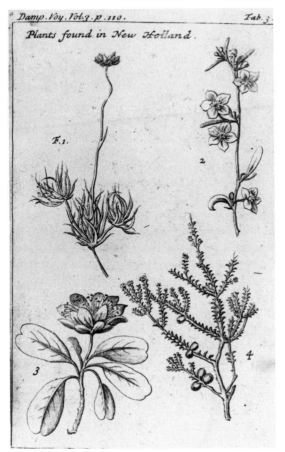

Damp. Voy. Vol. 3. p. 110.   *Tab. 3.*

Plants found in New Holland.

24. Anon. 'Plants found in New Holland', William Dampier, *Voyage to New Holland* (1703).

From Ascension Dampier's crew were picked up by an East India convoy, and Dampier himself was back in England by midsummer 1701. In September 1701 he faced court-martial for the loss of the *Roebuck*, but seems to have been acquitted. His journal of the voyage was handed in to the Admiralty at this time, but has not survived. In June 1702 Dampier faced a more difficult court-martial, relating to the problems on the voyage between England and Bahía. The verdict of the court was unequivocal. It found Dampier 'guilty of very Hard and cruell usage towards Lieutenant Fisher', fined him all his pay for the voyage and added, 'itt is further the opinion of ye Court that the said Capt. Dampier is not a Fitt person to be Employ'd as comdr of any of her Maty ships.'[66]

---

66. Printed in Masefield, *Dampier's Voyages*, II, p. 604. Baer, 'William Dampier at the Crossroads', shows that Fisher's suspicions about his captain were sharpened by Dampier's earlier association with the pirate Henry Every, and by the presence on the *Roebuck* of several men who had been with Dampier at La Coruña.

None of this seems to have disturbed Dampier's preparation of his journal for publication, and the first volume was issued by Knapton in 1703. It took the story up to Dampier's departure from the coast of New Holland in September 1699. There were, it seemed, few redeeming features about New Holland, apart from some 'sweet and beautiful flowers' and 'strange and beautiful Shells'. Dampier's references to the Aborigines reinforced the disparaging account of them given in the *New Voyage*, and some of his descriptions of other forms of life did little to dispel the overwhelming impression of backwardness, even monstrosity. A glimpse of dingoes left a distinctly unfavourable impression: 'two or three Beasts like hungry Wolves, lean like so many Skeletons, being nothing but Skin and Bones'. When a huge shark was caught, 'Its Maw was like a Leather Sack, very thick, and so tough that a sharp Knife could scarce cut it: In which we found the Head and Boans of a Hippopotamus [dugong?].' Shark's Bay was a predictable name for the stretch of water where this one, and many others, were caught and eaten 'very savourily' by the crew; but the fact that it was the only name given by Dampier to any part of mainland New Holland reinforced the impression of a featureless desert region. Even the innocuous stumptail lizard was described in a way that made it seem uniquely repulsive:

> a sort of Guano's, of the same Shape and Size with other Guano's, describ'd but differing from them in 3 remarkable Particulars: For these had a larger and uglier Head, and had no Tail: And at the Rump, instead of the Tail there, they had a Stump of a Tail, which appear'd like another Head; but not really such, being without Mouth or Eyes: Yet this Creature seem'd by this Means to have a Head at each End; and, which may be reckon'd a fourth Difference, the Legs also seem'd all 4 of them to be Fore-legs, being all alike in Shape and Length, and seeming by the Joints and Bending to be made as if they were to go indifferently either Head or Tail foremost. They were speckled black and yellow like Toads, and had Scales or Knobs on their Backs like those of Crocodiles, plated on to the Skin, or stuck into it, as part of the Skin. They are very slow in Motion; and when a Man comes nigh them they will stand still and hiss, not endeavouring to get away. Their livers are also spotted black and yellow. And the Body when opened hath a very unsavory Smell. I did never see such ugly Creatures any where but here.[67]

The events of the rest of the voyage, including the discovery of the more promising New Britain, had to wait for the second volume. This was not published until 1709, presumably because Dampier was away on yet another South Sea voyage from 1703 to 1707.

For the English reading public, from the scholar and merchant to the

---

67. Dampier, *Voyage to New-Holland*, pp. 285–6.

casual browser, Dampier's main contribution on his two voyages to New Holland was to make its western shoreline a real, if unattractive, place rather than a wavering line on the map. He added little to the Dutch discoveries, but his published descriptions of the scrubby coastal area and its inhabitants, the drawings of its flora and fauna, Moll's maps and the coastal profiles, gave solidity to what had been a phantom presence. Dampier was no Cook, and his unknown artist no Parkinson; but at least an attempt was being made to meet Tancred Robinson's criticism that the English did not send 'Painters, Naturalists and Mechanists' on their expeditions. Above all, whatever their deficiencies, at least accounts of the English voyages were being published. The contrast is marked with the Dutch voyage to New Holland in 1696–7 of three vessels commanded by Willem de Vlamingh. No proper description of the voyage was published until 1753, and the superb watercolour views of the west coast of New Holland by the artist Victor Victorszoon disappeared from view until 1970.

Apart from charting and describing previously unknown coasts, Dampier's voyage set a further precedent in that it was an Admiralty venture of Pacific exploration which had instructions to make careful observations, collect specimens and bring back 'some of the Natives, provided they shall be willing to come along'.[68] Another precursor of the expeditions of the Cook era of Pacific exploration were the voyages of Edmond Halley in the *Paramore* between 1698 and 1701. They were concerned with new navigational methods rather than with new lands, and in particular were intended 'to improve the knowledge of the Longitude and variations of the Compasse'.[69] They stand as a landmark in English oceanic enterprise, not least in the burgeoning relationship they revealed between the Admiralty and the Royal Society. Although there was originally some intention of reaching the East Indies and the South Sea, Halley's voyages took him no further than the South Atlantic, and the largest blank space in his magnificent world map of 1702 showing magnetic variation was the Pacific. As he explained, 'I durst not presume to describe the like Curves in the South Sea wanting accounts thereof.'

On the major geographical issues surrounding the South Land little progress had been made. Seen through Dampier's eyes, New Holland and Terra Australis resemble a case of intermittent double vision. Sometimes they are distinct and separate, sometimes they blur into one. By the time of the second voyage, and with a copy of Tasman's chart on board, Dampier had accepted the fact of the insularity of New Holland, and indeed seemed

---

68. Masefield, *Dampier's Voyages*, II, p. 331.
69. This and the next quotation are from Norman J.W. Thrower, ed., *The Three Voyages of Edmond Halley* (London, 1981), pp. 268–9, 60.

inclined to regard it as at least two large islands. That he had been reading accounts of earlier voyages to the area can be seen in his brief and cryptic statement as he swung off-course between Timor and Java on the homeward voyage in an attempt to find the Trial Rocks, 'which Discovery (when ever made) will be of great use to Merchants trading to these Parts'.[70] This is a reference to the disaster of 1622, when the *Trial* was wrecked on reefs off the Monte Bello Islands on the northwest coast of Australia. What value such a discovery might have – apart from identifying a danger spot – is unclear, but the detour says something about Dampier's continuing interest in the region. The most lasting effect of his voyage was to be his brief encomium on New Britain, ingeniously named, scarcely investigated, but thought by Dampier to 'afford as rich Commodities as any in the World'. It was the antidote to the image of the grim and barren west coast of New Holland – yet another example of the bipolarity that characterized the exploration of the region and that was to drive forward exploration of Terra Australis seemingly in defiance of rational considerations. In mid-century John Campbell in Britain and Charles de Brosses in France were to extol the potential of New Britain, no more explored in their day than in Dampier's.[71]

---

70. Dampier, *Continuation of a Voyage*, p. 243.
71. See Charles de Brosses, *Histoire des Navigations aux Terres Australes* (Paris, 1756), II, pp. 300–8; John Campbell, *Navigantium atque Itinerantium Bibliotheca: or, A Compleat Collection of Voyages and Travels* (London, 1744–8), I, p. 274, where Campbell claimed that New Britain was 'a Country, little, if at all, inferior to the Dutch Spice Islands'.

CHAPTER V

The 'Cruising Voyages' of Dampier and Rogers

The death of Carlos II of Spain in 1700 brought the long-impending Spanish Succession to crisis point, and war broke out in May 1702. In England the future of Spain's American empire was of concern to diplomats and merchants alike. To meet the growing interest in the vulnerability of that empire and the potential of its trade, the buccaneers' accounts provided first-hand information on the ports, anchorages and watering places of the South Sea. Readers were now spoilt for choice, for in 1699 Knapton brought out a fourth edition of Dampier's *New Voyage* to accompany an additional volume of his *Voyages and Descriptions*, Lionel Wafer's *New Voyage and Description of the Isthmus of America* and William Hack's *Collection of Original Voyages*. This last included Wood's journal from the Narborough voyage, descriptions of Sharp's Darien adventures of 1680–1 and Cowley's journal of his voyage round the world in 1683–6.

If Dampier is to be believed, the buccaneers collected the information printed in their accounts with scrupulous care:

> For they make it their Business to examine all Prisoners that fall into their Hands, concerning the Country, Town, or City that they belong to; whether born there, or how long they have known it? how many Families, whether most *Spaniards*? or whether the major part are not Copper-colour'd, as *Mulattoes*, *Mustesoes*, or *Indians*? whether rich, and what their Riches do consist in? and what their chiefest Manufactures? if fortified, how many great Guns, and what Number of small Arms? whether it is possible to come undescrib'd on them? . . . If any River or Creek comes near it, or where the best Landing with innumerable other such Questions, which their Curiosities led them to demand.

In reality, most of the published journals were careless and repetitive compilations, but in them readers found what they wanted to hear. The Spaniards in the South Sea were poor seamen and indolent traders; their ships and settlements were vulnerable; they were ready to engage in illicit trade; and they lived in fear of Indian insurrection. Dampier summed up the general impression: 'The *Spaniards* have more than they can well manage. I know yet, they would lie like the *Dog in the Manger*; although not able to eat themselves, yet they would endeavour to hinder others.'[1]

The misfortunes of the Scots in their attempts to colonize Darien in 1698, 1699 and 1700 seem to have excited rather than dampened English interest in the region. The attempted settlement of the Darien Company, which failed with the deaths of many hundreds of the colonists, was a Caribbean, not a South Sea, venture.[2] There can be no doubt, though, that if the colony had taken root the Scots would have followed the old buccaneering routes across the Isthmus and onto the Pacific coast. Lionel Wafer, whose manuscript of his travels across the Isthmus had much influenced William Paterson, the driving force behind the Darien Company, advocated a similar scheme in a long memorandum of 1698 or 1699 to the Duke of Leeds. This suggested establishing a base on Golden Island on the Caribbean side of the Isthmus and then seizing Panama, though this last was hurried over on the grounds that it was 'a matter of soe great Importance that I dare but Slightly Touch itt, Least I shold be thought to meddle with that which is above my Reach'. With more confidence Wafer turned to the South Sea proper. He provided Leeds with thumbnail sketches of the most important harbours on the Pacific coast and advocated that, if Spain persisted in keeping those ports shut against foreign traders, the English should establish settlements by force of arms. The seizure of the Chilean towns of Valdivia or Coquimbo would bring clear strategic and commercial advantages. Those ports were well-placed for English vessels rounding the Horn; the local Indian population was bitterly hostile to the Spaniards; and, above all, 'there [sic] Country abounds with all Sorts of Riches as Gold Silver &c.'[3]

Wafer was not the only advocate of such schemes. As international tension increased, that prolific pamphleteer and controversialist Daniel Defoe produced in 1701 his *Reasons against a War* with France, which argued in favour of a lucrative maritime war with Spain rather than a profitless continental struggle, and stressed the wealth and vulnerability of Spain's American colonies. It was at about this time that Defoe sent William III, to whom he acted as unofficial adviser in the last years of his reign, a plan resembling Wafer's. As a young merchant Defoe had gained first-hand experience of trading conditions in Spain, and he was well aware of the profits which an open trade with Spanish America might bring. Defoe always maintained that the King approved his scheme and that only his death in March 1702 prevented it being put into operation.[4]

1. The quotations are from Dampier, *New Voyage*, pp. 27–8, 273.
2. See John Prebble, *The Darien Disaster* (Harmondsworth, 1970).
3. The quotations are from Joyce, *Wafer's New Voyage*, pp. 142–3, 145.
4. See Defoe to Robert Harley, 23 July 1711, printed in G.H. Healey, ed., *The Letters of Daniel Defoe* (Oxford, 1955), pp. 345–6; D. Defoe, *The Essay on the South-Sea Trade* (London, 1712

When war came in 1702 it proved to be more continental than maritime, a matter of hard-slogging campaigns in Flanders and Spain rather than seaborne operations against distant colonies. It was the French who took advantage of Spain's weakness to exploit her overseas wealth, and nowhere more so than in the South Sea. There was no formal relaxation of Spain's prohibition of foreign traders within her American empire, but in practice French traders found it a simple and profitable matter to sail for Chile and Peru. The Spanish navy was unable even to protect home waters, and to patrol the South American littoral was beyond its capabilities. In 1707 only three Spanish naval vessels were available to guard the entire Pacific coastline from Chile to Lower California. From St Malo and other French ports increasing numbers of ships left for the South Sea, often with the connivance of the French authorities which issued them with permissions for China or for 'discovery'. Between 1698 and 1725 no fewer than 168 ships sailed for the South Sea (though by no means all reached there); and in the peak years of 1705, 1706 and 1707 a total of thirty-seven left France.[5] By opening a regular trade, and one that increasingly took the route round the Horn rather than through the Strait of Magellan, the French showed that the voyage was not as fearsome as some earlier mariners reported. At first they found an eager market, for during the war the whole elaborate structure of convoys, trade fairs and the rest had collapsed as the links snapped between Spain and her overseas empire. Only one Spanish fleet carrying trade goods for the South Sea reached Portobelo during the war years. Some of the French vessels that reached the Pacific continued their voyage to China and the East Indies, especially after the realization that the Spanish American market was a more limited one, and easier to glut, than had been thought.[6] Even so, the huge amounts of silver shipped back to France helped it continue the war, and from a different perspective justified the dreams of English projectors from Narborough's voyage onwards.

The number of French voyages to the South Sea in this period was not matched by published accounts of their achievements, adventures and misfortunes of the kind that accompanied the English voyages. This may have been a consequence of the relatively mundane nature of the trade, or perhaps be explained by a reluctance to publicize ventures that were diplomatically sensitive. Although only four English expeditions reached the South Sea in

---

[1711]), p. 46. But also note Peter Earle's warning: 'there is a problem of evidence. Defoe was always to stress the close relations, indeed the intimate friendship, that he had enjoyed with his hero, King William, and the important role that he played in his reign, but we have to rely, once more, mainly on his own unsupported testimony.' *The World of Defoe* (London, 1976), p. 12.

5. The standard work on this subject remains the first volume of E.W. Dahlgren, *Les Relations Commerciales et Maritimes entre la France et les Côtes de l'Océan Pacifique au Commencement du XVIIIe Siècle* (Paris, 1909). There are useful summaries in John Dunmore, *French Explorers in the Pacific*, I, *The Eighteenth Century* (Oxford, 1965), pp. 10–31; O.K.H. Spate, *The Pacific since Magellan*, II, *Monopolists and Freebooters* (London and Canberra, 1983), pp. 189–94.

6. See Louis Dermigny, *La Chine et l'Occident: Le Commerce à Canton au XVIIIe Siècle 1719–1833* (Paris, 1964), pp. 152–4.

the first twenty years of the eighteenth century (Dampier twice, Rogers and Shelvocke), they resulted in six books and several pamphlets and smaller pieces. By contrast, a mere three books appeared about the much more numerous French voyages in the same period: Froger's account (1702) of the de Gennes voyage, which never got farther than the Strait of Magellan; an important set of scientific and other observations by the mathematician and botanist Feuillet (1714); and finally Frézier's *Voyage* (1716), which alone was translated into English. Frézier was a capable mathematician and engineer, and his book, prompted by the possibility of a future war between France and Spain, contained detailed accounts and plans of Spanish defences along the Pacific seaboard.

Reports of French enterprise in the South Sea were slow to reach England, and when they did were greeted with incredulity and indignation. The first news arrived from the members of yet another Dampier expedition to the South Sea, for the disgrace of the *Roebuck* voyage was quickly overlooked as war came. In January 1703 Dampier was appointed to the command of a two-hundred-ton privateer, the *St George*, and in April the 'Old Pyrateing Dog' was ushered into the Queen's presence by her consort Prince George of Denmark, Lord High Admiral, to kiss hands.[7] The *St George* was a private man-of-war, a 'commissioned predator' that carried no cargo but 120 men.[8] It was 'an old ship but in very good Condition and strong', according to later evidence.[9] The size of its crew was much greater than that needed to work the ship (in this period the ratio was about one crew member to nine tons; ships larger than the *St George* crossing to the American seaboard colonies and the Caribbean would have crews of about twenty). The numbers on board allowed for casualties on the long 'cruising voyage', the boarding of enemy ships and the need for prize crews. But in the first instance they resulted in gross overcrowding, with deleterious effects on both health and morale. With the *St George* as it left Kinsale in September 1703 sailed the 130-ton *Cinque Ports* (eighty-three men), commanded by Captain Charles Pickering.[10] He died early on the voyage and was succeeded by Thomas Stradling, a young (twenty-one years of age) gentleman mariner. Also on the *Cinque Ports* as master or mate sailed Alexander Selkirk,[11] who later remembered that the vessel was 'a good new ship in very good Condition as to Body Masts Sayles . . . only wanted Sheathing'.[12]

---

7.   See the *London Gazette*, 16 Apr. 1703, reprinted in Masefield, *Dampier's Voyages*, II, p. 575.

8.   On the privateers of this period see David J. Starkey's essential work *British Privateering Enterprise in the Eighteenth Century* (Exeter, 1990).

9.   PRO: Chancery 24/1321, Pt. I. Deposition of Alexander Selkirk, 10 July 1712, para 2.

10. There is some uncertainty about the size of the *Cinque Ports*. The letters of marque issued to Pickering, not always a reliable guide, described her as 130 tons, 20 guns, 90 men. PRO: HCA 26/18, p. 64. According to William Funnell, *A Voyage Round the World* (London, 1707), p. 2, it was 90 tons, 16 guns, 63 men. Whatever the truth, it was a small craft for the voyage ahead.

11. For the puzzle about Selkirk's exact rank on board see C.D. Lee, 'Alexander Selkirk and the Last Voyage of the *Cinque Ports* Galley', *Mariner's Mirror*, 73 (1987), pp. 387–9.

12. Selkirk, 'Deposition', para 2.

The expedition's backers were a group of London and Bristol investors who were lured, one of them claimed later, by Dampier's promise of 'vast Profits and Advantages to the Owners'. The articles of agreement stipulated that decisions should be taken by a council of officers and that two-thirds of the plunder should go to the owners, one-third to the officers and crew on a 'no purchase, no pay' basis. With him as 'Purser and Agent', Dampier insisted, must sail Edward Morgan, a shipmate from his buccaneering days on the *Cygnet* fifteen years earlier; and the expedition was delayed until Morgan could be released from prison.[13] It was not a propitious start. Regarding what followed, the sources are unsatisfactory in both range and reliability. The only full-length account of the voyage was by William Funnell, mate on the *St George*. Its publication in 1707 was followed by an angry, incoherent *Vindication* by Dampier, which in turn was contradicted by John Welbe, a 'midshipman' on the voyage, in his *Answer*. Other insights come from legal proceedings taken by the owners against Dampier in 1712.

On the run down to Cape Horn Dampier – in what seemed to be a throwback to the quarrel with Fisher on the *Roebuck* – had 'some Disagreement' with his first lieutenant and put him ashore on the Cape Verde Islands, where he died.[14] The two ships became separated as they struggled to get round Cape Horn and into the South Sea, but met again at the rendezvous of Juan Fernández. There Stradling's behaviour led to the crew of the *Cinque Ports* abandoning ship to set up camp ashore. Only Stradling and the monkey were left on board. Dampier managed to persuade the would-be castaways to return, but the two privateering vessels cut a sorry figure in an action off the island against a thirty-six-gun French ship, the *St Joseph*. If Selkirk's evidence is correct, the crews thought the vessel was a Spanish merchantman, and in their eagerness to pursue it left a boat, sails, gear and some of their number on Juan Fernández. There was, Selkirk claimed, no consultation between Dampier and Stradling, and the engagement against the Frenchman was sadly mishandled. Dampier in the *St George* ran across the enemy's stern and so blocked the line of fire of the *Cinque Ports*, which was following its consort. The *St George* had nine of its crew killed before falling away.[15] Letters captured later revealed that the Frenchman had 'a great many' men killed and thirty-two wounded, and was about to surrender when the English called off the action.[16] Dampier later blamed his crew and claimed that they had fled below deck. Funnell in turn accused Dampier of breaking off the action against the wishes of the crew, and Welbe supported this with some circumstantial detail. Dampier, he wrote, failed to give the crew either encouragement or commands, 'but stood upon the Quarter-Deck behind a good

13. For the above see the legal documents cited in B.M.H. Rogers, 'Dampier's Voyage of 1703', *Mariner's Mirror*, 10 (1924), pp. 367–8.
14. See Funnell, *Voyage*, p. 6.
15. According to Selkirk, twelve were killed. For this and his evidence generally see his 'Deposition', para 8.
16. Funnell, *Voyage*, p. 49.

Barricado, which he had order'd to be made of Beds, Rugs, Pillows, Blankets, &c.'[17]

After this debacle the ships sailed towards the mainland. Their destination was the buccaneers' traditional plundering ground of Santa Maria and its gold mines, across the bay from Panama, but by time the crew mounted their attack little of value was left in the town. It was less this than the refusal to give the attackers brandy that set Welbe on edge as he remembered Dampier's words on this occasion: 'If we take the Town, they will get Brandy enough; but if we don't take the Town, I shall want it my self.'[18] The privateers seized a couple of prizes off the coast, and a triumphant Dampier 'asked his Men whether it was not better to take Spaniards without fighting than to fight Frenchmen'.[19] For privateers there was only one answer to this question, but these captures brought disagreements that were to result in the total disintegration of the venture. Selkirk claimed that from the beginning Dampier, Stradling and Morgan had 'managed all things in hugger mugger [clandestinely] among themselves without the knowledge of any of the said ships Company.'[20] As prizes were taken, this secretiveness pushed the crews' suspicions to breaking point. William Sheltram and Ralph Clift accused Dampier and Morgan of seizing from the prizes 'great Ingotts or wedges both of silver and also of gold', besides pearls and silk, and keeping them in the captain's cabin of the *St George*. Clift's deposition continued that after 'Dampier and Morgan had taken out what they Pleased they would not suffer the Men to rummage the sd Ships but turned them loose again with their Companys and what goods were left in them & would scarsly permit the Men of the sd ships St George & Cinque Ports Gally to take Cloaths tho' they were in great want of them.'[21] Through a combination of ineptitude and dishonesty (if his accusers are to be believed) Dampier missed much on the prize ships. On one he was in such a hurry that he overlooked eighty thousand dollars; on another he left much of value on board for 'a private consideration' from the Spanish captain.[22] Morgan, meanwhile, seems to have been taking and secreting silver plate whenever the opportunity arose.

In May 1704, 'having some disagreement', Dampier and Stradling decided to part company. Selkirk thought that Dampier's refusal to give the crews 'leave to rummage' the prize was the sticking point.[23] Stradling in the *Cinque Ports* returned to Juan Fernández to pick up his sails and men, only to find that both had been seized by the French. It was now that Selkirk determined

17. Ibid., pp. 25–6; William Dampier, *Captain Dampier's Vindication of his Voyage to the South-Seas, in the Ship St George* (London, [1707]), printed in Masefield, *Dampier's Voyages*, II, p. 581; John Welbe, *An Answer to Captain Dampier's Vindication* (London, [1708]), p. 3.
18. Welbe, *Answer*, p. 7.
19. PRO: Chancery 24/1321, Pt. I. Deposition of William Sheltram, 11 July 1712, para 9.
20. Selkirk, 'Deposition', para 2.
21. PRO: Chancery 24/1321, Pt. I. Depositions of Ralph Clift, 10 July 1712, para 9; William Sheltram, 11 July 1712, para 9.
22. Funnell, *Voyage*, p. 47; Rogers, 'Dampier's Voyage', pp. 369–70.
23. Selkirk, 'Deposition', para 9.

to maroon himself rather than continue the voyage. Though he regretted it at first, his decision was probably a wise one, for the *Cinque Ports* was riddled with worm and sank at sea. Thirty-two of her crew got away on rafts, but only eighteen of these (including Stradling) survived to reach the mainland, and a Spanish prison.[24] On the *St George*, also badly affected by worm, Dampier cruised aimlessly, first south, then north, along the coast, with the ship falling to pieces beneath him. Its bottom was 'in many places eaten like a Honey-Comb . . . [with] plank no thicker than an old Six-pence . . . in some places in the Hold we could thrust our Thumbs quite through with ease.'[25] It was one of the main accusations brought later against Dampier that he had failed to advise the owners that the ships should be sheathed, despite the fact that 'having been several Voyages to the South Seas before this Voyage, [he] must needs know that the worms there eat ships.'[26]

In September the chief mate, John Clipperton, decided to leave the expedition, and together with twenty-one men sailed away in a captured bark. With a decrepit ship and a dwindling crew Dampier attempted to salvage something from the wreckage of the expedition by aiming at the richest prize of all – the galleon from Manila as it neared Acapulco on the last leg of its long voyage. The confrontation with the Manila ship off Colima was described by Funnell, Welbe, Dampier and the deponents of the 1712 law suit. In the accounts of Funnell and Welbe, Dampier stood accused of missing an unexpected opportunity as the ships neared each other, for the galleon by hoisting its ensign and firing a signal gun showed that it had mistaken the *St George* for a Spanish ship. Dampier ignored the urging of his officers to hoist Spanish colours, return the signal and lay himself alongside the galleon, which had only two cannon clear of cargo and other clutter. Instead, he showed English colours and fired a single cannon at the great ship – uselessly, since the *St George* had only five-pounders. As the galleon cleared its decks, so it brought its own guns into action, hull-smashing eighteen- and twenty-four-pounders. An attempt to board might still have been successful, but 'the Capt. was so much against it, that when the Boatswain ordre'd the Man at the Helm to edge near her, in Order to clap her on Board, the Capt. swore he wld shoot the Man at the Helm through the Head.'[27] Ralph Clift later confirmed this, and did so with some feeling, for the helmsman in question was his brother.[28] As the galleon's cannon began to batter the *St George*, holing her through the bow on the waterline, Dampier stood away.

If an indignant Welbe is to be trusted, Dampier treated the whole affair with remarkable casualness as he beat an undignified retreat. According to Welbe, he commented: 'Well, Gentlemen, I will not say, as Johnny

24. Rogers, 'Dampier's Voyage', p. 396.
25. Funnell, *Voyage*, p. 68.
26. Selkirk, 'Deposition', para 17; and also Sheltram, 'Deposition', para 17.
27. Welbe, *Answer*, p. 6.
28. Clift, 'Deposition', para 13.

Armstrong said, I'll lay me down and bleed a while; but I will lay me down and sleep a while' – and proceeded to do so with such effect that he did not wake until the next morning.[29] Dampier's version of events, predictably, was rather different. The crew were 'drunk and bewitched', and refused to carry out his orders to disable the galleon by peppering her defenceless stern with the privateer's bow-chasers. And the encounter with the helmsman was crucially different as Dampier reported it: 'For the very Man at Helm contradicted my Orders, Edg'd her away to Leward once more; at which I offered to shoot him through the head.'[30]

A month later Funnell, Morgan and thirty-two others deserted, as Clipperton had done, in a prize vessel, leaving Dampier with 'no more than twenty-eight Men and Boys, and most of them Landmen'.[31] Evidence in the legal proceedings of 1712 described how after the unsuccessful action against the galleon, 'Dampier ordered all persons within the said ship St George to come on deck and having given them a dram of Rum or Brandy or some other strong Liquor desired all who were willing to go along with him *upon their own accounts exclusive of the Owners* to go on the quarter-deck, and prevailed upon 26 or 27 persons.'[32] In his evidence Clift deposed that Morgan demanded more information, but Dampier refused, saying only that he held the Queen's commission.[33] The parting was not amicable. According to Dampier, the master, Bellhash, 'took me by the Throat, and Swore if I spoke a Word they would Dash my Brains out'. When Dampier refused to hand over the keys of the powder room and arms chest, Morgan had an easy solution: '"We have Iron Crows on Board, they are as good Keys as we desire," and with that broke 'em open.' The final indignity came as the vessels drifted apart and, as Dampier recollected, 'that Buffoon Toby Thomas by name, said, Poor Dampier, thy Case is like King James, every Body has left thee.'[34]

During 1706 and 1707 the survivors straggled back to England a few at a time. Funnell, Clipperton and Dampier all lost or abandoned their ships, and after a variety of generally unpleasant experiences in China or Batavia were shipped home. Even Stradling got back in the end, after spells in a Peruvian

---

29. Welbe, *Answer*, p. 6. It was actually Armstrong's fellow-Scot, Andrew Barton, killed in a sea action against the English in 1511, whose last words were remembered in the ballad:

> I'll lay me down and bleed awhile
> And then I'll rise and fight again.

30. Dampier, *Vindication*, p. 584.
31. Funnell, *Voyage*, p. 221.
32. Rogers, 'Dampier's Voyage', p. 373; my italics.
33. Clift, 'Deposition', para 14. As Jonathan Lamb reminds me, there is something odd about this statement, because other accounts accuse Clipperton of having taken Dampier's commission with him when he deserted in September 1704. Certainly Dampier seems not to have had any commission with him when he reached Batavia, for the Dutch authorities there threw him into prison as a pirate.
34. Dampier, *Vindication*, p. 585.

prison and in France. How many of the crews returned is not known. The largest group, which included survivors from the vessels commanded by Funnell and Clipperton, reached England in August 1706, 'being but eighteen out of the one hundred and eighty-three which went out with us'.[35] For the owners the venture was a disaster: both ships lost, and little or nothing in the way of prize-money. For them there was little to choose between Dampier and his antagonists in the way of ineptitude, and worse. Morgan may have refused Dampier's offer of January 1705 off the Californian coast, but it was in his own interests, not those of the owners. When he and his fellow-deserters reached Batavia in the bark in February 1706 they sold the owners' share of the plunder for a mere £600.[36] According to Sheltram and Clift, who were among this group, when they reached Amboina some weeks later Morgan disposed of plate, bullion and jewels on his own account and made about £10,000 (Clift thought) from the transaction.[37]

The expedition confirmed what the *Roebuck* voyage had already indicated: that whatever his skills as a navigator and observer, Dampier lacked the qualities of an effective captain. Funnell's book, Welbe's pamphlet and the depositions of 1712 are all edged with malice in varying degrees; but there is a similarity between their accusations and those made on the *Roebuck* by Fisher. Welbe gave some examples of Dampier's language – '*Rogue, Rascal, Son of a Bitch*, and other such vulgar Expressions'. Sheltram noted that Dampier's language was 'very base and abusive'. Clift commented that, although Dampier met his officers on Saturday nights for a drinking session, in general he behaved 'very rudily & very villy both to his Officers & to Men on board'.[38] Once such complaints might have been dismissed by the historian as either trivial or sanctimonious, but not since Greg Dening has shown us the significance of 'bad language' on shipboard. On Bligh's *Bounty* 'it was his language that was seen to be his most offensive trait, not his violence.'[39] In other ways Dampier seems to have violated what his officers regarded as the conventions of orderly government. The owners accused Dampier of failing to hold councils of officers.[40] This does not seem to have been correct, but there is evidence that suggests that Dampier had a short way with his councils. Sheltram said that councils were held, but that their resolutions were never recorded, and as a result Dampier was guilty of 'disoblig[ing] all his Officers'. To this Clift added that only Morgan seemed to be in the captain's confidence.[41] Welbe allowed that Dampier 'sometimes' called councils, but claimed that he ignored proper procedures:

---

35. Funnell, *Voyage*, p. 300.
36. Rogers, 'Dampier's Voyage', p. 374.
37. Sheltram, 'Deposition', para 15; Clift, 'Deposition', para 18.
38. Welbe, *Voyage*, p. 8; Sheltram, 'Deposition', para 14; Clift, 'Deposition', para 9.
39. Greg Dening, *Mr Bligh's Bad Language: Passion, Power and Theatre on the Bounty* (Cambridge, 1992), p. 55.
40. Lee, 'Selkirk', p. 398.
41. Sheltram, 'Deposition', para 6; Clift, 'Deposition', para 6.

Now, it is usual in a Council of War for the youngest Officer to give his Opinion first; but, to the contrary, Captain Dampier would always give his own Opinion first; and then, if any of the Officers gave their Opinion contrary to his, he would fly out in a Passion, and say, *If you know better than I do, take you Charge of the Ship.*[42]

All this amounted to a guaranteed way of arousing suspicion among crews who were sailing on a 'no purchase, no pay' basis, and some of whom were old hands from their buccaneering days. The owners' worries about their commander must have been increased when they read about the occasion when (if Funnell is to be trusted) Dampier went into action flying, not the English ensign of a privateer bearing an official commission and a proud name, but 'the bloody flag' of his buccaneering past.[43]

If Dampier never actually lost his ship to mutineers as Bligh did, nonetheless successive desertions struck at his authority and dignity. His abandonment by his old shipmate and crony Edward Morgan would have cut especially deep. The confrontations were played out with the verbal pyrotechnics of stage dialogue rather than with actual violence; it was as though the wooden world of the ship had been transformed into the boards of a theatre stage. And the dialogue was important. The crew's bitterness against Dampier seems to have been fuelled, not only by his failures to take the rich prizes he had promised, but by his refusal (in public at least) to take those failures seriously. His insouciant behaviour before the assault on Santa Maria and his self-deprecating humour after the action against the galleon might have become the stuff of legend in a successful commander; but Dampier was never that.

In his book Funnell had written of 'the very great and profitable Voyages' made by the French, with reported profits of five thousand percent.[44] Further evidence came from captured letters from Spanish merchants at Lima, dated 1708, 'which clearly prove', a memorandum among the papers of Vice-Admiral Sir John Norris noted, 'that the French by carrying a Trade into the So. Sea and selling their goods at easier Rates to the Spaniards at Peru at their own doors than the South Galleonists can afford them at, have quite alter'd the Channel of that Trade.'[45] Another indication of the scale of the French trade came from the complaints of the Governor of Jamaica that his colony's long-standing if illicit commerce along the Spanish Main had almost vanished because of the competition from cheap French goods finding their way inland from the Pacific ports.[46]

42. Welbe, *Answer*, p. 5.
43. Funnell, *Voyage*, p. 55. From the wording it is not altogether clear whether the choice of the flag was Dampier's or the crew's.
44. Ibid., p. 147.
45. BL: Add. MS 28,140, f. 27d.
46. See *Calendar of State Papers Colonial: America and West Indies 1710–1711* (London, 1924), pp. 109, 111, 428.

Among those who read accounts of the 'vast Trade' driven by the French in the South Sea was a Bristol merchant and sea-captain, Woodes Rogers. He had managed to obtain a copy of the journal kept by Jacques de Beauchesne-Gouin, commander of the first of the French trading ventures to the South Sea (1698–1701), and he calculated that in all the French had brought back to Europe goods worth £25,000,000.[47] However much he made of this in his later book, Rogers and his backers were less interested in trading opportunities than in prizes and plunder. His letters of marque, dated 9 April 1708,[48] allowed him to wage war against both the French and the Spaniards, and officers on the expedition such as Edward Cooke hoped to recoup in the South Sea losses they had suffered from French privateers in home waters.[49]

The account of the voyage that follows is based on the published narratives of Rogers and Cooke, and also on the documents, most never used before, among the Chancery papers in the Public Record Office.[50] These were collected in relation to the long-running legal action over prize-money which followed the return of the expedition in 1711. Most of the documents are account books, bills, receipts, cargo lists and the like; but among them are letters from Rogers and other officers on the voyage, affidavits, complaints and abstracts of journals. Those that have been retrieved and read (not all are still legible) give a significantly different picture of a voyage generally acclaimed as the most successful and best-organized English venture in the South Sea since Drake. Dr John Campbell introduced his account of the voyage with the words 'There never was any Voyage of this nature so happily adjusted'. More recently, Woodes Rogers's biographer wrote that he 'had every reason for pride in what he had done . . . He had shown great nautical skill, a fine flair for leadership, and a blend of humanity and commercial acumen.'[51] This is by no means the whole story.

The expedition was one of the first to benefit from the Act of Parliament

---

47. Woodes Rogers, *A Cruising Voyage Round the World* (London, 1712), Introduction.

48. Now in PRO: HCA 25/20, Pt. 2.

49. Cooke had lost two ships within eight months. See Edward Cooke, *A Voyage to the South Sea, and Round the World* (London, 1712), Introduction.

50. The documents are in at least ten large cardboard boxes in the Public Record Office (the precise number is uncertain since Chancery 104/38, 39 and 40 are not open to inspection because of the poor condition of their contents, and each may contain more than one box). The seven boxes examined hold a bewildering miscellany of documents, most kept in no particular order. David Starkey used this material to establish the financial details of the venture in his *British Privateering Enterprise*, pp. 47, 61, 91, 96, 107, 278, 280. Chancery 104/160 (two boxes) has particularly interesting material, though much of it is only barely legible. The first box holds seventeen bundles of documents, each containing anything from a dozen to thirty or so separate documents, ranging from pieces of several pages to small slips of paper. The second box contains four account and letter-books, together with many loose papers. At some stage during the proceedings in Chancery an effort was made to sort the papers. Some bundles have notes attached that reflect varying degrees of clerical irritability: 'insignificant', 'unintelligible', 'useless'.

51. John Campbell, ed., *Navigantium atque Itinerantium Bibliotheca; or, A Compleate Collection of Voyages and Travels*, I (London, 1744), p. 150; Bryan Little, *Crusoe's Captain: Being the Life of Woodes Rogers, Seaman, Trader, Colonial Governor* (London, 1960), p. 148.

passed in March 1708 that encouraged privateers by relinquishing the right of the Crown to keep a proportion of the value of prizes. Copies of the Act were put on board the ships as evidence to the crews that 'All Prizes and Purchase which shall be Taken by the said Ships, is to be to the sole Use and Benefit of the Owners and Men, and not liable to pay Tenths.'[52] With the financial support of some of Bristol's leading merchants, two ships were bought, the *Duke* of 320 tons, to be commanded by Woodes Rogers, and the *Dutchess* of 260 tons, to be commanded by Stephen Courtney; in all, there were seventeen investors, holding 256 shares.[53] To allow for casualties on the voyage, to provide prize-crews and to guard against mutiny, the ships carried a double complement of officers and two agents (Carleton Vanbrugh and William Bath) to protect the owners' interests. When the ships returned, the spoils were to be divided between the owners (two-thirds) and the crews (one-third). Shares were allocated to the crews according to rank and duties: twenty-four for each of the captains, running down the scale (six shares for the master's mates and carpenters, for example) to the men. Here alternatives were on offer. Crew members could sail for shares only, as on Dampier's voyage in the *St George* (two and a half for seamen, one for landmen); or for part-shares (half the above), part-wages; or for wages only. Most opted for the part-shares, part-wages option.[54]

Also on board, once again, was William Dampier, who according to Cooke had been important in setting up the enterprise despite the 'great Discouragement' of his recent unsuccessful voyage.[55] This time he sailed in an advisory rather than executive position, as 'Pilot for the South Seas'. There has been much uncertainty concerning Dampier's status on the voyage, and especially the financial arrangements agreed with him.[56] Documents in Chancery help to elucidate these. The most significant document is a report of the proceedings of the Chancery Court on 21 November 1713 which refers to an agreement made between the owners and Dampier on 20 January 1708 concerning the terms on which he was to sail on the voyage.[57] The date goes some way towards confirming Cooke's assertion that Dampier was involved in the venture from the beginning, and its terms show the importance the owners attached to his services, for he was to receive one-sixteenth of the owners' net profits from the venture. Whether he also held shares is not quite clear. Cooke's list shows an allocation of eight shares to

---

52. Printed prospectus, 1 July 1708, in Chancery 104/160.
53. Starkey, *British Privateering Enterprise*, p. 91.
54. See the lists in C 104/37, Pt. II.
55. Cooke, *Voyage to the South Sea*, Introduction. One of the investors in the *St George* venture claimed that Dampier had secreted money from that voyage which he then put into the voyage of the *Duke* and *Dutchess*; however, the alleged go-between in this transaction denied the accusation. Rogers, 'Dampier's Voyage', p. 377.
56. On this see two articles by B.M.H. Rogers, 'Dampier's Debts', *Mariner's Mirror*, 15 (1924), pp. 322–4, and 'Woodes Rogers's Privateering Voyage of 1708–11', *Mariner's Mirror*, 19 (1928), pp. 196–211.
57. C 104/36, Pt. II: Account Book 1712–14, p. 14.

Dampier – a modest number, halfway between the master's ten and the carpenter's six, but a list in Chancery refers to eleven shares in Dampier's name.[58] This discrepancy would seem to be explained by another note in the Chancery records, intriguing in itself, which states that in 1708 Dampier promised three of his shares to John Ballett, his old surgeon from the *St George* (who had stayed with Dampier to the last). These would give Ballett nine shares, without which he refused to sail.[59] For a moment we are given a glimpse of perhaps a different side of Dampier's character. To add to the confusion, it is doubtful whether Dampier, or his heirs, actually collected on these shares. List after list in the Chancery records has Dampier's name firmly annotated 'no shares', or sometimes more explicitly 'no share but is to have one-sixteenth of the Owners' two thirds'. This seems to indicate that at some stage a decision had been made, either by the owners or by the court, that Dampier's one-sixteenth of the owners' profits cancelled out the shares he had originally been allocated. That Dampier, alone among the officers, was promised a share of the owners' profits was an acknowledgment of the fact that Dampier knew more of the South Sea than any other Englishman; though there is evidence that seems to show that his advice became less and less heeded as the voyage went on.

Despite being captain of the *Duke* and one of the prime promoters of the project, Woodes Rogers had not invested in it (though he later claimed both that he had negotiated Dampier's agreement with the owners, and had been promised something similar himself).[60] Stephen Courtney appears as an investor, though the number of shares he held was not specified. Rogers was not commander of the expedition in the normal sense, for a carefully worded Constitution of 14 July 1708 stipulated that all decisions should be made by a general Council of Officers. Its president (with a double vote) was Dr Thomas Dover, who as an investor had subscribed thirty-two shares to the expedition (more than any other investor except Thomas Goldney) and was also 'second captain' on the *Duke*, senior doctor and captain of marines.[61] The Constitution seems to represent an attempt to learn the lessons of Dampier's recent voyage and to guard against abuse of power by an individual officer; but the link between financial outlay and executive power was one of several features of the muddled command structure that led to increasing problems as the ships reached the South Sea and enemy waters.

The captains were given their sailing instructions on the same day that the Constitution was agreed; they are lacking in detail, but have some interesting

---

58. Cooke, *Voyage to the South Sea*, Introduction; for the Chancery list see Rogers, 'Rogers's Privateering Voyage', p. 208.
59. C 104/36, Pt. II: Account Book, 1712–14, p. 68.
60. See p. 155 below.
61. A copy of the Constitution is in C 104/36, Pt. II: John Parker's Letter Book, pp. 7–8. Long after the voyage, Dover achieved dubious fame with his recipe for a diaphoric powder known as Dover's Powder, while his exaggerated trust in mercury as a universal remedy gave him the nickname of the 'quicksilver doctor'. DNB.

features.[62] Rogers and Courtney were given discretion to use either the Cape
Horn or Strait of Magellan route; they were to consult the Council in all
cases of difficulty; and a rather fetching postscript exhorted them 'in Every
thing to behave yr. selves, one towards another as kind Duke regarding his
Beloved Dutchess.' Once in the South Sea they were to consider themselves
'under the Pilotage of Capt. Dampier', and this is explained more fully in a
later paragraph: 'Our grand Design Being to seeke out one or both the Ships
belonging to Acapulco in South America [sic]. You are to consult your pilot
Captain Dampier in Counsell on whose Knowledge in those parts we do
mainly depend upon for Satisfactory Success.'

Details about the voyage, explaining the sharing of prize-money, had been
printed and distributed as a fly sheet on 1 July in an effort to attract crews.
Although the officers had been appointed by early April, the search for
seamen went on through the summer. At a meeting of the owners in Bristol
on 23 June it was agreed that Captain Courtney should go to Portsmouth,
and third mate Simon Hatley to Ireland, 'to obtain what saylers they can to
go ye Voyage'.[63] These and other efforts produced what Rogers described as
a 'mix'd Gang' of 333 crew members. More than a third of them were
foreigners, and among the English on board were 'Tinkers, Taylors, Hay-
makers, Pedlers, Fidlers, &c.'[64] For their size, if not their function, the ships
were heavily over-crewed, or 'crouded and pester'd', as Rogers put it. The
ships sailed from Bristol on 2 August 1708, but by prior arrangement put in
at Cork, where there was a general shake-out; and some of the 'ordinary
Fellows' and 'fresh-water Sailors' were exchanged for stouter men.

From Cork the first hint of trouble to come reached the owners in a letter
of 3 September from their agents there:

> We are now to advise you that with the greatest difficulty that we met with
> in any affairs, we at last got the Duke and Dutches in a readyness to Saile the
> 1st Instant . . . God send them well, and that they may be Successfull to
> Answer the Vast expence they have beene for you . . . a Summe [£2000] we
> doubt not but will be as Surprizeing to you as it was dayly uneasye to us to
> Expend Soe much which could not be avoided, and would have Swelled
> vastly more, if we had not refused many things to both Captns. that they said
> was necessary . . . we cannot Express by our pens the fateagues and trouble we
> have had in this affaire.[65]

Confirmation of this came from one of the owners, Francis Rogers, who
complained in a letter of the same day that all his time in Cork had been

62. Curiously, the instructions were not printed in either the Rogers or the Cooke account of the
    voyage; there are copies in C 104/36, Pt. II, and C 104/160.
63. C 104/36, Pt. I.
64. Rogers, *Cruising Voyage*, p. 8.
65. C 104/160: bundle labelled 'SE/25'.

taken up with the privateers: 'Capt. Rogers Managmt. made ye Matters worse. It would be endless to relate what has hapened . . . I hope there will bee more regularity and a better harmony between ym when they gett into deep Water.'[66]

The ships left Cork on 1 September, and within two weeks came the first of several mutinies that occurred on the voyage. All, to a greater or lesser degree, were about the distribution of spoils; none led to a change in command, but the concessions made to the men brought significant changes to the original agreement. As Rogers explained, had this not been done, 'we must unavoidably have run into such continual Scenes of Mischief and Disorder, as have not only tended to the great Hindrance, but generally to the total Disappointment of all Voyages of this Nature.' Even more bluntly, he pointed out that 'it would be next to a miracle to keep the Men in both Ships under Command and willing to fight', if the articles of agreement drawn up by the owners had been insisted upon. Such a situation, he concluded, had not been 'duly consider'd at home'.[67] An exchange of blows between officers on the *Dutchess* and the putting of eight men in irons for refusing orders on the *Duke* showed that even so tensions still existed; and all this before the ships had reached Brazil.

At the harbour of Grande on the Brazilian coast the ships took in water and supplies, and Rogers reported home. After a long description of the mutiny, he evidently felt it was time to reassure the owners:

> I can assure you we are in perfect unity amongst ye Officers of each Ship, & every one is ambitious to shew himself forwardest in discouraging all practices yt may be any way detrimentall to ye good of ye Voyage. But this has been improvd by degrees, wn. we left Ireland I doubted having such a crew of straggling fellows of almost all Nations; how we should bring such Company of both Ships to a regular Command but that scruple is now cleard, and we can say it without vanity, that we never knew ships Companys better agree, & quieter than we now are . . . Capt. Dover reads a Sermon on Sundays & we have made Mr. Hopkins our Chaplain to read prayrs. every Day in the Week, the like is done by others on Board ye Dutchess.[68]

Rogers concluded with the hope that they would soon take their first prize, so that Edward Cooke, 'second captain' of the *Dutchess*, and some of the crews could be transferred from the overcrowded privateers: 'We are now too many in a Ship, I am sure more yn ever sayld so far as we are design'd in ships of ye like Burthen.'

66. Ibid.
67. Rogers, *Cruising Voyage*, pp. 28–9.
68. Rogers to owners, 28 Nov. 1708. C 104/160. Less than six months later, on 15 May 1709, Rogers was writing Hopkins's obituary. 'At 6 last Night Mr Samuel Hopkins, Dr. Dover's Kinsman and Assistant, died; he read prayers once a Day ever since we pass'd the Equinox in the North Sea.' *Cruising Voyage*, p. 206.

From Brazil the ships sailed south for Cape Horn, for it had been decided to follow the open water route around the Horn of the French traders rather than risk becoming entangled in the narrow channels and tidal races of the Strait of Magellan. After being blown as far south as lat. 61°53′S., the ships reached the waters of the Pacific in mid-January 1709 and turned towards Juan Fernández. The call at the island to recuperate and provision was by now almost a routine one for English expeditions entering the Pacific; but this particular visit was far from routine, for on the island the crews found the castaway Alexander Selkirk. The story of Selkirk was to have repercussions that none among the men who spotted the strange figure 'cloth'd in Goat-Skins' on 2 February 1709 could ever have imagined, and some of these will be dealt with elsewhere.[69] For the moment, Selkirk was seen as a useful addition to the expedition (he had been, Dampier said, the 'best Man' on the *Cinque Ports*),[70] and the two-week stay at Juan Fernández was also helpful in allowing many of the crew members suffering from scurvy to begin to recover. As the ships sailed away, Rogers noted – rather unoriginally – that the island 'might be at first of great use to those who would carry on any Trade to the *South-Sea*'.[71]

From Juan Fernández the expedition sailed northeast for the Lobos islands, fifty miles off the Peruvian coast. The taking of several coasting vessels, none of great value, was heartening in itself, but meant that secrecy could no longer be guaranteed. From Lobos the expedition was to head towards the important port of Guayaquil and take it by assault. This did not appeal to all those on board. As Rogers put it: 'We knew that Misfortunes attend Sailors when out of their Element: and hearing that they began to murmur about the Encouragement they were to expect for Landing, which they alledg'd was a risque more than they were ship'd for.'[72] Once again, the cooperation of the crews had to be bought by further adjustments to the rules on the distribution of booty – to the extent that Rogers later calculated that after all the modifications his and Courtney's share was only a tenth of what had originally been envisaged.

The attack itself was hardly a masterpiece of planning. As the assault boats rowed up the estuary of the River Guayas towards the port under cover of darkness, the fires and lights of a religious festival were taken as alarm signals; and Dr Dover, resplendent in his role as 'Captain of Marines', had second, and then third, thoughts about an attack. After arguments on the boats so noisy that the Spaniards on shore called in an interpreter to try to follow their gist,[73] the attack was called off, and instead negotiations were opened. When these broke down, an assault was finally launched on 24 April. It

69. See Ch. VI below.
70. Rogers, *Cruising Voyage*, p. 125.
71. Ibid., p. 137.
72. Ibid., p. 154.
73. See Cooke, *Voyage to the South Sea*, I, p. 141.

succeeded with few casualties on either side, but by then much of the treasure held in the town had been hurried away – perhaps as much as '2000000 Pieces of Eight in Money, wrought and unwrought, Gold and Silver, besides Jewels'.[74] The behaviour of the privateers seems to have been restrained,[75] certainly compared with their buccaneering predecessors (there had been a brutal sack of Guayaquil in 1687), but morale soon sagged as the Spaniards spun out the ransom negotiations, and armed men were seen in the woods. After five uneasy days it was decided to retreat to the boats with as much plunder as could be carried. Rogers was in command of the rearguard, but had a busier task picking up the weapons discarded by the privateers than in fending off the Spaniards – 'Pistols, Cutlashes and Pole-axes, which shew'd that our Men were grown very careless, weak, and weary of being Soldiers, and that 'twas time to be gone from hence'.[76]

Recriminations about the attack seem to have rumbled on for some time. Twenty months later and many thousand miles away, Carleton Vanbrugh, the owners' agent, was involved in an altercation with Woodes Rogers about the episode. Vanbrugh was at odds throughout with most of his shipmates and had been dismissed from the Council for misconduct just before the attack on Guayaquil. Even so, the general tenor of the conversation he noted in his journal on 11 December 1710 during the run from Batavia to the Cape of Good Hope carries some conviction:

> Last night upon Deck, as Capn. Rogers and I and others were Chatting, and ye main Subject the taking Guayaquill, my opinion made the Enterprise less daring and difficult than Captn. Rogers did – upon wch. he immediately retorted by Reflecting upon me, that I Chose to stay in the Bark where I was, to eat my dinner, and so to avoid by delay, the Danger, by landing after the others . . . I did tell Capn. R. yt whenever he charg'd me wth this I wou'd tell him openly of a worse charge on him; tell him my Author and swear to my Evidence – I will here Deliver it, in Case of Mortality[77] – Viz. that Capn. Thos. Dover told me, once in discourse (I can't say Just the time) that Capn. Rogers turn'd his back on ye Enemy and came Retiring towards the place he was at, under some sham Pretence of our mens being like to shoot him in the Back etc. God knows the Truth.[78]

The stay at Guayaquil not only opened up disputes among the officers; it introduced 'malignant Fever' to the crews, many of whom were still suffering

---

74. Rogers, *Cruising Voyage*, p. 185.
75. Though perhaps not as genteel as Rogers described it, for the Spanish sources examined by Little, *Crusoe's Captain*, pp. 92–5, give a rather more believable picture of drunkenness and at least mild debauchery.
76. Rogers, *Cruising Voyage*, pp. 183–4.
77. Vanbrugh had been ill for some time and died at the Cape a few weeks after this quarrel.
78. PRO: Chancery 104/160: 'Remarks' by Carleton Vanbrugh, Dec. 1710. This fragment of Vanbrugh's journal seems to have been kept among the papers in Chancery because it

from scurvy. To his dismay Rogers discovered that although the *Duke* had 'a regular Physician, an Apothecary, and Surgeons enough', they were running short of medicines.[79] When the ships reached the Galapagos Islands to refresh and rest the crews, Rogers was hard-pressed to find enough fit men to hoist out the ship's yawl. To add to his problems, one of the captured barks with Hatley and a small prize-crew on board became separated from the ships and was never seen again. Nor did the islands come up to expectations. Certainly, there was nothing to match the description by Edward Davis in the 1680s, and Rogers turned this disappointment into a broader assault on the tellers of tall tales:

> He says, that it had Trees fit for Masts; but these sort of Men, and others I have convers'd with, or whose Books I have read, have given very blind or false Relations of their Navigation, and Actions in these Parts, for supposing the Places too remote to have their Stories disprov'd, they imposed on the Credulous, amongst whom I was one, till now I too plainly see, that we cannot find any of their Relations to be relied on.

It seems very likely that much of this was a dig at Dampier, 'our Pilot', who seems to have been losing credibility fast. A return visit to the Galapagos Islands found Dampier insisting that the nearest ones lay only three hundred miles off the mainland. The ships had to sail over their supposed location and another two hundred miles farther west before he would admit his mistake. His identification of Cape Corientes when the Mexican coast was first sighted was treated by Rogers with what seems to be measured contempt – 'the Latt. directs us all to know it.' A few lines later Rogers returned to the subject: 'Capt. Dampier has been here also, but it's a long Time ago.' And it was surely mock-surprise rather than admiration with which Rogers greeted the expedition's safe arrival at an island 'which Capt. Dampier, I do believe, can remember he was at'.

Among the trading vessels taken in the weeks before the assault on Guayaquil was the *Havre de Grace*, almost as large as the *Dutchess*, and this prize was now refitted and renamed the *Marquess* to take its place as the third privateer in the little squadron. Among its mixed cargo were items that confirmed Protestant notions about 'the Ignorance and Credulity of the Papists'. There were, for example, no fewer than five hundred bales of papal bulls which, as far as Rogers could make out, allowed the eating of meat

---

contained some financial items. Among these was a note on a bet Vanbrugh won with Robert Fry, chief mate of the *Duke*, on the number of parishes in England and Wales: 'I affirm'd, above 2000 Parishes in England & Wales, He, not so many – £5:7:6.' This apparently inconsequential entry affords a tantalizing glimpse of shipboard conversation far from home and also raises the question of what sort of books the privateers had on board. Dr Dover, one suspects, had with him just the sort of reference work that could settle this question.

79. Quotations in this and the next two paragraphs are from Rogers, *Cruising Voyage*, pp. 209, 211, 266, 267, 230, 224.

during Lent — for those prepared to pay the right price. Some were used as firing material to burn the old pitch off the ships' bottoms; most were thrown overboard, as were thirty tons of relics found on board — 'Bones in small Boxes, ticketed with the Names of Romish Saints, some of which had been dead 7 or 800 Years; with an infinite Number of Brass Medals, Crosses, Beads, and Crucifixes, religious Toys in Wax, Images of Saints . . .' If Rogers allowed himself some easy fun about this assortment, he was insistent that there was 'Liberty of Conscience on board our floating Commonwealth' for the Spanish prisoners, who included priests. On both the *Duke* and the *Dutchess* the prisoners celebrated mass in the great cabin, while on the quarter-deck above an Anglican service took place — 'so that the Papists here were the Low Churchmen,' he commented wryly.

Another mutinous outbreak in early August 1709 over the distribution of booty was quelled by the arrest of four ringleaders and the making of further concessions. This came on top of what Rogers described as 'a general Misunderstanding amongst our Chief Officers' which had persisted since the attack on Guayaquil.[80] The Chancery papers have much on these disputes; predictably, there is little on the feeling below decks which now and again exploded into violence. A single document, of unknown reliability, gives some indication of the unrest among some members of the crews.[81] It takes the form of a two-page statement, with an undated covering letter, to Dr Dover from Richard Hitchman on the *Duke*. It describes a half-dozen 'cabals' or intrigues among members of the gunroom on the *Duke*, mostly directed against Dr Dover himself. The term 'cabal' is a significant one to find in this context. Used in the reign of Charles II to refer to the dominant group or junto in the government, it had by now acquired a more general meaning as a small body of men engaged in secret intrigue. The first of the cabals seems to have been provoked by a report, later found to be false, that Dover and Courtney were about to turn Rogers out of his command. Later developments led to threats to take over the *Marquess* prize, load into her the plunder from the *Dutchess* and let Dover and Courtney 'goe to ye Divell'. Hitchman noted down a speech by the malcontents (some named, some not): 'They swore God dam them thare should bee noe more Comittees nor Councell . . . Capt. Roggars was Comander, and hee that had ye Longest sword should carray it And his woard should be ye Law.' If the officers should unite, then the crew planned to retaliate by taking their share of the plunder by force. How much of this was gunroom talk, and how much was a serious threat, is impossible to say. What does seem certain is that knowledge of the disputes between the officers, noisy and public at times, could not be confined to the quarter-deck.

After consultations with Dampier and the prisoners taken in the previous months, the little squadron sailed north for Cape San Lucas at the tip of

80. Ibid., p. 237.
81. It is in PRO: Chancery 104/61, Pt. I.

Lower California. Here the expedition hoped to emulate Cavendish's achievement of 1587 and, with the assistance of more ships and men than Dampier had commanded during his unsuccessful attempt in 1704, capture the Manila galleon. As Rogers wrote, they had taken twenty prizes, but most were carrying only timber; for the Spaniards had embargoed all carriage by sea both of valuables and provisions.[82] Cavendish had intercepted the galleon in early November, but the privateers cruised off the Cape throughout November and most of December without sight of another sail. On 21 December 1709, with food running short, the expedition was on the point of giving up its vigil when a ship was seen far out to sea heading for land. This year there were two ships making the run from Manila to Acapulco, and the one in sight was the smaller of the two, the frigate-built *Nuestra Señora de la Encarnación Disengaño*. After a brisk action that left nine dead and ten wounded on the Manila ship but only two wounded on the *Duke* (one was Rogers with a shattered jaw), the Spaniard struck its colours. Rogers and Courtney agreed that 'except a small Number of good Officers (wch. were Europeans) we saw few men to manage yt fight.'[83] The second Manila ship, which came into sight on Christmas Day, proved a more formidable antagonist. The *Nuestra Señora de Begoña* was a new nine-hundred-ton galleon, with forty cannon mounted, a skilled master-gunner and an experienced crew. Its great hull easily withstood the cannon shot from the privateers' six-pounders, while boarding a ship defended by netting and a large crew was not a feasible option. Cooke wrote:

> Our Ships look'd like small Barks to the Enemy . . . we might as well have fought a Castle of 50 Guns, as this Ship which had about 40, and bear as many Brass Pedreros, each carrying as big a Shot as our great Guns; and, as some of the Prisoners told us, 600 Men, whereof 150 were Europeans, many of them English and Irish, some of which had been formerly Pirates.[84]

According to the French captain of the prize, the Spanish ships had received news before leaving Manila that two privateers under Dampier were on their way to the South Sea, and so were forewarned. The Frenchman also confirmed Cooke's wonder at the strength of the galleon as he recalled an engagement between a Manila-built ship and the Dutch in which the Spaniard 'had 90 Balls taken out of her Side, sticking there as it were in a Wall of soft Stone'.[85] The privateers suffered thirty men dead or wounded (Rogers was wounded again, in the foot) and considerable damage to masts and rigging. They could only watch as the galleon continued its stately way

82.   PRO: Chancery 104/160. Rogers, 'An Abstract of the Most Remarkable Transactions', 6 Feb. 1711.
83.   PRO: Chancery 194/36, Pt. II. John Parker's Copy Book, p. 95.
84.   Cooke, *Voyage to the South Sea*, I, p. 351.
85.   Ibid., I, p. 353.

south towards Acapulco and safety. It, too, was damaged, especially aloft, but with all its masts standing and its guns still run out, it was a testimony to the skill of the shipbuilders of the Philippines and to the determination of its crew.

The smaller Manila ship, with its cargo of gold plate and coin, textiles, silks and other oriental luxury goods, was renamed the *Batchelor*. Cooke's account has an inventory of its cargo of 'rich India goods', mostly fabrics.[86] After acrimonious arguments the prize was put under the formal command of Thomas Dover, but with two captains to look after the 'sole Navigating, Sailing and Ingaging' of the ship, helped by the experienced Selkirk as master. Rogers, wounded for a second time in the engagement with the galleon and unable to attend the critical meeting, sent his opinion on paper that Dover was not a fit person to be entrusted with the command 'because his Temper is so violent, that capable Men cannot well act under him, and himself is uncapable.'[87] This led to another outbreak of paper warfare as Dover and his supporters lodged a formal protest against Rogers's unwillingness to accept Dover's appointment – 'the like never having been refus'd by any before when Carried by Majority of Voices'.[88]

In his published account Rogers reflected on the problems that confronted long-range privateering expeditions:

> Privateering at so great a distance is but an indifferent Life at best, especially with so small a Force as ours, and when oblig'd to depend upon Chance or the Enemy's Courtesy for Provisions.
>
> Another Inconveniency we labour'd under, was the want of Power to try Offenders, as aboard her Majesty's Ships of War; which oblig'd us to connive at many Disorders and to be mild in our Punishments: but what was still worse, there was no sufficient Power lodg'd in any one hand to determine Differences amongst our chief Officers; which was a great Omission, and might have prov'd of dangerous Consequence, because of the Divisions which happen'd among us.[89]

The crossing of the North Pacific presented the usual gruelling problem to crews weakened by illness, shortage of food and wounds. Below decks men dropped at the pumps; others collapsed at the helm. It took two months to reach Guam, where the garrison was in no position to resist the privateers' demands for provisions. In his account of the island Rogers paid attention, as Dampier had done earlier, to its 'remarkable' breadfruit. Again like Dampier, he admired the speed of the proas, which 'passed us like a Bird flying'. The Governor presented one of these craft to the English,

---

86. Ibid., II, pp. vii–viii.
87. Rogers, *Cruising Voyage*, p. 310.
88. PRO: Chancery 104/160. Protest by Council, 6 Jan. 1710.
89. Rogers, *Cruising Voyage*, p. xix.

and from the wording of Rogers's account (not altogether clear on this matter) it seems that it was brought back to England on the *Duke*. Certainly, Rogers thought that this unusual craft would make a fine sight afloat in St James's Park.[90] For his hospitality, however enforced it might have been, the Governor was later called to account by his superiors in Manila, and imprisoned.[91] For his part, Captain Cooke picked up rumours about the Solomon Islands and their gold, but came no closer to discovering their location. As he wrote, it was not even clear whether they were north or south of the equator.[92]

From Guam the four ships sailed through the Moluccas to Batavia, where the *Marquess* was sold, 'eat to a Honey-comb by the Worms'.[93] Rogers reported to the owners that the ships had lost about seventy men by death or desertion, but that with the *Marquess* disposed of there were still enough to work the remaining three ships.[94] Among the few letters from the stay at Batavia that have survived were several from Vanbrugh. They could not have been very reassuring to the owners with their complaints that 'we have had great Jarring among us' and that Rogers had abused him during the whole voyage 'as such a Villainous Defamator as he, WR, deserved to be himself'.[95] Rogers himself, 'weak and thin', was still suffering from the effects of his wounds. A journal entry at Batavia shows something of the toughness of the man:

> 8 Days ago the Doctor cut a large Musket Shot out of my Mouth, which had been there near 6 Months, ever since I was first wounded; we reckon'd it a Piece of my Jaw-bone, the upper and lower Jaw being much broken, and almost closed together, so that the Doctor had much ado to come at the Shot, to get it out. I had also several Pieces of my Foot and Heel-bone taken out, but God be thanked, am now in a fair way to have the use of my Foot, and to recover my Health.[96]

Despite Rogers's confidence that they had enough crew to manage the ships, the *Duke*, *Dutchess* and *Batchelor* took on thirty or forty Dutch seamen at Batavia for the voyage home. They reached the Cape of Good Hope at the end of December, and stayed there more than three months waiting for the Dutch and English East Indiamen to arrive. While at the Cape, Rogers and Courtney sent home reports and letters. The owners would have been chiefly interested in the Manila ship, and especially the value of its cargo, but here both captains stressed the difficulties. They had made no attempt to

90.   Ibid., pp. 367–8.
91.   See Schurz, *Manila Galleon*, p. 329.
92.   Cooke, *Voyage to the South Sea*, II, pp. 16-17.
93.   Rogers, *Cruising Voyage*, p. 395.
94.   PRO: Chancery 104/160. Rogers to owners, 25 July 1710.
95.   Ibid. Vanbrugh to owners, 27 Aug., 8 Oct. 1710.
96.   Rogers, *Cruising Voyage*, pp. 390–1.

open up the cargo, and the original manifests had disappeared, probably thrown overboard before the action. Courtney thought the cargo was worth one and a half million dollars (Spanish), with private ventures adding another half-million; Rogers put the value at £200,000 sterling.[97]

Of the disputes on the voyage the two captains said nothing, at least in these reports; but Thomas Dover was not so reticent. After saluting the owners, he plunged straight into his story:

> Woodes Rogers a person of a different Intrest to ors, has proved a dead weight to all or. undertakings who Scorn's to lett his tongue utter anything but Satyr agst. his Country and Owners so Swell'd wth. pride yt He makes itt a Capitall offence for any officer or man to mention some of or. Names too often punishing merrit & too often advancing such as have prostituted their words and Consiences to his Exorbident desires and Commands his Sole Business has been to promote discord amongst us . . . He first made so strong an Intrest in both ships Company's by threats & promises yt he became as though master of both [ships] threateneing to cutt or. throats to make bloody Noses & warme work holding a Correspondence with or. Enemys . . . what can be Expected from a man yt will begin & drink ye Popes health, but I trust ye Divine power will still preserve Us.[98]

The nearest we have to a response from Rogers is a letter from him to three of the owners, written on 8 February:

> The World may believe I have procur'd a fortune, because itt's Customary the Commander of a Privateer has many Privilidges, and Plunder allowd in so much Purchase as we have gott, wch. would have been (according to Custom) considerable to any other Commandrs. But we have follow'd no Presidents from Privateers . . . What I have seperate from the Generall Interest is so insignificant, that itt's not Worth mentioning . . . I don't Expect that my shares (wch. is little more than what's given to nine common Sailors) will amount to more in this successful long Voyage, than what Joseph Eastmont's did, who told me he gott above a thousand pound in a Trip to Newfoundland . . . But what need I be afraid of this, when three such Gentlemen as your selves was pleas'd to assure me, I might Depend on the Advantage of a two and thirtieth part of the whole, tho' as things then were you told me itt could not be confirm'd to me any way before we saild . . . The Agreemt. wch. I promoted for Capt. Dampier very much to his Advantage; If you was sensible what has pass'd on the Voyage, You would pitty my hard fortune in not securing a better proposition for myselfe.

---

97. Rogers, 'Abstract', 6 Feb., and letter to owners, 8 Feb.; Courtney and Cooke, 'Abstract', 8 Feb. All in PRO: Chancery 104/160, while there are also copies in the Harley Papers in BL: Add. MS 70,163.
98. PRO: Chancery 104/60. Thomas Dover to owners, 11 Feb. 1711.

Hoping that the owners would settle the matter before he returned, Rogers signed himself 'Your most dejected Obedt. humble Servt.'[99]

From the Cape of Good Hope the little squadron of privateers returned to Europe in a convoy of Dutch and English East Indiamen. The final stages of the voyage were prolonged and frustrating. To avoid the dangers of interception by French ships in the Channel, the East India fleet sailed west of Ireland, picking up its escort of Dutch men-of-war off the Shetlands. As the convoy slowly made its way down the east coast of Britain the privateer captains sent letters in advance to the owners. Rogers, 'just recovered from ye jaws of death almost', wrote that it was better to have differences towards the end of a voyage than at the beginning. He hoped that their prize would 'make some Amends for what's past'. Courtney reported that the *Dutchess* was 'a very sickly ship', with forty of her crew ill, including himself. It was Dover, once again, who voiced the bitterest complaints: 'Or. Councell is att last of noe force. Woodes Rogers disposeing of wt He thinks fitt out of this Ship, We call'd a Councell & would have had a Chest out of Him of Pearl Jewells & Gold but he swore by Gd. we shoud not upon whch I propos'd to ye Councell to confine Him; according to His usuall Custom and was threatn'd with Death.' One might be disposed to discount this, were it not for the fact that the letter was also signed by Dampier, not before publicly involved in the disputes.[100]

The South Sea ships reached the Texel on 23 July 1711 and there spent dreary weeks anchored in the roadstead off Amsterdam waiting for instructions from Bristol. From Amsterdam a British agent sent Robert Harley, now Lord Treasurer, with a brief note on the ships' arrival: 'Dampier is alive, and one Captain Dover *alias* Doctor Dover seems to be the man of sense and conduct in all that affair.'[101] The owners had two distinct tasks. The first was to persuade the Admiralty to arrange to convoy the privateers and their prize to England. The second was to counter the suspicions of the East India Company that the expedition had been engaged in interloping activities within its chartered limits. The Company's directors had received advance warning of the activities of the Bristol ships from one of its captains at the Cape of Good Hope, who reported on 2 May that he thought the privateers had made 'an encroachment' on the Company's privileges. He went on to suggest to the directors that 'it might be highly advantagious to take the So Sea business into your own hands', including perhaps the opening of trade to Manila.[102] This was already a lost cause, for the same day that the letter was written at the Cape a bill was introduced in the House of Commons for a

99.   Ibid. Rogers to John Batchelor, Christopher Shuter and William [Thomas] Goldney, 8 Feb. 1711.
100. Ibid. Letters from: Rogers, 16 July 1711, off Shetland, and n.d., off Orkneys; Courtney, 'At sea', n.d. [July 1711]; Dover, near the Dutch coast [July 1711].
101. Robert Harley, *Letters and Papers*, III, in *Manuscripts of the Duke of Portland*, V (London, Historical Manuscripts Commission, 1899), p. 66.
102. OIOC: E 1/3, No. 103.

new chartered company, to be known as the South Sea Company. The East India Company watched the progress of the bill through Parliament with suspicion, but its objections were ignored, and in the end it had to be satisfied with a clause that the trade of the new Company should be limited to the Americas and to an expanse of ocean to the west not exceeding three hundred leagues.[103] The Bristol privateers were sailing, unwittingly, into a highly charged atmosphere as they neared Europe, and efforts by the Secretary of State, Henry St John, and the Attorney General, Edward Ryder, to mediate between Company and privateers failed.[104] The East India Company records for the late summer and early autumn of 1711 are full of references to the *Duke* and *Dutchess*, and to the steps to be taken to seize them once they reached home waters.[105]

Aware that the captains were on bad terms with each other, the owners sent one of their number, James Hollidge, to Amsterdam to take charge. He arrived on 7 August to find 'Captain Dover very well, Capt. Courtney out of Order wth. ye gout and Capt. Rogers under a great deal of Uneasiness . . . he seems desperate.'[106] There was a foretaste of this in one of Rogers's letters to the owners ten days earlier, where he complained that he had not heard from them and pleaded 'for Christs Sake dont lett me be torn to peices at home after I have been so rackt abroad.'[107] This brought a reassuring response from the owners, who wrote to Rogers that they hoped to meet 'any Reasonable Expectation' he might have; but clearly they were intensely suspicious of him. The same Francis Rogers who three years earlier had coped with the problem of fitting out the privateers in Cork spotted a letter from 'WR' to his mother among the mail that arrived in Bristol, and asked his associates whether he should open and read it before it was delivered.[108]

On board the ships problems grew as the weeks dragged by, and by 20 August Hollidge was reporting that 'our men are become mutinous'. Finally, in mid-September four warships arrived to convoy the ships across to England, and after further delays the privateers and what the London newspapers called 'the Aquapulca Ship' reached the Thames in the first week of October.[109] The East India Company held aloof from the general welcome, for declarations by the owners and captains that no trade had taken place at Batavia or elsewhere in the eastern seas had failed to soften its hardline attitude. It was just as well that the Company had not caught sight of a letter that Carleton Vanbrugh had written to Thomas Goldney, one of the owners,

---

103.   See OIOC: D/93, ff. 156, 158, 159, 162.
104.   See OIOC: E 1/3, No. 138.
105.   See Ibid. Nos. 204, 210; D/92, ff. 210, 211, 282.
106.   PRO: Chancery 104/60. James Hollidge to owners. Amsterdam, 7/18 Aug 1711.
107.   Ibid. Rogers to owners, 27 July 1711.
108.   Ibid. Owners to Rogers, 6 Aug. 1711; Francis Rogers to John Batchelor, Aug. 1711.
109.   See *Daily Courant*, 4 Oct. 1711; also *Post Boy*, 2–4 Oct. 1711, and *London Gazette*, 6–9 Oct. 1711. The best description of the events of these weeks is in Little, *Crusoe's Captain*, Ch. XI.

from Batavia in August 1710: 'I believe we shan't proceed directly hence for England, but try a market by the way for our Europe goods, wch. will else turn to a poor acct. I fear, if brought into Europe again.'[110] When the ships arrived in the Thames, the Company's agents were among the first to greet them and, although 'repulsed' in their attempts to board, they were at least able to throw notes of seizure onto the deck of the prize vessel.[111]

Financially, the voyage was at first sight a resounding success. It had been an expensive venture to fit out at just over £13,000, but the returns dwarfed the initial cost. The prize fund after the Spanish ship, its cargo and other assets had been disposed of amounted to £148,000,[112] though disputes about the proportions to go to the owners, officers and men not only soured any initial euphoria, but legal and other costs halved the profits (customs duties alone amounted to almost £27,000).[113] Among the extraordinary payments was one of £6000 to the East India Company to persuade it to drop its objections.[114] The cargo itself took time to sort and sell, and then there was the question of legal permission from the Chancery Court. Most was disposed of in nine sales between February and May 1713 at the Marine Coffee House, Cornhill;[115] but as late as September 1713 goods were still on offer. They ranged from bales of fabric to chests of cloves, down to 'One old Looking Glass'.[116] The Chancery Court was dealing with a whole series of interlocking disputes, which began in December 1712 and continued for several years – among the records in Chancery is an account dated 20 June 1719 which is still not the final one.[117] The problems were made more acute by the fact that both agents, Bath and Vanbrugh, had died on the voyage; accounts and copy-books had not been properly kept, or had disappeared; while some of the claimants were once more at sea. Accusations and counter-accusations, pleas and submissions, lay thick on the ground: that chests of treasure had been sold by the captains during the voyage 'after so clandestine and unfair a manner that he has no Room to doubt but it was intended the Crew shou'd be blinded and Kept in the Dark nay Defrauded' (a lawyer acting on behalf of the crew);[118] that although Thomas Dover was an owner, on the actual voyage he 'did noe service' and so was not entitled to any share as an officer (representatives of the crew);[119] that the agreement made on the voyage to pay 'Storm Money' (for storming Guayaquil and other places) was illegal (the owners);[120] that Dampier's one-

110. PRO: Chancery 104/60. Vanbrugh to Goldney, 27 Aug. 1710.
111. See OIOC: E 1/3, No. 218.
112. See Starkey, *British Privateering Enterprise*, pp. 48, 61, 65, 96, 107.
113. PRO: Chancery 104/36, Pt. I.
114. The first meeting between the owners and the Company seems to have been on 23 Nov. 1711. OIOC: D/92, f. 346.
115. PRO: Chancery 104/36, Pt. I: Account Book (beginning 27 Feb. 1712/13).
116. PRO: Chancery 104/37, Pt. I: Account Book (untitled) containing the cargo of the prize.
117. Ibid.
118. PRO: Chancery 104/160. Letter to James Hollidge, 15 Jan. 1712/13.
119. Ibid. 'Objections', 8 July 1713.
120. PRO: Chancery 104/36, Pt. II. Account Book, 1712–14, p. 31. 24 Apr. 1714.

sixteenth share should come out of the general account, not the owners' share (the owners).[121]

Not until August 1713 did the Master in Chancery feel sure enough of his ground to authorize a payment (£42.6s.od per share) on the shares held by the crew. Notices were put in newspapers, posted up at the Bank and the Exchange in the City and, more sensibly, displayed at Ratcliff, Wapping, Limehouse and Southwark, asking for seamen who had claims to come forward.[122] This marked a further stage rather than the end of the difficulties. There were seamen who had assigned their shares, or had raised credit on them, during or after the voyage; seamen who had deserted; seamen who had never sailed, but held share agreements from 1708; seamen who were back at sea; seamen who had died. Even those who were paid were disappointed at the amount. A petition from the crew to the House of Lords in the summer of 1714 alleged that the real value of the prize was £3,000,000 and that their shares should be valued accordingly at £1000 apiece. A second petition in August 1715 presented by thirty seamen and petty officers complained that their families were starving while the Master in Chancery refused to share out the proceeds of the voyage. Again, the accusation of fraud arose, with the crew claiming that the officers had sold off prize ships in the South Sea, at Batavia and at the Cape, as well as sending home 'much plate' in East India Company ships. None of this plunder had been reported to the High Court of Admiralty. 'In spite of the courage of the seamen, nearly 100 of whom lost their lives in the expedition, the owners and chief officers contrived to defraud them.' The men complained that during the four years the matter had been in Chancery the Master had refused to take evidence from them about possible embezzlement, and had made no attempt to determine the true value of the prize-money. The petition was rejected, but the repercussions were to linger.[123]

Among much else, the seamen claimed that Woodes Rogers had secreted some of the treasure, and that his departure for the Eastern Seas in 1713 was so that he could pick up his loot in Batavia.[124] Certainly, Rogers's attempts to persuade the owners to put him on the same footing as Dampier seem to have failed, and most of the £1500 or so paid to him came from his twenty-four shares as captain. Dampier's accounts are completely baffling, as is so much else relating to this enigmatic wanderer. Sorting out his one-sixteenth of the owners' share, deciding whether he also held crew shares in the venture, whether he could claim 'Storm Money' and other special payments and what exactly had been advanced to him before and during the voyage proved almost an impossible task even for the patient Master in Chancery. In

121. Ibid., p. 61.
122. Ibid., p. 11.
123. For the petitions see Rogers, 'Privateering Voyage', pp. 209–10; David L. Johnson, ed., *Manuscripts of the House of Lords*, 12 (New Ser.), *1714–1718* (London, 1977), pp. 235–6.
124. In an affidavit of 8 October 1713 Rogers denied all intention of 'piracy' and claimed that his voyage was to buy slaves in Madagascar for sale in the East Indies. OIOC: D/93, f. 511.

1717, two years after Dampier died, just over £1000 was paid to his executrix, but it is still not clear whether this was a final settlement or not.[125]

For many who had sailed on the *Duke* and *Dutchess*, 'the Success and Profit of this Long and Hazardous Voyage' (the words of Woodes Rogers in the Dedication of his book) had turned sour. What to the outside world was a spectacular triumph, in which the capture of the Manila ship made it second only to the voyages of Drake and Cavendish in terms of South Sea success, became for the seamen in the Thameside taverns and lodging-houses a byword for deception and fraud. When in 1719 the privateer *Speedwell*, bound for the South Sea, reached Brazil, its crew refused to 'stir a step' further until Captain Shelvocke agreed to their demands that any plunder should be distributed as soon as it was seized. As the crew's letter put it, 'it is known to all, how the people on board the ships *Duke* and *Dutchess* were treated, and if we carry our money to London, can expect no better treatment.'[126] Behind this, if Shelvocke is to be believed, was Simon Hatley, who had sailed with Woodes Rogers as third mate before losing company with the *Duke* and *Dutchess* in his prize bark. Hatley and four other Englishmen who were captured by the Spaniards underwent terrible hardships before finding themselves in the same Lima prison as Stradling and other survivors from the *Cinque Ports* of the Dampier expedition. After the declaration of peace in 1713 Hatley was released, only to sign on again for the South Sea in 1718 as 'second captain' to Shelvocke on the *Speedwell*. He soon reminded the crew how the sailors on the Rogers voyage were treated, 'being paid not one tenth of their due'.[127] The expectations of those who had sailed on the *Duke* and *Dutchess*, fuelled by rumour, by distrust of their officers and by the promptings of unscrupulous agents, were unrealistic; but they were long remembered.

125. See Rogers, 'Privateering Voyage', p. 208. B.M.H. Rogers found no record of Storm Money being paid to Dampier, but an account book in PRO: Chancery 104/37, Pt. II, shows that he was in fact paid £80 Storm Money (only the captains received more, £100).
126. George Shelvocke, *A Voyage Round the World* (London, 1726), pp. 31–2.
127. Ibid., p. 38.

Chapter VI

'A Gross, Palpable Illusion': The Founding of the South Sea Company

The appearance in the Thames in October 1711 of a captured Manila 'galleon', the very incarnation of the wealth of the South Sea, coincided with the enthusiasm that greeted the establishment that summer of the South Sea Company. The origins of the company are to be found more in the political and financial situation than in a genuine intention to open new overseas trade.[1] Even so, the very name of the new company, and the surge in interest that accompanied it, testify to the appeal of those distant lands and seas that had attracted generations of Englishmen since Drake. The central figure in the establishment of the company was Robert Harley, Chancellor of the Exchequer in the Tory administration that had come into office in August 1710 at a time during the war when a credit collapse had made more acute the growing problem of the 'floating' or unsecured debt, which stood at the alarming figure of £9,000,000. By late autumn Harley was considering the setting up of a new joint stock company as a way of funding this massive debt and was also in touch with William Paterson, the originator of the ill-fated Darien scheme, about 'the Indies'. By the spring of 1711 Harley seems to have reached a firm decision to link the proposed new company with the opening of trade with Spanish America, and was encouraged in this by the apparent readiness of the French Foreign Minister, the Marquis de Torcy, to accept a peace settlement that would include guarantes for British trade in the Spanish Indies as well as in Europe.[2]

1. Good accounts of the origins and history of the South Sea Company are J.G. Sperling, *The South Sea Company: An Historical Essay and Bibliographical Finding List* (Boston, 1962) and John Carswell, *The South Sea Bubble* (2nd edn, Stroud, Glos., 1993). Glyndwr Williams, ' "The Inexhaustible Fountain of Gold": English Projects and Ventures in the South Sea, 1670–1750', in John E. Flint and Glyndwr Williams, eds, *Perspectives of Empire* (London, 1973), pp. 27–53, represents my first attempt to disentangle some of the complexities surrounding the early years of the South Sea Company.
2. Robert Harley, *Letters and Papers*, II, *Manuscripts of the Duke of Portland*, IV (London, Historical Manuscripts Commission, 1897), pp. 583–4; F.G. Davenport, ed., *European Treaties Bearing on the History of the United States and its Dependencies*, III (Washington, 1929), p. 141.

25. Coat of arms
of the South Sea
Company.

On 2 May 1711 Harley presented his scheme to the House of Commons, and the next day a pamphlet was published which described the riches of South America, set out the extent of French activity there and argued in urgent terms the case for British intervention.[3] In the Commons a bill was introduced on 17 May by which the government's unsecured creditors were to be incorporated as 'the Governor and Company of Merchants of Great Britain Trading to the South Seas and other parts of America and for running the Fishery'; and on 12 June it received the royal assent. Much later, after the South Sea Bubble had burst, a contemporary observer pointed out that the project was 'a gross, palpable illusion; Nevertheless, the same being gilded over by the glittering Prospect of having a Share in the Trade of the South-Seas (by which the French got immense Riches) Mr Harley's Scheme was received with general Applause.'[4] At the time it had the appearance of a

3.   [Anon.], *A Letter to a Member of Parliament on the Resolution of the House to Settle a Trade to the South Sea* (London, 1711).
4.   Abel Boyer, *The History of the Life and Reign of Queen Anne* (London, 1722), p. 495.

master-stroke by Harley, who before the end of May had become Earl of Oxford and Lord Treasurer. He had disposed of the immediate problem of the floating debt; had founded a company with a directorate he could pack with those Tory merchants, financiers and politicians who were excluded from the Whig-dominated Bank of England and East India Company; and was sure of support from the Tory country gentry and the mercantile community for his move away from endless continental campaigns towards the more alluring prospect of war or trade, or both, in Spanish America.

Under the terms of the Act the South Sea Company's privileges were gargantuan. The company was granted:

> the sole trade and traffick into, unto, and from all the kingdoms, lands, countries, territories, islands, cities, towns, ports, havens, creeks, and places of America, on the east side thereof from the river of Aranoca, to the southermost part of the Terra del Fuego; and on the west side thereof, from the said southermost part of the said Terra del Fuego, through the South Seas, to the northermost part of America, and into, unto, and from all countries, islands, and places within the same limits, which are reported to belong to the Crown of Spain, or which shall hereafter be found out or discovered within the said limits, not exceeding three hundred leagues from the continent of America.[5]

How these paper concessions were to be transformed into commercial practice, and how they could possibly be accepted by a Spain still clinging to its doctrine of *mare clausum*, was left unsaid. As an opening move in diplomatic negotiations they might have had some merit; as part of the formal terms of establishment of a chartered company they represented fantasy rather than reality. It was doubtful if enlightenment would come either from the Company's (honorific) first governor, Harley, or from its thirty-three directors, none of whom had any experience of trade with Spanish America. A hostile versifier lampooned them in his *South Sea Whim*:

> We are a wretched motley crew,
> More various than the weather,
> Made up of debtors old and new,
> Tumbled and rocked together;
> Tars, soldiers, merchants, transport, tallies,
> Chained in a row like slaves in galleys.[6]

Such comments could be put down to the envy of the government's Whig opponents, and certainly most of the public discussion during the summer and autumn of 1711 exuded lighthearted optimism about the

5. Parliamentary Statutes: 9 Anne, cap. XXI.
6. Quoted in Carswell, *South Sea Bubble*, p. 49.

potentialities of the new company. Among Harley's papers are a number of memoranda sent to him about the South Sea and its trade at this time, some at least in response to his request for information.[7] In June one memorialist advocated both an overland trade with Chile and Peru from the Atlantic coast and a coastal trade enforced by a powerful expedition sent from England into the South Sea. Another told Harley that he could see no reason why a dozen well-armed ships should not glean as much profit along the Pacific coasts as the French had done, particularly if they could be supplied across the Isthmus. In July, Sir George Byng, future victor of Cape Passaro and at this time one of the Lords Commissioners of the Admiralty, submitted a list of practical points designed to ensure the success of any expedition sent to secure a base in the South Sea. He remarked that if Dampier's ships returned in time (a reference to the *Duke* and *Dutchess*), experienced seamen might be found in them for the new venture.

Some time during the year John Pullen, later governor of Bermuda, who claimed that he had 'convers'd with more of our Buccaneers that have been in the South Seas than any one Man of her Majesty's Subjects', wrote to Harley with advice on how to exploit the concessions – not yet granted, of course – by Spain. Earlier he had proposed the sending of a powerful squadron to the South Sea which would occupy Juan Fernández, attack Arica and Panama, seize both the westbound and eastbound galleons off Acapulco and occupy Chile.[8] A more speculative point was made by the writer of the 'Observations on the South-Sea Trade and Company', who reminded Harley that 'We have also a Right to the great Island of California, as having been first discover'd by our Country Man Sir Francis Drake', and other islands northwest of Mexico might also be worth exploring. In September Dampier's old associate from the East Indies, Thomas Bowrey, sent in a series of proposals about which ports should be seized in Spanish America.[9] A harbour on the Atlantic seaboard was essential, and his preference was for Anegada Bay in lat. 39°S., described by Drake 130 years earlier. On the Pacific coast, Valdivia was Bowrey's choice. It lay only five hundred miles overland from Anegada Bay on the Atlantic coast; the Spanish population of the region was scattered, and hemmed in by hostile Indians; the country was productive, with a temperate climate (and therefore offered good prospects for the sale of English woollens); and the hinterland was rich in gold. Like other advocates of overland trade between Pacific and Atlantic coasts, Bowrey seemed to have no knowledge of the problems presented by the Andes and other physical obstacles. Even so, pride of place among

7. Unless otherwise indicated, these memoranda are in BL: Add. MS 70,163 (no page or folio numbers).
8. See John Pullen, *Memoirs of the Maritime Affairs of Great-Britain* (London, 1732).
9. As well as copies in the Harley papers in BL: Add. MS 70,163 there are further copies in Add. MS 28,140, ff. 31–33d, and among the Bowrey Papers in the Guildhall Library, London: MS 3041/2.

the lunatic fringe of pamphleteers must go to the anonymous writer who advocated the establishment of a settlement colony on the barren, galeswept coasts of Tierra del Fuego, which he referred to as 'a fruitful and pleasant country'.[10]

A more sceptical note is to be found in an unsigned memoir of the same period among Harley's papers. The writer pointed to earlier unsuccessful attempts to establish trading contacts with South America. He described the way in which Captain Swan had been forced to turn buccaneer, and how the failure of Captain Strong's later trading venture 'utterly dismay'd the Merchants from any further Attempts'. He was full of foreboding about the fate of vessels, which after an arduous voyage might reach the South Sea to find closed ports and a hostile population. Whether he was considering the Atlantic or the Pacific seaboards, navigational hazards or trading difficulties, the writer could see little reason for optimism. The southern extremities of the continent formed 'an Iron Coast' with few harbours, and even if English vessels did secure a base farther north along the Chilean or Peruvian coasts they would find the market glutted with French goods.[11] If Harley read all the 'Essays', 'Memorials' and 'Observations' addressed to him, he would have been the best-informed man in England about the South Sea.

It was left to the cartographer-geographer Herman Moll to try to meet the particular demand for reliable information about the vast region that lay within the charter rights of the South Sea Company. Moll was one of a group of geographers, navigators and writers that often met at Jonathan's Coffeehouse in Change Alley, and whose interest in the South Sea extended back to the 1690s.[12] He was responsible for the maps in many of the best-known 'voyages' of the period, including Dampier's *New Voyage* (1697), Hack's *Collection of Original Voyages* (1699), Funnell's *Voyage Round the World* (1707) and Rogers's *Cruising Voyage* (1712). He drew on much of the knowledge he had acquired over the previous fifteen years to produce in 1711 two editions of *A View of the Coasts, Countrys, & Islands within the Limits of the South-Sea Company*. His sources were mostly English, and printed; for someone with so wide a range of contacts, it is surprising that he seems to have had no access to, or at least to have made no use of, any of the manuscript copies of Hack's great 'South Sea Waggoner'. In Moll's work the deficiencies of the buccaneers' accounts were plain to see. It would have been a rash seaman who took his vessel into the Bay of Guayaquil with Moll's book as his only guide: 'If you fall in there in the Night, keep your head going, and mind your depth, till you either can get out, or with

10. See Anon., *The Considerable Advantages of a South-Sea Trade to our English Nation* (London, c. 1711).
11. BL: Add. MS 70,164 (no page numbers).
12. See Dennis Reinhartz, 'Shared Vision: Herman Moll and his Intellectual Circle and the Great South Sea', *Terrae Incognitae*, 19 (1988), pp. 1–10.

Conveniency come to an Anchor.'[13] Moll was under no illusions about the inadequacies of his sources, lacking as they did 'exactness, accuracy and curiosity'. Cowley on one voyage, and Sharp on another, were criticized for their 'Vanity' in altering the names of places on their charts, 'to the puzling those that use 'em'. As Woodes Rogers complained a few months later, the flamboyance of the buccaneers' accounts gave a misleading impression of English enterprise in the South Sea. It was

> a particular Mistake which attends Voyages to the South-Sea, that the Bucca-
> neers, to set off their own Knight-Errantry, and to make themselves pass for
> Prodigies of Courage and Conduct, have given such romantick Accounts of
> their Adventures, and had such strange Stories, as to make the Voyages of
> those who came after (and cannot allow themselves the same liberty) to look
> flat and insipid to unthinking people.[14]

Though Moll made intelligent use of the voyage narratives to produce a comprehensive survey which he hoped would be of value to navigators and merchants alike, his main aim was to reveal 'the Countries, Commerce and Riches which are the Subject of our present Views and Expectations'. Chile was singled out as 'that part of the Continent of South America that most tempts the Europeans to try their Fortunes there, and is on many Accounts the properest Place for Settlements.'[15] The frontispiece of the book displayed an early version of what one scholar has called 'Moll's greatest contribution to the vision of the South Sea',[16] his 'New & Exact Map of the Coast, Countries and Islands within ye Limits of ye South Sea Company', dedicated to Robert Harley (Ill. 26). It showed the Pacific coasts of South and Central America in as much detail as any map of the time; its insets depicted some of the more important ports and islands; and a dotted line marked the extent of the South Sea Company's charter privileges. To its readers it presented in vivid form the opportunities that seemed to await Britain and its traders, and such was the demand for copies that Moll complained that they 'were being pirated to Holland, reprinted there, and resold in London at a profit'.[17]

Interest in the new company and its potential was stimulated by lively press comment. The lapsing of the Licensing Act in 1695 had given rise to a new generation of newspapers, many of them politically partisan. To the *London Gazette*, the only newspaper regularly published before 1695, could be added another twenty or so newspapers by 1711. In addition, an array of

---

13. This and the next two quotations are from [Herman Moll], *A View of the Coasts, Countrys, & Islands within the Limits of the South-Sea Company* (2nd edn, London, 1711), pp. 113, 137, 124.
14. Rogers, *Cruising Voyage*, p. xvi.
15. Moll, *View*, preface, p. 43.
16. Reinhartz, 'Shared Vision', p. 5.
17. Burton J. Fishman, 'Defoe, Herman Moll and the Geography of South America', *Huntington Library Quarterly*, 36 (1973), p. 236.

26. Herman Moll. Map showing the limits of the South Sea Company, 1711.

literary talent found outlet in the new periodicals of the period – Swift's
Examiner, Defoe's *Review* and Steele's *Tatler*. In these public prints the fullest
and most perceptive discussion of the South Sea matter apppeared in the
pages of Defoe's thrice-weekly *Review*, founded in 1704 to lend journalistic
support to Harley's political ambitions.[18]

For all his long-standing interest in the South Sea, Defoe's position was an
awkward one. Although uneasy about some of the policies and personalities
of the new Tory administration, he was trying to re-establish close relations
with Harley. At the same time, he was concerned about several features of
the new company and the adulatory public response to its launch. He had to
pick his way with care between 'your wild Expectations on the one Hand,
or your Phlegmatick Discouraging Notions on the other', and did not
mention the scheme until the issue of 28 June 1711, eight weeks after
Harley's introduction of the subject in the House of Commons. There is no
evidence that Harley had consulted Defoe about his scheme. Between early
March and early August 1711 the two men did not meet, and no correspondence exists between them from early March to early June.[19] In a letter of 26
June to Harley, Defoe's tone is one of reproach: 'I would gladly have spoken
six words to your Lordship on the subject of the South Sea affair, in which
I persuade myself I might do some service in print.'[20] In four consecutive
numbers of the *Review* Defoe limited himself to a factual account of the trade
of Spanish America, which forms as good a summary of the state of informed
knowledge as can be found in any English publication, provided one ignores
those passages where Defoe's fear of French activities in the South Sea led
him into the realms of fantasy. The French, he wrote, had taken possession
of Lima, were fortifying bases along the coast and had been promised any
unoccupied regions they wanted south of Potosí. At the time of writing, fifty
French ships were on the Pacific coast and would each bring home up to
£200,000 in silver, thereby allowing Louis XIV to wage war indefinitely. As
long as the war continued, French influence would stiffen Spanish resistance
in America to English interlopers, and even when peace came Defoe could
not envisage any reversal by Spain of her traditional policy of exclusion.
'New Spain is the Spouse of Old Spain, and they will no more prostrate her
to be debauch'd in Trade by us, than they, the most Jealous People in the
World, should allow us to come to Bed their Wives.' He derided current
speculation that convoys would soon be leaving England for South America
and within a matter of months would 'bring Home Potosi, and the Gold of
the Andes'. Rather, any attempt to break into the trade of Chile, Peru and
Mexico would meet countermeasures, both against the English and any

18.   The relevant issues in the summer of 1711 are *Review of the State of the British Nation*: no. 41,
      28 June; no. 42, 30 June; no. 43, 3 July; no. 44, 5 July; no. 45, 7 July; no. 47, 12 July; no. 49,
      17 July; no. 50, 19 July; no. 53, 26 July; no. 54, 28 July; no. 58, 7 August; no. 68, 30 August.
19.   See J.R. Moore, 'Defoe and the South Sea Company', *Boston Public Library Quarterly*, 5 (1953),
      p. 177.
20.   Ibid., p. 182.

Spaniards who had been tempted to trade with them. Under these conditions a profitable trade would be impossible.

Defoe did not put forward his own proposals until the *Review* of 17 July, and even then they were presented in a way that was guarded and vague. Instead of incursions into Spanish-held territories, he supported the establishment of a trade along the Pacific coast 'without Injuring, Encroaching on, or perhaps in the least Invading the Property or Commerce of the Spaniards', but the location of such an area of trade was nowhere mentioned. The reason for his secretiveness was revealed in a letter of the same date to Harley in which he explained: 'I have put a Stop to what I was saying in Print Till I may kno' if my Thoughts are of any Consideration in your Ldpps Judgemt.'[21] In this, and two other letters to Harley in the next week, Defoe gave more details of his plan. This proved little more than a copy of the scheme he had put to William III ten years earlier advocating the settling of colonies in Chile and on the Atlantic coast of southeast America, well away from the main centres of Spanish power. The Chilean colony would form the lynchpin of the new trade, with its temperate climate, friendly Indians, fertile land and gold mines. With the opportunities it offered for private trade it would play in the South Sea the role of Jamaica in the Caribbean – 'Tho' the Spaniards will Not Open Their Ports and Markets for us to Sell, we Shall allways have an Open Port and Market for Them to buy.'[22]

Harley's reaction to these proposals is not known, but it could not have reassured Defoe, for in the late summer of 1711 he launched an open attack on the very essence of the minister's South Sea scheme. In later numbers of the *Review*, and in his *Essay on the South-Sea Trade*, published in September, he lamented lost opportunities:

> There has not been in our Memory an Undertaking of such Consequence, and so generally to be engaged in; nor has there been an Undertaking, about which the People, even those who are to be concern'd, have been so uneasie, their Opinions of it so confused, and their Knowledge of the Manner and Circumstances of it so small . . . How this Golden Ball, now it is in our Hands, [is] toss'd up and down among us, with Contempt, with Regret, with Reproach; Envy on the one Hand, Stock-Jobbing on the other, and ill Management on both Hands.[23]

Defoe regretted that the whole South Sea project had become entangled in the fierce political conflicts of the day, 'Party-curst' as he put it. The problem of the floating debt and the opening of Spanish America had become fused, and the attempt by the politicians 'to cure them both with One Plaister, or as we say more vulgarly, Kill both these Birds with One Stone' threatened

---

21. Defoe to Harley, 17 July 1711; printed in Healey, *Letters of Defoe*, p. 338.
22. Defoe to Harley, 23 July 1711; ibid., pp. 347–8.
23. [Defoe], *Essay on the South-Sea Trade*, p. 5; *Review*, no. 68, 30 Aug. 1711.

disaster. Although disillusioned with the government's approach, Defoe retained his belief in the potential of the Pacific trade:

> not only probably to be Great, but capable of being the Greatest, most Valuable, most Profitable, and most Encreasing Branch of Trade in our whole British Commerce . . . a Trade, which had it been offered to the Merchandizing Part of Mankind, who understand Trade, who were emply'd in Commerce, and accustom'd to Adventures, and not unhappily join'd in and tied down to a Rabble of casual Subscribers, neither inclin'd to, capable of, or in the least having a Genius to trade, it would no doubt have met with another kind of Reception than now it has.[24]

Again, the location of his own preferred region of settlement was not specified, but it was an open secret that it was Chile. The reasoning that tempted Defoe and his associates towards that part of Spanish America was by now clear. Unlike Peru and New Spain, its key ports were only thinly held by the Spaniards, and much of it was not under Spanish control at all. A colony in Chile, perhaps linked with a settlement on the opposite Atlantic coast, would change the whole tenor and thrust of the English approach to the South Sea. No longer would it be a matter of privateering or plundering expeditions, of raids on coasts and shipping, of ventures warlike and often disreputable in character. Instead, what was envisaged was a release of English capital and skill in an environment with immense natural advantages which had been shamefully neglected by the Spaniards. The new venture would redound to the wealth and power of the nation, even if there was no tapping into Spanish commerce to the north. There was a lack of realism about much of this, but in essence the plans of Defoe, Moll and the rest looked forward, not back. To them, the images of Drake, Manila galleons, ransoms and prizes had little relevance in the coming age of more constructive British enterprise in the South Sea.

Away from the flurries of pamphlets and memorials, the fate of all the South Sea schemes depended on the peace negotiations upon which Harley had staked his political future. Diplomatic conversations between Matthew Prior and the Marquis de Torcy during the summer of 1711 had revealed the difficulties of turning the hints by the French in the spring about guarantees for British commerce into specific concessions. Defoe soon got wind of this and wrote to Harley warning him against 'laying any (or not so great) weight on an immediate commerce through the Spanish dominions (which people have already a notion cannot be obtained)'.[25] British attempts to secure four bases, two in the Caribbean and two on the Pacific coast of South America,

24. [Defoe], *Essay on the South-Sea Trade*, pp. 37–8.
25. *Harley Letters*, III, *Portland Manuscripts*, V, p. 67.

were rebuffed; and the possibility that Juan Fernández could be offered
instead soon disappeared when the French negotiators speculated that under
its new masters it might become 'the greatest entrepot in the world for the
manufactures of Europe and Asia'. Torcy's hostile response to successive
British suggestions reduced Prior to despair. 'My heart ached extremely and
I was ready to sink,' he reported home. Torcy brought the negotiations to an
end with a blunt warning to Prior that 'Your demands in the Indies are
such as the crown of Spain, by all the laws, maxims, and interests of the
kingdom, can never consent to.'[26] Faced with this refusal to negotiate on the
matter of Spanish American bases, the Harley government dropped its
demands, and in October it accepted instead a fifteen-percent reduction in
the duties on English goods entering Spain, and the transfer of the *asiento* (the
agreement to supply slaves to Spanish America) from France to Britain for
thirty years.[27]

This limited concession was a far cry from the ambitious hopes of domi-
nating a vast market from Chile to Mexico that had accompanied the
formation of the South Sea Company only a few months earlier. Ironically,
it was at this moment that the return of the *Duke* and *Dutchess* from the
Pacific, complete with their Manila prize and a balance-sheet showing a
healthy profit, seemed to justify the enthusiasts for commercial enterprise in
the South Sea. Rogers and the second captain of the *Dutchess*, Edward
Cooke, spent the winter writing rival accounts of the venture, and these
were published in 1712. Cooke's two volumes were dedicated to Harley, a
gesture that prompted Admiral John Baker to put into verse the enthusiasm
of the moment for Harley's scheme:

> Our Trade revives, our Traffick doth prevail
> Wealth shall imported and Exported be
> To unknown Coasts, Britannia's Fleets shall Sail
> And always Ride in a Pacific Sea.

Both Rogers and Cooke stressed the potential of Chile for settlement,
though on the voyage they had seen nothing of it. They did have the
advantage of having at their disposal the translation in the *Collection of Voyages
and Travels* recently issued by Awnsham and John Churchill of part of the
history of Chile by Alonso de Ovalle, first published in 1646. Generally they
repeated the arguments of Defoe, Bowrey and Moll, and before them
Narborough (whose narrative had been reprinted in 1711). Once more,
readers heard how in these southern reaches of Spain's Pacific empire the
climate was healthy; the Spaniards were few, and intimidated by the Indians;

26. See ibid., pp. 34–41; L.G. Wickham Legge, 'Torcy's Account of Matthew Prior's Negotia-
     tions . . . in July 1711', *English Historical Review*, 29 (1914), pp. 525–32; Spate, *Monopolists and
     Freebooters*, p. 200.
27. Davenport, *Treaties*, III, pp. 147–51.

and in the interior were mines of gold and silver. Most of the second volume of Cooke's account was taken up with a description of the coasts of the South Sea from the Strait of Magellan to Acapulco,[28] using information from sailing directions or Waggoners seized on the Manila ship in 1709 – the equivalent of Sharp's great trophy of 1681, but this time made public. Cooke also reproduced a large number of Spanish charts, coastal profiles and plans of harbours to give the most detailed and up-to-date guide available in English at this time. In Cooke's more general sections, it was again Chile that took pride of place: 'one of, if not the wealthiest and most delightful Provinces in the Universe'; 'the most happy Country in the World for Temperature of Air'; 'the subterraneous Wealth is immense, consisting in Mines of Gold, Silver, Copper, Tin, Quick-silver, and Lead.'[29]

In his book Rogers shifted the emphasis a little from the current preoccupation with Spanish America to wider oceanic exploration. He acknowledged that he had no 'new and wonderful Discoveries' to put before his readers, since the voyage was 'only design'd for cruising on the Enemy'; but this did not prevent him from speculating:

> I have often admir'd that no considerable Discoveries have yet been made in South Latitude from America to the East Indies: I never heard the South Ocean has been run over by above three or four Navigators, who varied little in their Runs from their Course, and by consequence could not discover much. I give this Hint to encourage our South Sea Company, or others, to go upon some Discovery that way, where for ought we know they may find a better Country than any yet discover'd, there being a vast Surface of the Sea from the Equinox to the South Pole, of at least 2000 Leagues in Longitude that has hitherto been little regarded, tho it be agreeable to Reason, that there must be a Body of Land about the South Pole, to counterpoise those vast Countries about the North Pole.[30]

During the winter months both Rogers and Cooke were consulted by the South Sea Company. Cooke submitted a list of the best harbours on the Pacific coast and advised that a trading factory might be set up at either Valdivia or Juan Fernández.[31] Bound up immediately in front of Cooke's report is a manuscript 'Essay on the Nature and Methods of Carrying on a Trade to the South Sea', written by Robert Allen, a Scottish survivor from Darien who had subsequently worked for the Spaniards in Quito, Guayaquil and Panama.[32] He was able to give first-hand evidence of the French

28. Cooke, *Voyage to the South Sea*, II, pp. 109–328.
29. Ibid., I, pp. 49, 61, 62.
30. Rogers, *Cruising Voyage*, pp. 314–15.
31. BL: Add. MS 28,140, ff. 29–30.
32. See J.D. Alsop, 'A Darien Epilogue: Robert Allen in Spanish America, 1698–1707', *The Americas*, 43 (1986), pp. 197–201.

penetration of the Peruvian market. On the fly-leaf of the essay is scribbled the name Hubert Tassell, which is intriguing, for Tassell later became a factor of the South Sea Company and in 1740 sailed on Anson's circumnavigation.[33] Rogers for his part met the sub-governor of the Company, Sir James Bateman, and notes of their conversation have survived.[34] Rogers gave much practical advice about the dispatch of an expedition to the South Sea, and there are indications that if one had gone he would have sailed with it. With him, possibly, might have sailed Alexander Selkirk, for on 3 July 1712 the Court of Chancery, enquiring into Dampier's conduct on the *St George/ Cinque Ports* voyage, heard that Selkirk was 'a material witness . . . in a short time going a long voyage to some remote Isles beyond the Seas'.[35] In consulting Cooke and Rogers, the Company seems to have been prompted by more than idle curiosity; and one of the most baffling aspects of the convoluted early years of the Company's existence is the evidence that throughout 1712 it was collaborating with ministers to send an expedition of force to the Pacific coasts of Spanish America – despite the diplomatic decisions of the previous autumn that seemed to have put an end to the hope of securing bases, or even trade, in the region.

The evidence is contained in the minutes and letter-books of the Court of Directors, which show that at the end of January 1712 the Company submitted a plan to Harley for an expedition to the South Sea.[36] It was to be of prodigious size: one eighty-gun ship; four of seventy; five of sixty; five of fifty; two of forty; three of fewer than forty; forty transports; bomb vessels; hospital ships; and four thousand soldiers. For its part the Company would supply merchantmen and cargoes. What exactly this sledgehammer of an expedition was intended to do was not made clear, though the directors hoped (quite unrealistically) that the ships would be ready to sail by mid-June. The year before they had acquired one of William Hack's copies of the great Waggoner seized by Sharp in 1681, and this may have excited them.[37] In March, Secretary of State Henry St John wrote pledging government support for 'their making a Settlement in the South Seas for their security and better carrying on the Trade to those Parts', but his letter was studiously vague about the size, destination and date of departure of the force.[38] Further minutes show the directors busy hiring vessels and men and collecting cargo; but by May they were showing signs of anxiety about the government's silence. Letters written 'in pressing Terms' to Harley and the Queen, about the lateness of the season and the fact that the Company had laid out £120,000 in trading goods, evidently brought no response; and the only

33. See Chap. IX below.
34. BL: Add. MS 28,140, f. 30.
35. PRO: Chancery 33/317, f. 451v.
36. BL: Add. MS 25,559, ff. 8d–9.
37. See Howse and Thrower, *A Buccaneer's Atlas*, Table 3.
38. BL: Add. MS 25,494, ff. 66, 68.

other mention of the venture comes in a reproachful note of February 1713 which informed Harley that the cargoes bought the previous year would soon decay unless they were sold.[39]

It is difficult to see rhyme or reason behind this exercise. Time and money had been spent in organizing an expedition that was never likely to sail after the diplomatic agreements of the previous autumn. Why Harley and St John allowed the farce to continue, and why the directors devoted energy to playing it out, is a mystery. It may have been connected with the jockeying for position within the government of the two politicians. Possibly the paper expedition was intended as a reminder to France and Spain of the likely consequences of a breakdown in the negotiations for a definitive peace treaty that had begun at Utrecht in January 1712. Whatever the explanation, the projected expedition was the first and last attempt by the South Sea Company to take advantage of the Pacific privileges outlined in the Act of 1711. In putative size it exceeded the wildest dreams of the South Sea fantasists. For more sober men, the thought of a hurriedly mounted expedition of sixty or so warships and transports, together with an unknown number of merchantmen, attempting the Cape Horn route into the Pacific was a chilling prospect. It was as well that the attention of the Company turned to the more realistic, if still difficult, business of exploiting its *asiento* concession.

---

39. Ibid., ff. 69, 69d, 75, 78, 87, 89, 93, 94; Add. MS 25,559, ff. 8, 9, 10–11, 14.

Chapter VII

The Age of the Bubble (1): Castaways and Projectors

As a peace of exhaustion settled over the warring nations of Europe in 1712–13, practical men of business in England abandoned schemes for trading into the South Sea. Others were less willing to give up their fascination with a region that seemed to promise so much. The editorial preface to the *Collection of Voyages and Travels* published by Awnsham and John Churchill in 1704 had stressed the double utility of travel accounts – 'as an incentive to stir up another to imitate him, while the rest of mankind, without stirring a foot, compass the earth and seas, visit all countries, and converse with all nations'.[1] It was this second possibility, later described by Defoe in his *Compleat English Gentleman* as the ability to make 'the tour of the world in books . . . [to] go round the globe with Dampier and Rogers',[2] that began to exert an influence over writers and readers alike in the years after the founding of the South Sea Company. So, for the time being at least, the narratives by Woodes Rogers and Edward Cooke of their recent privateering expedition to the South Sea seemed less important as guides for further ventures than as revelations of worlds and events that appealed to the imagination. In the rescue of Alexander Selkirk from his lonely sojourn on Juan Fernández enterprise in the South Sea took on a new and dramatic shape.

Scholarly interest in tracing the links between Selkirk's experiences and Defoe's *Robinson Crusoe* (1719) has tended to obscure the more immediate contemporary interest in the story. The title-pages of the books of both Rogers and Cooke show that Selkirk's island exile was expected to be a selling point fit to be set alongside the taking of the Manila ship. First to be published in March 1712 was Volume I of Cooke's *Voyage to the South Sea*, which covered the events of the voyage up to the capture of the galleon. Among these, the title-page proclaimed, 'an ACCOUNT is given of Mr.

---

1. The introduction to the Churchill collection may have been written by John Locke. See Steele, *Interpreters*, pp. 113–14.
2. Quoted in Earle, *World of Defoe*, p. 47.

Alexander Selkirk, his Manner of living and taming some wild Beasts during the four Years and four Months he liv'd upon the uninhabited Island of *Juan Fernandes*'. The title-page of Rogers's single-volume *Cruising Voyage Round the World*, published at the end of June, also promised 'An Account of *Alexander Selkirk's* living alone four Years and four Months in an Island' and devoted seven pages to the episode.

As told in Rogers's book, the story unfolds – for an unsuspecting reader at least – with a strong element of tension. Juan Fernández was sighted at 7 am on the morning of 31 January 1709 (ship's time),[3] with some among the more sickly members of the crews near death. At 2 pm in the afternoon, although the island was still four leagues distant, Thomas Dover insisted on taking the pinnace ashore, much 'against my Inclination', Rogers wrote.[4] An impending sense of danger grew as darkness fell and a light appeared on the land, with the pinnace still a league offshore and the wind rising. The fear on board the ships was that the French were in occupation of the island and that 'we must either fight 'em or want Water'. The pinnace turned back as soon as the light was spotted, but it was late at night before Dover and his men got back on board the *Duke*. The next morning, in gusting winds, the ship's yawl was sent in to investigate, followed by the pinnace when the first boat failed to return. The delay was explained when 'our Pinnace return'd from the shore and brought abundance of Craw-fish, with a Man cloth'd in Goat-Skins, who looked wilder than the first Owners of them.' In this way – crayfish first, wild man second – Rogers's readers were introduced to Alexander Selkirk, the castaway sailing master of the *Cinque Ports*. 'The Governour', as he was called ('tho we might as well have nam'd him the Absolute Monarch of the Island') proved a useful acquisition. On the recommendation of Dampier, who of course had known him on the *Cinque Ports*, he was appointed mate, and in the meantime he made himself useful by catching goats whose meat made a nourishing broth for the sick. There would have been eagerness to hear his story, though his telling of it must have been a slow and halting business; for 'at his first coming on board us, he had so much forgot his Language for want of Use, that we could scarce understand him, for he seem'd to speak his words by halves.'

He had several times seen sails out to sea, but on the only occasion when ships anchored they had proved to be Spanish, and he had to flee for his life. Rogers's account of what they heard from Selkirk was a miscellany of information, but a single paragraph contained the central experience of Selkirk's solitary existence:

---

3. Until 1805 nautical or ship's time differed from civil time in that the twenty-four-hour day extended from noon to noon, not midnight to midnight. Rogers kept to ship's time even in the published version of his journal, explaining that 'Every day's Transactions begin at the foregoing Day about twelve a clock, and end at the same Hour the following Day carrying that Date.' *Cruising Voyage*, p. 2.

4. The quotations in the following paragraphs are taken from Rogers, *Cruising Voyage*, pp. 123–31.

He had with him his Clothes and Bedding, with a Fire-lock, some Powder, Bullets, and Tobacco, a Hatchet, a Knife, a Kettle, a Bible, some practical Pieces, and his Mathematical Instruments and Books. He diverted and provided for himself as well as he could; but for the first eight months he had much ado to bear up against Melancholy, and the Terror of being left alone in such a desolate place. He built two Hutts with Piemento Trees, cover'd them with long Grass, and lin'd them with the Skins of Goats, which he kill'd with his Gun as he wanted, so long as his Powder lasted, which was but a pound; and that being near spent, he got fire by rubbing two sticks of Piemento Wood together upon his knee. In the lesser Hutt, at some distance from the other, he dress'd his Victuals, and in the larger he slept, and employ'd himself in reading, singing Psalms, and praying; so that he said he was a better Christian while in this Solitude than he ever was before, or than, he was afraid, he should ever be again. At first he never eat any thing till Hunger constrain'd him, partly for grief and partly for want of Bread and Salt; nor did he go to bed till he could watch no longer.

Further details followed. Once his powder was exhausted and his shoes worn out, Selkirk caught goats by chasing them across the rocky terrain in his bare feet. He made clothes for himself out of goat skins and linen cloth, using an iron nail for a needle and making a knife out of iron hoops. To deal with the rats that had come ashore from the ships, he tamed some of the cats that had also found their way off the ships until hundreds of them surrounded him in a cordon as he slept. For relaxation, apart from carving his name and the date on trees, Selkirk made the most of local resources as he 'tam'd some Kids, and to divert himself would now and then sing and dance with them and his Cats.' After this dip into sentimentality Rogers settled back with some conventional moralizing:

By this one may see that Solitude and Retirement from the World is not such an unsufferable State of Life as most Men imagine, especially when People are fairly call'd or thrown into it unavoidably, as this Man was . . . We may perceive by this Story the Truth of the Maxim, That Necessity is the Mother of Invention, since he found means to supply his Wants in a very natural manner, so as to maintain his Life, tho not so conveniently, yet as effectually as we are able to do with the help of all our Arts and Society. It may likewise instruct us, how much a plain and temperate way of living conduces to the Health of the Body and the Vigour of the Mind, both of which we are apt to destroy by Excess and Plenty, especially of strong Liquor, and the Variety as well as the Nature of our Meat and Drink: for this Man, when he came to our ordinary Method of Diet and Life, tho he was sober enough, lost much of his Strength and Agility. But I must quit these Reflections, which are more proper for a Philosopher and Divine than a Mariner.

Much has been made of the links between Selkirk's experiences and those of Robinson Crusoe. From a different perspective, if we look back from Selkirk rather than forward from him to Crusoe, his story forms the climax to a sequence of castaway narratives on Juan Fernández, perfect in shape and form. Many of the elements of his story are there in the personal histories of those in front of him in the queue of castaways – the resourcefulness shown by 'Will', marooned for three years with far less in the way of material resources than Selkirk; the turning to religion for consolation of the four buccaneers set ashore from Davis's *Batchelor's Delight*, who were, like Selkirk, kings of all they surveyed.

Given the greater prominence that Edward Cooke, at least on the title-page of his account, seemed to attach to the Selkirk story, it is surprising to find his first volume dedicating only a few lines to the castaway. Oddly, he gave more space to the rather stale story of 'Will' on Juan Fernández, copied from Dampier. This cursory treatment was evidently not to the liking of Cooke's readers, for in the second volume, rushed out in June 1712 (and forestalling Rogers's book by a few weeks), he acknowledged complaints that 'That short Hint rais'd the Curiosity of some Persons to expect a more particular Relation.' In defence of the lack of attention he had given Selkirk, Cooke asked: 'Is he a natural Philosopher, who, by such an undisturb'd Retirement, could make any surprizing Discoveries? Nothing less, we have a downright Sailor, whose only Study was how to support himself, during his Confinement, and all his Conversation with Goats.'[5] Despite these caveats, rather grudgingly, and with asides to the effect that 'it is the most barren Subject', Cooke relented enough to give more details about Selkirk's stay on the island and his rescue. Of most interest – for it was not mentioned by Rogers – was the evidence of Selkirk's intense dislike of one of the officers on the *Duke* or the *Dutchess*. On his first encounter with the boat's crew he was reluctant to be taken out to the *Duke*:

> he first enquir'd whether a certain Officer that he knew was Aboard; and hearing that he was, would rather have chosen to remain in his Solitude, than come away with him, 'till informed that he did not command . . . They had much Difficulty to perswade him to venture himself Aboard, so great was the Aversion he had conceiv'd against the Officer aforesaid; yet, upon Promise of being restor'd to his former Dwelling, if not satisfy'd, he at length comply'd.[6]

Most commentators have taken it for granted that the officer concerned was Dampier, who might well have been expected to be in command of the expedition (as the Spaniards in the region assumed). Certainly the quarrels on both his previous expeditions had shown him to be a man who made

5. Cooke, *Voyage to South Sea*, II, p. xix.
6. Ibid., pp. xx–xxi.

enemies easily. Yet there are puzzling aspects about this episode. Despite Selkirk's critical deposition of 1712, there is no evidence of bad relations between Dampier and Selkirk on the St George/Cinque Ports voyage, though there were enough witnesses hostile to Dampier to recall any such. Instead, it was Stradling whose behaviour provoked Selkirk to the point of abandoning the Cinque Ports at Juan Fernández. After Selkirk came on board the Duke at Juan Fernández there seems to have been no attempt to keep him on a different ship from Dampier, though this would have been easy enough to arrange. Finally, there is the brief but telling compliment by Dampier that Selkirk had been the 'best man' on the Cinque Ports.[7]

The continuing interest in the castaway's experience is shown by the account given by the essayist and politician Richard Steele in his periodical The Englishman.[8] Although not published until December 1713, the piece was based on conversations Steele had with Selkirk soon after his return two years earlier, and it contains material not in the Rogers and Cooke books. The story of the dancing goats was put into a more practical context when Selkirk explained that he had goats around him because he had lamed them when they were kids so as to have a constant food supply to hand. Selkirk was even more emphatic that his problems on the island were those of loneliness rather than physical necessity – 'the Desire of Society' and 'eager Longings for seeing again the Face of Man'. Deprived of company, he 'grew dejected, languid, and melancholy, scarce able to refrain from doing himself Violence, till by Degrees, by the Force of Reason, and frequent reading of the Scriptures, and turning his Thoughts upon the Study of Navigation, after the Space of eighteen Months, he grew thoroughly reconciled to his Condition.' So acceptable did he find his 'Disengagement from the World' that his initial reaction on seeing the English ships was how he could help their crews rather than the opportunity for rescue which they presented. For Steele the Selkirk experience provided evidence of the happiness of man in a state of nature, and his concluding sentences can be placed with many other examples of nostalgic escapism that crowd this period: 'This plain Man's Story is a memorable Example, that he is happiest who confines his Wants to natural Necessities; and that he goes further in his Desires, increases his Wants in Proportion to his Acquisitions; or to use his own Expression, I am now worth 800 Pounds, but shall never be so happy, as when I was not worth a Farthing.' The events of Selkirk's few remaining years added poignancy to this reflection, for before he died in 1721 he had been summoned for assault in Bristol and on a charge of bigamy in Plymouth.[9]

This is not the place to venture into the thickets of scholarship that surround the issue of the sources used by Defoe for Robinson Crsuoe. That the story of Alexander Selkirk was known to Defoe and provided material for

7. Rogers, Cruising Voyage, p. 125.
8. Printed in Rae Blanchard, ed., The Englishman (Oxford, 1955), pp. 106–9.
9. See Little, Crusoe's Captain, p. 160.

Crusoe's experiences seems beyond dispute. In the same way material from Dampier's *New Voyage*, and his later writings, helped Defoe with some of the detail both of *Robinson Crusoe* and of the second part, *The Further Adventures of Robinson Crusoe*, published later in 1719.[10] What degree of primacy can be given to Selkirk, as against a host of rival claimants, ranging from Robert Knox, whose *Historical Relation of Ceylon* (1681) is alleged to have the main inspiration, to the Dutch Crusoe described in Hendrik Smeek's *Krinke Kesmes* (1708), is a different and more difficult matter.[11] For all his interest in the South Sea, Defoe made a conscious decision to distance the travels of Crusoe from that region, not only in the location of his original island, set somewhere off the mouth of the Orinoco, but in his subsequent wanderings. In *The Further Adventures* these took Crusoe across the Indian Ocean, into the East Indies, and through Asia, but at no point did he touch the Pacific. It was only in his last novel, *A New Voyage Round the World* (1724), that Defoe again returned to the South Sea, but the didactic thrust of that book shows that he had lost none of his earlier interest in the region.

The experiences, real or fictional, of 'Will', Selkirk, Crusoe and the rest brought a new emphasis to perceptions of the South Sea, in that islands rather than continents became the object of attention. It was a reversion in one sense to the fascination with the Solomons which marked the earlier period of Spanish exploration, an extension in another sense of utopian romances such as Nevile's *Island of Pines*. For mariners islands had always held a double significance. Looming out of open water they posed a threat to any ship, especially if their presence was unknown or unsuspected. But on the long ocean voyages to and across the Pacific they also represented a haven for crews short of food and water, and often suffering from scurvy. Guam in the North Pacific, Juan Fernández in the South Pacific became standard calling places for ships of all nations. For English buccaneers and privateers Juan Fernández also had the advantage that the Spaniards had not occupied it, and it was known to have plenty of goats, seals and turtles. Finding it, however, was not always easy. As late as 1709, after thirty years of visits by English ships, Woodes Rogers noted that 'We are very uncertain of the Latitude and Longitude of *Juan Fernandez*, the Books laying 'em down so differently, that not one Chart agrees with another; and being but a small Island, we are in some doubts of striking it.'[12] Whether in despair or out of frivolity, John Seller in his 'Chart of the South-Sea' (1675) had marked a 'Flying Island' in mid-Pacific, almost a prefiguration of Gulliver's Laputa.

Farther north, straddling the equator, the Galapagos Islands offered another

10. See Pat Rogers, *Robinson Crusoe* (London, 1979), pp. 30–2.
11. As a general investigation A.W. Secord, *Studies in the Narrative Method of Defoe* (Urbana, IL, 1924; repr. New York, 1963) still holds much value. One of the most recent among many books that challenge Secord's conclusions is David Fausett, *The Strange Surprizing Sources of Robinson Crusoe* (Amsterdam and Atlanta, GA, 1994).
12. Rogers, *Cruising Voyage*, p. 122.

possible refuge for predators. They were near enough to the mainland to allow a descent within a few days, distant enough to offer security from Spanish forces. The Galapagos group possessed an overlay of mystery, almost of magic. Accidentally discovered by the Spaniards in 1535, they were first called the 'Islas Encantadas', or Enchanted Isles, and then (on the great Ortelius world map of 1570) 'Insulae de los Galepego' after the giant tortoises found there.[13] Their location on the Cowley map printed in Hack's *Collection* of 1699 had little more than a two-degree error in longitude (reasonably good for the period); yet the archipelago proved remarkably hard to find. Spanish prisoners on board Cowley and Eaton's ships in 1684 followed the example of Sharp's captives in 1680 with a series of tales designed to deter their captors from making for the islands.[14] Dampier, who had been with Cowley, further muddied the waters with his insistence that the maps showed the islands too near the mainland, and it needed much embarrassing tacking backwards and forwards with Woodes Rogers in 1709 before he would admit that he was a couple of hundred miles out.[15] Moll grumbled more than once at the errors and inconsistencies in Dampier's books, but thought such were inevitable as long as men of 'Learning and Judgment' were reluctant 'to expose themselves so long to the Hardships, Terrors and Barbarous Conversation of the Sea'.[16] He kept his severest censure for the way in which Dampier's buccaneering associates, especially Cowley and Sharp, sprinkled names on the map. The former

> having it seems a particular fancy to christen the Places he came to, as Seamen generally affect to do, by which means they are oft confounded, Charts render'd different one from another, to the puzzling those that use 'em . . . yet when a Name has prevail'd, 'twill always stand, The Vanity of Sharp, to call John Fernando Queen Catherine's Island, has not lost the old Name.[17]

The experiences of those marooned on an island, like Selkirk, or cast away on one, like Crusoe, revealed shifting perceptions of their predicament. For Selkirk a time of terror was followed by one of happiness and tranquillity; for Crusoe 'the Island of Despair' became a secure refuge in time, even 'Deliverance' when he managed to struggle back to it after drifting away in his canoe.[18] Defoe's great novel was followed by a host of 'Robinsonades' which supplanted the utopian novel 'as a vehicle for allegorical commentaries on society . . . The hero no longer bore news of another society, whether better or worse than his own. He bore in his own person a body of experience;

---

13. See Howse and Thrower, *A Buccaneer's Atlas*, pp. 258–9.
14. See pp. 95–6 above.
15. See p. 150 above.
16. Moll, *A View*, p. 137.
17. Ibid., p. 124.
18. See Seidel, *Robinson Crusoe*, p. 119.

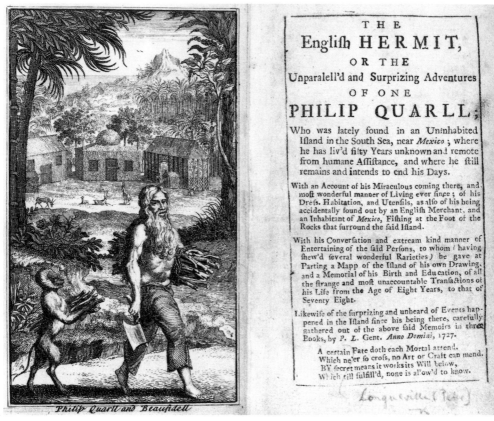

Philip Quarll and Beaufidell

27. Title-page and frontispiece of Peter Longueville, *The English Hermit* (1727).

experience not so much of an exotic social world, as of survival in the world at the most basic, physical level.'[19] One of the earliest of the successors to *Crusoe*, little-known now but a book that went through a dozen editions in the eighteenth century, was *The English Hermit* (1727) by Peter Longueville. Its frontispiece shows idyllic island scenes, peaceful and benign (Ill. 27). The title-page explains all: 'The English Hermit, or the Unparalell'd and Surprizing Adventures of One Philip Quarll; Who was lately found in an Uninhabited Island in the South Sea, near Mexico; where he has liv'd fifty Years unknown and remote from humane Assistance, and where he still remains and intends to end his Days.' This is the logical extension of the stories of Selkirk and Crusoe; there will be no rescue, for none is wanted.

A new vision of the South Sea was appearing, 'A Dream of Islands'.[20]

---

19. Fausett, *Strange Surprizing Sources of Robinson Crusoe*, p. 126.
20. To borrow from Gavan Daws, *A Dream of Islands: Voyages of Self-Discovery in the South Seas* (New York, 1980).

Before the end of the century there would be Tahiti, and much else. Perhaps not too much should be made of this anticipation, for the island refuges of the buccaneers and privateers were uninhabited. There were no welcoming, garlanded islanders thronging the beaches of Juan Fernández, Tinian or the Galapagos Islands. They were deserted, silent places, except for the beating of the surf and the calling of the sea-birds. They were a reminder that for Europe, two hundred years after Magellan, the Pacific remained a vast, empty ocean. Of Polynesia there was some premonition, but little know-ledge. Escapist writings there might be, but as Richard Steele's description of Selkirk's adjustment to life on Juan Fernández showed, they celebrated the pleasures of solitude rather than those of the flesh.

> Disengagement from the World, a constant, chearful, serene Sky, and a temperate Air, made his Life one continual Feast, and his Being much more joyful than it had before been irksome. He now taking Delight in every thing, made the Hutt in which he lay, by Ornaments which he cut down from a spacious Wood, on the side of which it was situated, the most delicious Bower, fanned with continual Breezes, and gentle Aspirations of Wind, that made his Repose after the Chase equal to the most sensual Pleasures.[21]

The period between the publication of the accounts of the Woodes Rogers expedition in 1712 and the appearance of *Robinson Crusoe* in 1719 saw a lull in both practical and literary interest in the South Sea. Not until 1720 would pamphleteers rouse themselves once more on South Sea issues, and then in the very different atmosphere of financial collapse and growing panic. Dampier, who as buccaneer, privateer, explorer and author had been the key figure in South Sea enterprise for thirty years, died in 1715, 'diseased and weak in body but of sound and perfect mind'.[22] However sound his mind, Dampier seems to have made no effort to emulate the success of his earlier books. His disastrous privateering expedition of 1703–6 on the *St George* had resulted only in the few pages of his brief *Vindication*, and as far as we know he made no attempt to produce an account of his experiences with Woodes Rogers on the *Duke*. Yet there was to be a curious sequel to his South Sea voyages in the shape of proposals put forward for the discovery of 'Terra Australis Incognita' by his former shipmate, John Welbe. The story is a tangled one, which has to be teased out of scattered documents from the period, and much of it remains obscure. In a bizarre way Welbe's scheme resurrected some of the older elements of Pacific discovery; at another level it was altogether appropriate to an age marked by the frenzy of the South Sea Bubble.

Welbe had been one of the mutineers, as Dampier called them, who had sailed away from the *St George* in a small bark. He had also participated in the

21. Blanchard, *The Englishman*, pp. 107–8.
22. Rogers, 'Dampier's Debts', p. 322.

war of words between the two sides on their return to England with his *Answer to Capt. Dampier's Vindication*, published in 1707. The same year Welbe left England for Denmark, where he urged on the Danish court a discovery expedition to the spice islands. However, because of the outbreak of war in the Baltic this scheme came to nothing, and in the summer of 1712 Welbe seems to have written to Harley from Copenhagen asking for employment by the South Sea Company.[23] When he returned home in 1713, bearing testimonials from Danish officials that they found his proposals 'plausible',[24] Welbe had changed tack. He now tried to interest the British government in a full-fledged 'Scheme of a Voyage Round the Globe for the Discovery of Terra Australis Incognita'. He asked for the command of two naval vessels, a fourth-rate and a brig, which he proposed to take into the Pacific by way of the familiar buccaneers' route of Cape Horn, Chile, Juan Fernández and Peru:

> Thence take my departur and Stear west to the Solomons Islands, which are reported by the Spanyards to abound in Gold. They were discoverd above 150 years ago, but the Court of Spain did not think fit to setle them, by reason they had not intirely setled the main land of Peru . . . as soon as I come to these Islands, I propose to go a Shore with about 150 Men, and search and discover what the Country abounds in, and then trapan[25] some of the inhabitants on board, and bring them for England, who when they have learned our language, will be proper Interpreters.
>
> From the Solomons Islands I propose to sail west to the Coast of Nova Guinea, which is the East Side of Nova Hollandia in the East Indies and make a true discovery of that coast, and search what the Country abounds in, it lying North and South as Peru does, and in the same lattd. I belive it abounds in Gold and Silver Mines (the Spanyards having found some there above 150 years ago) which if discovered and setled may be of vast advantage to great Britain. This Coast is full of Harbours, according to the account I have had out of Spanish Journals, of the Discovery of the Solomon Islands.
>
> After I have made discovery of the Coast of Nova Guinea, and taken away some of the Inhabitants, I propose to make a farther discovery of Nova Britannia, and the adjacent Islands, and search what they abound in, and take off some of the Inhabitants likewise, for tho Capt Dampire discover'd Nova Britannia, yet he never was a Shore at any place except port montague, and only as far as the watering place, he having only 50 Men in his Ship, was not strong enough to search the Country.[26]

However appealing Welbe found this blend of the voyages of Mendaña, Quiros and Dampier, others were less impressed. He spent fourteen months

23. See BL: Add. MS 70,042, f. 295.
24. See BL: Sloane MS 4044, f. 214.
25. Trepan, or (in this context) lure away.
26. Ibid., f. 214v.

being sent from pillar to post with his scheme, trying without success to interest the new monarch, George I, the South Sea Company, Secretaries of State Stanhope and Townshend, and the First Lord of the Treasury, Robert Walpole. In a note to the latter Welbe evidently hoped to strike a sympathetic chord by claiming to 'have studied Chymistry, and the Natur of Gold and Silver Mines, the want of which Qualifications, rendred the Discoverys of Capt Dampire of little or no efect, and retarded a farther Search of those Countrys'.[27] The Committee of the South Sea Company granted Welbe an interview in March 1715 but took fright when it heard that he would begin his search twelve hundred leagues out into the Pacific from the coast of South America.[28] This was well outside their limits, and inside the limits of the charter of the East India Company, which had already shown by its attitude to the Woodes Rogers expedition in 1711 that it was neurotically suspicious of possible interlopers. As a letter from the backers of that voyage to the ships' captains noted, the Company was 'incens'd against us'.[29] By 1716, having failed to enlist direct government support for his project, Welbe outlined the prospectus for a new company, the London Adventurers. With a proposed joint stock of £2,500,000 it would establish a trade to Terra Australis, settle colonies there and exploit the region's gold and silver mines. These last, he was confident, would 'enrich the British Nation upwards of 50,000,000 [pounds] sterling'.[30] Welbe's own circumstances went ill with so grandiose a scheme, for at some time during 1716 he was committed to prison for a debt of £6. From his cell he sent pleading letters for support and money to Hans Sloane. In one he asked for his case to be laid before the Royal Society, in another he told Sloane that he had 'expended my whole Substance to serve my Native Country', and as though to prove the point enclosed a recipe for 'an Anti-venerial Water'.[31]

John Welbe had his counterparts elsewhere in Europe, notably in the person of Jean Pierre Purry, a Swiss employee of the Dutch East India Company. On his return from Batavia in 1717 Purry drew up a plan for the settlement of Nuyts Land, so called from the explorations of Pieter Nuyts along the southern coast of (present-day) Western Australia in 1627. In a classification of the regions of the earth based on a rigid climatic determinism, Purry hit on lat. 33° (south or north) as the ideal: 'to find the best Countries of the Earth, we should look for them in the Middle of the fifth Climate, under the 33d Deg. of Latitude.' On this basis, the southern part of New Holland discovered by the Dutch was well worth investigating. 'Who knows what there is in New-Holland, and whether that Country does not

27.   Ibid., f. 217.
28.   BL: Add. MS 25,550, f. 18.
29.   Cooke, *Voyage to the South Sea*, II, p. 100.
30.   The 1716 proposal is printed in George Collingridge, *The Discovery of Australia* (Sydney, 1895), pp. 301–2.
31.   BL: Sloane MS 4044, ff. 212–13, 241.

contain richer Mines of Gold and Silver, than, perhaps, Chili, Peru, or Mexico.' Even if gold and silver were not found in Nuyts Land, its climate would be suitable for the production of silk, wine, fruit, corn and much else. After failing to interest the VOC, Purry approached the French government, which referred his scheme to the Académie Royale des Sciences. Unlike those French investors being attracted by John Law's vision of an El Dorado in Louisiana, the Académie took a robustly sceptical attitude towards Purry's project: 'they could not pass a Judgment on a Country which they had never seen, and . . . therefore it would not be advisable to make expensive Settlements in Places they were unacquainted with.' Undaunted by this rebuff, Purry next turned to the British government with proposals for a new settlement in the Carolinas, but again failed to attract official support.[32]

In England, John Welbe was showing equal perseverance. Discharged from prison, he next appears in 1719 as 'Master of a small ship in the River of Thames'.[33] A fresh attempt to promote his discovery scheme, one of many being pushed in these months of the South Sea Bubble, was frustrated when he was once more sent to prison. This time, according to his own account, Welbe's only offence was the exposure of a marine insurance fraud organized by Edward Morgan, a former shipmate from his privateering days. Welbe described him as 'Mr Edward Morgan a Roman Catholick lieving in Bloomsbury Square who was Round the Globe with Capt Dampire the same voyage that your Petitioner was . . . the said Morgan was afterwards the Ruin of the said Expedition and now endeavours to Ruin your Petitioner and thereby overthrow his Intended discovery.'[34] Whether in or out of prison, Welbe continued to bombard ministers with details of his scheme – Townshend and Walpole again, the King, the Lords Commissioners of Trade and Plantations – in the hope of being granted a charter. In May 1720 he went so far as to issue shares in his proposed company, though a couple of newspaper items the next month indicate that something untoward had happened. On 17 June the *Daily Post* carried a notice:

Welbe's *Gold and Silver Mines*

All those Persons who have Permits for 10,000l. Stock in Capt. Welbe's Company of London Adventurers for the carrying on a Trade to (and settling Colonies in) Terra Australis, for working and improving the Gold and Silver

---

32. Purry's original *Memoir sur le Pais des Caffres, et la Terre de Nuyts* was published at Amsterdam in 1718. It was translated into English in 1744 as *A Method for Determining the Best Climate of the Earth*. The citations here are taken from this edition, pp. 4, 6, 32, which also provided several of the legends displayed on Emanuel Bowen's 'Complete Map of the Southern Continent' (1744); see pp. 251–2 below. Purry himself ended his days, as presumably he would have wished, in a Swiss settlement in South Carolina, not far off lat. 33°N.

33. BL: Add. MS 33,054, f. 75.

34. PRO: Treasury 1/240, No. 38, f. 182.

Mines, are desired not to fail Meeting at the South Sea House to Morrow being Saturday the 18th Instant, at 12 a Clock in the Forenoon, upon special Affairs relating to the said Company.

This notice was not as official as it appeared – it was presumably the work either of a practical joker or a disgruntled shareholder – for the next day the advertisement was repeated, this time accompanied by a note stating: 'I do hereby certify, that the said Advertisment was made without my Knowledge, Privity, or Consent. Written my Hand this 18th Day of June 1720. John Welbe.'

At the end of the year, months after the Bubble had burst to leave the country's credit system in ruins and its whole political edifice at risk, Welbe was still pursuing his obsession. On 6 December he petitioned the Crown in Council 'on behalf of himself and several Persons of distinction Merchants and others of the City of London touching the Establishing a Company by way of Charter for carrying on a Trade to Terra Australis'.[35] There were indications other than the inept timing of this approach that suggested that Welbe was now veering towards total delusion. From his early, quite correct, claims that the normal track of sailing ships in the Pacific took them away from the supposed location of the Solomon Islands and Terra Australis, he had now moved on to implying that he had seen those lands himself. In 1716, with his old commander Dampier safely dead, he had claimed that the 2500 leagues from Peru to the East Indies 'south of the line *is undiscovered to any European, Captain Welbe excepted*'.[36] The wording of the supporting detail both in 1716 and 1720 seems to show that he was using 'discovery' in the sense of an intellectual process in which the application of logic had revealed a great truth hidden to others. So he set out his

proposed discoverys (viz) the Snt Georges Islands (so named by your Petitioner) which abound in Gold formerly Calld the Solomons Islands being within and between the Equinoctial Line and the one and twentieth degree of South Latd about twelve hundred Leagues West from the Coast of Peru . . . and likewise New Wales so named by your Petitioner abounding with Gold and Silver Mines and several other adjacent Islands being farther West.[37]

A further petition to the Crown asserted that 'Columbus had nothing nigh the grounds to go upon as the said Captain hath who can plainly demonstrate the Situation of his intended Discoveries which is an undoubted sign of his knowing the same.'[38] Welbe was putting forward his own commercialized,

35. Ibid., f. 192.
36. Collingridge, *Discovery of Australia*, p. 301.
37. PRO: Treasury 1/240, No. 38, f. 191.
38. Ibid., ff. 195–6.

English version of Quiros's mystical early seventeenth-century vision. It is not likely that Welbe had seen the full English translation of Quiros's celebrated eighth memorial, *Terra Australis Incognita: OR, A New Southern Discovery, Containing A Fifth Part of the World*, which was published in 1617; and by the time it was reprinted in 1723 Welbe had disappeared from public view. Much more probable is that he had seen the abbreviated version printed in the Churchills' *Collection of Voyages and Travels* (IV, 1704), or that in Moll's *Compleat System of Geography* (V, 1717). Faced with the problem of identifying the various lands discovered by the Spaniards and Dutch, Moll divided Terra Australis Incognita into New Holland, Carpentaria, Terra Austral del Spiritu Santo and Solomon's Islands to the north, and Diemen's Land and New Zealand to the south. In quite traditional terms he suggested that the whole mass was 'as large as Europe, Asia, and Africa' combined, and repeated Quiros's representation of it as a region which 'produces Nutmegs, Mastick, Pepper, Ginger, Cinammon, Gold, Silver, Pearls, Silk, Sugar, Anniseed, Honey, Wax, Ebony-Wood, Turpentine, Lime-Pits, and Marble, with Stones, and other Materials for Building. Here are no snowy Mountains, drown'd Land, Croco-diles, or any other hurtful Creature.'[39] From Quiros to Welbe there is a clear line of descent. The reported words of Quiros's appeal to the King of Spain in 1608 might as easily have been those of Welbe petitioning the King of England more than a hundred years later: 'If upon a bare suspicion *Christophorus Columbus* did pursue his Design with so much Obstinacy, you are not to account it strange in me if the Things which I have beheld with mine Eyes, and touch'd with mine Hands, do put some of Constraint upon me to be importunate.'[40]

At the end of 1720 Welbe's petition was referred to the Lords Commissioners of Trade and Plantations. It requested permission to issue stock to the amount of £3,000,000, a sum decried by Welbe as insignificant compared with the riches that his discoveries would produce, and of which the Crown would retain one-fifth. With this wealth the government could maintain the balance of power in Europe, even pay off the National Debt.[41] When he wrenched himself away from this fantasy world Welbe was writing anxiously to the Lords Commissioners about the efforts of his rivals 'to delude the people and extract their money by giving out shares, and all under a pretence of going on those discoverys', and finally in July 1721 he gained an interview at the Board of Trade. After 'some discourse' with him about his complaint that the charters of the East India and South Sea companies 'were an obstruction to his making the discoveries', and about his request for a rival charter, the Lords Commisioners told Welbe that they could give him 'no

39. [Herman Moll], *Atlas Geographicus* (London, 1711–17), V, pp. 1–6.
40. *Terra Australis Incognita . . . Lately Found Out by Ferdinand De Quir* (London, 1617, repr. 1723), p. 30.
41. PRO: Treasury 1/240, No. 38, ff. 195–6.

encouragement as to the Charter desired'.[42] This final blow seems to have scattered what wits and fortune Welbe had left, and in 1722 he was once more writing from a debtors' prison, the King's Bench. His file in the Treasury Papers comes to an end with a series of distraught letters containing mingled appeals and threats. A letter to a legal adversary concluded with the archaic offer, 'What does you think of a fiery Tryall'. His last known letter, of August 1722, appealed to Townshend for help, and offered him 'a Treatise of Philosophy proving the possibility of Regeneration and Transmutation called the Philosophers Stone which I wrott since my confinement in the Kings Bench to show what pains I have taken to qualify my self to serve my native country.'[43]

The frustrated and increasingly manic Welbe is more interesting as a psychiatric case than as a potential explorer. His scheme itself, perhaps like Dampier's of 1698–9, had more to do with gold, spices and shares than with geographical discovery. Since, despite his claims, he had never been near the regions of his projected enterprises, Welbe probably owed something to Dampier's writings, and perhaps something to conversations on the *St George*. Certainly the insistence on sailing west across the Pacific from the South American coast towards the unknown southern lands reflected Dampier's strong preference. It is not without significance that during the closing stages of this particular saga that other old crew member from the *St George*, Edward Morgan, was also pushing his own, rival scheme for a chartered company. These dimly glimpsed manœuvres and intrigues no doubt owed more to stock manipulation than to genuine commitment to overseas discovery, and in this they resembled the much greater schemes swirling around the South Sea Company at this moment.

42. *Journal of the Commissioners for Trade and Plantations, 1718–1722* (London, 1925), p. 301.
43. Both letters are in PRO: Treasury 1/240, No. 38, f. 198.

CHAPTER VIII

The Age of the Bubble (2): Voyages Real and Fictitious

The period of the South Sea Bubble was not merely one of abortive projects. During 1719 two expeditions left England for the Pacific, though their planned routes were very different. The privateers *Success* and *Speedwell* sailed from Plymouth in February 1719, heading for the Strait of Magellan and the South Sea, and were away more than three years. A few months later, in June, two Hudson's Bay Company vessels, the *Albany* and *Discovery*, left the Thames bound for Hudson Bay and the Strait of Anian on a gold-seeking quest as bizarre and improbable as anything conjured up in the imagination of Welbe or Defoe. In command of the expedition was Captain James Knight, a veteran officer who had served the Hudson's Bay Company since the 1670s and was now at least seventy years old. In 1714 he had returned to Hudson Bay after a period as one of the directors of the company to take up the post of Governor at York Factory, where he re-established the company's position after a period of French occupation during the war. With him he took 'Cruseables, Melting Potts, Borax &c for the Trial of Minerals',[1] for during his time in England, or possibly during his travels on the continent, he had heard of a strait beyond Hudson Bay that led to a land of treasure, a veritable El Dorado which might be located on the Pacific coast of North America.[2]

Knight's first years at York were taken up restoring the fort and renewing contacts with the local Cree and more distant Indians. Among the latter, the 'Northern' or Chipewyan Indians brought Knight news of copper deposits away to the northwest, but as the Governor wrote in his journal for May 1716: 'that is not Still what I am Endeavouring to gett or Endeavour to

---

1. HBC Archives: A 1/33, f. 97v.
2. Much of the following is based on my *The British Search for the Northwest Passage in the Eighteenth Century* (London, 1962), Ch. 1, 'James Knight and the Strait of Anian'; updated by the report of recent attempts to find the remains of the Knight expedition in John Geiger and Owen Beattie, *Dead Silence: The Greatest Mystery in Arctic Discovery* (London, 1993).

Discover thare is a Parcell of Indians as lyes upon the west Seas as has a Yellow Mettle as they make us of as these do Copper.'[3] The mysterious metal, Knight concluded, was gold; and for the few remaining years of his life he was absorbed in the search for it. Since the quickest way to reach the land of gold was by sea, it was urgent for Knight to find the answer to the question that had perplexed geographers for centuries: was there a strait through or around the North American continent which led to the Pacific? From his factory on the shores of Hudson Bay Knight was peering into the unknown, for this period before Bering's voyages of 1728 and 1741 was one of complete ignorance in Europe about the northwest coast of America above lat. 43°N. On most maps the vast region between Hudson Bay and the dimly known lands of eastern Asia was simply marked *incognita*. Knight studied the rough maps the Indians drew for him and interpreted them as showing seventeen rivers along the coast of the Hudson Bay to the north. The fourteenth, he was told, ran into the western ocean, while the seventeenth and largest might well be the strait itself.[4] One Indian had ventured down this river to a large bay, where he met the tide from the sea and saw the islands with yellow metal. This bay was far to the north, but Knight was convinced that it was open to ships because he was told that its inhabitants 'every Summer see Sevll Ships in the Western Seas wch I cannott think to be Spaniards . . . I rather take them to be Tartars or Jappannees Vessells and they see 'em go to Some great Islands that lyes within Sight of the Land and that there is very little Ice in them Seas in the Winter.'[5]

Knight interpreted the reports he collected in the light of his own preconceptions. The 'sea' of the Indians, which Knight took to be the Pacific, was probably Great Slave Lake. The large rivers they described and drew were no doubt the Slave, Mackenzie and Coppermine rivers, flowing north towards the Arctic Ocean, not west to the Pacific. The yellow metal might have been any one of a half-dozen ores from the rich mineral deposits of the northwest. It was not only Knight who listened eagerly and uncritically to Indian reports. A French officer, Nicolas Jérémie, spent many years in Hudson Bay during the French wartime occupation of York Factory and in 1720 published an account of his experiences. Like Knight, he was interested in the geography of the interior and repeated the information given him by the Indians about a strait that ran from Hudson Bay to the western sea. Along the shores of that sea, Jérémie was told, bearded white men from ships collected gold.[6] The Indians who made the long journey from the Athabaska and Great Slave Lake region to York were not

---

3. HBC Archives: B 239/a/2, f. 28v.
4. For an interpretation of such maps see June Helm, 'Matonabbee's Map', *Arctic Anthropology*, 26 (1989), especially pp. 29–30.
5. HBC Archives: B 239/a/2, f. 45v.
6. R. Douglas and J.N. Wallace, eds, *Twenty Years of York Factory 1694–1714* [1720] (Ottawa, 1926), p. 21.

disappointed when they reached the factory, for Knight was pathetically eager to glean any scrap of information about their country. More than thirty years later, one of the men who was with him when he interrogated the strange Indians about the mines of gold and copper remembered how the Governor 'was very earnest in this Discovery, which was always his Topic, and he took all Opportunities of making Presents to the Natives'.[7]

After attempts by Knight to establish overland contacts with the lands of gold to the west failed, he returned to England in 1718 and persuaded the Hudson's Bay Company to fit out an expedition of two discovery vessels. These were the frigate-built *Albany* of a hundred tons, commanded by George Berley, and the tiny *Discovery* sloop under David Vaughan. Knight himself would sail on the *Albany*, and he also contributed one-eighth of the cost of the fitting out of the expedition. This was an unusual departure from normal practice and raises the whole question of the company's attitude towards the expedition. One historian has concluded that the trebling of stock by the company in 1720 shows that the company and its governing committee 'were as much carried away by the dreams of copper and gold as their overseas Governor'.[8] The timing of the operation creates doubts about the validity of this supposition. Knight's ships sailed in June 1719, and allowing for a wintering they might be expected to return in the autumn of 1720. If the trebling of stock stemmed from hopes aroused by the Knight expedition, then it is difficult to see why the decision was delayed for fifteen months after its sailing and was then taken in August 1720, only a few weeks before the return of Knight's ships, or news concerning them, might be expected. These financial manœuvres were more probably connected with the boom in South Sea Company shares during the summer of 1720; and in December, after the crash of those stocks, and with, as the governing committee expressed it, 'The Present Scarcety of Moneys, and the Deadness of Publick Credit', much of the scheme was abandoned.[9] What evidence there is suggests that the company fitted out the Knight expedition with some reluctance, and under pressure. One of the company's ship-captains, Christopher Middleton, later reported that 'The Company were against him going; but as he [Knight] was *opiniatre*, they durst not disoblige him, lest he should apply elsewhere.'[10] Clearly, the ageing ex-Governor, dreaming of a land of gold, would be a hard man to dissuade once his mind was set on the venture. And his threat to 'apply elsewhere' would be a most effective one, for it raised the spectre of interloping expeditions, rival charters and much else.

7. *Report from the Committee Appointed to Inquire into the State and Conditions of the Countries Adjoining to Hudson's Bay* (London, 1749), p. 49.
8. A.S. Morton, *A History of the Canadian West to 1870–71* (London, 1939), p. 140.
9. HBC Archives: A 1/119, f. 7v; and for an authoritative examination of the company's financial transactions in this period see E.E. Rich, *The History of the Hudson's Bay Company 1670–1870* (London, 1958), I, Ch. 36.
10. Arthur Dobbs, *Remarks upon Capt. Middleton's Defence* (London, 1744), p. 9.

Since the control of the venture rested in Knight's hands no detailed instructions were given by the company to the two captains about their route, but as Knight was sailing in the *Albany* an outline of the intended explorations had to be supplied to Vaughan in the sloop in case of separation. If this happened, Vaughan was to proceed in Hudson Bay 'to the Latitude 64 Degrees North Latitude and from thence Northward to Endeavour to find out the Streights of Anian'.[11] An entry in the minute-book of the committee as it assembled at Gravesend on 4 June 1719 to bid farewell to the ships noted that Knight 'is gone with the Albany and Discovery sloop in order to A Discovery of a NW Passage beyond Sir Tho' Buttons which is supposed to Lye to the northwards of 64 degrees.'[12]

These fragments of evidence help to show the way in which Knight integrated the Indian information he had received at York with the current speculative European geography of northwest America. When the Strait of Anian first appeared on maps in the second half of the sixteenth century it was shown as a narrow strait separating Asia from America, roughly in the position of the modern Bering Strait. By the late seventeenth century the legendary strait had moved farther south, and it is possible that Knight had seen one of the maps of the period indicating a connection between the Strait of Anian and Hudson Bay. In 1700 and 1708 a French cartographer, J.B. Nolin, published different versions of his *Globe Terrestre*, which showed, in tentative fashion, a Strait of Anian leading from the Pacific to the northwest of Hudson Bay (Ill. 28). Such maps would be treated with more than usual attention at this time because of the long French occupation of York Factory during the war. Knight's propensity for naming the route he was seeking the Strait of Anian, rather than the more normal term used by English explorers, the Northwest Passage, suggests that he had made some study of French or Dutch maps, perhaps during the time he spent in Holland in 1710 as one of the company's representatives at the peace negotiations. It was also at this time, in 1708, that the extraordinary Fonte letter was printed in *The Monthly Miscellany or Memoirs for the Curious*. The letter appeared to have been written by a Spanish admiral, Bartolomew de Fonte, and described a voyage north from Lima in 1640 during which Fonte and his officers had discovered a network of straits, rivers and lakes leading inland from the northwest coast of America. The entry point of these waterways was the Archipelago of St Lazarus in lat. 53°N. (roughly in the position of the present-day Queen Charlotte Islands off the coast of British Columbia), much farther north than any known exploration had reached. At the eastern end of one stretch of water, the Sea of Ronquillo, the Spaniards encountered a Boston fur-trading ship commanded by Captain Nicholas Shapley, which seemed to have come in through Hudson Bay. If the story was true,

11. Sailing orders to Captain Vaughan. HBC Archives: A 6/4, f. 38v.
12. HBC Archives: A 1/117, f. 24v.

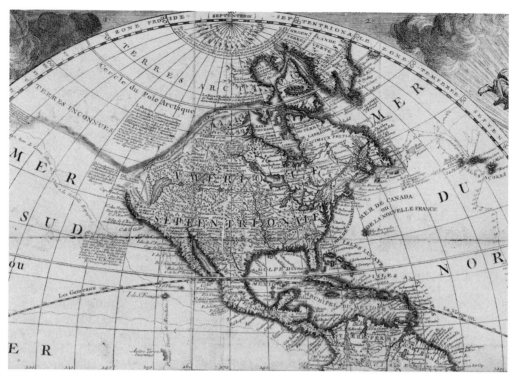

28. J.B. Nolin. Section from 'Globe Terrestre', 1708.

there seemed to be a Northwest Passage after all, and one in temperate latitudes.[13]

The Monthly Miscellany was a periodical edited by James Petiver which made its first appearance in January 1707. It was by no means a collection of trivialities: its contents varied from observations on the origins of English laws to an account of the conversion of the Muscovites from the Greek Church, from the translation of papers delivered to the Academy of Sciences in Paris to a description of the lifestyle of crustaceans. It contained little that was frivolous, and its audience was the 'curious' in the sense of the learned. A biography of Petiver mentions the short-lived run of *The Monthly Miscellany*, but throws no light on the source of the Fonte letter, although it shows that Petiver had correspondents in most parts of the world. His library included a fair number of 'voyages and travels', as well as maps and atlases, but most of his collection related to natural history and his other professional interests.[14] The picture that emerges of an earnest botanist is hard to reconcile

13. The best discussion in English of the Fonte letter and voyage remains Wagner, 'Apocryphal Voyages', pp. 179–234.
14. See R. Stearns, *James Petiver: Promoter of Natural Science* (Worcester, MA, 1953); BL: Sloane MS 3367.

with the suggestion that Petiver himself composed the letter as a hoax. In the age of Defoe and Swift imaginary voyages and fabulous journeys had become a recognized genre. In his *Advice to an Author* (1710) the 3rd Earl of Shaftesbury admitted that travel books had become 'the chief materials to furnish out a library', but complained about the way in which 'Histories of Incas or Iroquois, written by friars and missionaries, pirates and renegades, sea-captains and trusty travellers, pass for authentic records.'[15] It was in this period that Mandeville's *Travels* was reprinted ten times in England, and in 1704 George Psalmanazar, passing himself off as a Formosan, published his fantastical but well-received *Description of Formosa* in which he invented his own language. Since Dampier's *New Voyage* the South Sea and its exploration had come back into fashion, and some unknown writer perhaps hoped to cause a stir, or turn a dishonest penny, with the Fonte letter.

Whatever expectations rested on the writing and publishing of the letter, they seem to have been disappointed. In mid-century the account was to make a great impact on the world of geography, but at the time of its first publication it seems to have vanished without trace. There is no telling whether Knight ever saw the account – he makes no reference to it – but if he did it would have seemed to confirm both the Strait of Anian thesis and those Indian reports he had collected at York which seemed to indicate an ice-free sea on the northwest coast of America. At the Hudson Bay entrance of the supposed passage, the 'Sir Tho' Buttons' mentioned in the company's record of Knight's sailing was a rather imprecise geographical location along the northwest coast of the Bay in about lat. 64°N. The same area was called (pessimistically) Ne Ultra or (optimistically) Roe's Welcome by the English explorers of the early seventeenth century. Some maps showed this feature as a closed bay, but others marked it as a large opening on the strength of Foxe's observation on his voyage of 1631–2 that the run and height of the tides might indicate a passage nearby. Knight's intention was clear. The ships would sail to the Welcome, far to the north of the company posts along the southern shores of Hudson Bay, and then turn west along a strait or great river that would take them to the Pacific. On board were building materials, ten 'Landmen Passengers', who if a newspaper report about 'Artificers' was correct were probably miners and smiths, and, a later account rumoured, large iron-bound chests in which to bring back the gold.[16]

Knight's vessels left the Thames together with the *Hudson's Bay* and *Mary*, making their regular voyage to the Bay posts. The company ships were the last to see the discovery vessels and their crews; for once they separated (presumably on reaching Hudson Bay, when the company ships would turn

15. Quoted in R.W. Frantz, *The English Traveller and the Movement of Ideas 1600–1732* (repr. New York, 1968), p. 8. See also Percy G. Adams, *Travelers and Travel Liars 1660–1800* (Berkeley and Los Angeles, 1962).

16. HBC Archives: A/117, f. 24v; *Saturday's Post*, 6 June 1719; Joseph Robson, *An Account of Six Years Residence in Hudson's-Bay* (London, 1752), p. 37.

southwest) Knight and his men disappeared from view. The first definite news of the fate of the expedition came three years later when a company sloop on a voyage along the northwest coast of Hudson Bay found wreckage at Marble Island, a barren island of white rock twenty-five miles off the mainland. On the sloop's return its master, John Scroggs, reported to his superior, Richard Staunton, that 'he had been where the Albany and Discovery where both Ship-wracked and he doth Affirm that Every Man was Killed by the Eskemoes, wch I [Staunton] am heartily Sorry for their hard fortune.'[17] Not until 1767 was more discovered. In that year the crew of a company whaling sloop at Marble Island came across the ruins of a house with implements scattered around, human bones, and in a small harbour nearby the hulks of two ships. It was the graveyard of the Knight expedition. Two years later the whalers returned, and one of them, Samuel Hearne, soon to become an explorer of note himself, heard through their Inuit interpreter what purported to be a description of the last days of the survivors in their second winter trapped on the island:

> two survived many days after the rest, and frequently went to the top of an adjacent rock, and earnestly looked to the South and East, as if in expectation of some vessels coming to their relief. After continuing there a considerable time together, and nothing appearing in sight, they sat down close together, and wept bitterly. At length one of the two died, and the other's strength was so far exhausted, that he fell down and died also, in attempting to dig a grave for his companion.[18]

Recent excavations on Marble Island suggest that this is not the whole story, perhaps not even part of the story;[19] but it was all that eighteenth-century readers would learn of the disappearance of the Knight expedition. There are several aspects of the tragedy that bear an ironic relation to these years of frenzied speculation and greed at home. The final desperate recourse to Marble Island as winter closed in must have come after weeks of searching the northwest coast of Hudson Bay for an opening that would take the ships into the Strait of Anian, and on to Knight's land of gold far to the west. It was a project too far, one that resulted not simply in the financial distress of investors but in the deaths of men caught up in Knight's dream. It was a story of castaways and an island which replicated, in nightmare fashion, the

---

17.　HBC Archives: B 42/a/2, f. 51v. For Marble Island see Map 2, p. 50 above.

18.　Richard Glover, ed., *A Journey from Prince of Wales's Fort in Hudson's Bay to the Northern Ocean . . . by Samuel Hearne* [1795] (Toronto, 1958), pp. lxiii–iv.

19.　See Geiger and Beattie, *Dead Silence*, especially Chs. VIII–X. Perhaps I can quote from my own preface to the book (p. xii) in which I point out that Geiger and Beattie 'have scrutinized every scrap of documentary evidence, and have matched this with four seasons of land and underwater investigation at the harbour on Marble Island. Much has been found at that ominous site, and a sounder interpretation of many aspects of the expedition is now possible; but the central issue of what happened to the forty men of the expedition remains as much a puzzle as ever.'

saga of Robinson Crusoe, which was seizing readers' attention at home during the months that Knight's men were dying. And if the transition from Crusoe's tropical island to the sub-Arctic wastes of Hudson Bay should be thought too abrupt, then a stray piece of evidence indicates something of the universality of Defoe's story. In the 1750s one of the Cree hunters employed by the Hudson's Bay Company was named Robinson Crusoe; and his son was called Friday.[20]

While Knight's men were perishing on Marble Island, the *Success* and the *Speedwell* were heading for the South Sea by a more conventional route. However, neither ship returned home, the casualties were heavy, and this last of the English privateering expeditions into the Pacific was marked by an extraordinary degree of acrimony and tumult. Nowhere is this more evident than in the rival accounts of the venture: *A Voyage Round the World by Way of the Great South Sea* by George Shelvocke, captain of the *Speedwell*, published in 1726; and *A Voyage Round the World* by William Betagh, a former naval purser, who was captain of marines on the *Speedwell*. His book was published in 1728 and was partly based on the journal kept by George Taylor, mate of the *Success*, whose captain, John Clipperton, died soon after his return. Of Shelvocke and Betagh, Oskar Spate has written, 'Hard liars both . . . it would be as difficult as unprofitable to decide which was the more atrocious traducer.'[21] Shelvocke's account, the better known of the two, was (another scholar has commented) 'a histrionic appeal for sympathy'.[22] It told a heart-rending story of hardship, mutiny and shipwreck, in which the fast-diminishing crew of the *Speedwell* were kept alive only by their captain's prodigious efforts. Whatever the truth of the accusations and counter-accusations, the accounts reinforce the observations of Woodes Rogers about the problems of authority endemic in any non-naval expedition, especially one to distant seas. At another level they unwittingly reveal the contrast between the grandiose national expectations surrounding the South Sea trade and the grubby reality of English enterprise there.

The expedition took place in the context of the brief bout of hostilities that broke out between Britain and Spain in December 1718. If war had not been declared, the ships would have sailed under Austrian colours. Clipperton, who had been Dampier's mate in 1704, was captain of the larger ship (about 350 tons), and was made senior to Shelvocke, who had served in the Royal Navy until the peace of 1713. The mix of regular navy and privateer was not likely to be a comfortable one, and Shelvocke later accused Clipperton of having 'been always a stranger to regular discipline' and showing contempt for anyone who had served in the navy.[23] John

20. See *Dictionary of Canadian Biography* (Toronto and Quebec, 1974), III, p. 151.
21. Spate, *Monopolists and Freebooters*, p. 383.
22. Jonathan Lamb, 'George Shelvocke's Jacobite Pretences in the South Sea', unpublished paper.
23. Shelvocke, *Voyage*, pp. xxii–iii.

Campbell, writing later, described Clipperton more sympathetically as 'an able Pilot, an experienced Seaman . . . a blunt, rough, free-spoken Sailor, [who] had not much the Air of a Gentleman'.[24] The instructions given to the two captains were mostly routine: raids on Spanish ports and shipping in the South Sea; refreshment at Juan Fernández; cruising for the galleon off Acapulco. The only surprising note was the instruction to make for the Strait of Magellan, for this route into the South Sea had by now been generally discarded. And on the return voyage home the captains were told that they might sail between New Holland and New Guinea into the Indian Ocean – as though Torres Strait was marked on every map of the Eastern Seas. Finally, the owners presented the expedition with copies of Woodes Rogers's *Cruising Voyage Round the World*, which had been reprinted the year before.[25]

The expedition got off to a calamitous start, for within a week of sailing from Plymouth the ships parted company in a storm and made separate voyages into the South Sea. On board the *Speedwell* Shelvocke began to lose men as they slipped away at various ports of call, the chief mate, gunner and boatswain among them. At St Catherine's on the coast of Brazil the crew demanded a different distribution of the plunder from that set out in the agreement with the owners. Led by the 'second captain', Simon Hatley, and with the support of three mates, the petty officers and thirty-six 'chief foremast-men', the crew complained that the articles of agreement pinned up at Plymouth had since been altered and expanded without their consent: 'Three times as much in writing in them . . . and written by several hands, and intertwined in a great many places, which we do not know the meaning of . . . how dangerous is it for poor men to trust their fortune in the hands of rich men?' Reminding Shelvocke of the way in which Woodes Rogers's men had been treated on their return in 1711, the *Speedwell*'s crew demanded that 'the whole cabin plunder' and other personal possessions from prizes should be divided among them at the time of capture. Refusing to carry out their duties, milling around Shelvocke on the quarter-deck and abusing the absent owners 'with a thousand scurrilous expressions', the men soon won the day.[26] There may have been more in this episode than meets the eye, for Matthew Stewart, the crew's representative in the dispute, had earlier been inexplicably promoted from cabin steward to mate by Shelvocke. According to Betagh, Stewart was an *agent provocateur* in a mutiny whose real purpose was to gain for the captain part of the owners' share of the booty. Shelvocke proclaimed his innocence of this charge and went on to lament that 'it was a melancholy reflection to me, that after having been 30 years an Officer in

24.   Campbell, *Navigantium atque Itinerantium Bibliotheca*, I, p. 186.
25.   The instructions are written out at the beginning of Shelvocke's manuscript journal in the Admiralty Library (Taunton): MS 18, f. 2v, and are printed in W.G. Perrin, ed., *A Voyage Round the World: Captain George Shelvocke* (London, 1928), pp. xii–xiv.
26.   Shelvocke, *Voyage*, pp. 32, 34–6, 42.

the service, under the best regulated discipline in the world, I should now be harass'd with continual mutinies.'[27]

As the *Speedwell* sailed south from Brazil, Betagh seems to have been the chief culprit in terms of 'insolence' and 'mutinous behaviour'. When the ship neared the Strait of Magellan, he sent Shelvocke a half-hearted letter of apology, insisting that 'I never entertained any thoughts of ever being a party man, for it is my aversion.'[28] At this time Shelvocke had other problems to occupy him, for the only charts were with Clipperton on the *Success*. Eventually he decided to take the Strait of Le Maire and Cape Horn route into the Pacific, thereby allowing Hatley's encounter with the 'disconsolate black albatross' which eighty years later was immortalized by Coleridge in his 'Rime of the Ancient Mariner'. Once in the South Sea the *Speedwell* took a few minor prizes, while off Arica on the Peruvian coast Shelvocke claimed to have had a conversation with a local merchant who 'made a great enquiry after English commodities, and offer'd great prices for them, and complain'd that the French only supply'd them with paltry things and trifles, for which they ran away with many millions from them, and asked whether all the English merchants were asleep, or grown too rich.'[29] Two months later Hatley and Betagh set off in a cruise on the *Mercury* prize, taking the *Speedwell*'s pinnace with them, and never returned. According to Shelvocke, the two officers determined to desert with their ship, only to be captured by a Spanish man-of-war. He accused Betagh of then displaying his true colours as an Irish Catholic by entering Spanish service and informing his new masters of Shelvocke's plans.[30] In response Betagh claimed that the cruise of the *Mercury* was a deliberate move by Shelvocke to get rid of several of his officers, who otherwise would have claims on the prize-money. And, for good measure, he accused Shelvocke of being a Jacobite who celebrated the Pretender's birthday.[31]

After taking and burning Paita, Shelvocke headed for Juan Fernández, but there in heavy seas the *Speedwell* was driven onto the rocks and wrecked. The stranding of the crew at Juan Fernández forms the dramatic centrepiece of Shelvocke's book. Betagh's later accusation that Shelvocke had deliberately wrecked his ship in order to sever his legal tie with the owners does not ring true. The plight of the crew, and the hardships and dangers they experienced in the next six months, would seem to make that a peculiarly pointless, if not suicidal, action. Predictably, once the ship had gone so did all semblance of discipline. Shelvocke's attempt to persuade the men to build a small bark out of wood on the island and from the wreck faltered and came to a halt. Most of the officers joined the men, leaving Shelvocke with the support only of

27. Ibid., p. 26.
28. Ibid., pp. 62–4.
29. Ibid., pp. 167–8.
30. Ibid., p. 179.
31. William Betagh, *A Voyage Round the World* (London, 1728), pp. 104–5, 118.

the third lieutenant, the lieutenant of marines, the agent, the surgeon and his son. Remembering what had happened to Dampier on the *St George* voyage, Shelvocke entrusted his commission to his son to hide in a safe place among the trees or rocks. Commission or no commission, Shelvocke's position came under direct attack. Among the ringleaders determined to adopt 'the Jamaica discipline' of the buccaneers was the cobbler William Morphew, who had been in the South Sea before. He told the captain 'that my Command was too lofty and arbitrary for a private ship, that I should have continued in men of war, where people were obliged *quietly to bear* all hardships impos'd upon them, whether right or wrong.'[32] Shelvocke's number of shares in the expedition was reduced from sixty to six (and he was told that he was lucky to have so many since under the Jamaica system captains normally held only four); the few weapons retrieved from the wreck were taken from him; and he was fed last. In spite of all of his tribulations, Shelvocke was able (if Betagh, who was not on the island, is to be believed) to celebrate the Pretender's birthday, though not exactly in style. A bonfire was lit, the men wore roses made out of rags and paper and the Pretender's health was drunk in a punch of vinegar, sugar and water.[33] A semblance of authority was only restored when a large ship came into sight, and although it passed the island without anchoring, the fright its appearance caused led to work being resumed on the bark. So crazy a craft was this 'bundle of boards', with only a rock for an anchor, that eleven of the crew refused to leave in her, saying that 'they were not yet prepar'd for the other world'.[34]

The remaining forty or so sailed in the *Recovery* on 6 October 1720. First attempts to seize large trading vessels failed, but at last the privateers captured a two-hundred-ton merchant vessel off Pisco, renamed it the *Happy Return* and sailed north. The twists and turns of Shelvocke's story continued unabated, for early in 1721 Clipperton's *Success* came into sight north of Panama. The reunion was neither a warm nor a long one: by March the two ships had separated once again as they were lying in wait for the galleon off Acapulco. Shelvocke accused Clipperton of 'the most perfidious piece of treachery' by deliberately deserting him, while Betagh insisted that there had been a quarrel over prize-money.[35] In May Shelvocke took another prize, the *Concepción*, laden it seemed with a cargo of foodstuffs: 'flour, loaves of sugar, bales of boxes of marmalade, jars of preserved peaches, grapes, limes, &c.' To Shelvocke's prosaic list Betagh added a postscript: 'Now, Be it known to ALL MEN, that, that et caetera was A hundred and eight thousand six hundred and thirty six pieces of eight'; and later events seem to confirm Betagh's charge.[36]

32.   Shelvocke, *Voyage*, pp. 219–20.
33.   Betagh, *Voyage*, pp. 179–80.
34.   Shelvocke, *Voyage*, p. 242.
35.   Ibid., p. 324; Betagh, *Voyage*, pp. 191–3.
36.   Shelvocke, *Voyage*, p. 371; Betagh, *Voyage*, p. 203; and see p. 202 below.

In yet another prize Shelvocke and the remnants of his crew headed across the North Pacific after careening it at Puerto Segura, just north of Cape San Lucas in Lower California. So thinly manned was the vessel that Shelvocke dared not call at Guam, the normal first stopping place after the long ocean run, but made for Canton instead. There Shelvocke had further news of Clipperton, who had, it seemed, cut a sorry figure in an action with a Spanish ship off Guam before making for Macao. From China he had sailed to Batavia, where he had sold the *Success* before taking passage in a ship for England. He was soon followed by Shelvocke in an East Indiaman from Canton. Of the hundred or so men who had sailed in the *Speedwell* in February 1719 eighty-four had been lost in one way or another – killed by enemy action, died of illness or deserted.

The aftermath of the voyage was in keeping with much that had occurred during it. Clipperton died in Ireland a few days after his return in June 1722, and when Shelvocke reached London in August, he was pursued through the courts by indignant owners trying to recover prize-money. They had been alerted by Betagh, who after a spell in a Lima prison had arrived in London in August 1721, bearing with him tales of Spanish discoveries in the ocean west of Peru which were thought to be the long-lost Solomon Islands. As set out in his book of 1728, Betagh's report was just credible enough to carry conviction, and it may have had some bearing on the Admiralty's plans twenty years later for a South Sea discovery expedition.[37] Certainly, to put the matter at its lowest, there was nothing in Betagh's mixture of second-hand information and tentative speculation that could be shown to be false:

The viceroy [of Peru] having lately had certain notice by a Spanish ship, that they accidentally made an island in the South-Seas till then unknown to them, tho' markt in several drafts by the name of Solomon's island; it made his excellency curious to persue the discovery. He thereupon ordered the ketch to be fitted out for two months under Thaylet's command;[38] who accordingly saild into ten degrees south, in which latitude the island was said to lye. He cruised thereabout till his provision was nigh expended; and returned without success. However as the same account came by two different ships who touched there, the Spaniards verily believe there is such a place; for the men reported, that the natives, as to their persons and behaviour, were much like the Indians on the continent; that they had many gold and silver things among them, but that their language was new and unintelligible. The reason why Mr. Thaylet could not meet with Solomon's island might be from the uncertainty of the latitude, and his inability of making further search, being provided for only two months; for I have been informed in London that the said island or

---

37. See p. 263 below.
38. Thaylet was a French private trader from St Malo.

islands lye more southerly in the Pacific ocean than where they are laid down by the Dutch maps.[39]

Betagh's more immediate objective was the pursuit of his feud with Shelvocke, and he gave damning details from an account book in the possession of Shelvocke's confidant on the voyage, Matthew Stewart. This contained a record of the missing prize-money of 108,000 pieces of eight taken from the *Concepción* and its division between Shelvocke and the thirty-three surviving members of the crew.[40] For a time Shelvocke was in the King's Bench prison, almost certainly at the same time that Welbe was incarcerated there. After a spell of lying low, Shelvocke emerged to enjoy his prize-money – possibly as much as £7000[41] – and to retrieve his reputation. This latter process began with the presentation to the Admiralty in about 1724 of a copy of his journal of the voyage. References in it to 'your Lordships' suggest that this version, an abbreviated and bland affair, was adapted to its particular audience.[42] A published account of the journal appeared in 1726, full of special pleading and self-justification which absolved Shelvocke of any blame for the disasters of the voyage. In a letter to the Admiralty in May 1726 Shelvocke enclosed additional material which (he explained) he had omitted from the book, 'fearing it might be made use of, to the advantage of such as [are] or would be our Rivals in Trade'.[43] The main purpose of these confidential additions, which were not of any great moment, was probably to ingratiate himself with the Admiralty.

With war against Spain looming once more, Shelvocke may have hoped for a possible command, but his only offer in this direction came from the Duke of Chandos who for a time contemplated fitting out a voyage to the South Sea.[44] There is some indirect evidence that the government was considering a South Sea expedition. Woodes Rogers, who was being consulted by ministers at this time, submitted an ambitious plan to conquer Chile with a mixed force of navy and private ships.[45] Admiral Charles Wager, soon to become First Lord of the Admiralty, found time while cruising off Cadiz to write to Robert Walpole, the first minister, wondering whether the ships sent to the Caribbean might not have been better employed in the South Sea in attacks on Lima or Panama.[46] That some such venture seems to have been under consideration is revealed in a letter of November 1726 from Horace

39.   Betagh, *Voyage*, pp. 227–8 (misnumbered 277–8 in some copies).
40.   Ibid., p. 205.
41.   See Perrin, *Shelvocke's Voyage*, p. xviii.
42.   See, for example, Shelvocke's remarks on missing the Acapulco galleon. Admiralty Library: MS 18, f. 119v.
43.   BL: Add. MS 19,034, f. 84.
44.   See C.H.C. Baker and M.I. Baker, *The Life and Circumstances of James Brydges, First Duke of Chandos* (Oxford, 1949), p. 338.
45.   See BL: Add. MS. 19,034, ff. 70–1.
46.   See William Coxe, *Memoirs of the Life and Administration of Sir Robert Walpole* (London, 1798), II, p. 514.

Walpole, British ambassador at Paris, to the Duke of Newcastle, Secretary of State for the Southern Department. Walpole expressed concern about 'the Project of a Settlement in the South Seas', and warned that 'the Execution of it at this critical Juncture may give perhaps too much Jealousy and Umbrage to the French Nation.'[47]

In the end there was no expedition and no further employment for Shelvocke, but his book, *A Voyage Round the World*, kept his name before the reading public. Whatever his personal deficiencies, Shelvocke had a good eye for commercial gain. In three different parts of the book he hinted at the possible opening of new trades, though their exploitation would have to wait for a later generation of seafarers and projectors. As he coasted along the Patagonian coast he noticed the number of whales, so many and so close to the ship that it would be 'impossible to escape striking them on every send [plunge] of a sea'. Shelvocke continued: 'I am a stranger to the Greenland fishery, therefore cannot say why a trade for blubber might not be carried on here. I may venture to affirm it is a safer navigation, and I am apt to believe that here is a greater certainty of success.'[48] It was 1786, after Cook's voyages, before Parliament passed an Act for the Encouragement of the Southern Whale Fishery. Off the Peruvian coast Shelvocke captured a vessel laden with a noisome cargo of guano, and he described its use as a fertilizer. This was one of the first published references in English to the importance of guano, which in the nineteenth century attracted ships from Europe and the United States.[49] Finally, in Lower California, Shelvocke washed out some gold-dust from the earth, though it was later 'lost in our confusions in China'.[50]

Shelvocke's narrative was cleverly written, with few of those 'dry and jejeune' details of navigation that had clogged other accounts. Its author emerges as a heroic figure who had surmounted 'inexpressible troubles and hardships' and now had time for broader reflections.[51] These were cast in terms becoming routinely fashionable. The story of the stranding on Juan Fernández was accompanied by an enthusiastic description of the island: the soil was fruitful, the water good and the air wholesome. So healthy was the environment that during the six months the crew spent there not one hour's sickness occurred among them. Shelvocke himself 'became one of the strongest and most active men on the island, from being very corpulent, and almost crippled with Gout'. He concluded with comments very much in line with the period's emphasis on the picturesque:

47. BL: Add. MS. 32,748, f. 232.
48. Shelvocke, *Voyage*, p. 65.
49. Ibid., pp. 166, 171. Frézier had anticipated Shelvocke by a few years; his description of 'guana' is in the English edition of his *Voyage to the South-Sea* (London, 1717), p. 147.
50. Ibid., pp. 400–401.
51. The first quotation is from Dampier, *Voyage to New-Holland*, preface; the second from Shelvocke, *Voyage*, p. 468.

In short, every thing one sees or hears in this place is perfectly romantick; the
very structure of the Island, in all its parts, has a certain savage irregular beauty,
which is not to be expressed; the many prospects of lofty inaccessible hills and
the solitariness of the gloomy narrow valleys, which a great part of the day
enjoy little benefit from the sun, and the fall of waters, which one hears all
around, would be agreeable to none but those who would indulge themselves,
for a time, in a pensive melancholy.[52]

Even more in conformity with eighteenth-century sentimentality were
Shelvocke's comments on the 'Indians' of Lower California, where the
expedition spent five days. In his manuscript journal Shelvocke briefly
acknowledged the help the natives had given there; in the book this was
expanded into a panegyric on the virtues of the simple life. I have argued
elsewhere that James Cook's surprising declaration on the Aborigines of the
east coast of Australia in 1770 – 'far more happier than we Europeans' and
so on – perhaps owed something to Shelvocke, whose book was on board
the *Endeavour*.[53] Shelvocke in turn seems to have been reading the accounts
of his contemporaries on the other side of the North American continent,
and his remarks on the 'Indian' inhabitants of the Pacific coast of
Lower California could have been taken from any one of a half-dozen such
books:

> There is a wide difference between what one would, upon the first sight,
> expect to find from them, and what they really are; for by all that I could
> discern in their behaviour towards one another, and their deportment towards
> us, they are endued with all the humanity imaginable, and they make some
> nations (who would give these poor people the epithet of Savages and
> Barbarians) blush to think that they deserve that appellation more than
> they . . .
>
> In the main they lead a careless life, and have everything in common
> amongst them, and search for nothing except the necessary supports of life,
> viz., meat and drink, by which means they are free from the anxious troubles
> to which those nations are subject where Luxury and Pride have got any
> footing; a solid content seems to dwell in the midst of them, so that they covet
> (and have no reason for it) nothing belonging to one another; and never
> offered to pilfer or steal any of our tools, and other utensils, which might have
> been of great service to them . . .
>
> In a word they seem to pass their lives in the purest simplicity of the earliest
> ages of the world, before discord and contention were heard of amongst
> Men.[54]

52. Ibid., pp. 248, 257.
53. See Williams, '"Far More Happier than We Europeans"', p. 507.
54. Shelvocke, *Voyage*, pp. 405–7. These extracts can be usefully compared with *New Voyages to
     North-America by the Baron de Lahontan*, reprinted from the English edition of 1705, ed. R.G.
     Thwaites (Chicago, 1905), especially pp. 420–1; or *A New Voyage to Carolina by John Lawson*

29. 'Indian' of Southern California.
George Shelvocke, *Voyage* (1726).

At the opposite edge of the Pacific rim to Dampier's landing places in New
Holland, Shelvocke (or his editor) had come up with a very different
representation of a primitive lifestyle. The contrast between Dampier on the
Aborigines and Shelvocke on the Californian Indians is too episodic to bear
any weighty generalizations. Even so, there is a hint here that writers found
it easier to follow one or other of those artificial categories – noble or
ignoble savages – than to cope with the problem of describing an exotic
lifestyle without the help of such familiar value judgments.

The survivors of the Clipperton–Shelvocke expedition had returned to a
country where for years to come mention of the South Sea raised the spectre

[1709], ed. H.T. Lefler (Chapel Hill, 1967), especially pp. 243–4. Betagh described Shelvocke's
comments as written in 'comical stile . . . He would fain give us great ideas of the good
breeding and gentility of those savages.' *Voyage*, p. 215.

of the Bubble of 1720. The financial speculation and chicanery that led to the
crisis had little to do with the overseas trade, actual or potential, of the South
Sea Company; but the collapse of its shares had a chastening effect on
promoters and investors alike. The only discovery expedition of the period
to the Pacific was Dutch. In 1721 the West India Company fitted out three
ships under the command of Jacob Roggeveen to search for the 'long Tract
of pretty high Land' supposedly seen by the buccaneer Edward Davis, and
represented in the Wafer and Dampier accounts as, possibly, the coast of
Terra Australis Incognita.[55] Roggeveen failed to find 'Davis Land' and vented
his wrath on Davis, Wafer and Dampier alike – 'as much robbers of the truth
as of the goods of the Spaniards'.[56] Though the expedition was a commercial
failure and lost many men through scurvy, Roggeveen went on to make
landfalls of some importance: Easter Island, where Europeans saw for the first
time the great stone statues; the northern Tuamotus; the fringes of the
Society Islands; and Samoa. A few more pieces had been added to the jigsaw
of the map of the Pacific, though no details of the voyage were available in
English until 1744.

The main English riposte to Roggeveen was a paper one, Defoe's last
work of significance on the South Sea, his *New Voyage Round the World by
a Course Never Sailed Before* of 1724. The implicit acknowledgment to
Dampier in the title is followed by an account of a fictitious voyage that left
England at the end of 1713. The date is significant: peace had come to
Europe, and with it a cessation of those predatory expeditions in search of
Spanish wealth. It was a 'dream-fulfilment' of Defoe's earlier plans for South
Sea trade, never carried out in the way he wished.[57] As in 1711, he stressed
the opportunities awaiting British merchants in Chile. Following an error in
Moll's maps, Defoe postulated an overland journey of only eight days from
Valdivia, across the Andes, and onto the Atlantic coast.[58] In command of the
venture was a man who summed up all that Defoe looked for in a leader:
'reasonable, restrained, courageous, far-seeing and resourceful, with rational
and humane views on the handling of men. The orders given to his captain
are those which Defoe would have loved to issue in reality.'[59] The expedition represented Defoe's frustration that for all the talk of the South Sea in
previous years, nothing had been done in terms of discovery. If an article in
a periodical in August 1720 was indeed his, then it summed up this frustration: 'nor, as I can find, did all our Bubble Projectors ever propose one
Subscription for making Discoveries'.[60]

55. See p. 101 above.
56. Spate, *Monopolists and Freebooters*, p. 224.
57. Moore, 'Defoe and the South Sea Company', p. 186.
58. See Fishman, 'Defoe, Herman Moll, and the Geography of South America', pp. 227–38.
59. Jane H. Jack, 'A New Voyage Round the World: Defoe's *Roman à Thèse*', *Huntington Library
      Quarterly*, 24 (1960–1), p. 325.
60. See P.N. Furbank and W.R. Owens, *Defoe De-Attributions: A Critique of J.R. Moore's Checklist*
      (London, 1994), p. 124.

Although the book's emphasis was on Chile, Defoe took his voyagers away from South America and onto a wider prospect of 'New Worlds and new seas, which had never been heard of before'. By 1715 they were at the Ladrones, and from there they sailed south to find a succession of unknown lands. Given the state of knowledge at the time, there was nothing inherently improbable about the discoveries made. In lat. 17°S. east of the Moluccas and New Guinea they found 'not an Island, but a vast Tract of Land', much the same that Dampier had hoped to come across in 1699. Farther south, they found in lat. 32°S. lands never before visited by Europeans, where the inhabitants wore gold ornaments, and the crew found lumps of gold. Farther south still they reached the Pearl Islands, probably the long-sought Solomon Islands, Defoe thought. Only Le Maire and Schouten in 1616 had followed a track close to this; others had been blown along the trade wind belts, and so had found nothing new. With this in mind, Defoe anticipated a succession of mid-century advocates of Pacific discovery:

> I lay it down as a Foundation; that whoever, Sailing over the South-Seas, keeps a stated Distance from the Tropick to the Latitude of fifty six, to sixty Degrees, and steers Eastward towards the Straights of Magellan, shall never fail to discover new Worlds, new Nations, and new inexhaustible Funds of Wealth and Commerce, such as never were yet known to the Merchants of Europe.

'This is the true Ocean call'd the South-Sea,' Defoe added, a great ocean stretching from the equator to the South Pole, 'this unknown Part of the Globe'.[61]

By now the didactic had taken over from the descriptive as Defoe laid out a more gainful programme of commercial opportunities than that represented by the East India Company, its bullion-driven trade and its restrictive outlook. The numerous peoples of the newly discovered southern countries, lacking manufactures of their own, would take 'a very great Quantity of English Woollen-Manufactures . . . we shou'd have Gold in Specie, and perhaps Spices; the best Merchandize and Return in the World.'[62] If the trade of Defoe's discoveries was closer to the national interest than that of the monopolistic East India Company, so commerce in general was to be preferred to piracy. Defoe expressed his contempt for the pirates of the time – a leaderless, anarchic bunch, 'a Crew of unresolv'd divided Rogues . . . never two Days of a Mind . . . had no Body to command, and therefore no Body to obey.'[63] Instead, as Robert Markley has argued, 'Defoe offers his readers a vision of trade and exploration as an idealized extension

---

61. Daniel Defoe, *A New Voyage Round the World by a Course Never Sailed Before* (London, 1725 [1724]), Pt. I, p. 178.

62. Ibid., I, p. 177.

63. Ibid., I, p. 73.

of upper-class existence: many labor, few profit. At the heart of Defoe's novel lies a dream of explorers, pirates, merchants, and venture capitalists that does not die with the Bubble: getting something for nothing.'[64] Finally, Defoe turned to the moral dimensions of exploration and exploitation, though he did not probe very deep:

> it is our People, I mean the Europeans, breaking Faith with them, that first teaches them Ingratitude; and inures them to treat their new Comers with Breach of Faith, and with Cruelty and Barbarity. If you once win them by Kindness, and doing them good, I mean at first, before they are taught to be Rogues by Example, they will generally be honest, and be kind also to the uttermost of their Power.[65]

The Pacific kept its attraction for compilers of travel accounts and for writers looking for a safe haven in which to pitch their satires and fantasies; but it dropped out of the reckoning as a sphere of actual British activity for almost twenty years after Shelvocke's voyage. This raises the question of the links, if any, between literary interest and practical enterprise. One scholar has put the conundrum thus: 'If nothing more than curiosity and enthusiasm were needed to launch expeditions, a flurry of exploratory activity in the Pacific, led by the English, should certainly have commenced by about 1720. Nothing of the sort occurred.'[66] As far as the relationship between literature and enterprise in Britain is concerned, the issue can be argued in rather different ways. There is a temptation to see the South Sea setting of *Gulliver's Travels* of 1726 as evidence of strong contemporary interest in the Pacific, and as a way in which that interest was transmitted and increased through the wide readership of Swift's book. Swift began it in 1721; and in July 1722 he wrote that he was reading 'I don't know how many diverting Books of History and Travels'.[67] And it showed. Houyhnhnms Land was situated near the coast of New Holland (Ill. 30), the island of Lilliput (oddly) was northwest of Van Diemen's Land, which would place it firmly in the interior of Australia, and other islands of the *Travels* were scattered about the vast ocean. There was even room in the North Pacific for the monstrous bulk of Brobdingnag, whose three-thousand-mile coastline could be accommodated in the unexplored seas north of California and the 'Streights of Annian', and whose curious shape may have been an ironic comment on the insular/

---

64. Robert Markley, ' "So Inexhaustible a Treasure of Gold": Defoe, Capitalism, and the Romance of the South Sea', in Jonathan Lamb, Robert P. Maccubbin and David F. Morrill, eds, *The South Pacific in the Eighteenth Century: Narratives and Myths* (Baltimore, 1995), p. 150.
65. Defoe, *New Voyage*, II, p. 202.
66. Daniel Baugh, 'Seapower and Science: The Motives for Pacific Exploration', in Derek Howse, ed., *Background to Discovery: Pacific Exploration from Dampier to Cook* (Berkeley and Los Angeles, 1990), p. 2.
67. Harold Williams, ed., *The Correspondence of Jonathan Swift*, II, *1714–1723* (Oxford, 1963), p. 430.

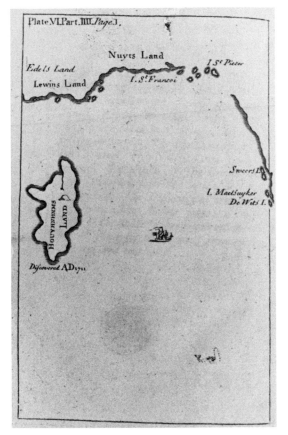

Plate VI.Part.IIII.Page.1.

Nuyts Land

Edels Land   I. St Pieter

Lewins Land   I. St Francoi

HOUYHNHNMS LAND

Smeers I.

I. Maetsuyker
De Wits I.

Discovered AD 1711

30. Houyhnhnms' Land, from
Gulliver's Travels (1726).

peninsular debate centred on California.[68] The artist who drew the maps for
the book almost certainly used Moll's 'New & Correct Map of the Whole
World' (1719) as his basis, and since Swift retained the maps in the definitive
Dublin edition of 1735 it may well be that their 'mistakes' were deliberate.[69]

Although the regions of the *Travels* are 'suspiciously extreme',[70] there are
echoes and hints of real voyages and real people throughout. The name of
Gulliver's ship on his first voyage to the Pacific was the *Antelope*, and he left
England in 1699, the same year as Dampier's departure in the *Roebuck*. On
3 June Dampier sighted a sail off the Cape of Good Hope, which turned out
to be the *Antelope*, though both its captain and port of origin were different

68. See Polk, *Island of California*, pp. 311–12.
69. See David Fausett, *Images of the Antipodes in the Eighteenth Century: A Study in Stereotyping*
     (Amsterdam, 1994), p. 46n.
70. Michael Seidel's words in 'Strange Dispositions: Swift's *Gulliver's Travels*' in Frank Palmeri, ed.,
     Critical Essays on Jonathan Swift (New York, 1993), p. 81.

from those of Gulliver's ship. The 'resolutely empirical, unimaginative style'[71] used by Gulliver to record his adventures ran close to Dampier's, for which the latter had been much criticized. Dampier referred to 'this plain piece of mine'; the publisher of the *Travels* to a style 'very plain and simple'. If Gulliver was Swift, then Gulliver's admission that he had corrected the style of Dampier's first book completes the chain. But the admission could be as much a trap as a clue. All that we can say is that, like Defoe, but perhaps not in person, Swift knew his Dampier and his Moll – and he acknowledged the debt. Of identifiable persons in the *Travels* 'My cousin Dampier' was the first, 'my worthy friend Mr Herman Moll' the last.

A contrary view might argue that Swift's choice of the Pacific for Gulliver's exploits firmly categorized it as a region outside the sphere of reality, a never-never land approachable only in fiction and satire. In this reading the inconsistencies of distances, bearings and locations that confuse the geography of *Gulliver's Travels* are not the result of printers' errors or an artist's carelessness,[72] but intentional, a deliberate parody of travel accounts that was part, though perhaps a minor part, of Swift's task. The reference to Dampier is not an acknowledgment in the normal sense, certainly not a question of Swift tipping his hat to a mentor, as has been suggested.[73] Rather it is 'a satiric jab' at travellers and their representations, for if 'Dampier is the age's Scientific Hero; Gulliver is Swift's Antihero'.[74] If this interpretation is correct, then the Pacific setting of *Gulliver's Travels* lacks any intended significance as a signpost pointing the way for future voyages. Further, the casting of the book as a voyage narrative does not imply even the neutrality of a literary device, for the elements of mockery and parody are as applicable to the form of Swift's book as to its content. 'I thought we were already overstocked with Books of Travels,' Gulliver replies when the sea-captain who rescues him from Brobdingnag expresses the hope that he will publish an account of his adventures.[75]

There is further evidence in Swift's earlier writings that Terra Australis Incognita had long been one of his targets – though again, one hesitates over the word. In *A Tale of a Tub*, published in 1704, but probably written seven or eight years earlier (about the time of the publication of Dampier's *New Voyage*), Lord Peter's first undertaking was 'to purchase a Large Continent, lately said to have been discovered in *Terra Australis*

71. Ricardo Quintana's description in '*Gulliver's Travels*: Some Structural Properties and Certain Questions of Critical Approach and Interpretation', in Claude Rawson, ed., *The Character of Swift's Satire: A Revised Focus* (Cranbury, NJ, 1983), p. 301.
72. As is ingeniously argued in Arthur E. Case, 'The Geography and Chronology of Gulliver's Travels', in his *Four Essays on Gulliver's Travels* (Princeton, 1945), pp. 50–68.
73. By Ross Gibson, *The Diminishing Paradise: Changing Literary Perceptions of Australia* (Sydney, 1984), p. 14.
74. Charles L. Batten, Jr, 'Literary Responses to the Eighteenth-Century Voyages', in Howse, *Background to Discovery*, pp. 153, 156.
75. This is quoted from p. 189 in the Penguin edition of *Gulliver's Travels*, ed. Peter Dixon and John Chalker (Harmondsworth, 1967).

Incognita.[76] This may have been a reference to Dampier; to the discovery of 'James Sadeur', for Gabriel de Foigny's *La Terra Australe Connue* had appeared in an English translation in 1693; or to nothing specific at all. Foigny's book might have appealed to Swift, for it was fantasy based on fantasy insofar as it was an elaboration of the claims of Quiros: 'We found a Country much more Fertile and Populous than any in Europe; that the Inhabitants were much Bigger and Taller than the Europeans; and that they lived much longer than they.'[77] Lord Peter's Terra Australis was of more benefit to its proprietor than to the emigrants. Because all the purchasers of land who went there were shipwrecked, he was able to sell the land over and over again. Even so, although he never got round to embodying him in book form, Swift's exotic visitor to Europe – the equivalent of Lahontan's Huron or Montesquieu's Persian – was to come from Terra Australis.[78]

Rather later, among Swift's pieces published in 1720, was *A Project, for the Universal Benefit of Mankind*. It promised 'to print by Subscription in 96. large volumes in folio, an exact Description of *Terra Australis incognita*, collected with great care & pains from 999.learned & pious Authors of undoubted veracity.' It was to have maps and views, including one of its capital city, 'from a known Author who took an exact survey of it in a dream'. The first edition would run to 100,000 copies, and with translations into most languages of the world millions of copies would be sold. In a prophetic flash, Swift announced that this was 'the spacious Country, where by a general Doom all transgressors of the law are to be transported'. The project, he announced, 'will tend to the great benefit of all Mankind, & produce a handsom Revenue to the Author'.[79] The sentiments would have been familiar to anyone that year reading the prospectuses of the various Bubble projects. At a more individual level, from his debtor's prison poor deluded John Welbe was making much the same claims at much the same time. The line between fact and fiction, fantasy and reality, was a wavering one in the London of 1720.

When Swift turned to *Gulliver's Travels* he seemed determined to pit those natural allies, Dampier and Defoe, against each other – though at no time did he directly acknowledge the existence of *Robinson Crusoe*.[80] On his fourth and final voyage Gulliver appears to be trying to emulate Crusoe as he explains that, on leaving the land of the Houyhnhnms, 'My design was, if possible, to discover some small island uninhabited, yet sufficient by my

76. Jonathan Swift, *A Tale of a Tub*, ed. A.C. Guthketch and D. Nichol Smith (2nd edn, Oxford, 1958), pp. 106–7.
77. *A New Discovery of Terra Incognita Australis, or the Southern World, by James Sadeur* (London, 1693), preface; see also p. 74 above. For more on the influence of Foigny on Swift, see Fausett, *Images of the Antipodes*, pp. 39–54.
78. Swift, *Tale of a Tub*, p. 352.
79. Ibid., p. 310.
80. See Seidel, *Robinson Crusoe*, p. 19.

labour to furnish me with the necessaries of life.' What follows owes much
to Dampier as Gulliver pointed his canoe eastwards and after two days
paddling reached 'the south-west point of New Holland'. 'The maps and
charts placed this country at least three degrees more to the east than it really
is,'[81] his account ran – a reference to Moll's maps, and a gloss on Dampier's
note that the west coast of New Holland 'is less by 195 Leagues [from the
Cape of Good Hope] than is usually laid down in our common Draughts'.[82]
Again, uncertainty arises. Is this a recognition by Swift that the inability to
determine longitude at sea was one of the main navigational hazards of the
age, though it is of precious little relevance to Gulliver in his canoe; or is it
a tilt at the supposedly scientific cartographers of his day who cannot even
get a continental coast right to within a few hundred miles? Once ashore,
Gulliver began to venture inland, but on the fourth day after landing went
'a little too far' and encountered twenty or thirty natives. In the account
that follows there is much that resembles Dampier's brush with the Aborigines in 1699 – the nakedness, the hostility, the fear of poisoned weapons.[83]
'They were stark naked, men, women, and children . . . five of them
advanced toward me . . . ran after me, and before I could get far enough
into the sea, discharged an arrow . . . I apprehended the arrow might be
poisoned, and paddling out of the reach of their darts . . . I made a shift
to suck the wound.'[84] A Crusoe-like solitary life had brought pain and
despair.

Only a few pages later, in the last chapter of the book, Swift launched an
attack on the veracity of travel accounts and, more sombrely, on discovery
and its consequences:

> a crew of pirates are driven by a storm they know not whither, at length a boy
> discovers land from the topmast, they go on shore to rob and plunder; they see
> an harmless people, are entertained with kindness, they give the country a new
> name, they take formal possession of it for the King, they set up a rotten plank
> or a stone for a memorial, they murder two or three dozen of the natives,
> bring away a couple more by force for a sample, return home, and get their
> pardon. Here commences a new dominion acquired with a title by *divine
> right*.[85]

From this indictment Swift excluded the British, but in language so extravagant – 'an example to the whole world for their wisdom, care and justice in
planting colonies . . . utter strangers to corruption . . . have no other views
than the happiness of the people over whom they preside' – as to add weight

81. The two quotations are from the Penguin edition of *Gulliver's Travels*, pp. 332, 333.
82. Dampier, *Voyage to New-Holland*, p. 107.
83. See pp. 108–9 above.
84. Swift, *Gulliver's Travels*, p. 333.
85. Ibid., p. 343.

to those scholars who consider this another example of Swiftian parody.[86] The sharpest thrust of Swift's condemnation of 'this execrable crew of butchers employed in so pious an expedition' looks back to an earlier age, to the conquest of America and to Montaigne's accusation that the true savages were the Europeans. But there is also an anticipation of the anti-colonial critics of the later eighteenth century – of Raynal, Diderot and Georg Forster – moved by the plight of distant peoples as they endured a process of 'discovery' by Europe.

86. Ibid., p. 344; and see Claude Rawson, *Order from Confusion Sprung* (London, 1985), p. 101 n. 10. Neil Rennie, *Far-Fetched Facts: The Literature of Travel and the Idea of the South Sea* (Oxford, 1996) has much of interest on Swift, Defoe and other writers of this period, but was published too late for the present writer to make use of it.

CHAPTER IX

'Our Second Drake': Anson's Circumnavigation

Although financial and mercantile confidence slowly recovered in Walpole's Britain after the catastrophe of 1720, little was heard of the sort of wild speculative ventures that had characterized the period of the Bubble. Defoe summed up the new mood of caution when he wrote that it seemed as if 'the enterprising Genius was buried with the old Discoverers, and there was neither Room in the World nor Inclination in our People to look any farther.'[1] Growth and expansion there were, but within known limits. The important trade with Old Spain once more reasserted itself as the fulcrum of Anglo–Spanish relations, which at least implied a commitment to peace between the two countries in the New World. Instead, a revival of the long-standing disputes over the terms of the Treaty of Utrecht, in particular the concession of the *asiento* to the South Sea Company and the right to send a yearly ship to the trade fairs of the Spanish Main, began to sour the atmosphere. Both sides had justifiable grievances, and although diplomats put together a settlement of the various issues in 1738, the obstructiveness of the South Sea Company backed by a warlike clamour from opposition politicians brought about a breakdown in the negotiations. In the summer of 1739 both governments ordered fleets to sea, and in October war was declared.

In London there was a general expectation that the new war would not see a repetition of the costly continental campaigns of Marlborough's day; instead it would be a maritime struggle in which the navy would be used to strike at Spanish colonies and shipping. In June, well before the formal declaration of hostilities, the Admiralty sent ships to seize the Spanish *flota* as it sailed from Cadiz, while in July Vernon was ordered to the Spanish Main. To go further and set in motion operations involving seizure of territory needed more thought. At least there was no shortage of plans for the

---

1. [Daniel Defoe], *A Plan of the English Commerce* (2nd edn, London, 1730), pp. xiii–xiv.

government to consider, and the files of ministers bulged with plans for conquering Spain's overseas territories: Havana, Vera Cruz, Cartagena and Darien in the Caribbean; Panama, Lima and Manila in the Pacific. So wide and beguiling was the choice of objectives that the two main offensive schemes that emerged by the autumn of 1739 were still couched only in general terms. The first, and more important, was a plan to follow Vernon's expedition with a large-scale attack on Spanish colonies somewhere in the Caribbean.

The second, which led to Anson's voyage, was a proposal to send one or more expeditions to the Pacific. Although a meeting of the Cabinet Council as early as 3 June seems to have looked at a plan for a venture into the South Sea,[2] it was September before the two senior naval advisers to the government, Sir Charles Wager, First Lord of the Admiralty, and Sir John Norris, Admiral of the Fleet, gave it any detailed consideration. Both men had shown interest in the region thirty years earlier, during the War of the Spanish Succession, and Wager had turned over in his mind the possibility of a South Sea venture in 1727.[3] Another link with the past was provided by two former factors of the South Sea Company who helped to plan the Anson voyage, Hubert Tassell and Henry Hutchinson. Tassell had served as a Company factor in Havana, while Hutchinson had been a Company factor at Panama and Portobelo, and had also visited Lima, probably in 1736 or 1737.[4] Although neither trader was still in the employ of the South Sea Company – and Hutchinson had been in dispute with the Company over his accounts for several years – the two men brought a practical dimension to the discussions on the proposed South Sea expedition.

The twists and turns of those discussions from September 1739 to January 1740 can be followed in the pages of Norris's private journal, a valuable source of information about the preparations for war.[5] On 11 September Tassell and Hutchinson wrote to Walpole suggesting that a squadron carrying fifteen hundred soldiers should be sent around Cape Horn to attack the Pacific coasts of Spanish America, and at the end of the month they put their plan in person to Wager and Norris.[6] To anyone who had read Defoe or Rogers, much of it had a familiar ring: the force was to conquer Chile, plunder Lima and perhaps establish a government there that was well disposed to the British, seize other coastal towns and then attack Panama. Smaller craft might be detached from the squadron to fortify Juan Fernández as 'a settlement, retreat, or as a place of rendezvous'. In a separate

2. BL: Add. MS 32,993, f. 59.
3. See BL: Add. MS 28,140, ff. 20–34, and p. 202 above.
4. See BL: Add. MSS 25,510 and 25,558 passim.
5. 'A Journal of my Proceedings' by Sir John Norris, 1739–40. Add. MS 28,132. Extracts from it, together with some of the other sources relating to the Anson expedition, are printed in Glyndwr Williams, ed., Documents Relating to Anson's Voyage Round the World 1740–1744 (London, Navy Records Society, 1967). This will be referred to hereafter as Documents.
6. BL: Add. MSS 32,694, ff. 41–5 and 28,132, 17, 29 Sep. 1739 (Documents, pp. 7–8, 18–21).

memorandum Hutchinson noted that he had in his possession 'a modern manuscript coasting pilot of all the South Sea coast from Cape Horn to California', together with first-hand information on the state of Spanish defences in the South Sea. So, for example, Callao might be stormed in one night and then

> Lima six miles from it would be taken with little or no resistance with the treasure in it, or the greatest part, there being only two or three hundred peaceable soldiers and a militia unused to arms except for the parade of processions and church festivals. The city is surrounded by a wall of unburnt brick except the side towards a river and suburbs. There are no cannon nor anything more on the wall than a parapet of unburnt brick of about two foot thick.[7]

Despite the insistence of the two traders that Spanish defences along the Pacific seaboard were weak, and rebellion among the Creole or Indian inhabitants probable, the reaction of Wager and Norris to these sweeping proposals was cautious. Both were doubtful about the wisdom of sending land forces to the Pacific and thought that an attack on Panama would be better mounted across the Isthmus, Henry Morgan style; but in mid-October they endorsed the principle of a raiding expedition along the coasts of Chile and Peru.[8]

With a South Sea expedition agreed on 16 October, two days later Wager and Norris met James Naish, a former supercargo of the East India Company, with long experience (since 1713 at least) of trading to China and the Eastern Seas. His service with the Company had come to an end in 1731 when he was accused of fraud and smuggling, and the dispute had only been settled in March 1739. If a letter by him of 9 August 1739 among the Wager Papers was indeed written to Wager, then it is clear that the two men knew each other and that Naish had 'often' talked to the First Lord of the Admiralty about the possibility of capturing Manila, the great Spanish entrepôt in the North Pacific and the destination of the Acapulco treasure galleon.[9] At the meeting of 18 October Naish produced detailed proposals and volunteered to accompany the expedition. Summaries of the scheme are in the Newcastle and Wager Papers, and by a fortunate chance Naish's views have survived in a fuller version as a long note written by him some years later in his copy of the authorized account of the Anson expedition, *A Voyage Round the World by George Anson* (1748). Like Hutchinson and Tassell, Naish was alert to the wider implications of a predatory expedition to the Pacific. The conquest of the Philippines, he argued, would give British traders in the East a decisive

7. PRO: SP 42/88, ff. 37–41 (*Documents*, p. 23).
8. BL: Add. MS 28,132, 16 Oct. 1739 (*Documents*, pp. 8–9).
9. Wager MS, f. 45,846 (*Documents*, p. 27).

advantage over their foreign rivals 'for extending of commerce to Cochin-China, Cambodia, Siam, Ichore, the coasts of China, and in any islands upon them; and to Japan, and even to the coasts of Mexico, Peru, and Chile; and to every island and place in the vast Pacific Ocean.'[10]

Wager and Norris evidently caught some of Naish's enthusiasm, and despite a frosty comment by the Duke of Newcastle, Secretary of State for the Southern Department, that 'this was a small affair, and that greater matters had been under consideration',[11] they put both the South Sea and Manila schemes before a meeting of leading ministers on 29 October. Hutchinson and Tassell had already written to a minister (probably Newcastle) a few days before trying to enlist his support by supplying a brief abstract of their proposal. A squadron of four men-of-war, two snows and two victuallers would be sufficient, they claimed, 'to settle some island in the South Sea; to succeed in a descent on Peru; to take two men-of-war and the Lima fleet; to take Panama and their treasure; to take several valuable towns; to take the Acapulco ship; and to induce the Peruvians to throw off their obedience to the King of Spain.'[12] At the meeting of 29 October Naish's proposals were approved in principle, but commitments elsewhere made it impossible to send a land force of any size into the South Sea. Instead of the fifteen hundred or two thousand soldiers Hutchinson had in mind, only two hundred could be spared. Norris's private journal makes it clear that some ministers, Newcastle and the Earl of Harrington (Secretary of State for the Northern Department) in particular, had reservations about both Pacific expeditions. Norris himself was beginning to suspect that trade as well as war might be involved. He was not informed of at least one meeting to discuss details of the South Sea squadron – an oversight, he was assured – and when he asked Wager whether trading goods were to be carried on the ships he was told that 'Mr. Tassell would take care of that, by which methods I saw it was a voyage to cover some adventure I was not let into, as well as to annoy the Spanish navigation in those seas.'[13] Finally, after a further fortnight of uncertainty, Walpole came to a decision. Although the squadron for Cape Horn and the South Sea was to go ahead, the forces needed for the Manila enterprise could not be found. He had at first thought it 'a proper enterprise, but . . . everybody's thoughts were upon an undertaking in the West Indies as the place where it was thought that the Spaniards could be most affected.'[14] The debates in Parliament that November on the prosecution of the war certainly confirmed this. Speaker after speaker urged the government

10. Notes by Naish on his copy of *A Voyage Round the World by George Anson* (London, 1748), now in BL 10,025, f. 8 (pp. 1–13); see also BL: Add. MS 28,132, 18, 20 Oct. 1739 (*Documents*, pp. 9–10).
11. BL: Add. MS 28,132, 23 Oct. 1739 (*Documents*, p. 10).
12. BL: Add. MS 32,694, f. 47 (*Documents*, pp. 33–4).
13. BL: Add. MS 28,132, 10 Nov. 1739 (*Documents*, p. 12).
14. Ibid., 5 Dec. 1739 (*Documents*, p. 14).

to attack in the Caribbean, and there was no hint that 'side-shows' in the
Pacific were considered necessary or desirable.[15]

At Wager's suggestion George Anson, an experienced naval captain forty-
two years old, had been chosen for the Manila project, and on its abandonment he was given command of the Cape Horn expedition. His orders were
drawn up personally by Wager[16] and reveal that the expedition was still
regarded as something more than a plundering raid. Attacks on Spanish
American ports and shipping, and the capture of the Acapulco galleon, were
the routine buccaneering and privateering objectives of an earlier time; but
the clauses that dealt with the encouragement of rebellion in Peru and the
establishment there of a government sympathetic towards British merchants
had much wider implications. A draft manifesto drawn up before Anson
sailed promised British protection, freedom of trade and religious liberty to
all who rose against the authority of the Spanish crown.[17] There was also a
suggestion that if the wealthy Creole inhabitants did not rebel, then an
attempt might be made to win over the mulattos and oppressed Negro slaves
by offering them their freedom – by the standards of the time an incendiary
proposition, and one that in the end did not find its way into Anson's official
orders.[18] Although the possibility of rebellion within the Spanish colonies had
often been mentioned in earlier proposals, Anson's instructions are the first
evidence of any awareness in government circles that the most promising
openings for British merchants would come if Spain's American empire, with
or without British help, moved towards independence.

At the same time that Anson's ships were preparing for sea, Wager
signified his approval for another, less publicized expedition which hoped to
reach the Pacific by way of a Northwest Passage. The venture was the
brainchild of Arthur Dobbs, Surveyor-General of Ireland and a confidant of
Walpole's. Since 1731, when he had drafted a seventy-page memorial on the
subject, he had sought support for a voyage to Hudson Bay to find a
Northwest Passage. Opposition from the Hudson's Bay Company, whose
directors still remembered the disaster of James Knight's voyage of 1719, and
an initial lack of interest by the Admiralty failed to quench Dobbs's enthusiasm. To the readers of his memorial he outlined a glittering prospect which
appealed to national pride, to commercial acquisitiveness and to old fantasies
about the South Sea:

> What great Advantages might be made by having a passage to California in
> three or four Months & so down the Western Coast of America into the
> South Sea where a New and beneficial Commerce might be carry'd on along

15.   See W. Cobbett, *The Parliamentary History of England*, XI (London, 1812), pp. 16–19, 24, 87, 91,
      93–4, 138, 152, 251–2, 286.
16.   PRO: SP 42/81, ff. 293–8, 42/88, ff. 2–10 (*Documents*, pp. 34–9).
17.   BL: Add. MS 19,030, ff. 470–2 (*Documents*, pp. 39–41).
18.   BL: Add. MS 32,694, ff. 88–93 (*Documents*, p. 20).

the Spanish Coasts & among many Islands & Countrys in the Great Southern Ocean not yet fully discover'd Such as the Islands of Solomon etc. How Great would be the benefit in time of War to be able in a Short time to send Ships of War or Privateers into the South Sea to intercept the Spanish Commerce. How great would be the benefit to send Ships an Easy & short way to Japan & Even to China, & to be able to send a Squadron of Ships, Even to force Japan into a Beneficial Treaty of Commerce with Britain. How great would be the Advantage of opening a New Trade for our Woollen Manufactures in the Temperate & Cold Regions near California in America & along the Country of Yedso[19] & other Countrys in our Passage yet unknown . . . By making a few Settlements there we should ingross All their Commerce & open a New Market for our Manufactures vastly advantagious to us, Inlarge our Trade for furs, increase our Navigation, and Employ all our Poor.[20]

The more Dobbs read about the earlier explorations of Hudson Bay, the more convinced he became that a passage existed in the area of Roe's Welcome in lat. 64°N. on the west coast of Hudson Bay. By 1736 he had enlisted the support of Christopher Middleton, one of the Hudson's Bay Company sea-captains, whose navigational skills and scientific knowledge were recognized the next year when he was elected a Fellow of the Royal Society. Official support was less easy to come by. In March 1738 Sir Charles Wager wrote to Dobbs agreeing that 'if a Passage could be found into the South Sea, it would open a very large Field, and very probably of a very profitable Commerce'; but although he had himself long been interested in the possibility of a passage, 'I have found but very few that were willing to bestow any Thoughts about it.' With tension with Spain increasing, he doubted whether such a venture would attract government interest, since 'Parliament may think, especially at this Time, that we ought not to play with the Money they give us, for other and particular Services.'[21] When war actually came the next year, Dobbs tried to turn it to the advantage of his scheme, as he reminded Wager that if a passage were found 'we might intercept their Acapulco Ships, and make many Prizes from California to Panama, before they would suspect our being upon their Coasts.'[22] Whether this argument had any effect,

---

19. Yedso or Yezo (present-day Hokkaido) had been the subject of speculation since Jesuit reports from Japan in the sixteenth century. In the 1730s Yedso was often shown as a landmass somewhere between the 'Company Land' of the seventeenth-century Dutch explorers of the North Pacific and Kamchatka.

20. There are at least five manuscript copies of Dobbs's 'Memorial' extant. See the present writer's note on these in William Barr and Glyndwr Williams, eds, *Voyages to Hudson Bay in Search of a Northwest Passage 1741–1747*, I, *The Voyage of Christopher Middleton 1741–1742* (London, 1994), p. 9 n. 1. The extract given here is printed ibid., pp. 34–5.

21. Wager to Dobbs, 4 March 1738. Printed ibid., pp. 49–50.

22. Dobbs to Wager, 30 Oct. 1739. Printed ibid., pp. 55–6.

or whether the fitting out of Anson's expedition for the same region brought a change of mind, is uncertain; but in May 1740 Wager told Middleton that he had mentioned the scheme to the King (George II) who 'seemed to approve it very well'.[23]

The next year Middleton, now a captain in the Royal Navy, commanded two vessels which sailed in June 1741 for Hudson Bay and, it was hoped, the Northwest Passage. Once through the passage, Middleton was to explore the Pacific coasts of North America, negotiate alliances with native rulers and take possession of 'convenient Situations' in the King's name. On the coast of California he was to watch out for Anson, who by December 1741 was expected to be off Cape Saint Lucas, lying in wait for the Manila galleon. But if Middleton encountered ships from Japan or any other power he was to bear away for home, 'that Ships of Sufficient Force may be sent out next Season to begin a Trade, or make a Settlement'. Breathtaking in their easy optimism, Middleton's instructions anticipated events of the next reign, when naval vessels ranging the Pacific on survey work were on the alert for opportunities of trade and settlement.[24]

The fitting out of Anson's squadron and the approval of the smaller discovery expedition under Middleton resurrected older plans of a twin approach to the Pacific by a southern and a northern route. The plans noised abroad in the War of the Spanish Succession had, it seemed, come to fruition at last. It was no longer a matter of projects advanced by gadfly pamphleteers or by memorialists with dubious buccaneering backgrounds. The South Sea plans of the autumn of 1739, though in scope not much different from earlier ones, had found their way to the heart of government. With Wager and Norris acting, in a sense, as guarantors, the schemes were taken seriously by ministers from Walpole downwards. Although the decision not to go ahead with the Manila venture and to reduce the size of the Cape Horn expedition disappointed their promoters, what was agreed in late 1739 was still impressive – not a couple of small privateering vessels, but a naval squadron of some force. For the first time British warships were to be used as instruments of commercial imperialism in the Pacific. The wheel, it seemed, had come full circle since Defoe's rather hopeless admission in the years after the South Sea Bubble that future enterprise in such distant regions would have to rely on 'the little Adventures of single Men, and the small Undertakings of a few'.[25]

Hindsight would show that the hopes that prompted the sending of Anson to the Pacific were as unrealistic as those behind earlier ventures. The projects of Tassell, Hutchinson and Naish paid little attention to the likely reactions in Old and New Spain to foreign incursions; nor did they take

23. Middleton to Dobbs, 1 May 1740. Printed ibid., p. 66.
24. Middleton's instructions are in PRO: Adm 2/37, pp. 98–100 and are printed ibid., pp. 86–9.
25. [Daniel Defoe], *A General History of Discoveries and Improvements* (London, 1726–7), p. iii.

account of the diplomatic pressures that would be brought to bear (as they had been in 1711 and would again be in 1762) on any attempts at territorial adjustment within the Spanish colonial empire. Anson's sailing instructions revealed more immediate difficulties. In one hand he held instructions to destroy Spanish American towns and shipping; in the other exhortations to gain the confidence of all Spanish Americans ready to rebel against viceregal rule. The inquiries of Antonio de Ulloa and Jorge Juan in Peru at this time were providing disturbing evidence for the Spanish government of discontent in its American possessions;[26] but there was little likelihood that any substantial section of the colonial population would welcome marauding heretics with open arms. The problem remained that explained by St John in 1711 when he pointed out that 'the prospects of opening a new trade with the Spaniards and of attacking their colonies at the same time tended to be repugnant one to another'.[27]

The squadron put under Anson's command at the beginning of 1740 consisted of the flagship *Centurion* (1005 tons, 60 guns, 521 men), the *Gloucester* (866 tons, 50 guns, 396 men), the *Severn* (833 tons, 50 guns, 384 men), the *Pearl* (595 tons, 40 guns, 299 men), the *Wager* (559 tons, 24 guns, 243 men), the *Tryal* (200 tons, 8 guns, 96 men) and two merchant vessels, the *Anna* and *Industry*, carrying supplies.[28] To see the ships' names on a royal commission was one thing; to get the vessels to sea, manned and in fit condition for a voyage to the other side of the world, was another. With large forces fitting out for the Caribbean and for home waters, naval dockyards and victualling departments were strained to the utmost in the first full year of the war.[29] Anson's squadron at Spithead came low on the list of priorities. In June 1740 major repairs to his largest ships were still at the discussion stage, and in despair at the slowness of the work Anson wrote to Wager's secretary, 'as Sir Charles Wager is so fully employed when in town, and has so many people continually seizing him'.[30] A complaint from Anson that twenty pressed men had been taken out of his tender and sent on board another ship was shrugged aside by the Admiralty. In July the only response to his request for more men was an order to make up his complement with men discharged from hospital, drafts brought in by the press gang, and marines quartered in the neighbourhood.[31]

26.   See Jorge Juan and Antonio de Ulloa, *Relación Histórica del Viaje a la América Meridional* (Madrid, 1758).
27.   See Williams, 'The Inexhaustible Fountain of Gold', p. 52.
28.   These details are from Boyle Somerville, *Commodore Anson's Voyage into the South Seas and Around the World* (London, 1934), p. xvi. The ships' complements noted above included about 470 land forces.
29.   See Daniel A. Baugh, *British Naval Administration in the Age of Walpole* (Princeton, 1965), Ch. IV.
30.   PRO: Adm 1/4109, f. 164.
31.   PRO: Adm 1/1439, letters of 9 June, 11 July, 25 July, 28 July 1740.

Fleets fitting out for sea in the eighteenth century were accustomed to receiving their share of human flotsam and jetsam, men with neither aptitude nor enthusiasm for life at sea. It was one of the grim achievements of the Georgian navy that this unpromising material was knocked into shape; but nothing could be done with the pitiful procession of pensioners from Chelsea Hospital who straggled on board Anson's ships in place of the regiment of regular soldiers originally envisaged. Eight years later the authorized account of the voyage written under Anson's supervision conveyed something of his feelings at this time: 'As these out-pensioners consist of soldiers, who from their age, wounds, or other infirmities, are incapable of service in marching regiments, Mr. Anson was greatly chagrined at having such a decrepit detachment allotted him; for he was fully persuaded that the greatest part of them would perish long before they arrived at the scene of action.'[32] Worse was to follow, for Anson discovered that of the two thousand pensioners at Chelsea Hospital, those selected for the voyage were the oldest and weakest, and 'instead of five hundred, there came on board no more than two hundred and fifty-nine; for all those who had limbs and strength to walk out of Portsmouth deserted, leaving behind them only such as were literally invalids, most of them being sixty years of age, and some of them upwards of seventy.'[33] Not one of them appears to have survived the voyage, and their presence on board the ships added to the problems of health and morale that afflicted the expedition from the beginning. To help these invalids storm the bastions of Spanish America 210 'marines' arrived, so raw that most of them had never fired a musket. These were thought fit for shipboard service on the grounds advanced by the Secretary at War in November 1739: 'In fighting a ship there is no part of the land discipline required but that of loading and firing a musket, and a country fellow from the plough may be in three days taught to do this.'[34]

When the ships were at last ready for sea further delay followed from the decision that the squadron should act as escort to a fleet sailing for the West Indies, itself held up by unfavourable winds. Not until mid-September could Anson sail from Spithead, and even then he was given convoy duties. The effect of all this was explained by Lieutenant Philip Saumarez in the private journal he was keeping on the *Centurion*:

These several disappointments not only harassed and fatigued our men, but likewise disabled and shattered our ship in their attempts to get out, more especially the transports, who in the confusion of dark nights with blowing weather through the mistakes of signals frequently ran on board each other

---

32.　[Richard Walter and Benjamin Robins], *A Voyage Round the World in the Years MDCCXL, I, II, III, IV by George Anson* (London, 1748), p. 6. For a discussion of the authorship of the book see pp. 255–6 below.

33.　Ibid.

34.　*A Collection of Parliamentary Debates*, XVIII (1741), p. 462.

and contributed much to dispiriting our new raised marines who were novices to such accidents.[35]

A more worrying aspect of the delays was that they cost the expedition any chance it had of surprise. Before Anson sailed he knew that attempts to keep his destination secret had failed. In June two British naval vessels intercepted a Dutch ship in the Caribbean with Spanish officials on board. Papers seized from them showed that 'the King of Spain had notice of our fitting out six ships, with 700 land forces on board, for to go round Cape Horn to the South Sea, and expresses have been sent to the Viceroys of Peru and Mexico to be upon their guard.'[36] The source of this information is revealed in the French Foreign Ministry archives. As early as 30 January (New Style date) a letter was dispatched to the French ambassador at Madrid informing him that the English 'are sending six frigates under the command of M. Hanson [sic], which are under orders to round Cape Horn and enter the South Sea'.[37] Since these details had been agreed by the British government only two weeks earlier, the letter is an impressive testimony to the efficiency of the French secret service. Further correspondence shows that the French government, officially neutral, was bringing pressure to bear on Spain to intercept Anson,[38] and in October a force of five powerful warships under the command of Admiral Don José Pizarro left Santander for Madeira, Anson's first port of call.

In the event, the main forces of the two squadrons never encountered each other, though the *Pearl* was sighted and chased by Pizarro's ships off the Patagonian coast. Desperately short of provisions, the Spanish squadron was dispersed as it tried to round Cape Horn, and only Pizarro's flagship, the sixty-six-gun *Asia*, returned to Europe. Of the others the fifty-four-gun *Hermiona* sank at sea with no survivors, the seventy-four-gun *Guipuscoa* was run ashore by her mutinous crew, the shattered forty-gun *San Estevan* was abandoned at Montevideo, and only the fifty-gun *Esperanza* got round the Horn (in 1742) and reached Chile. As the 1748 account commented, 'The calamities of all kinds, which this squadron underwent in this unsuccessful navigation, can only be paralleled by what we ourselves experienced in the same climate, when buffeted by the same storms.'[39] Because of his late start, Anson was approaching Cape Horn in the southern hemisphere autumn, when the equinoctial gales were at their fiercest. The squadron confronted this ordeal with crews already weakened by sickness. Dysentery, typhus and malaria had swept through the ships as they crossed the Atlantic to the

---

35. Saumarez Papers: 'Historical Remarks', Sep. 1740 (*Documents*, p. 57).
36. PRO: Adm 1/1695, f. 272 (*Documents*, p. 52).
37. Archives du Ministère des Affaires Etrangères (AMAE): Corr. Pol./Espagne: Vol. 460, f. 46 (*Documents*, p. 53). The English date, given in the Julian or Old Style, for this letter would be 19 January 1740.
38. Ibid., Vol. 460, f. 192; Vol. 462, ff. 119, 149, 238v (*Documents*, pp. 53–4).
39. [Walter and Robins], *Anson's Voyage*, p. 22.

Brazilian coast. The worst casualties were on the *Centurion* and *Severn*, which between them lost seventy-five men in this period.[40] The passage round the Horn brought the even more fearsome scourge of scurvy, whose ravages were increased by the poor health of many of the crews and especially the pensioners, by overcrowding (with five hundred land forces on board, hammocks were slung even less than the regulation fourteen inches apart), and by inferior provisions.

The journal writers all had their own descriptions of scurvy and their own remedies, ranging from exposure to land breezes to various forms of diet and medicine. Scurvy took a different form in almost every sufferer, the authorized account noted, but the

> common experiences are large, discoloured spots dispersed over the whole surface of the body, swelled legs, putrid gums, and above all, an extraordinary lassitude . . . the whole body, but more especially the legs, were subject to ulcers of the worst kind, attended with rotten bones, and such a luxuriancy of fungous flesh, as yielded to no remedy.[41]

Pascoe Thomas, the schoolmaster on the *Centurion*, gave a more personal account as he described how his legs and thighs turned black, his teeth fell loose and his whole body was racked by such insupportable pains that 'one week more at sea would have ended me'.[42]

During the forty days of continuous gales as they tried to beat into the Pacific, men died in their hundreds, the *Wager* was wrecked and the *Severn* and *Pearl* turned back. Account after account dwelt on the monstrous seas, and this was not just a case of timorous landlubbers aghast at their first sniff of rough weather. Captain Legge on the *Pearl* thought that the size of the waves 'by much exceeds anything that I ever saw, or that I could find any man in my ship had ever seen in the northern hemisphere'.[43] Pascoe Thomas's description of conditions on the *Centurion* can stand for the rest:

> The Sea went Mountains high . . . our Ship was nothing to them, but notwithstanding her large Bulk, and deep Hold in the Water, was toss'd and bandy'd as if she had been no more than a little pitiful Wherry; those Seas often broke in upon her Decks, and even upon her very Quarter Deck, with the most prodigious Violence. Her Decks were almost always full of Water; washing from Side to Side, the Gratings of the Head were torn up, the necessary Houses there wash'd down . . . The Ship rolled almost Gunnel-to continually, the Sails were almost always splitting and blowing from the Yards;

40.   See James Watt, 'Commodore Anson's Circumnavigation (1740–1744): the Bequests of Disaster at Sea', *Transactions & Studies of the College of Physicians of Philadelphia*, Ser. 5, Vol. 7 (1985), p. 227.
41.   [Walter and Robins], *Anson's Voyage*, pp. 101–2.
42.   Pascoe Thomas, *A True and Impartial Journal of a Voyage to the South Seas* (London, 1745), p. 141.
43.   PRO: Adm 1/2040, section 11 (*Documents*, p. 90).

the Yards themselves frequently breaking; the Shrouds and other Rigging cracking and flying in Pieces.[44]

In the freezing weather men lost the use of their limbs from frostbite. Water and food ran short, and the crew's misery was increased by the lice which covered the living, the dying and the dead – a peck (two gallons) on each man, the purser on the *Tryal* estimated.[45] On the *Centurion* the crew were so weak that dead bodies washed about the deck, for no man had the strength to heave them overboard.

The most disheartening shock was still to come. By the end of March 1741 the ships of the squadron, miraculously it seemed all still afloat and in company, were thought to have sailed ten degrees of longitude clear of the most westerly point of Tierra del Fuego. Secure with this margin of safety, they now headed north for the open waters of the Pacific, only to find themselves running at night straight onto a rocky lee shore (probably Cape Noir). The ships were almost three hundred miles east of their estimated position, and they had no alternative but to turn back into southern latitudes before beginning the wearisome business of beating west in far southerly latitudes again so as to clear Cape Horn. It was a terrifying example of the perils consequent upon the difficulty of determining longitude at sea, for the allowance made by the sailing masters on Anson's ships for wind and current had proved totally inadequate – and this was despite Frézier's earlier warning about ships that 'find themselves upon the Land, when they thought they had weather'd the Cape, and were 40 or 50 Leagues out at sea'.[46] The problem was illustrated in the authorized account by a detailed chart which marked 'both the real track which we described, and the imaginary track exhibited by our reckoning' (Ill. 31).[47]

Not until 22 April did Anson on the *Centurion* think it safe to turn north again, and by now his ship was alone. With 'our men dying four, five and six in a day', Anson headed for the first rendezvous of Nuestra Señora de Socorro in the Chonos Archipelago on the Chilean coast, but found no sign of the other ships. From there the *Centurion* headed out to sea again, making for the second rendezvous, the old privateer haven of Juan Fernández. The decision to sail west along the latitude until the destination was reached was wrecked by uncertainty over the island's longitude. Afraid that he had sailed past the island, Anson turned back east, only to sight once more the coast of Chile. It took another nine days to beat back west, and the delay cost the lives of eighty or ninety of the sick. When Juan Fernández came into sight on 9 June, only just over two hundred men were left alive, and most of them

44. Thomas, *True and Impartial Journal*, p. 21.
45. Lawrence Millechamp, 'A Narrative of Commodore Anson's Voyage into the Great South Sea and Round the World', NMM: MS 9354/JOD 36 (no page numbers) (*Documents*, p. 77).
46. Frézier, *Voyage to the South-Sea*, p. 42.
47. [Walter and Robins], *Anson's Voyage*, p. 97.

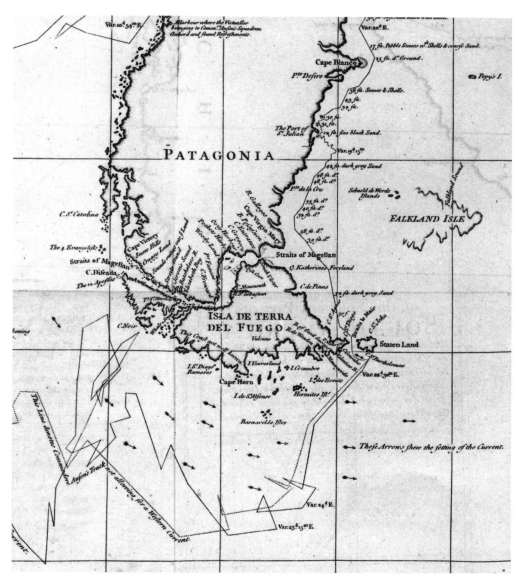

31. Track of the *Centurion* around Cape Horn, 1748.

were sick: 'the Lieutenant could muster no more than two Quarter-masters, and six Foremast men capable of working; so that without the assistance of the officers, servants and the boys, it might have proved impossible for us to have reached the Island, after we had got sight of it.'[48]

A few days later the *Tryal* reached Juan Fernández. Millechamp's story of

48. Ibid., p. 110.

the weeks since the sloop had parted company from the rest in late April was a familiar one: 'sometimes we had no more than the captain, lieutenant, surgeon, myself and two boys, with now and then one marine, to work the sloop, mend the sails, bury the dead . . .'[49] The sighting of the *Gloucester* on 21 June brought excitement and rejoicing on the island, but this was dampened when it took the sickly remnants of its crew almost a month to beat against the wind into harbour. Three-quarters of her men had died. The final, and most surprising, arrival was that of the victualler, the *Anna*, whose small crew had recuperated in a harbour on the Chilean coast before taking their vessel to Juan Fernández. Of the *Severn*, *Pearl* and *Wager* there was no sign.

The *Severn* and *Pearl* had lost company with the rest of the squadron, though not with each other, during the night of 10 April as the squadron sailed north, almost to its doom three days later on the rocks of Cape Noir. Edward Legge on the *Pearl* and George Murray on the *Severn* experienced the same fearful shock of sighting a lee shore when they thought they were hundreds of miles out to sea, but unlike the other captains within a few days they gave up the attempt to gain a westering by sailing south again. Their letters and minutes of consultation with their officers survive.[50] Legge wrote that his ship was 'in the utmost distress, and unable to strive against the wind and seas that were again come upon us, having no sails but what were worn to pieces and though mended and patched in the best manner we were able (the sailmaker dead and his mate sick) by no means sufficient to contend with such weather as we had met with for the last six weeks.'[51] Murray wrote at greater length and with more emotion about the state of affairs on the *Severn* after narrowly avoiding being driven ashore:

> Those poor men who had stood the deck with a resolution not to be met with in any but English seamen, though they were very thinly clad, having sold their clothes at St. Catharines, and when chased by the Spaniards [Pizarro's squadron] had thrown half ports, bulkheads and tarpaulins overboard, for want of which they were continually wet in their hammocks, the tarpaulins I made being of little service for want of sun to dry them. Yet under all these difficulties and discouragements they behaved beyond expectation hitherto, but being now quite jaded and fatigued with continual labour and watching, and pinched with the cold and want of water, on discovering how far we were out in our computation they became so dejected as to lay themselves down in despair, bewailing their misfortunes, wishing for death as the only relief

49. Millechamp, 'Narrative' (*Documents*, p. 78).
50. PRO: Adm 1/2040, section 11 (Legge's letters); Adm 1/2099, section 3 (Murray's letters); all printed in *Documents*, pp. 88–106.
51. PRO: Adm 1/2040, section 11, 4 July 1741 (*Documents*, p. 90).

to their miseries, and could not be induced by threats or entreaties to go aloft.[52]

On 17 April Legge, Murray and their officers agreed to retrace their track round Cape Horn, and the ships bore away southeast. On 6 June they reached Rio de Janeiro. The *Pearl* had only three casks of water left on board, and the *Severn* was in a worse state, with 114 men 'sick and absolutely unable to stir' and only thirty men able to carry out any duties. These were the only survivors out of the 384 who had sailed from England (the casualties were even heavier than these figures indicate, for in the intervening months forty or more extra men had been sent on board the *Severn*). Within a month the two captains were in disagreement over Murray's request to be allowed to make another attempt to get round the Horn and perhaps rejoin Anson. As his senior, Legge overrode this suggestion; instead the two ships with their much-diminished crews sailed for home, and to less than a heroes' welcome. There was no formal investigation into the concerted separation of the two vessels, but this did not stop comment. In April 1742 *The London Magazine* noted that Anson had arrived in the South Sea, 'notwithstanding the dismal accounts brought to us from the *Severn* and *Pearl* men-of-war, who parted from him in a storm, on the other side Cape Horn, and seems to have suffered more by returning than he did by proceeding'. The most damaging reference to the separation was made by Pascoe Thomas in his 1745 book of the voyage when he wrote that on the day of their disappearance the *Severn* and *Pearl* 'seemed to me to lag designedly'.[53] The accusation was not repeated in the authorized account of the voyage published in 1748. This stressed the 'great joy' with which news of the survival of the two ships was greeted by the *Centurion*'s crew at Macao in 1742, and the 'exemplary punctuality' with which Legge had kept station until his crew were affected by 'extraordinary sickness'.[54] By now Legge was dead, but his brother Henry wrote to Anson thanking him for protecting Edward's memory 'against coffee-house cen-surers, and the cavils of those children of ease who sit at home and, without risking themselves, blame every man's conduct they do not and cannot understand'.[55]

Any controversy surrounding the actions of Legge and Murray paled into insignificance compared with the furore over the loss of the *Wager*, an episode of melodramatic horror.[56] Under Captain David Cheap the *Wager*, in shattered condition and with almost half its crew dead, lost sight of the other

52.   PRO: Adm 1/2099, section 3, 10 July 1741 (*Documents*, p. 102).
53.   Thomas, *True and Impartial Journal*, p. 24.
54.   [Walter and Robins], *Anson's Voyage*, pp. 364–5.
55.   John Barrow, *The Life of George Lord Anson* (London, 1839), pp. 408–9.
56.   All accounts of Anson's voyage have a section on the loss of the *Wager*. S.W.C. Pack, *The Wager Mutiny* (London, 1964) is a detailed, rather over-written narrative. A more perceptive and critical account of the events following the loss of the vessel is given in Edwards, *Story of the Voyage*, pp. 53–79.

ships on the second thrust north in late April 1741. On 14 May, as it edged along the Chilean coast towards the rendezvous at Socorro, it was wrecked on an island (now Isla Wager or Wager Island) in the Gulf of Peñas. Cheap was lying disabled in his cabin after a heavy fall, and the vessel was under the command of Lieutenant Baynes. As the ship struck all semblance of authority disappeared; some of the crew smashed open wine casks and arms chests, while those sober enough to take to the boats managed to get ashore. As the ship began to break up, a midshipman, John Campbell, went back on board to persuade those still on the wreck to get ashore: 'I . . . found them all in such Confusion as cannot be imagined by any who were not Eye-witnesses of it. Some were singing Psalms, others fighting, others swearing, and some lay drunk on the Deck.'[57] On shore matters were not much better, and in the days after the last of the men left the wreck Cheap and his officers found it impossible to re-establish control. Henry Cozens was among the more troublesome of the malcontents. He had evidently read his South Sea narratives, and infuriated Cheap with his references to Shelvocke and his mutinous crew. 'Though Sh-lv-k was a Rogue, he was not a Fool; and by G-d, you are both,' he shouted at Cheap on one occasion.[58] Matters reached a head on 10 June, and as Cozens, truculent but unarmed, rampaged around the beach the captain shot and fatally wounded him.

During the confusion of the following weeks the carpenter, John Cummins, worked steadily to lengthen the longboat. This seemed to offer the best chance of escape, but here again disagreements surfaced. Much taken with Narborough's account, a copy of which had been brought ashore, the gunner John Bulkeley persuaded most of the crew that they should sail south along the coast, through the Strait of Magellan and then north to Brazil. A semblance of legality was observed, with the arguments in favour of this route being put on paper and signed 'by all the Officers on the Spot, except the Captain, Lieutenant, Purser, and Surgeon, and by all the Seamen in general, except the Captain's Steward'.[59] As Bulkeley explained later, though 'Persons of our Stations' would not normally take the lead, since Cheap was unable or unwilling to do this, 'There was a Necessity for Action, and a great deal of it too.'[60] Cheap, it became clear, preferred a shorter run north to capture a Spanish vessel on which they could sail to Juan Fernández; and according to Bulkeley, he tried to bribe the seamen with rum to accept this course. Such manipulation reminded Bulkeley of how things were done at home – 'There is a Sort of Party-rage among the People, fomented by a kind of Bribery.'[61] Even if Cheap joined the southern party it was made clear that

57. Pack, *Wager Mutiny*, p. 47.
58. John Bulkeley and John Cummins, *A Voyage to the South-Seas, In the Years 1740–1* (London, 1743), p. 27.
59. Ibid., p. 47.
60. Ibid., p. xvi.
61. Ibid., p. 69.

he would not be allowed to make any decisions without consultation, and his protests at such proposed restrictions were met with the reply: 'Sir, we will support you with our Lives, as long as you suffer Reason to rule.' A later justification by Bulkeley was also attuned to political sensitivities in England when he remarked of Cheap that 'We think him a Gentleman worthy to have a limited Command, but too dangerous a Person to be trusted with an absolute one.'[62]

Eventually, after five months, for part of which time Cheap was kept bound, the two groups parted company. On 13 October 1741 eighty of the crew sailed south in the schooner *Speedwell* (the converted longboat) and cutter, and the following February after a series of misadventures and hardships about thirty of them reached Rio Grande in Brazil in a state of starvation. The story of their ordeal does not make pretty reading, as men bought and sold flour at a guinea a pound, only to starve to death later. In one episode eight men seem to have been deliberately left ashore. Of this little group two were killed, two disappeared and only four survived to be taken captive, first by local Indians and then by the Spaniards at Buenos Aires. After further disputes, and delays at Rio de Janeiro and Bahía, Bulkeley and Cummins reached England on 1 January 1743, but were on board ship while the Admiralty considered their fate.

On Wager Island it was December 1741 before Cheap and his group of nineteen got away on their northern venture in the barge and yawl, but after losing the yawl and several men they were forced back to the island. In the end, Cheap and his three surviving companions were taken across land and water by the Indians to the Spanish garrison at Chiloé, and finally back to England. Among the group was midshipman John Byron, eighteen years old at the time of the wreck. Many years later he published an account of his experiences. It gave a harrowing description of the mental and physical collapse of Captain Cheap among the Indians, unable to remember his own name, covered with thousands of ants, his beard as long as a hermit's and his face filthy with train-oil.[63] The others among the survivors disappeared without trace, but were not quite forgotten. Twenty-three years after the wreck of the *Wager*, Byron was back in the Pacific as captain of the discovery vessel *Dolphin*. Among his sailing orders was an instruction 'to make enquiry after the People who were Shipwrecked in His Majesty's Ship the Wager and left upon that Coast, and use your best endeavours to bring them home'.[64]

Cheap, accompanied by Byron and Hamilton, did not get back to England until April 1746. That same month the Admiralty held a court-martial on the loss of the *Wager*. The hearing, despite some threatening noises made in the direction of Bulkeley and Cummins about mutiny being a hanging offence,

62.   Ibid., pp. 58, 88.
63.   See Edwards, *Story of the Voyage*, p. 75.
64.   Cited ibid., p. 53.

confined itself to the actual circumstances of the shipwreck on 14 May 1741; and the gunner and carpenter were present only as witnesses to the events of that day.[65] The whole episode was an embarrassment to the Admiralty, and to bring charges of mutiny against Bulkeley and other members of the crew might have raised awkward questions about the conduct of Cheap and his officers, and in particular the shooting of Cozens. Then, too, there was a legal grey area. Since entitlement to wages in the navy ceased when a ship sank, did a crew's duty to observe naval discipline continue after that point? The authorized account of Anson's voyage is interesting here. Although the words 'mutiny' and 'mutineers' are freely used, there is also what appears to be an escape clause: 'For the men conceived, that by the loss of the ship, the authority of the officers was at an end.'[66] That a loophole did seem to exist was shown by the passing in 1747 of an Act 'for extending the discipline of the Navy to crews of His Majesty's ships, wrecked, lost, or taken, and continuing to receive their wages upon certain conditions'.[67]

The wreck of the *Wager* gave rise to more books at the time than Anson's voyage itself – five in all, published over a twenty-five-year period from 1743 to 1768. They had in common a revelation of the behaviour of men released, under circumstances of the utmost danger, from the normal restraints and guides of a disciplined environment. In this context the earliest account, that of Bulkeley and Cummins, is of most interest. As Philip Edwards has written, its importance lies 'in their attitude to the naval hierarchy. Basically, their story is of the re-creation of authority after its collapse and disintegration in the wreck of the king's ship.'[68] The remaining narratives are a gloss on that story, viewing it from different perspectives. Their subtext is one of frustration and disappointment, the shipwreck serving as the final evidence of the falsity of the hopes that lay behind the Anson expedition. This is best expressed in the account attributed to John Young, cooper of the *Wager*, who wrote: 'I flatter'd myself with nothing less than a Fortune sufficient to buy a Peerage . . . The Grief we expressed at this Disappointment was proportionate to the Hope we had conceived.'[69]

This latter sentiment was undoubtedly the dominant one as the remnants of Anson's force limped one by one into the harbour of Juan Fernández. In the words of the authorized account, the squadron had been reduced 'from the formidable condition in which it passed Straits Le Maire, to a couple of

---

65. For the court-martial see Pack, *Wager Mutiny*, Ch. XVI.
66. [Walter and Robins], *Anson's Voyage*, p. 147.
67. Pack, *Wager Mutiny*, p. 246.
68. Edwards, *Story of the Voyage*, p. 78.
69. [John Young], *An Affecting Narrative of the Unfortunate Voyage and Catastrophe of His Majesty's Ship Wager* (London, 1751). Philip Edwards has made a convincing case that this book was the work of a hack rather than a first-hand narrative (*Story of the Voyage*, pp. 75–7); this does not invalidate the point made here about the contrast between expectation and reality, though it would have more force if the words were those of Young himself.

32. Peircy Brett. 'The Commodore's Tent on Juan Fernandes', 1748.

shattered half-manned cruisers and a sloop, so far disabled that in many climates they scarcely durst have put to sea.' The loss of three vessels was a crippling blow. The *Severn* and the *Pearl* were two of Anson's most powerful fighting ships, while the *Wager* carried field-guns, mortars and ammunition for land operations. The weakening of the squadron made the full execution of Anson's orders impossible, and together with the death rate on the surviving ships wrecked any hopes of aggressive operations against the important cities of Spanish America. On the three warships 335 men were left alive out of an original complement of 961, not enough to man even the *Centurion* at normal crew levels.[70] The best that could now be expected was a series of hit-and-run raids on coastal shipping and some of the smaller towns.

After weeks of slow recovery on Juan Fernández, Anson set sail again in September 1741. The island had been a haven for his scurvy-stricken crews, and earlier praise by buccaneers and privateers was pushed to new heights in the authorized account. The writer described his feelings as the *Centurion* slowly sailed towards the island, and its appearance was transformed from 'broken craggy precipices' to 'the finest vallies' and 'the most beautiful verdure'. Weeks of living ashore increased the sense of wonderment at a landscape that afforded satisfaction to both body and mind, a refuge where abundant supplies of life-saving greenstuffs were set amid romantic valleys

70. [Walter and Robins], *Anson's Voyage*, p. 160.

and cascading streams. These 'presented scenes of such elegance and dignity, as would perhaps with difficulty be rivalled in any other part of the globe'. The writing became even more ecstatic when it came to describing the park-like surroundings of the spot where Anson pitched his tent. 'I despair', the writer remarked, 'of conveying an adequate idea of its beauty', and he was glad to have the help of Lieutenant Peircy Brett's drawing to give 'some faint conceptions of the elegance of this situation' (Ill. 32).[71] Pascoe Thomas was even more effusive, concluding with words from Milton's *Paradise Lost* and the thought that 'there can scarce anywhere be found a more happy Seat for the Muses, and the Flights of Fancy, or Pleasures of the Imagination.'[72]

Although his ships were thinly manned, Anson seems to have had no thought of returning home. News from the first prize captured that Pizarro's shattered squadron had failed to round Cape Horn, and that the authorities assumed that Anson's ships had shared the same fate, brought hope that the Spanish coastal trade might be attacked before the alarm was raised. The interminable zig-zag haul around the Horn had brought one consolation. After cruising off Juan Fernández until just a few days before the *Centurion*'s arrival there, a squadron of ships fitted out in Chile had returned to port convinced that Anson had not reached the South Sea. Before the Spaniards were disabused about this, Anson's squadron took several prizes and destroyed the little town of Paita when no ransom was forthcoming (Ill. 33). The assault was no great feat of arms, and if Pascoe Thomas is to be believed the casualties among the attackers were probably caused by wild firing from among their own ranks.[73]

At the end of 1741 the squadron, now without the *Tryal*, which had been scuttled, but strengthened by three prizes, sailed north for Acapulco, there to lie in wait for the Manila galleon. This richest of the regular Spanish treasure galleons, 'the Prize of all the Oceans', had been taken by Thomas Cavendish in 1587, and its smaller companion vessel by Woodes Rogers in 1709. It was characteristic of the ill-luck that seemed to dog Anson that he arrived off Acapulco three weeks too late to intercept the eastbound galleon as it reached the coast from the Philippines. His squadron was then sighted from the shore, and the galleon was kept in port. Nor was Anson to be astounded by the sight of two Royal Navy vessels bearing down from the north to join him; for Middleton's expedition was experiencing a miserable, scurvy-ridden winter in Hudson Bay, and its attempts to find a passage through to the Pacific the following summer were as unsuccessful as those of all its predecessors.[74] After a long vigil outside the harbour, Anson decided to abandon his

71. Ibid., pp. 112, 119.
72. Thomas, *True and Impartial Journal*, p. 36.
73. Ibid., p. 56.
74. Although in the circumstances a creditable amount of useful exploration was carried out. See Barr and Williams, *Voyages in Search of a Northwest Passage*, I, and Map 2, p. 50 above.

33. Peircy Brett. 'The burning of Payta', 1748.

wait for the galleon and instead to sail westwards across the North Pacific to China. Macao and Canton, though eight thousand miles distant, were the nearest neutral ports for refitting and victualling.

Before leaving the Mexican coast Anson gave orders for the scuttling of the three prizes, including the *Tryal Prize*, formerly a thirty-two-gun Spanish frigate. The authorized account makes it clear that the sinking of this useful addition to the squadron was carried out to strengthen the crews of the *Centurion* and *Gloucester*, but makes no mention of the strenuous opposition to this move by the officers appointed to the *Tryal Prize*. Millechamp's journal contains copies of the petitions and letters exchanged between Anson and the aggrieved officers, the latter fearful that they would lose not only their existing posts but also any share in future prize-money. Writing after the event, Millechamp made much of the blow that he felt this decision had dealt to the unity of the expedition:

> God knows we had at that time had a thousand difficulties to encounter, and the least of them full as terrible as engaging the galleon. We had above half the compass of the globe to sail, most of which was in unknown seas; and our

staying too long in search of the Manila ship had made us lose the season in which the trade blows to the westward. So that we were sure we had the longest passage in the whole world (I mean that from Acapulco to China) to make in a wrong season, where we were also sure the winds would be contrary.[75]

The long trail of misfortune was not at an end. Light or contrary winds and damage to the mainmast of the *Gloucester* and to the foremast of the *Centurion* slowed the progress of the ships so that it was seven weeks before they picked up the Northeast Trades. Most depressing of all, scurvy appeared again almost as soon as the ships put to sea, despite the warm weather, the plentiful stocks of fresh provisions and water on board and the amount of space for the crews. Henry Ettrick, surgeon on the *Centurion*, declared himself helpless in the face of this new outbreak, and the writer of the authorized account concluded that 'in some instances, both the cure, and

75. Millechamp, 'Narrative' (*Documents*, p. 120).

prevention of this disease, is impossible to be effected by any management, or by the application of any remedies which can be made use of at sea.' The crew were left with 'the melancholy prospect, either of dying by the scurvy, or perishing with the ship for want of hands to navigate her'.[76] Further damage to the masts and hull of the *Gloucester* turned it into a leaking, unmanageable hulk, with sixty-eight of the crew sick and only sixteen men and eleven boys able to keep the deck. With difficulty its crew and bullion were transferred by boat to the *Centurion* – nothing could be done about most of its stores – and in case it remained afloat long enough for the Spaniards on Guam to find her, the vessel was set on fire.

According to the authorized account, the operation was carried out 'with as much care as the circumstances of that time would permit'.[77] Something of the reality behind this cautious statement was revealed in the journal of Lieutenant Philip Saumarez on the *Centurion*. As the heavily laden boats rowed back from the sinking wreck, Saumarez realized that their crews 'were most of them drunk with the liquor they had rumaged'. They arrived on the deck of the *Centurion* just as a squall struck, and attempts to shorten sail were hampered by 'sick and dying men, the hurry and shortness of time had not permitted us to take care of and with casks and lumber received from the other ship which filled up the decks and entangled all our running ropes'. It was a nightmare scene as darkness fell, with 'the last ship of our squadron blazing within two miles of us'.[78]

For Millechamp, unbothered by the practical duties of Saumarez, the end of the *Gloucester* was a sight both dramatic and moving:

> She burnt all night, making a most grand, horrid appearance. Her guns, which were all loaded, fired so regularly at about the distance of a minute between each as the fire came to them, that they sounded like mourning guns, such as are fired at the funeral of some great officer. At six o'clock the next morning, the fire having reached her powder room, where was upwards of two hundred barrels of gunpowder, she blew up. That action made an odd appearance, for we first saw a quick streak of smoke fly up with an incredible swiftness, and a prodigious height, and when it had reached a particular region of the air, its velocity ceased, and the top of it grew into a monstrous large cloud, that it seemed for about an hour to be an overgrown column, whose base was fixed to the sea and whose capital supported the clouds. We soon after heard the report, which sounded like a great clap of distant thunder. Thus ended the Gloucester, a ship justly esteemed the beauty of the English navy.[79]

76. [Walter and Robins], *Anson's Voyage*, pp. 293–4.
77. Ibid., p. 300.
78. Leo Heaps, *Log of the Centurion. Based on the Original Papers of Captain Philip Saumarez* (London, 1973), p. 175.
79. Millechamp, 'Narrative' (*Documents*, p. 128).

Storms now forced the *Centurion* north of its intended track towards
Guam. Lieutenant Peter Denis recollected how 'Our men by this time died
like rotten sheep . . . six, eight, ten or twelve in a day.'[80] As the leaks gained
upon the pumps, it was a race against time to find port. The seriousness of
the ship's plight was shown by the fact that 'the Commodore and all the
officers were frequently obliged to work as common seamen.'[81] At the
uninhabited island of Tinian, 150 miles north of Guam, the *Centurion* at last
anchored on 28 August 1742 after sixteen weeks at sea. Philip Saumarez, first
lieutenant on the ship, thought that within ten days they would have taken
to the boats, so serious were the leaks and so weak the crew.[82] Only seventy-
one men were capable of even the lightest duties, and so few could go aloft
that it took five hours to furl the sails when the ship reached its anchorage.
In all 128 sick were carried on shore – again Anson and the officers were
among those engaged in this task – but once there the sufferers had to fend
for themselves. Pascoe Thomas was one of those weak with scurvy, and he
wrote that

> nor could those who carry'd us up to the Tent assist us any farther, but left us
> there half naked on the cold Ground, or a hard Hide, to help ourselves, of
> which we were utterly uncapable; nor had we for the greatest Part any Person
> to get us a sour Orange, or a Lime, or one Drop of Water; tho' all these
> Things abounded within our View, and almost our Reach.[83]

A further twenty-one men died during the landing or soon after, but then
fresh meat and fruit worked what Millechamp called 'a miracle' and 'those
who were brought on shore in their hammocks, and were so ill as not to be
able to move, in two or three days would be crawling along in the sun.'

Depopulated as a result of disease among the native inhabitants and the
forced migration to Guam of the survivors, Tinian attracted the most
extravagant praise from the *Centurion*'s journal-keepers – in some cases even
before landing. Millechamp wrote: 'to us it was a perfect paradise, for besides
a great quantity of coconut and orange trees that we could discover by the
help of our glasses as we sailed along the shore, we saw numbers of beautiful
cattle grazing on the most delightful plains full of herbage.'[84] The cattle were
for the use of the Spaniards on Guam, and a party of one Spaniard and four
'Indians' was seized with its flying proa and a small bark used to carry beef.
The double-ended, outrigger proa, often described but rarely drawn by
earlier voyagers, was of particular interest. Peircy Brett took this particular
specimen to pieces before making a detailed scale drawing of it for the

80. *The Gentleman's Magazine* (June 1743), p. 326.
81. NMM: 39/MS 9416/HAR 4 (*Documents*, p. 260).
82. Saumarez MSS: 'Abstract of a Journal' (*Documents*, p. 168).
83. Thomas, *True and Impartial Journal*, p. 154.
84. Both references in Millechamp, 'Narrative' (*Documents*, p. 131).

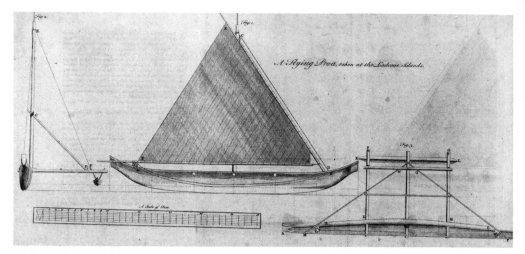

34. Peircy Brett. 'A Flying Proa', 1748.

authorized account (Ill. 34); and the accompanying text speculated that in such craft the inhabitants of the archipelago (the Northern Marianas) might have island-hopped as far as New Guinea. Tinian itself was represented as 'this delightful island . . . this little paradise', which did not resemble 'an uninhabited and uncultivated place, but had much more the air of a magnificent plantation, where large lawns and stately woods had been laid out together with great skill'.[85] Once more Brett was called on to draw the scene, complete with picturesque ruins, a well, the Commodore's tent and in the foreground a large breadfruit tree (Ill. 35).

Brett's sketch also hints at one of the drawbacks to Tinian – the open roadstead at the southwest end of the island which was the only place where ships of any size could anchor. On 18 September the *Centurion*, with only a skeleton crew on board, was blown out to sea and was not able to claw its way back to the island for nineteen days. Saumarez as first lieutenant was in command of the ship and later described what happened:

a storm came on and rose so mountainous a sea as none of us ever saw before. The ship being in danger of being pooped as we lay at anchor; at last we parted both our bower-cables and drove out to sea, with the sheet-anchor hanging in the hawse, with a cable and two-thirds of another, and narrowly escaped driving on a ledge of rocks very near, leaving the Commodore and all the rest behind. The ship, by her labouring in such a troubled sea, made so much water that I was in doubt whether she would not have foundered, our ports being but ill-secured, as were likewise the guns, by the suddenness of the storm, which likewise overset the longboat. In these circumstances I drove out

85. [Walter and Robins], *Anson's Voyage*, p. 306.

35. Peircy Brett. 'The Watering Place at Tenian', 1748.

having 109 men on board and boys, not knowing whether I should not be a captain in spite of my teeth at last.[86]

For Anson and the 113 crew members stranded on shore the situation seemed desperate, for the probability was that the *Centurion* had gone down. The only alternative to a Spanish prison was to attempt to reach Macao, two thousand miles distant, in the bark seized on arrival. In an echo of the operation carried out by the *Wager*'s crew the year before, they began to lengthen and refit the tiny craft. Anson and the other captains once more joined in the task, 'working with an axe, cross-cut saw, or carrying timber'.[87] Although there was to be no repetition of the lurid events on Wager Island, there was clearly some challenge to Anson's plan, if not to his overall authority. Millechamp referred to objections and arguments, and even the authorized account hinted at problems. Pascoe Thomas later picked up a rumour that 'most of the common People had resolved to desert us in four or five Days more if the Ship had not appear'd in that Time, and to have built themselves Huts in the Woods, and run the Risk of staying on the Island, rather than venture themselves to China in that Bark.'[88] With the reappearance of the *Centurion* any rumbles of discontent vanished, and within nine days it was at sea again, heading for Macao.

As the *Centurion* cautiously entered the crowded Macao roadstead in early November 1742 Anson's troubles were by no means over. The frustrations he encountered in his efforts to get supplies and refit the ship during his five-

86. Saumarez MSS: 'Abstract of a Journal' (*Documents*, p. 169).
87. Millechamp, 'Narrative' (*Documents*, p. 133).
88. Thomas, *True and Impartial Journal*, p. 159.

month stay at Macao are tartly described in the authorized account. The East
India Company records for their part reveal the predicament the Company
traders were placed in by the sudden and unexpected appearance of a British
man-of-war.[89] Ever since its establishment a half-century earlier the Company's trade at Canton had experienced difficulties, for it depended on a
fragile triangular relationship between the Company, the local Hong merchants and the watchful Chinese authorities. Subject to stringent restrictions
and sometimes under threat of suspension, the Company's trade was still a
delicate enough plant to be uprooted by any display of force by an impatient
naval commander unfamiliar with local conditions. The partial dislocation of
the Company's China trade in 1744 with the arrival on the coast of Spanish
warships from Manila hunting for Anson was to provide a sharp reminder of
the damage that commerce could suffer from the spread of war to a place as
remote from Europe and its conflicts as Canton.

It took the presence of Anson himself at Canton to extract a grudging
permission for essential work to be carried out on the *Centurion*. His letters
to Philip Saumarez on board the ship show that if any Spanish vessels had
come into sight all considerations of diplomacy and the East India Company's trade would have gone by the board.[90] In this correspondence the
shortage of men was a constant theme. Not even the chaplain Richard
Walter could be allowed to return home until he had found a replacement,
for though 'rather a puny, weakly, and sickly man, pale and of a low stature',
he had done the work of an ordinary seaman on the desperate voyage across
the North Pacific.[91] In a private letter home to James Naish in December
1742, Anson revealed something of his despair about the protracted negotiations in which he was entangled and the state of weakness of his men:

> I am certainly unfortunate, and a fatality attends me! What an opportunity I
> lose . . . of doing service to my country and gaining credit for myself, for two
> Acapulco ships will arrive at Manila the next June! . . . I have but five-and-
> forty men before the mast and some of them have not recovered their senses,
> for numbers turned mad and idiots with the scurvy. I cannot pretend to
> describe that terrible distemper, but no plague ever equalled the degree we
> had of it.[92]

This letter is the only private communication written by Anson on the
voyage known to have survived; its uninhibited language is very different
from the dispassionate prose of Anson's long official report of the same time

89.   See OIOC: Factory Records: China II, 3, pp. 11–17, 37–40 (*Documents*, pp. 144–8).
90.   Saumarez MSS: letters of 24 Nov., 28 Nov., 30 Nov., 1 Dec., 5 Dec., 6 Dec. 1742 (*Documents*,
      pp. 148–52).
91.   See *Documents*, p. 285.
92.   Letter originally in possession of the late Commander C.G. Pitcairn Jones (who kindly supplied
      a copy to the present writer); now in the Staffordshire County Record Office: Anson Deposit,
      D615 – P(S) 1/10, item 4A (*Documents*, p. 152).

to the Duke of Newcastle.[93] In revealing for a moment the frustration Anson was feeling after the disasters of the previous two years, the letter to Naish lifts the edge of the close mask of reserve and composure with which Anson normally faced the world.

One source of concern to Anson and his officers was their assumption that no reports about their fate had reached England and their families. It is a sign of the difference between this expedition and its privateering predecessors that Anson and his ships had in fact not disappeared from view. A surprising amount of news had filtered back to England long before the first letters from Macao reached there on East India Company ships in the summer of 1743. In the Caribbean Vernon intercepted and sent home correspondence from Panama and elsewhere about Anson's movements, and Jamaica proved a sensitive seismograph for picking up Spanish tremors about Anson's exploits on the other side of the Panama isthmus. By the spring of 1742 ministers and newspapers in London knew about the shattering of Pizarro's squadron, Anson's stay at Juan Fernández, the assault on Paita and the turning back of the *Severn* and *Pearl*. By the autumn news had reached England of the wreck of the *Wager*.[94] By contrast, Anson, who by now had reached the coast of China, knew nothing of the *Wager*'s fate. Among the letters he wrote at this time was one addressed to Captain Cheap at Batavia: 'Having information by letters from Manila Directed to this Place, that in July last, there was a ship seen off the Boccadeiro in the entrance of the Straits of Manila [the San Bernardino Strait], which was not the Galleon she not being Arrived, make me imagine that ship might be the Wager.' Anson then went on to instruct Cheap to raid Spanish shipping before rejoining the *Centurion* when it reached Batavia on its homeward voyage.[95] At home, fuller information about the expedition came from an unexpected source, the French cook on the *Centurion*, Louis Leger, who after being captured by the Spaniards near Acapulco escaped and reached England in the spring of 1743. The long letters, official and private, written at Macao and Canton, were of course welcome. Their contents were summarized in newspapers and periodicals, and at least one letter, from Lieutenant Peter Denis to his brother, was printed in full; but even before these arrived an outline of the expedition's fortunes up to the time it headed across the North Pacific was known in England.[96]

In April 1743 the *Centurion*, refitted but manned by less than half its complement, left Macao. Ostensibly it was bound for England, after a

93. See PRO: SP 42/88, ff. 77–85 (*Documents*, pp. 154–64).
94. See *The Gentleman's Magazine*, 12 (Sep. 1742), pp. 496–7; PRO: Adm 1/3827, letter of 1 Oct. 1742 from A. Castres in Lisbon to Admiralty.
95. Anson to Cheap, 28 Feb. 1743. BL: Add. MS 15,855, f. 133.
96. For these various letters and reports see *Documents*, pp. 169–79. The long letter from Denis was printed in *The Gentleman's Magazine*, 13 (June 1743), pp. 325–6.

36. Peircy Brett. The engagement between the *Centurion* and the *Covadonga*, 1748.

voyage in which catastrophe had become commonplace, success rare and fleeting. Left with only one ship out of a squadron of six, Anson could show little for his losses: the capture of a few prizes and the sacking of an unimportant Peruvian town. While at Canton he had not been able to bring himself to write a single line to his patron, Lord Hardwicke. As he explained later, 'I ought to have wrote to your Lordship on my arrival at Canton . . . but . . . these misfortunes gave me an uneasiness I could not express.'[97] One exploit alone could redeem the story of repeated disaster – the capture of the treasure galleon from Acapulco on its way into Manila. As the *Centurion* sailed south from Macao, Anson assembled the crew on deck to tell them that he was making, not for home, but for Cape Espiritu Santo, the normal landfall of the westbound galleon. After a month's tense wait off the Cape, the lookouts sighted the galleon at daybreak on June 1743. Slowly the two ships closed with each other, soon after noon they opened fire, and after a ninety-minute action at twenty or thirty yards' range the galleon, the *Nuestra Señora de Covadonga*, struck its flag.

97. BL: Add. MS 35,359, f. 360 (*Documents*, p. 224).

The authorized account of the voyage gives the accepted English version of the action – of a triumphant action against the odds by a smaller vessel with well under half the complement of the Spaniard. Peircy Brett's sketch of the action, printed in the book, gives the same impression as it shows the tall masts and high hull of the galleon looming over the *Centurion* (Ill. 36). In reality, the odds were heavily weighted against the Spaniard; this was no English David slaying a Spanish Goliath. Saumarez went on board the *Covadonga* immediately after the action and was 'amazed to think what he could propose against our weight of metal and a ship of our appearance'.[98] The *Centurion* was a specialist fighting ship mounting sixty guns, twenty-four of them heavy twenty-four-pounders firing a ball that would smash through a ship's side and send a hail of splinters ricocheting across the decks. Its weakness was that it carried only 227 men. From this number men were needed to work the ship, man the guns, act as marksmen in the tops, carry ammunition, take away the wounded and be ready to extinguish fires or repel boarders. With less than half its normal complement, it was impossible to meet these calls in conventional fashion. Since it was a single-ship action, guns were manned on one side of the ship only, and instead of a normal gun-crew of eight or ten, two men were posted at each gun to load and sponge it out, while gangs of a dozen men ran from gun to gun opening the ports, laying and firing, and bringing up ammunition for the next loading. Broadsides were out of the question, but the erratic nature of the *Centurion*'s fire proved highly effective against an enemy that was anticipating broadsides every few minutes, with intervals of comparative safety between salvoes.

Nor was the *Covadonga* the larger vessel: it was twenty feet shorter on its gun-deck, with a tonnage of about seven hundred tons (compared to the 1005 tons of the *Centurion*). Certainly it did not have the giant dimensions of the *Santísima Trinidad*, captured by Admiral Cornish's ships off the Philippines in 1762 – at two thousand tons one of the largest vessels afloat. The *Santísima Trinidad* was hit by more than a thousand shot, none of which penetrated its hull timbers.[99] By contrast, when an East India Company factor went on board the *Covadonga* at Canton a few months later, he was shown 'a Hole in the Starboard Quarter where one of the Centurions four and twenty pounders had penetrated and gone through the Larboard Bow, and near a pistol Shot beyond'.[100] The fact was that the *Covadonga* was a trading rather than a fighting vessel. Spanish accounts and the reports of British officers who inspected it after the action show that, although it was pierced for sixty-four guns, there were only forty-four on board, and twelve of these were lying useless between decks or in the hold. The heaviest of the thirty-

98. Saumarez MSS: Log IV, 20 June 1743 (*Documents*, p. 198).
99. See Schurz, *Manila Galleon*, p. 340.
100. See Glyndwr Williams, 'Anson at Canton, 1743: "A Little Secret History"', in Cecil H. Clough and P.E.H. Hair, eds, *The European Outthrust and Encounter* (Liverpool, 1994), p. 284.

two that were in position were twelve-pounders; the rest were eight- or six-pounders. The *Covadonga* had low bulwarks, which gave its crew on deck little protection, and narrow gun-ports, which made it difficult to aim its cannon at the *Centurion* except when it lay directly alongside. Unless the Spaniards could board the *Centurion* and overwhelm its crew by sheer numbers, there could be only one result. Even the Spaniards' numerical superiority, on which the authorized account laid such stress, was not quite what it seemed. A later statement made by the galleon's Portuguese commander, Don Gerónimo Montero, showed that of the 530 on board only 266 were crew members, about half of them Filipinos. Apart from a company of forty soldiers, the rest were passengers, servants and convicts.[101] The fact that Montero made no attempt to board the *Centurion* does not suggest that he had much confidence in his crew. Certainly they did not have the same incentive to fight as Anson's men. Of the 227 on board the *Centurion* during the engagement, about two-thirds had sailed from England with Anson; the rest were Lascars, Negroes and Peruvian Indians picked up at various stages of the voyage, plus some European seamen who had joined at Macao. Of the original crews of the *Centurion*, *Gloucester* and *Tryal*, only the hardiest had survived, and confronted with the alternatives of a fortune in prize-money or the inside of a Spanish gaol they fought with grim ferocity. Their temper was noted by an observer on the *Centurion*, who wrote that hours before there was any possibility of action, 'the ship was cleared and the guns unlashed in an instant, anything standing in the way, let it belong to who, or be it of what value it would, the sailors immediately threw it overboard.'[102]

The *Centurion* lost two men killed, seventeen wounded, had a few shot in the hull and suffered damage to its rigging. Of the *Covadonga*, Anson wrote, 'her masts and rigging were shot to pieces, and 150 shot passed through her hull, many of which were between wind and water, which occasioned her to be very leaky.'[103] The Spanish accounts give a chilling impression of the effect of the *Centurion*'s cannon and small-arms fire as it swept across the galleon's exposed deck.[104] They show that resistance was already weakening when Montero was struck down by a musket-ball. His second-in-command took over and remained on deck though hit in the thigh; but when another officer was killed, and the captain of soldiers badly wounded, the crew began to desert their posts. The galleon's steering failed, and as the *Centurion* moved across the galleon's bows the Spaniards ignored Montero's final order from the cockpit to blow up the ship and instead struck their flag. In all, the *Covadonga* had lost more than sixty killed and seventy wounded, and

101.　PRO: HCA 32/135, Bundle A, 21 July 1743 (*Documents*, p. 220).
102.　Millechamp, 'Narrative' (*Documents*, p. 186).
103.　PRO: SP 42/88, f. 87 (*Documents*, p. 222).
104.　See, in particular, Juan de la Concepción, *Historia General de Philipinas*, XI (Manila, 1791), pp. 152–61.

when Saumarez went on board to accept the galleon's surrender he found the deck 'covered with carcasses, entrails, and dismembered limbs'.[105] The vessel, he was told, was seventy-two days out from Acapulco and had on board silver amounting to one and a half million dollars, 'besides private money'.

The value of the cargo makes the actions both of the galleon's officers and the authorities at Manila hard to understand. Spanish sources reveal a sorry story of ineptitude and rashness. The *Centurion*'s movements were known in Manila: an informant in Canton told the Governor of the Philippines in December 1742 of Anson's arrival and refit, and in a later letter warned him that Anson was preparing to sail – 'And for all the commander's exaggerated remarks about the sad condition of his ship, wanting to take advantage of the remainder of the monsoon to cross to Batavia, and of not being in any state to attack a galleon, but rather to continue his voyage to Europe – it is feared he has other plans . . . if I am not mistaken he intends to cruise for either the incoming or the outgoing galleon.'[106] Councils of war were held in Manila which decided to fit out the galleon *Pilar* and other smaller vessels to escort the *Covadonga* into port; but little urgency was shown, despite reports that a strange vessel had been sighted off the coast. The *Pilar*'s progress was slow, and a week after the galleon's capture the relief force was still a hundred miles west of Cape Espiritu Santo. On the *Covadonga* itself there seems to have been little awareness of the seriousness of the threat. After hearing news at Guam of Anson's stay at Tinian the year before, the galleon's commander Montero suggested to his council that they stop at Guam or make a detour. His advice was ignored, for the news of the weakness of Anson's crew at Tinian 'reassured our men unduly, and left them without the slightest apprehension of any danger. They accepted all too readily that Anson's ship was incapable of going into action.' The council of officers also refused to mount cannon on the lower deck, and insisted that if Anson had sailed towards the Philippines he would have been intercepted by cruisers sent out from Manila. This proved to be the final, and fatal, error; for when the Spaniards first sighted a distant sail on the morning of 20 June they assumed that it was an escort or supply vessel coming out from Manila. By the time the mistake was realized a change in the wind had made it impossible for the galleon to escape.[107]

From the Philippines the *Centurion* returned with her prize to the Canton River, where once more Anson became involved in protracted disputes with agitated East India Company factors and obstructive Chinese officials. No part of the authorized account aroused more comment in Europe than the

105. Saumarez MSS: Log IV, 20 June 1743 (*Documents*, p. 199).
106. Archivo de Indias, Seville (AI): Audiencia de Filipinas/256, items 4, 5 (*Documents*, pp. 208–9).
107. See Concepción, *Historia General de Philipinas*, XI, pp. 152–61 (*Documents*, pp. 215–19). Investigations into the loss of the *Covadonga* continued until 1754, when her officers were cleared of negligence, unlike Gaspar de la Torre, Governor of the Philippines at the time, who was found guilty of that charge in 1749.

sections on the expedition's two visits to the Chinese coast, where some forthright comments challenged the prevailing view that China was a blessed land free from the superstition, bigotry and corruption of Europe. Arraigned alongside incomprehensible Chinese officials were the East India Company traders at Canton, whose behaviour the book condemned as unhelpful, if not downright unpatriotic. To contemporaries ready to expect the worst of a monopolistic trading company these remarks would have come as no surprise, but recently discovered documents which show the Company's side of the affair give a rather different picture. King's officer and Company trader were always going to have different priorities, and nowhere would these be more evident than in the charged atmosphere of Canton as Chinese officials and Company traders tried to ignore the distant clamour of European war.[108]

Just before leaving Macao, the galleon, emptied of her treasure, was sold to local merchants, and in December 1743 the *Centurion* put to sea. The rest of the voyage was a welcome anti-climax. Leaving behind Spanish punitive expeditions, which were scouring the seas off Juan Fernández in one hemisphere and the Chinese coast in another, the *Centurion* slipped home by way of the Sunda Strait and the Cape of Good Hope. At the Cape Anson took on another forty men and arrived in England in June 1744 with 145 of the original members of the expedition among the *Centurion*'s motley crew. 'Besides these English there were men of eighteen other different nations, viz. Dutch, French, Spaniards, Italians, Germans, Swedes, Danes, Muscovites, Portuguese, Lascar Indians, Malays, Persians, Indians of Manila, Timor and Guam, Negroes of Guinea, Creoles of Mexico and Mozambique.'[109] On the six vessels of Anson's squadron that had sailed from Spithead almost four years earlier, only four men had died from enemy action, but more than 1300 had perished from disease. In England these sombre figures were swept from sight by the news that on board the *Centurion* was treasure worth 'not much short of £400,000'.[110] To attempt to put this sum into modern currency would be an exercise in futility, but some indication of its worth is given by the value of the cargoes brought home from Canton by the two East India Company ships *Haeslingfield* and *Harrington* the same year. These included 800,000 pounds of tea, 400 chests of china, 7000 pieces of wrought silk, 60 chests of raw silk and £20,000 in bullion – amounting in all to a total value in England of £240,000.[111]

★

108.   See OHS: MSS 2892, 2893, 2894; also Williams, 'Anson at Canton, 1743', pp. 271–90.
109.   BL: Add. MS 35,396, f. 217 (*Documents*, p. 237).
110.   [Walter and Robins], *Anson's Voyage*, p. 384. Most of this came from the *Covadonga*, whose treasure consisted of 1,313,843 pieces of eight and 35,682 ounces of virgin silver. For the rest of her cargo see the ship's register (in Spanish, with a contemporary English translation) in PRO: HCA 32/135, Bundle C. Other estimates differ. Pascoe Thomas (*True and Impartial Journal*, Appendix, pp. 4–5) estimated an overall total of more than £478,000, but this included the face value of some of the prize goods rather than the amount that was actually realized.
111.   Williams, 'Anson at Canton, 1743', p. 286.

Anson, an almost unknown naval captain when he left England in 1740, returned home a celebrity. After the Mediterranean fleet's failure off Toulon in February the navy stood in need of a popular triumph, and in the public mind the capture of a treasure galleon was the next best thing to a fleet victory. If the celebrations were not quite as exuberant and certainly not as nationwide as those that followed Admiral Vernon's successes in the Caribbean in the early years of the war, this might be explained by the important difference that Vernon was an opposition hero, who had focused resentment against an unpopular government.[112] In 1744, on the other hand, ministers were eager to claim a share of the glory. On 15 June Newcastle, no great enthusiast for the voyage four years earlier, wrote to Anson at Spithead to convey the King's 'great approbation of your conduct' and added a postscript: 'I take a great part in the good fortune, and in the honour you have acquired to yourself, and the service you have done your country.'[113] On 18 June Anson was received by the King, and by the end of the year he was a member of the new Board of Admiralty and Rear Admiral of the Blue. His professional competence, political connections and, not least, his new-found wealth assured Anson a dominant position in naval affairs.

During the late summer of 1744 the newspapers were full of reports of the voyage and what followed: the procession from Portsmouth to London, which finally arrived at the Tower on 4 July (Ill. 37). The *General Advertiser* of the next day described the scene:

> Yesterday the money taken by Admiral Anson was carried through the City in thirty-two wagons, preceded by a kettle-drum, trumpets, and French horns, guarded by the seamen, commanded by the officers richly dressed, and was lodged in the Tower. On the first wagon was the English colours, with the Spanish ensign under it, and every third or fourth wagon carried some trophy of honour, which had been taken from the Spaniards in the South Sea, as well as from the Acapulco ship. Their Royal Highnesses the Prince and Princess of Wales, and Admiral Anson, were at a house in Pall Mall to see the procession.

To Horace Walpole, watching from his window, it was 'a trumpery sight',[114] but another spectator thought it 'a sight more rare and not less agreeable to an Englishman than the secular games to a Roman'.[115] The analogy with

---

112. For more on this see Kathleen Wilson, 'Empire, Trade and Popular Politics in Mid-Hanoverian Britain: the Case of Admiral Vernon', *Past & Present*, 121 (1988), pp. 74–109; *The Sense of the People: Politics, Culture and Imperialism in England, 1715–1785* (Cambridge, 1995), pp. 140–65.
113. PRO: SP 42/88, f. 89 (*Documents*, p. 233).
114. W.S. Lewis, ed., *The Yale Edition of Horace Walpole's Correspondence*, XXX, W.S. Lewis and R.A. Smith, eds, *Horace Walpole's Correspondence with George Selwyn et al.* (New Haven and London, 1961), p. 53.
115. BL: Add. MS 35,396, f. 217 (*Documents*, p. 237).

37. 'England's Glory', 1744 (the treasure reaching the Tower of London).

Rome was carried on in celebratory verses printed in the *Daily Advertiser*, which described the great Roman empire before pointing out:

> But round the Globe her eagle never flew,
> Thro' every clime is Albion's thunder hurled,
> And Anson's spoils are from a tribute world.

Officers and crew from the *Centurion* were guests of honour at Sadlers Wells and at the rival New Wells – which inserted into its current production a new song 'in honour of their glorious commander taking the Acapulco ship from the Spaniards'. By 18 July one paper at least had taken to referring to 'our immortal Anson'. He had already been compared with Drake in verses written for the *London Evening Post* 'after the death of Mr. Pope' (Alexander Pope had died in May). They concluded:

> But what to Anson's were Ulysses' toils?
> Or what, to India's wealth, were Ilion's spoils?

The world surrounded, all her nations viewed,
Each climate tried, each danger now subdued,
Our second Drake, arrived on British ground,
Requires no Pope his honours to resound.

To satisfy the demand for more detail on the voyage, an unauthorized narrative written by 'John Phillips', allegedly a midshipman on the voyage, was rushed through the press and was quickly followed by several pirated editions. Another pseudonymous account by 'an officer of the *Centurion*' was published in two parts in *The Universal Spectator* of 25 August and 1 September.

Not all the comment was favourable. The first critical note in the public prints came in the *Daily Post* for 6 July, two days after the triumphant procession through the streets of London. Its sentiments, if not its verse style, have a surprisingly modern touch:

Deluded Britons! Wherefore should you boast
Of treasure, purchased at a treble cost?
Will this, while centering in a private hand,
Restore to wealth, your much impoverished land?
To purchase this, think how much treasure's gone;
Think on the mighty mischiefs it hath done.
In this attempt, count o'er the numerous host
Of Albion's sons, unprofitably lost.
Then will your boastings into sorrow turn,
And injured Britons, Albion's fate shall mourn.

By the late summer a more general change of tone was noticeable in some of the newspapers, outraged by the brawls started by the *Centurion*'s sailors on their jaunts through the capital. The issuing of the first instalment of the prize-money in late August − if the reported amount of £171 for each seaman was correct, it represented the equivalent of twelve years' wages for an able seaman − could not have helped matters. In the newspaper reports of these weeks Anson's men emerge from the anonymity in which they had remained on the long voyage, where no chronicler had recorded the lower-deck point of view. For the first time they begin to appear as individuals, celebrating, marrying, fighting and dying in the streets of London, prize-money in pocket and all too often knife in hand: John Maddox marrying Mrs Simms, a widow with a fortune of £1000, at a ceremony at Dulwich which was attended − perish the thought − by forty of his shipmates from the *Centurion*; a murderous attack by 'some of the New Gentlemen belonging to the *Centurion*' on the Aldgate watch; a Dutch sailor from the *Centurion* stabbing a soldier; Martin from the *Centurion* found drowned in the Thames after 'being in liquor. Fifteen guineas and some silver were found in his pocket'; Burton from the *Centurion* robbed and seriously wounded by a gang between Stratford and Bow.[116]

For the officers the return to London brought uncertainty and bitterness over the allocation of the prize-money between the officers of the *Centurion* on the one side, and those of the *Gloucester* and *Tryal* on the other. The dispute, which fills many hundreds of pages of documentation, revolved around two main issues: the legal question of whether the officers from the scuttled ships could hold any position on the *Centurion* other than that of supernumeraries; and the practical one of the precise duties performed by those officers on the flagship. All prize-money disputes seem difficult and perplexing at this remove; this one more so than most. Since Anson's share was not affected by the outcome,[117] the list of the *Centurion*'s officers (the Apellants) was headed by Philip Saumarez, its first lieutenant. His view of the matter was expressed in a grim little letter to his brother in August 1744: 'The answer as to the survivorship of our countrymen is very concise. They are all dead, few entitled to any prizes, and none to the galleon.'[118] After almost three years, the matter was finally settled in May 1747 in favour of the *Centurion*'s officers when the Lords Commissioners for Appeals in Prize Causes reversed an earlier decision of the High Court of Admiralty and ruled that the officers of the *Gloucester* and *Tryal* were entitled only to an ordinary seaman's share of the prize-money. Millechamp, purser of the *Gloucester* and one of the unsuccessful Respondents, added a last, rueful comment: 'We had more terrible engagements in the courts of law than ever we had in the South Seas.'[119]

---

116. All these newspaper and periodical references will be found in *Documents*, pp. 233–49.

117. Prize-money was divided into eight parts, shared as follows: 2 parts – captain; 1 part – admiral or commander-in-chief (in this case Anson, who would therefore take 3 parts); 1 part – sea lieutenants, marine captains, master; 1 part – marine lieutenants, boatswain, gunner, purser, carpenter, master's mate, surgeon, chaplain; 1 part – midshipmen, carpenter's mates, boatswain's mates, gunner's mates, quartermaster; 2 parts – able and ordinary seamen, volunteers, marines, cooper, armourer.

118. Saumarez MSS: 15 Aug. 1744. Later letters from Philip indicate some change of attitude about 'this fatal law suit'. See Heaps, *Log of the Centurion*, p. 255.

119. Millechamp, 'Narrative' (*Documents*, p. 194). The main points at issue are contained in the 'Allegations' of 2 Aug. 1744 and 10 June 1745 in the Hartwell Papers (NMM: 39/MS 9416/HAR 4); extracts printed in *Documents*, pp. 249–67.

CHAPTER X

Widening Horizons

Some observers looked beyond the immediate excitement and controversy of the *Centurion*'s return and began to consider the long-term implications of Anson's exploits in the Pacific. In the first volume (1744) of his revised edition of Harris's monumental work *Navigantium atque Itinerantium Bibliotheca*, Dr John Campbell included an account of Anson's voyage based on the *Authentic Journal* just published under the pseudonym of 'John Phillips'. To Campbell, a prolific writer on mercantile affairs and an enthusiastic advocate of overseas enterprise, the voyage was evidence of the opportunities awaiting Britain in the South Sea. It was 'an expedition that has demonstrated to the whole world, that a train of unforeseen and disastrous accidents may be remedied, and even turned to advantage'; and a follow-up venture, he argued, would surely learn from Anson's experiences.[1]

In his edition Campbell juxtaposed the narratives of Quiros, Tasman, Dampier and Roggeveen (the first account of the latter's voyage to appear in English) to prove the existence of a fertile southern continent. The concept was illustrated by the maps of Emanuel Bowen which Campbell included, in particular his 'Complete Map of the Southern Continent' (Ill. 38). One of its legends stated that 'the Country discovered by *Ferdinand de Quiros* lies according to his description on the east Side of this Continent directly Opposite to *Carpentaria*.' Another legend gave an ecstatic account of the new continent and its potential, and with references to the silver of Peru, the spices of the Moluccas and the diamonds of Java, took the hopes expressed by Jean Pierre Purry[2] a quarter of a century earlier a stage further:

It is impossible to conceive a Country that promises fairer from its situation than this of *Terra Australis*; no longer incognita, as this Map demonstrates, but

1. John Campbell, ed., *Navigantium atque Itinerantium Bibliotheca; or, A Compleat Collection of Voyages and Travels* (London, 1744–8), I, pp. 364–5.
2. See p. 185 above.

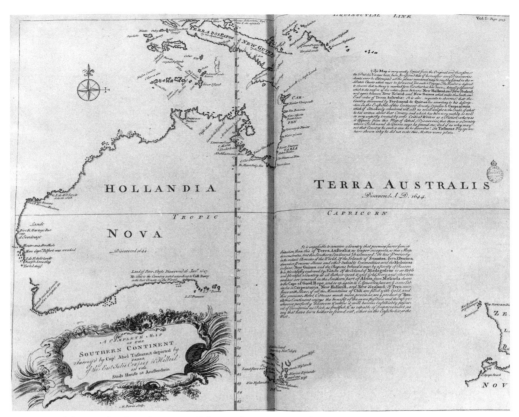

38. Emanuel Bowen. 'A Complete Map of the Southern Continent', 1744.

the Southern Continent Discovered. It lies Precisely in the richest Climates of the World . . . and therefore whoever perfectly discovers & settles it will become infallibly possessed of Territories as Rich, as Fruitful, & as capable of Improvement, as any that have hitherto found out, either in the East Indies, or the West.

To substantiate his 'new Indies' Campbell had only the dismal and frag-mentary reports of the Dutch, Dampier's brief remarks on New Holland and New Britain, and the hallucinations of Quiros. The latter he took at face value, noting that Quiros reported that Espiritu Santo 'abounds with Gold, Silver, Pearls, Nutmegs, Mace, Ginger, and Sugar-canes of an extraordinary Size'. He explained that these reports had not been followed up because of the lethargy of the Spaniards: 'It has been now, for many Years, a settled Maxim in the *Spanish* Politics, not only to lay aside all Thoughts of prosecut-ing these Discoveries, but even to treat the Relations published of them by their best Authors as absolute Romances.' The more formidable Dutch could hardly be dismissed in the same way. Campbell saw their reports as part of a devious plan 'to frighten other Nations from approaching so inhospitable a Coast, every-where beset with Rocks, absolutely void of Water, and inhabited by a Race of Savages more barbarous, and, at the same time, more miserable, than any other Creatures in the World.' For the present, Campbell thought, the Dutch were a satiated power, but if driven out of the Spice Islands they would retreat south towards New Holland and New Guinea to 'avail themselves effectually of this noble Discovery, which lies open to them, and has been hitherto close shut up to all the World beside.' To prevent this, Campbell suggested a twin process of exploration and settlement. Ships should be sent out to explore the 'back Coast of New Holland and New Guiney', and to establish a settlement on New Britain, for 'a great Trade might be carried on from thence through the whole *Terra Australis* on one Side, and the most valuable Islands of the *East Indies* on the other.' To the east Juan Fernández ought to be garrisoned, perhaps by the South Sea Company, both as a trading entrepôt and as a base for discovery vessels. These might explore the true Terra Australis Incognita, the great landmass that probably stretched from the west coast of New Zealand reached by Tasman to the 'Davis Land' sighted by the buccaneers in 1687.[3]

The South Pacific was also much to the fore in the *Complete System of Geography* of 1747, published under Emanuel Bowen's name, and successor to the various editions of Moll's *Compleat Geographer* (Bowen in fact was responsible only for the maps, and this revision of Moll was undertaken by Stephen Whatley). The reader was told that 'it is very probable, that *New-Guiney*, *New-Holland*, *Van Diemen's Land*, and the *Land of the Holy Ghost*, the Country discovered by *De Quiros*, make all together one great Continent, separated from *New-Zealand* by a Streight.' The traditional southern continent, by contrast, was viewed in an altogether more sceptical manner than it had been by Campbell:

> What Countries there may be, nearer the South Pole, or round it, is intirely unknown; tho' a large Tract of Land is set down in several Maps of the whole World, under the Name of *Terra Australis incognita*, or *The unknown Southerly Countries*. Well may they be stil'd *unknown*, since we have no manner of Knowledge of them, and it is still uncertain whether there be any Land, or only an open Sea, from the 56th Degree of South Latitude, all round quite to the Pole.[4]

For Campbell the sending of expeditions to the South Pacific was only one part of his general plan to encourage British overseas trade 'as the surest Means of making us a great, wealthy, powerful and happy people'. The most important single step towards this end would be to find the Northwest Passage – 'a kind of maritime Philosopher's Stone' – for its discovery and

3. Ibid., I, pp. 65, 325, 328, 332.
4. [Stephen Whatley], *A Complete System of Geography* (London, 1747), II, pp. 777, 784.

exploitation would bring a new vitality to British overseas trade. With memories of Anson's voyage still fresh, Campbell pointed out how British naval vessels could sail quickly and undetected through a northern passage to Spain's Pacific possessions. He also stressed the new areas that would be opened to British trade by such a route: the unknown lands north of California; the rich islands thought to lie between the American coast and Japan; and parts of the East Indies. To this end he lent his support to Arthur Dobbs, 'a Man born to revive the old heroic Spirit, of turning all our Endeavours to the Service of the Public'.[5] Undismayed by the failure of Captain Middleton to find a strait through Hudson Bay during his explorations of 1742, Dobbs was busy preparing a new expedition to make the discovery. He blamed Middleton's failure on bribery of the captain by the Hudson's Bay Company and, although a prolonged bout of pamphlet warfare failed to settle the issue, went ahead with his plans. In 1745 Parliament passed an Act offering a reward of £20,000 for the discovery of a navigable passage; by chance, perhaps, it was the same amount Parliament had offered in 1714 for a reliable and precise way of determining longitude at sea, a reward as yet unclaimed. Encouraged by the prospect of an official reward, enough investors came forward to fit out two ships for another attempt on the passage. In 1746 the *Dobbs Galley* and the *California*, carefully named, sailed for Hudson Bay commanded by William Moor and Francis Smith. Something of the air of optimism that surrounded the new expedition is conveyed in Whatley's *Complete System of Geography*, published before Moor's ships returned. The editor remarked that 'there has been no News of them, that we know of; but it is suppos'd they are gone thro' the Passage, and an Account of them is expected by the first homeward-bound East-India Ships.'[6] Rather less sensationally, the ships brought their own news back with them in October 1747, and it was of failure; though the half-discovery of Chesterfield Inlet was to keep alive hopes of a passage through Hudson Bay for years to come.

It was in the context of this renewed interest in Pacific exploration and trade – among geographers, merchants and parliamentarians – that in May 1748 the long-awaited authorized account of Anson's voyage was published. In 1745 Pascoe Thomas had published a lively, at times acerbic, account, *A True and Impartial Journal of a Voyage to the South Seas and Round the Globe in His Majesty's Ship the Centurion*; but his standing on the voyage as 'Teacher of the Mathematicks on board the Centurion' made it clear that this was very much an *un*authorized account. *A Voyage Round the World . . . by George Anson* was an altogether weightier, more official affair. Its first edition attracted more than 1800 advance subscribers, including some of the leading figures in the land, and it had gone through four further editions by the end

5. See Campbell, *Navigantium atque Itinerantium Bibliotheca*, II, pp. 399–404, 440, 1039–41.
6. [Whatley], *Complete System of Geography*, II, p. 799.

of the year. Translations into French, Dutch and German were published in 1749, while in London extracts from the book appeared in serial form in newspapers and periodicals. The book was in its fifteenth edition by 1776, and abridged versions were included in most of the collections of voyages and travels published in the second half of the century. Its importance and popularity make it the more puzzling that the question of its authorship has long remained in doubt. The title-page of the first edition is clear enough: the book was 'Compiled From Papers and other Materials of the Right Honourable George Lord Anson, and published under his Direction, By Richard Walter, M.A. Chaplain of his Majesty's Ship the Centurion.' Nor does the fact that Walter left the *Centurion* at Canton in December 1742 necessarily invalidate that statement. On page 365 of the first edition the author noted that several officers returned to England in East India Company ships and that 'I, having obtained the Commodore's leave to return home, embarked with them.' At this point the narrative changes from first to third person, and becomes more summary – precisely what one would expect in the circumstances. On publication the book was accepted by newspapers and reviews as Walter's work.

The first indication that this might not be so came in 1761 when the claim was made that most of the book had been written by Benjamin Robins, a mathematician, engineer and pamphleteer known to Anson through his work on naval gunnery, who had died at Madras in 1751.[7] In contradiction to this was the recollection of Walter's widow Jane of her husband's 'constant attendance upon Lord Anson at six every morning for his approbation, as his Lordship overlooked every sheet that was written'.[8] Evidence that has emerged since supports Robins's authorship, though it is clear that Walter began the work and perhaps continued to see it through to publication. In September 1746, by which time it might have been expected that an account of the voyage would have appeared, the Rev. Thomas Birch wrote to Philip Yorke, eldest son of the Lord Chancellor, the Earl of Hardwicke, and from 1748 Anson's brother-in-law, that 'Mr. Anson has now put his papers into the hands of Mr. Robins, Mr. Walter, the first undertaker, having made scarce any progress in the work.'[9] Independent confirmation of Anson's dissatisfaction with Walter comes in the recollections of the Rev. Alexander Carlyle, who was a young man at the time of Anson's return. Among his friends was Captain David Cheap of the *Wager*, who had arrived back in England in April 1746 and 'was employ'd by Ld Anson to look out for a Proper Person to write his voyage, the Chaplain whose Journal furnish'd the Chief Materials being unequal to the work.'[10]

7. See James Wilson, ed., *Mathematical Tracts of the Late Benjamin Robins, Esq; Fellow of the Royal Society and Engineer-General to the Honourable the East India Company* (London, 1761), preface.
8. *Notes and Queries*, 8th Series, II (London, 1892), pp. 86–7.
9. BL: Add. MS 35,397, f. 20.
10. James Kinsley, ed., *Anecdotes and Characters of the Times* (Oxford, 1973), p. 99.

The evidence suggests that the literary style of the book derived from Robins's contribution to it in 1746–7. Given Anson's preoccupation with war and politics at this time, and his known aversion to writing, there is no justification for the claim that 'the book was virtually written by Anson himself'.[11] But the probability that the co-author (at least) was a man who was not on the voyage, Birch's assertion that Anson initially had intended 'to give the world an account himself' and Jane Walter's memory of Anson's close scrutiny of the work in progress all point to the *Voyage* as being in everything except stylistic terms Anson's own account. It is valuable not as an impartial account – for that was not its purpose – but as a narrative that reflects the views of the expedition's commanding officer.

The book was a classic story of adventure at sea, and a reasoned plea for the expansion of British power and commerce in the South Sea; and in both aspects it retained the interest of the British reading public for the rest of the century. To the modern reader the literary style may seem to veer uneasily between the pedestrian and the turgid, but the narrative has unmistakable power as it unfolds its terrible story of catastrophe and death.[12] The circumstances of its composition are reflected in the fact that it is decorous in tone and eulogistic whenever it refers to Anson. Compared with the slipshod literary efforts of most of Anson's privateering predecessors in the South Sea, the book was a detailed, unsensational work; and although the expedition was bent on war, not exploration, the number of charts and views (forty-two in all) showed Anson's concern to provide a guide to future voyagers in a region that was still largely unknown to British navigators. And, as was noted in the Introduction, these 'were not copied from the works of others, or composed at home from imperfect accounts, given by incurious and unskilful observers, as hath frequently been the case in these matters, but the greatest part of them were drawn on the spot.' In this and other ways it anticipated the narratives of Cook and his contemporaries later in the century, for the *Voyage* was above all a work of information, whose intent was summed up in the Introduction as the encouragement of 'the more important purposes of navigation, commerce, and national interest'. In this task the writer (from the nature of the material, almost certainly Robins) stressed the value of accurate charts, global recordings of magnetic variation and proper surveys taken from naval vessels.[13]

Given that part of the purpose of the Introduction was to contribute to 'the safety and success of future navigators', one quite mystifying omission was the lack of any discussion of the threat posed to future expeditions by

---

11. *DNB*, II, pp. 31–5 (Sir John Knox Laughton's entry on Anson).
12. I do not share Philip Edwards' astonishment that this 'tedious and bland official narrative' became a best-seller. *Story of the Voyage*, p. 56.
13. Despite such exhortations and Anson's growing influence, the Royal Navy failed at this time to establish any surveying service, or even a hydrographic office to classify and publish charts.

scurvy. It was as though the pessimistic, almost fatalistic comments in the body of the narrative about the difficulty, if not impossibility, of either prevention or cure represented the final word on the subject.[14] Even to those familiar with terrible losses at sea from disease, the ravages of scurvy on Anson's expedition seemed particularly difficult to explain or accept. Far worse than on any previous English voyage into the South Sea, they threw doubt on the whole practicality of the schemes proposed by Campbell and other projectors of the period. It was one of the unforeseen consequences of Anson's losses from scurvy, and the publicity given to them in the accounts of the voyage, that they prompted James Lind, in 1747, to begin his investigations into scurvy. In 1753 his *Treatise of the Scurvy* was published (dedicated to Anson) and was followed four years later by *An Essay on the Most Effectual Means, of Preserving the Health of Seamen*. It was to take the rest of the century for Lind's researches and recommendations to be officially accepted, but they marked the beginning of a modern, scientific approach to the problem of scurvy.[15]

In some sections the *Voyage* moved away from the task of recording and informing: 'I have thought it my duty not only to recite all such facts, and to inculcate such maxims as had the least appearance of proving beneficial to future navigators, but also occasionally to recommend such measures to the public, as I conceive are adapted to promote the same laudable purpose.' In this spirit the author urged the surveying of the Falkland Islands, Patagonia and Tierra del Fuego to make 'all that southern navigation infinitely securer than at present'. With this done, the passage from the Falklands to Juan Fernández should take little more than two months. 'This, even in time of peace, might be of great consequence to this nation; and, in time of war, would make us masters of those seas.'[16]

The same theme was followed in Chapter XIV, 'A brief account of what might have been expected from our squadron, had it arrived in the South-Seas in good time'. This postulated a summer passage round the Horn with little loss of men 'and without any damage to our ships and rigging'; the taking of Valdivia and other Spanish ports which, hopefully, would be followed, first by an Indian rising in Chile, and then by 'a general insurrection' which would give 'a violent shock to the authority of Spain on that whole Continent; and might have rendered some, at least, of her provinces independent'.[17] This unabashed piece of special pleading provoked Horace

---

14. See pp. 235–6 above.
15. There has been much revisionist work on this subject since the publication of Christopher Lloyd and J.L.S. Coulter, *Medicine and the Navy*, III, *1714–1815* (Edinburgh, 1961); for example, Kenneth J. Carpenter, *The History of Scurvy and Vitamin C* (Cambridge, 1986), and Christopher Lawrence, 'Disciplining Disease: Scurvy, the Navy, and Imperial Expansion, 1750–1825', in David P. Miller and Peter H. Reill, eds., *Visions of Empire: Voyages, Botany and Representations of Nature* (Cambridge, 1996), pp. 80–106.
16. [Walter and Robins], *Anson's Voyage*, pp. 90–4.
17. Ibid., pp. 279–89.

Walpole, no friend of Anson's, into a response that had at least an element of justification:

> He sets out with telling you that he had no soldiers sent with him but old invalids without legs or arms; and then in the middle of the book there is a whole chapter to tell you, what they would have done if they had set out two months sooner; and that was no less then conquering Peru and Mexico with this disabled army.[18]

Walpole's was a rare critical voice amid a general chorus of approval for Anson's conduct, both on the circumnavigation and after. He was one of only a few national heroes to emerge from a costly and disappointing war. His fleet victory over the French off Finisterre in 1747 confirmed his reputation as a fighting admiral, and he was raised to the peerage in 1748. His dominance on the Board of Admiralty was recognized when in 1751 he was appointed First Lord, a position that he held (with one brief interlude) until his death in 1762. Evidence has now emerged that shows that after the end of the War of the Austrian Succession in 1748 he was involved in the planning of a further expedition to the South Sea.[19] In the end, it never sailed, but in many ways the thinking behind it anticipated the beginning of more serious official interest in the Pacific which came to fruition in the voyages of the next reign.

In January 1749 Anson reported to his colleagues on the Board of Admiralty (where the Earl of Sandwich was First Lord) 'His Majesty's Pleasure that Two Sloops should be forthwith fitted to be sent on Discoverys in the Southern Latitude'.[20] By the end of February the sloops had been chosen (the *Porcupine* and *Raven*), and during March and April they were sheathed, a new deck was added to each, and John Campbell (who had sailed with Anson on the circumnavigation) was appointed to command the expedition.[21] By now the Spanish government had got wind of the venture, and its ambassador in London, General Wall, asked for further details. These came from Sandwich, who explained to the Duke of Bedford, Secretary of State for the Southern Department, that the vessels were to sail

> to the Coast of Brasil to wood & Water, and from thence go in Search of Peppy's Island[22] which is supposed to be to the Eastward of Cape Blanco, from thence to go to Falkland's Islands, & after having made what Discoveries they

18. W.S. Lewis, ed., *The Yale Edition of Horace Walpole's Correspondence*, IX, W.S. Lewis and R.S. Brown, eds, *Horace Walpole's Correspondence with George Montagu*, I (New Haven, 1941), p. 55.
19. What follows is based on the research carried out jointly with Professor Alan Frost of La Trobe University.
20. Adm 3/60: Minutes of the Board of Admiralty, 19 Jan. 1749.
21. See ibid., 28 Feb. 1749; also Adm 2/214, ff. 265, 301, 321, 353, 399.
22. Pepys Island, allegedly discovered by Ambrose Cowley in 1684, does not exist. See p. 93 above.

can in those Parts, to return to Brasil to clean & refit for the farther intended discovery, on which they are to set forward in the proper Season, they are then to double Cape Horn, & to water at Juan Fernandez, from Thence to proceed into the Trade Winds keeping between the Latitudes of 25 & 10 Sth. & steer a traverse Course for at least 1000 Leagues or more if they have an opportunity of recruiting their Wood & Water.[23]

Sandwich then went on to offer to abandon the second, or Pacific, part of the voyage, which he thought would 'be misrepresented at the Spanish Court'. As Bedford explained to Benjamin Keene, Britain's special envoy there, the King had approved this partial abandonment, for 'as this latter Part of the Scheme cannot be carried into Execution without wooding and watering, at the Island of Juan Fernandez, & possibly coming sometimes within Sight of the Spanish Coasts of Chili and Peru, it is apprehended here, that an Attempt of this Nature may alarm the Court of Madrid.' In addition, Bedford stressed that the expedition would limit its activity at Pepys Island and the Falklands to survey work – 'there is no intention of making any Settlement in either.'[24] Keene's reply showed that the Spanish government was far from reassured by these concessions. The Foreign Minister, Don Joseph de Carvajal, warned that 'neither He nor any one else could be a Stranger to the Rise and Intent of such an Expedition, since it was so fully explained in the printed Relation of Lord Anson's Voyage.' He went on to express doubt about British intentions as far as Pepys Island and the Falklands were concerned, for 'if We did not intend to make any Establishment there, What Service could this bare knowledge be of to us?' To save Britain the trouble, he offered to show Keene papers about Spanish discoveries in those islands. If his report to Bedford can be trusted, Keene was undiplomatically forthright in his response to Carvajal: 'I told him it would be difficult to take any Step for the Improvement of Navigation, and procuring a more perfect Knowledge of the World in general, that might not be subject to twisted Interpretations, and imaginary inconveniences.'[25]

By June British ministers, anxious not to upset the delicate negotiations with the Spanish government on the *asiento* and other issues, ordered the Admiralty to drop the entire expedition 'for the present'. The immediate point at issue had been conceded in deference to diplomatic and commercial considerations, but on the wider question 'His Maty cannot in any respect give into the reasonings of the Spanish Ministers, as his right to send out Ships for the discovery of unknown & unsettled Parts of the World, must indubitably be allowed by every body.'[26] Keene added a postscript, noting

23. Earl of Sandwich to the Duke of Bedford (Secretary of State for the Southern Department), 14 Apr. 1749. BL: Add. MS 43,423, f. 81.
24. Bedford to Keene, 24 Apr. 1749. PRO: S.P.94/135, ff. 177–8.
25. Keene to Bedford, 21 May 1749. Ibid., ff. 265–9.
26. Bedford to Keene, 5 June 1749. Ibid., ff. 271–2.

39. Edward Holding. A chart of
the Fonte voyage, 1749.

that if the Spaniards continued to be obstructive, 'We have Matters and Ways
to vex them in our Turn . . . one of my first Steps should be, setting out
upon discoveries in the South Seas.'[27]

The matter did not quite rest there. Scattered fragments of evidence point,
not very conclusively, to attempts by Anson to redirect the aborted expedition. The context of these attempts seems to have been the realization, after
the failure of two expeditions (in 1741–2 and 1746–7) to find a Northwest
Passage through Hudson Bay, that an attempt to locate the Pacific entrance
might be more practical. The idea was not new: it dated back to Grenville
and Drake in the 1570s and had since been advocated by, among others,
Dampier.[28] The notion of a Pacific approach was given a new lease of life at
this time by the rediscovery of the Fonte letter of 1708. Arthur Dobbs had
plucked it from obscurity by reprinting it in 1744, and this was followed in

27. Keene to Aldworth, 29 June 1749. Ibid., f. 330.
28. See pp. 16, 28, 49 above.

February 1749 by the publication of the first chart purporting to show Fonte's discoveries (Ill. 39). This was part of a detailed study of the Fonte account by T.S. Drage, who had sailed with the unsuccessful Northwest Passage expedition of 1746–7 and on his return published a two-volume account of the voyage under the pseudonym of 'The Clerk of The *California*'.[29] The most novel part of Drage's examination was his identification of Fonte's Archipelago of St Lazarus with the Strait of Anian. The latitude of the southern shore of the Archipelago was the same, according to Drage's thesis, as that of the southern shore of the Strait of Anian in lat. 51°N., long. 141°47′W. He did not acknowledge the source of such a precise location, but it came from the account by Pascoe Thomas of Anson's voyage. At the end of his book Thomas appended, without comment, a list captured from the Spaniards of the latitudes and longitudes of various places in the South Sea; and this included 'The Point of Suesta del Estrech Danian' in lat. 51°N., long.147°47′W.[30] The exactness of this location, contained as it was in an otherwise mundane table of observations, further strengthened the long-standing suspicion in Britain that the Spaniards had discovered the Strait of Anian, but had kept its location secret.

In September 1749, four months after the original expedition to the Falklands and beyond had been cancelled, it was noted that 'The *Porcupine* sloop of war has been greatly alter'd, and provided with double-chain pumps, &c., adapted to the *South Sea*.'[31] This continued work on the sloop may explain the meetings that one newspaper reported in December 1749 taking place between the Admiralty and Henry Ellis. He had sailed as agent on the Northwest Passage expedition of 1746–7, had written an account of the voyage in which he held out continuing hopes of a passage and was soon to publish a pamphlet arguing specifically for the next attempt on the passage to be made from the Pacific side.[32] The reports in the *London Evening Post* were brief and factual:

12–14 December Capt. Ellis, who went as Agent with the Dobbs and California Gallies to find out the North-West Passage, has, we hear, on being examin'd and approv'd of by Lord Anson and others, obtain'd a Commission from his

---

29. The preceding two sentences are brief summaries of two difficult and complicated matters: the puzzle of how Dobbs came across the Fonte letter, and the identity of T.S. Drage. Neither is fundamental to the present argument, but readers who are interested in following them further should consult Barr and Williams, *Voyages in Search of a Northwest Passage*, II, Appendix I (pp. 353–6) and Appendix II (pp. 357–63). The Fonte letter was reprinted in Arthur Dobbs, *Account of Hudson's Bay* (London, 1744), pp. 123–8, while 'A CHART for the better understanding DE FONT'S Letter' appeared in Clerk of the *California* [T.S. Drage], *An Account of a Voyage for the Discovery of a North-West Passage*, II (London, 1749).

30. Thomas, *True and Impartial Journal*, Appendix, p. 36.

31. *The Gentleman's Magazine*, 19 (1749), p. 427.

32. Henry Ellis, *A Voyage to Hudson's-Bay* (London, 1748), especially pp. 327–31; Captain [sic] Henry Ellis, *Considerations on the Great Advantages that Would Arise from the Discovery of the North West Passage* (London, 1750), especially p. 5.

Majesty, as Commodore of three Sloops of War, to make the same Attempt again; as also to try other Discoveries.

14–16 December Commodore Ellis, who is going to attempt the North-West Passage, is to go, by his own Desire, first to Japan, and from thence to the Back of America, where, as the Sea is open and the Weather mild, he would have better Opportunities of coasting, and passing from thence into our Northern Seas; if any Passage can be found.

26–28 December We hear that MR. ELLIS, who went Agent on board the *Dobbs Galley*, in the Last Attempt to discover a North-West Passage by *Hudson's Bay*, in the Years 1746 and 1747, has been examin'd in relation to the farther Pursuit of that Discovery by the Lords of the Admiralty: And having given entire Satisfaction as to the *Probability* of such a Passage, he is now to be sent out, not by *private Subscription*, but with three of his Majesty's Ships of War, which will sail early in the Spring. Something more than the bare *Discovery* of a Passage is said to be in View in this Enterprize, founded upon some *Hints* that arose in Lord ANSON's *Voyage*.[33]

There is no note of such meetings in the Admiralty records, though this does not necessarily mean that they did not take place. What is unlikely is that Ellis, who had no experience of command at sea, would have been offered a commission. If an expedition was planned and Ellis was indeed approached, then it would have been because of his experience of Hudson Bay, the destination of the vessels once into the passage. His capacity on the expedition would probably have been as agent or other supernumerary, rather as Tassell and Hutchinson had been on Anson's voyage.

That some sort of northern expedition was under consideration is suggested not only by these newspaper entries – never a very reliable source – but by evidence that, though much later in the form it has come to us, clearly refers to the 1749–50 period. In December 1772 a retired merchant named Cramond remembered how at a time when all the talk was of the Northwest Passage he had approached Lord Halifax, President of the Board of Trade, with a plan for an expedition to find a North*east* Passage. At that stage, Cramond recollected, 'I had a Visit from Lord Anson . . . his Lordship approv'd very much of my Plan – but was of opinion that it ought to be executed by Government, Said that he had two Ships which had been intended to be sent to the South Seas and that he would get Capt Dennis and Captain Campbell to take the Command of them.'[34] On the advice of Henry Pelham (then First Minister) Cramond consulted the directors of the East

33. See also *The Gentleman's Magazine*, 19 (1749), pp. 570–1.
34. J.C. Beaglehole, ed., *The Journals of Captain James Cook: The Voyage of the Resolution and Discovery 1776–80* (Cambridge, 1967), I, p. li. Like Campbell, Denis had sailed with Anson on his circumnavigation; both were captains in 1749.

India Company, and there the venture stalled. 'I . . . found them of various and very different Sentiments concerning the Expediency of making the discovery; So that it was deferr'd from time to time till the breaking out of the [Seven Years] Warr which put an end to our Speculation.'[35]

Rumours about the proposed expedition of 1749 led to a predictable outbreak of speculative newspaper reports. So close in timing that it seems not to be a coincidence came a long-running saga in the *London Evening Post* about the discovery by a Danish ship that had been blown off-course on a voyage from the East Indies of 'a new World' in lat. 50°S. The land seemed to form part of a continent, the captain reported, and among the people seen there were two Portuguese, 'all that remain'd alive of a Crew driven there in 1696, many of which were English'. By December the paper was insisting that 'there is a Project actually on Foot for attempting New Discoveries towards the South or Antarctic Pole', and another entry described it as an expedition intended to rival Bouvet's French discovery voyage of 1739 into the South Atlantic.[36]

Of the plans for the Admiralty expedition as originally conceived, the most intriguing was the proposed track of the two sloops west into the Pacific from Juan Fernández for three thousand miles or more, steering 'a traverse course' between lat. 10°S. and lat. 25°S. If followed long enough, this would have taken the vessels into the heart of Polynesia (Tahiti lies in lat. 17°30'S.). It is not argued here that Anson or his contemporaries had some premonition of the Society Islands; much more likely was that they had been scrutinizing Roggeveen's track through the northern Tuamotus (as set out in Campbell's volumes), or had picked up the rumours of Spanish half-discoveries of islands far out in the ocean west of Peru.[37] A more direct influence may have been Henry Hutchinson, who fell on hard times after his return from Anson's voyage.[38] He remained an indefatigable memorialist, and in his memoranda now among the papers of the Earl of Egmont (First Lord of the Admiralty from 1763 to 1766) is one entitled 'Colony in South America'. It is undated, and it could have been written at any time after his return to England in 1744. It covers well-trodden ground in its listing of the advantages to Britain of establishing a settlement in Chile; but then opens up a prospect of oceanic expansion:

> We might hereafter if necessary, from this Colony carry on a Trade to China and the East Indies, without Carrying out any Bullion out of Great Britain . . . besides the great and many advantages that may probably arise, by

35. Ibid.
36. *London Evening Post*, 3–5 Oct., 16–18 Nov., 12–14 Dec., 23–26 Dec. 1749. For Bouvet's voyage see p. 264 below.
37. As related, for example, by William Betagh in his *Voyage Round the World* of 1728; see p. 201 above. This report had recently been reprinted in Campbell, *Navigantium atque Itinerantium Bibliotheca*, I, p. 246.
38. See his letter to the Duke of Newcastle, 26 Feb. 1751. BL: Add. MS 32,724, f. 145.

making discoverys of some Good Islands, which have been seen, and are often talkd of by the Spaniards in Peru, who say, through Policy, those Islands have not been sought after in a proper manner . . . I have been informed by some judicious persons of Peru, that the declining searching after several Islands, which have been seen in South America, is owing to the fear of their being discover'd to other Nations.[39]

In the event, the 'Right to send out Ships for the discovery of unknown and unsettled Parts of the World' was not exercised for another fifteen years. As far as Spanish sensitivities about its territories on the other side of the world were concerned, what Keene called 'their whimsical notions of exclusive rights in those seas'[40] were to be respected, at least for the time being.

If there were no further voyages to the South Sea from Britain in the years after Anson's return, the period was nonetheless one of intense speculation about the Pacific by geographers. Paris had long since replaced Amsterdam as the main centre of European cartography, and in the 1750s French scholars took the lead in interpreting discoveries, real and imaginary, in a way calculated to promote new French enterprise in the South Sea. Inspired, it seems, by the voyage of Bouvet de Lozier in 1739, Philippe Buache republished the 'Hémisphère Méridional' (first issued in 1714) of his father-in-law, Guillaume de l'Isle, and added to it the 'Cap de la Circoncision' sighted by Bouvet in the South Atlantic. Shown in Buache's map of 1755 as the outlying cape of a great continent, in reality Bouvet's discovery was a speck of land so small (less than five miles across and more than a thousand miles from its nearest neighbour) that it was not sighted again until 1898. Buache's interpretation of the discovery was as fanciful as the supposition that had inspired Bouvet's expedition: that the mysterious voyage of the Frenchman, Paulmier de Gonneville, to the 'south Indies' (probably Brazil) in 1503–4 had reached Terra Australis.[41] Grappling with Britain for global supremacy, the French were anxious to stake any claims that seemed possible to lands in the southern hemisphere. In his *Histoire et Théories de la Terre* (1749), the Comte de Buffon had thrown his considerable scholarly weight in favour of a southern continent as large as Europe, Asia and Africa combined.[42] When in the mid-1750s Charles de Brosses issued his great collection of Pacific voyages, *Histoire des Navigations aux Terres Australes*, he argued for the existence and potential of such a continent in words similar to those of Campbell and Bowen in Britain:

39. BL: Add. MS 47,014C, f. 122.
40. PRO: SP 94/135, f. 267v.
41. See Leslie R. Marchant, *France Australe* (Perth, 1982), pp. 15–19, 37–42.
42. Louis Leclerc Buffon, *Histoire et Théories de la Terre* (Paris, 1749), Art. VI, pp. 98–9.

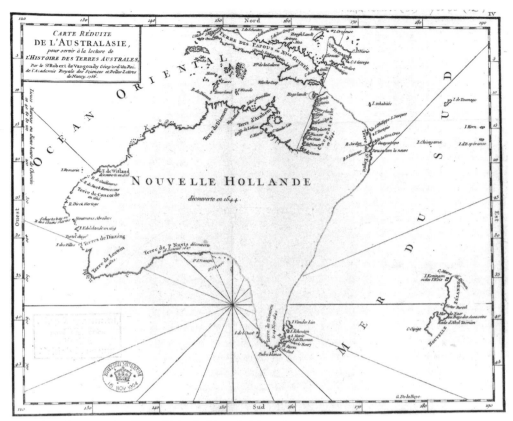

40. Robert de Vaugondy. 'Carte réduite de l'Australasie', 1756.

It is not possible that there is not, in such a vast sea, some immense continent of solid land south of Asia, capable of keeping the globe in equilibrium in its rotation . . . How can we doubt that after its discovery such a vast expanse of land will supply objects of curiosity, opportunities for profit, perhaps as many as America furnished in its novelty?[43]

As far as the shape of the South Land was concerned, de Brosses was not totally convinced by Quiros's description of Espiritu Santo. He suspected that the Spaniard's discovery might be insular rather than continental, and noted that no European had seen it since Quiros. The map by Robert de Vaugondy that accompanied this section, however, allowed of little ambiguity (Ill. 40). The unknown east coast of New Holland was marked by a broken line, slanting north–northeast from Van Diemen's Land as far as the mainland bulge of the Quiros discoveries. It was a natural development of the trend started by Sanson and Guillaume de l'Isle in the late seventeenth

43. Charles de Brosses, *Histoire des Navigations aux Terres Australes* (Paris, 1756), I, pp. 13, 16.

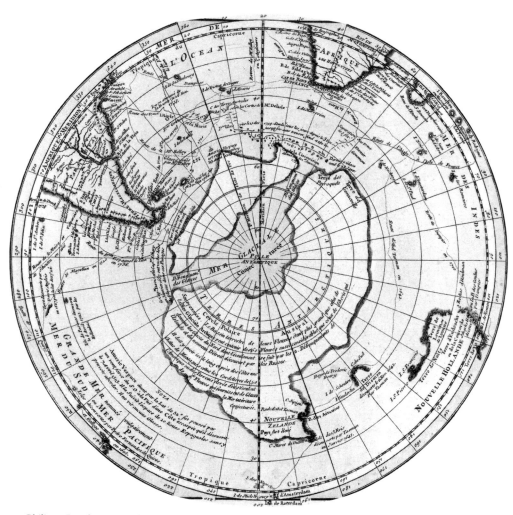

41. Philippe Buache. 'Carte des Terres Australes', 1754.

century, and gave the image of an extended Australian continent a greater circulation than ever before. In one form or another it was repeated in many of the atlases of the mid-eighteenth century – a tantalizing union of the known barrenness of the west coast with the expected but still unknown riches of the east. This concept took its most extreme form in Philippe Buache's adaptation of his father-in-law's maps, especially his world map, 'Mappe par Guillaume de l'Isle . . . augmentée par P.B.' (1755). Here Buache pushed Espiritu Santo almost as far east as the longitude of New Zealand. If this was correct (and it *is* roughly the longitude of the New Hebrides/ Vanuatu), and if Quiros's discovery was indeed part of the mainland, then New Holland stretched a thousand miles farther east than most of the maps suggested – a mighty landmass indeed. Farther south the Buache maps (Ill. 41) were by now showing New Zealand as the western extremity of a great continent, whose misty shapes swirled around his polar projections in imposing, if ill-defined, fashion. 'We have the impression', a French scholar writes, 'of seeing a new world recently emerged from the oceans.'[44]

For the North Pacific the French interpretations of recent explorations were even more startling. In 1747 Joseph Nicholas de l'Isle, younger brother of Guillaume, returned to France after twenty years in Russia, during which he had helped to plan the second Bering expedition of 1741–2. In April 1750 de l'Isle read a paper on Bering's voyages before the Académie Royale des Sciences in Paris and accompanied it with a map drawn by his nephew, Philippe Buache. The publication two years later of de l'Isle's memoir and Buache's map marked the beginning of a controversy which exercised a bizarre but important influence upon the course of exploration in the North Pacific for the rest of the century.[45] The French geographers juxtaposed the real, if fleeting, sightings of the northwest coast of America by the Russian expeditions with the sweeping discoveries alleged to have been made by Admiral de Fonte in 1640 and by Juan de Fuca in 1592. So on Buache's map northwest America was shown penetrated by the great inland seas, straits and rivers said to have been discovered by Fonte and Fuca. By 1752 de l'Isle and Buache were in disagreement over the starting point of Fonte's discoveries and issued separate maps and memoirs.[46] These were examples of hypothetical geography at its most complex and fantastic (Ill. 42). Accounts of voyages, some genuine, some apocryphal; reports and rumours, French, English, Spanish, Russian, even Chinese: all were welded together in the construction of their fanciful systems. De l'Isle and Buache divided the world of French cartography with their theories. Jean Janvier and Louis Denis were among the geographers who fell in line; two of the best-known French geographers, Bellin and de Vaugondy, remained sceptical. In Russia Gerhard Müller of the St Petersburg Academy of Sciences refuted much of what de l'Isle and Buache had said about Bering's discoveries and thought the Fonte letter 'calculated only for amusement'.

The most thorough of the early criticisms of de l'Isle and Buache came from the British geographer known as John Green, whose 'New Chart of North and South America' was published in 1753, together with an

44. Numa Broc, *La Géographie des Philosophes: Géographies et Voyageurs Français au XVIIIe-Siècle* (Paris, 1974), p. 180.

45. For a recent discussion see Lucie Lagarde, 'Le Passage du Nord-Ouest et la Mer de l'Ouest dans la Cartographie Française du 18e Siècle, Contribution à l'Etude de l'Œuvre des Delisle et Buache', *Imago Mundi*, 41 (1989), pp. 19–43.

46. See J.N. de l'Isle, *Nouvelles Cartes des Découvertes de l'Amiral de Fonte* (Paris, 1753); Philippe Buache, *Considérations Géographiques et Physiques sur les Nouvelles Découvertes au Nord de la Grande Mer* (Paris, 1753).

42. J.N. de l'Isle. 'Carte des Nouvelles Découvertes', 1752.

explanatory booklet of *Remarks*.[47] In contrast to the elaborate maps of de l'Isle and Buache, Green's depiction of the northwest coast of America was austere – blank spaces, a few dotted lines and the legend, 'These parts, as yet wholly unknown are filled up, by Messrs Buache and Del'Isle, with the pretended Discoveries of Adml. De Fonte and his Captains in 1640.' Far to the east on Green's chart another annotation in the Hudson Bay area pointed out that the distance to the Pacific of at least 430 leagues 'hath long cry'd aloud that there is no Passage, at least for Ships'. Green's accompanying *Remarks* took de l'Isle and Buache to task for, at best, carelessness, at worst, deception. He showed that whereas the Fonte letter stated that the Archipelago of St Lazarus lay in lat. 53°N., on Buache's 'Carte des Nouvelles Découvertes au Nord de la Mer du Sud' of June 1752 it was marked in lat. 63°N., with the result that all the subsequent explorations were shown too far north. Having challenged Buache on his own ground, Green returned to the real point at issue: 'The Discoveries ascribed to Admiral De Fonte have no real Existence in Nature; and that however commodiously they may help to fill-up a Map of the North-West Part of America, they ought in reality to have no Place there.'[48]

In the South Pacific, Green struggled, as others had done, to reconcile the differing reports of discoveries brought back by voyagers from Mendaña and Quiros onwards: 'There are doubtless many large Countries or Islands in this Part of the South-Sea: But the published Account of De Quiros is so imperfect, that there is no laying-down any Thing from it with Certainty.'[49] With unusual candour, Green admitted that much of his own placement of islands in the region was 'Guess-Work'. As he explained, some navigators had seen no islands in their track across the South Sea, and those who had

> have left such imperfect Accounts, that they are scarce of any Use: For they seldom mention the Longitude or Distances; and rarely the Latitude with any Accuracy; contenting themselves to say that they saw such an Island about the 16th Degree of Latitude, or between 10 and 12 Degrees. As if they thought so vague a Direction sufficient; or that the Places might be found again by the capricious Names which they imposed upon them.[50]

Green's attack on de l'Isle and Buache was unusual in an age when French cartographers were esteemed for their critical approach and technical excellence. Maps and books by French geographers reached England soon after

---

47. For more on John Green see two articles by G.R. Crone, 'John Green. Notes on a Neglected Eighteenth-Century Geographer and Cartographer', and 'Further Notes on Bradock Mead, Alias John Green, an Eighteenth-Century Cartographer', *Imago Mundi*, 6 (1949), pp. 85–91, and 8 (1951), pp. 69–70.

48. John Green, *Remarks in Support of the New Chart of North and South America* (London, 1753), p. 84.

49. Ibid., p. 42.

50. Ibid., p. 43.

publication, and newspaper advertisements show that London sellers of maps and prints normally stocked both the standard and latest foreign maps.[51] Often it was possible to obtain atlases direct from the continent at the time of publication, and the list of subscribers given in the opening pages of de Vaugondy's prestigious *Atlas universel* of 1757 included English scholars and librarians. Nor was interest confined to specialist circles. Within a month of the publication in Paris in June 1752 of the first of Buache's Fonte maps, information about it appeared in English newspapers:

> The Sieurs de Lisle and Buache have presented to the King [of France] a Chart of Mr. Lisle's late Discoveries to the Northward of the South Sea, containing all the Space hitherto unknown, betwixt North America and the Eastern Extremity of Asia; a Performance certainly of as great Importance as any which Geography has for a long Time afforded, both by the vast Extent of Seas and Lands it exhibits, and the Insight for a shorter Cut to the East Indies.[52]

Copies of the map were eagerly awaited in England, where the Royal Society received one of the de l'Isle productions before the end of 1752. Early in 1753 Peter Collinson, London merchant and Fellow of the Royal Society, wrote to Benjamin Franklin in Philadelphia describing the new French map, which showed 'a River from about Hudsons bay Derived from a Great Inland lake full of Islands and another river falling from that lake into the Eastern Ocean above California'.[53] In 1754 translations of de l'Isle's original memoir and Müller's riposte were published in London, while an engraving of one of de l'Isle's maps, and a long summary of the controversy, appeared in *The Gentleman's Magazine* for March and April. Despite Green's criticism of the Fonte account, and a conclusive refutation of it by a Spanish scholar in 1757,[54] belief in the extraordinary voyage it described was to have a long life. The Fonte letter was reprinted many times in the second half of the century; it played a part in the instructions given to the discovery expeditions of Cook, La Pérouse and Malaspina; and not until George Vancouver's comprehensive survey of the northwest coast in 1792–4 was its fictitious nature finally recognized.[55]

---

51. For example, in March and May 1748 the following advertisements were inserted in *The General Advertiser* by Overton, the Fleet Street mapseller: 23 March: 'Just arrived from Holland the following Foreign Maps; Several Atlas's of 110, 118 and 132 Maps, by the celebrated Mons. D'Lisle, First Geographer to the present King of France.' 16 May: 'Just imported from Amsterdam, A Large Parcel of Foreign Maps done by the Royal Academy at Paris, also by Mons. De Lisle, Sanson . . . and other celebrated Geographers.'

52. *London Daily Advertiser*, 16 July 1752.

53. See Bertha Solis-Cohen, 'Philadelphia's Expeditions to Labrador', *Pennsylvania History*, 19 (1952), p. 159.

54. See Glyndwr Williams, 'An Eighteenth-Century Spanish Investigation into the Apocryphal Voyage of Admiral Fonte', *Pacific Historical Review*, 30 (1961), pp. 319–27.

55. A personal note might be permitted here. The present writer received in July 1996 a courteous enquiry from a descendant of Captain Nicholas Shapley (the 'real-life' New Englander whose vessel Fonte was supposed to have encountered in 1640) asking for further information about the meeting between his ancestor and the Spanish admiral.

Geographers, cartographers and projectors continued to busy themselves with new books, new charts, new schemes; but as war battered Europe and its overseas empires, governments had little time or money for distant ventures of exploration. The nearest British approach to the Pacific came with a scheme for the capture of Manila, approved by Anson as First Lord of the Admiralty shortly before his death. As he sat through three days of meetings in January 1762, echoes of the discussions of 1739 may have come back to him as he listened to the advantages that would follow the seizure of Manila and the establishment of a British base on Mindanao. 'All trade or intercourse betwixt the E. Indies and the Spanish American provinces in the South Seas will be efectually cut off during the war, at least . . . from such proposed settlement the Spanish provinces in the South Seas, both of South and North America may with great success be insulted and plundered on the part of Great Britain.'[56]

With peace, ministerial thoughts turned again to exploration, and in 1764 the first discovery expedition of George III's reign, commanded by Commodore John Byron, sailed for the Pacific. Perhaps because of the new reign, perhaps because an account of it appeared in Hawkesworth's *Voyages* in company with those of Wallis, Carteret and Cook, Byron's voyage has conventionally been linked with the succeeding discovery expeditions. In reality it was a throwback to an earlier period; it was the abortive 1749 expedition writ large. Byron had been a midshipman on the unlucky *Wager*, so it was appropriate that he was to command an expedition whose aims would be familiar to Anson and to Anson's generation. Anson had died in June 1762 – still regretting, so Shelburne claimed, that he had not pressed ahead with the Falklands project[57] – and Byron received his instructions from a new First Lord of the Admiralty, the Earl of Egmont. The Admiralty seems to have planned the voyage, in direct communication with the King, without keeping other ministers informed. This may have been a deliberate move by Egmont to avoid a repetition of the 1749 imbroglio when intervention by Bedford had forced the cancellation of the intended expedition of that year.

Certainly Byron's 'Secret Instructions' seem to have been more secret than most. Their opening lines struck a new note as they proclaimed that 'nothing can redound more to the honor of this Nation as a Maritime Power, to the dignity of the Crown of Great Britain, and to the advancement of the Trade and Navigation thereof, than to make Discoveries of Countries hitherto unknown.'[58] The body of the instructions, however, contained little fresh.

56. Nicholas P. Cushner, ed., *Documents Illustrating the British Conquest of Manila 1762–1763* (London, 1971), p. 12. There were other resonances from an earlier period about this operation, for in October 1762 British warships captured the *Santísima Trinidad*, one of the last and greatest of the Manila galleons.

57. See Helen Wallis, ed., *Carteret's Voyage Round the World 1766–1769* (Cambridge, 1965), II, p. 309.

58. Quotations in this paragraph are from Robert E. Gallagher, ed., *Byron's Journal of his Circumnavigation 1764–1766* (Cambridge, 1964), pp. 3, 161.

They represented the bringing together of the plans of earlier generations. 'Trade and navigation' were to be the chief beneficiaries; of science there was as yet no mention. Drake and Dampier were the forerunners, and the Northwest Passage appears as an alternative route home. Egmont's report to the Cabinet when he received news of Byron's arrival in the Falklands confirms the anti-Spanish aim of the expedition. The enterprise was of 'very great Moment & of the most secret nature'. The Falklands, he insisted, were *'the Key to the whole Pacifick Ocean'*, for they 'must command the Ports & Trade of Chili Peru, Panama, Acapulco, & in one word all the Spanish Territory upon that Sea. It will render all our Expeditions to those parts most lucrative to ourselves, most fatal to Spain.' Clearly, the earlier nervousness of Spanish ministers when they heard details of the proposed expedition of 1749 had some justification.

Only once did Egmont raise wider considerations of oceanic explora- tion, when he mentioned the possibility of further 'Discoverys in all that Southern Tract of Ocean both to the East & West of the magellanick Streights'.[59] But it was these wider considerations that came to the fore in the voyage that immediately followed Byron's, that of Captain Samuel Wallis (accompanied by a consort vessel commanded by Captain Philip Carteret). For the first time since Dampier, *Terra Australis Incognita* appears in official Admiralty instructions: 'whereas there is reason to beleive [sic] that Lands, or Islands of great extent, hitherto unvisited by any European Power may be found in the Southern Hemisphere between Cape Horn and New Zeland, in Latitudes convenient for Navigation, and in Climates adapted to the product of Commodities usefull in Commerce.'[60] In this new and portentous directive, Byron, usually dismissed as an inadequate explorer, played an important role. Sailing through the northern fringes of the Tuamotu Archipelago in June 1765 he was convinced that there was land to the south, and but for unfavourable winds 'I should have fell in with it, & in all Probability made the discovery of the So Continent.'[61] On his return to England Byron became involved with Egmont's planning of the Wallis expedition, and his 'posative oppinion' on the existence of 'a Continent of Great Extent never yet Explored or seen' seems to have persuaded Egmont to point Wallis towards its discovery.[62] In the event, Wallis showed little initiative on his track across the Pacific, but his voyage was marked by his stay at Tahiti, a chance encounter whose impact on the European imagination was out of all proportion to its geographical significance. James Cook was at Tahiti by 1769, on a voyage prompted by motives of scientific investigation as well as of trade

59. Ibid., p. 161.
60. Wallis, *Carteret's Voyage*, II, p. 302.
61. Gallagher, *Byron's Journal*, p. 105.
62. See Hugh Carrington, ed., *The Discovery of Tahiti* (London, 1948), p. 4; Wallis, *Carteret's Voyage*, II, pp. 311–12.

and navigation, and a new era of European exploration and exploitation had opened.

Egmont had resigned as First Lord of the Admiralty before Wallis had sailed, but the continuing insistence on the importance of the Falklands was a blind alley that led Britain close to war before in 1774 it abandoned its tiny base there. For British navigators it was too close to centres of Spanish power, and it was on the wrong side of the passage through the Strait of Magellan or round Cape Horn. The bases for the new explorers of the Pacific were not even names on the map when Byron sailed: Matavai Bay, Queen Charlotte Sound, Kealakekua Bay, Nootka Sound. Although Spain made increasingly forlorn attempts to extend dominion over these far-flung bays and coves, the blocking manœuvre of 1749 never succeeded again. Out of deference to Spanish sensitivities the Admiralty might change the names of its discovery vessels from *Drake* and *Raleigh*, but they still made their voyage under Cook in 1772–5 (renamed *Resolution* and *Discovery*).

Thoughts of raiding Spanish American settlements and trade still attracted ministers whenever war loomed, and did so even as the Spanish empire was disintegrating in the French Revolutionary and Napoleonic Wars.[63] The assault on Buenos Aires in 1806 was a direct descendant of the schemes and projects going back to Anson, Defoe and Drake, and had as little permanent success. It was that other stream of South Sea enterprise, visible from the beginning, that in the later eighteenth century pushed forward and influenced the course of exploration. It was wider, more beguiling and more truly oceanic. It drew on theories, speculations and myths – of a great southern continent, mysterious islands, an ice-free northwest passage. None of these existed, at least in the form anticipated, but it was the search for them – rather than predatory designs on Spanish possessions – that lay behind the voyages of Cook and his successors.

---

63. See Vincent T. Harlow, *The Founding of the Second British Empire 1763–1793*, II, *New Continents and Changing Values* (London, 1964), pp. 615–61; Alan Frost, *Arthur Phillip 1738–1814: His Voyaging* (Melbourne, 1987), pp. 105–15.

Bibliography

Manuscript Sources

Rather than follow the more normal method of listing the manuscript sources by archive, this section arranges the documents by chapter.

[III] The British Library holds a large collection of journals from the buccaneering and other South Sea voyages of the late seventeenth century. The following were found particularly useful:

> Sloane MS 3833: John Wood's journal of the Narborough voyage, 1669–70
> Add. MS 21,539: Spanish reports by the Viceroy of Peru and others relating to the Narborough voyage
> Sloane MS 3820: Basil Ringrose's holograph journal of Bartholomew Sharp's voyage, 1680–1
> Sloane MS 48: William Hack's edited copy of the Ringrose journal (above)
> Add. MS 11,410: anonymous journal of Sharp's voyage, 1680–2
> Sloane MS 54: Ambrose Cowley's journal of his voyage, 1683–6
> Sloane MS 3236: William Dampier's journal, 1681–91 (incomplete)
> Sloane MS 3295: John Strong's journal of his voyage, 1689–90
> Sloane MS 86: Richard Simson's journal of the same, 1689–90

[IV] Documents on the genesis of Dampier's *Roebuck* voyage (1699–1701) are contained in PRO: Adm 2/1692. Although Dampier's original journal has not survived, the log of the ship's master, Jacob Hughes, is in Adm 52/94.

[V] Some light is cast on Dampier's troubled voyage in the *St George* (1703–6) by the depositions given in 1712 by crew members in the legal proceedings brought against Dampier by the owners. These are in PRO: Chancery 24/1321 and 33/317.

The Chancery papers contain a wealth of material, much of it ill-organized and some of it illegible, on the Woodes Rogers voyage (1708–11), especially Chancery 104/36, 37, 61, 160. It should be noted that Chancery 104/38, 39, 40 were unavailable for inspection. The reactions of the East India Company to the return of the expedition are scattered through OIOC: E 1/3 and D/92, 93.

[VI] The British Library holds a number of memoirs and proposals on the South Sea c. 1711, in Add. MS 28,140 and among Robert Harley's papers in Add. MSS 70,163 and 70,164 (formerly the Portland Loan). Papers of the South Sea Company relating to the proposed expedition of 1712 are in Add. MSS 25,494, 25,559. The Bowrey Papers in the Guildhall Library, London: MSS 3041, 3042 also have material of interest.

[VII] The erratic career and South Sea proposals of John Welbe can be followed in BL: Add. MSS 70,042, 25,550, 33,054; and in PRO: Treasury 1/240.

[VIII] The Archives of the Hudson's Bay Company, Winnipeg, hold much material about the voyage of James Knight in 1719. Knight's journals at York Factory are in B 239/a/1, 2, 3, and his correspondence with the Company at this time is in A 11/ 114. Preparations for the expedition are in A 1/117 and A 6/4. The first news of the expedition's fate is given in B 239/a/5 and B 42/a/2; later and fuller information is in 42/a/68, 69.

Shelvocke's manuscript journal of his voyage of 1719–22 is in the Admiralty Library (Taunton): MS 18. Correspondence on the brief revival of interest in the South Sea c. 1726, and including memoranda by Shelvocke and Woodes Rogers, can be found in BL: Add. MSS 19,034, 32,748.

[IX] On Anson's voyage the main collections are at the British Library, Public Record Office and the National Maritime Museum. The planning of the expedition is dealt with in PRO: SP 42/88; BL: Add. MSS 28,132, 32,694; while there is also relevant material in the Wager MSS at the Library of Congress. Anson's instructions, together with draft manifestoes, are in PRO: SP 42/81, 42/88 and BL: Add. MS 19,030. Preparations for the voyage are covered in PRO: Adm 1/4109, 1439. Details about enemy knowledge of the voyage will be found in PRO: Adm 1/1695, and in AMAE: Corr. Politique/Espagne 460.

For the voyage itself Millechamp's journal in NMM 9354/JOD 36 provides a continuous record, though one clearly written after the event. Anson's own correspondence, before and during the voyage, is in BL: Add. MSS 15,855, 35,359 and PRO: SP 42/88. Legge's journal and letters are in PRO: Adm 1/2049, Section 11; and Murray's letters are in Adm 1/2099, Section 3. Spanish reactions to the capture of the *Covadonga* are in AI: Audiencia de Filipinas, 256; while PRO: HCA 32/135 has material on the capture and the resultant booty, including a deposition by the galleon's commander. A mass of evidence about the legal dispute over prize-money is contained in NMM: 39/MS 9416/HAR 4. Details of Anson's visits to Macao and Canton are in OIOC: Factory Records: China II, 3; and also in recently discovered documents now in the Library of the Oregon Historical Society (OHS), MSS 2892, 2893, 2894.

It should be said that much valuable information about the voyage and its aftermath is included in the papers of Lieutenant (later Captain) Philip Saumarez, consulted by the present writer many years ago when they were in family possession at Sausmarez Manor, Guernsey; but their present whereabouts are not known.

The journal of Middleton's discovery voyage of 1741–2 is in PRO: Adm 51/379;

his instructions are in Adm 2/57; and much other information about the expedition and the controversy after its return in Adm 1/2099.

[X] BL: Add. MSS 35,396, 35,397 hold intriguing evidence about the authorship of the authorized account of Anson's voyage (1748). There is a considerable amount of rather scattered material about the projected expedition of 1749 to the South Sea in PRO: Adm 2/214 and 3/60 (practical arrangements), and in PRO: SP 94/135 and BL: 32,724, 43,423 and 47,014C (diplomatic considerations).

Printed Sources

i) Official

Calendar of State Papers, Spanish, III, 1580–6 (London, 1896); IV, 1587–1603 (London, 1896).

Calendar of State Papers, Colonial: America and West Indies, 1696–7 (London, 1904); 1697–8 (London, 1905).

Cobbett, William, ed. *The Parliamentary History of England*, XI (London, 1812).

Davenport, F.G., ed. *European Treaties Being on the History of the United States and its Dependencies*, II, III (Washington, 1929).

Johnson, David L., ed. *Manuscripts of the House of Lords*, XII (New Ser.), 1714–1718 (London, 1977).

Journal of the Commissioners for Trade and Plantations 1718–22 (London, 1922).

ii) Journals, Memoirs, Correspondence &c.

Amherst, Lord, ed. *The Discovery of the Solomon Islands* (London, 1901).

[Anon]. *An Account of Several Late Voyages & Discoveries to the South and North* (London, 1694).

———. *The Considerable Advantages of a South-Sea Trade to our English Nation* (London, c. 1711).

Asher, G.M., ed. *Henry Hudson the Navigator* (London, 1860).

Ayres, Philip. *The Voyages and Adventures of Captain Barth. Sharp and Others, in the South Sea* (London, 1684).

Barr, William, and Williams, Glyndwr, eds. *Voyages to Hudson Bay in Search of a Northwest Passage*: I, *The Voyage of Christopher Middleton 1741–1742* (London, 1994); II, *The Voyage of William Moor and Francis Smith 1746–1747* (London, 1995).

Beaglehole, J.C., ed. *The Journals of Captain James Cook: The Voyage of the Endeavour 1768–1771* (Cambridge, 1955).

———. *The Journals of Captain James Cook: The Voyage of the Resolution and Discovery 1776–80* (Cambridge, 1967).

———. *The Endeavour Journal of Joseph Banks 1768–1771* (Sydney, 1962).

Betagh, William. *A Voyage Round the World* (London, 1728).

Blanchard, Rae, ed. *The Englishman* (Oxford, 1955).

Brosses, Charles de. *Histoire des Navigations aux Terres Australes* (Paris, 1749).

Buache, Philippe. *Considérations Géographiques et Physiques sur les Nouvelles Découvertes au Nord de la Grande Mer* (Paris, 1753).

Buffon, Louis Leclerc. *Histoire et Théories de la Terre* (Paris, 1749).

Bulkeley, John, and Cummins, John. *A Voyage to the South-Sea, In the Years 1740–1* (London, 1743).

Campbell, John, ed. *Navigantium atque Itinerantium Bibliotheca: or, A Compleat Collection of Voyages and Travels* (London, 1744–8).

Christy, Miller, ed. *The Voyages of Captain Luke Foxe of Hull, and Captain Thomas James of Bristol* (London, 1894).

Churchill, Awnsham and John. *A Collection of Voyages and Travels* (London, 1704).

Collinson, Richard, ed. *The Three Voyages of Martin Frobisher* (London, 1894).

Concepción, Juan de la. *Historia General de Philipinas*, XI (Manila, 1791).

Cooke, Edward. *A Voyage to the South Sea, and Round the World* (London, 1712).

Coxe, William. *Memoirs of the Life and Administration of Sir Robert Walpole*, II (London, 1798).

Cummins, J.S., ed. *Sucesos de Las Filipinas by Antonio de Morga* (Cambridge, 1971).

Cushner, Nicholas P., ed. *Documents Illustrating the British Conquest of Manila 1762–1763* (London, 1971).

Dampier, William. *A New Voyage Round the World* (London, 1697). Also: ed. Sir Albert Gray (London, 1927), and with a new Introduction by Percy G. Adams (New York, 1968).

———. *Voyages and Descriptions*. Vol II (London, 1699).

———. *A Voyage to New-Holland, &c. In the Year 1699* (London, 1703).

———. *A Continuation of a Voyage to New-Holland, &c. In the Year 1699* (London, 1709). Also: both vols ed. J.A. Williamson (London, 1939), James Spencer (Gloucester, 1981).

———. *A Collection of Voyages*, I–IV (London, 1729). Also: John Masefield, ed., *Dampier's Voyages* (London, 1906).

———. *Captain Dampier's Vindication of his Voyage to the South-Seas, in the Ship St George* (London, [1707]).

Defoe, Daniel. *The Essay on the South-Sea Company* (London, 1712 [1711]).

———. *The Essay on the South-Sea Trade* (London, 1712 [1711]).

———. *The Life and Strange Surprizing Adventures of Robinson Crusoe* (London, 1719). Also: ed. Angus Ross (Harmondsworth, 1965).

———. *A New Voyage Round the World by a Course Never Sailed Before* (London, 1725 [1724]).

———. *A General History of Discoveries and Improvements* (London, 1726–7).

———. *A Plan of the English Commerce* (2nd edn, London, 1730).

Dobbs, Arthur. *Remarks upon Capt. Middleton's Defence* (London, 1744).

Donno, Elizabeth S., ed. *An Elizabethan in 1582: The Diary of Richard Madox* (London, 1976).

[Drage, T.S.]. *An Account of a Voyage for the Discovery of a North-West Passage* (London, 1748–9).

Eden, Richard. *The Decades of the Newe World* (London, 1555), reprinted in Edward Arber, ed., *The First Three English Books on America* (Birmingham, 1885).

———. *The History of Trauayle in the West and East Indies* (London, 1577).

Ellis, Henry. *A Voyage to Hudson's-Bay* (London, 1748).

————. *Considerations on the Great Advantages that Would Arise from the Discovery of the North West Passage* (London, 1750).

[Exquemelin, A.O.]. *Bucaniers of America . . . Inlarged with two Additional Relations, viz. the one of Captain Cook, and the Other of Captain Sharp* (London, 1684)

[Foigny, Gabriel de]. *A New Discovery of Terra Australis, or the Southern World. By James Sadeur* (London, 1693).

Frézier, A.F. *A Voyage to the South-Sea, and Along the Coasts of Chili and Peru* (London, 1717).

Funnell, William. *A Voyage Round the World* (London, 1707).

Gallagher, R.E., ed. *Byron's Journal of his Circumnavigation 1764–1766* (Cambridge, 1964).

Green, John. *Remarks in Support of the New Chart of North and South America* (London, 1753).

Hacke [Hack], William, ed. *A Collection of Original Voyages* (London, 1699).

Hakluyt, Richard. *The Principall Navigations, Voiages & Discoveries of the English Nation* [1589]: facsimile edn with an Introduction by D.B. Quinn and R.A. Skelton, and new index by Alison Quinn (Cambridge, 1965).

————. *The Principal Navigations Voyages Traffiques & Discoveries of the English Nation* [1598–1600] (reprinted Glasgow, 1902–5).

Harley, Robert. *Letters and Papers*, II, III, in *Manuscripts of the Duke of Portland*, IV, V (London, Historical Manuscripts Commission, 1897, 1899).

Healey, G.H., ed. *The Letters of Daniel Defoe* (Oxford, 1955).

Heeres, J.E., ed. *Abel Janszoon Tasman's Journal of his Discovery of Van Diemen's Land and New Zealand in 1642* (Amsterdam, 1898).

Heylyn, Peter. *Cosmographie* (2nd edn, London, 1657).

Howse, Derek, and Thrower, Norman J.W., eds. *A Buccaneer's Atlas: Basil Ringrose's South Sea Waggoner* (Berkeley and Los Angeles, 1992).

[Hyde, Thomas]. *An Account of the Famous Prince Giolo* (London, 1692).

Isle, J.N. de l'. *Nouvelles Cartes des Découvertes de l'Admiral de Fonte* (Paris, 1753).

Joyce, L.E. Elliott, ed. *A New Voyage and Description of the Isthmus of America by Lionel Wafer* [1699] (Oxford, 1934).

Juan, Jorge, and Ulloa, Antonio de. *Relación Histórica del Viaje a la América Meridional* (Madrid, 1758).

Kelly, Celsus, ed. *La Austrialia del Espíritu Santo* (Cambridge, 1966).

Kinsley, James, ed. *Anecdotes and Characters of the Times* (Oxford, 1973).

Mackaness, George, ed. *Some Proposals for Establishing Colonies in the South Sea* (Sydney, 1943).

Major, J.H., ed. *Early Voyages to Terra Australis, Now Called Australia* (London, 1859).

Markham, C.R., ed. *The Voyages and Works of John Davis* (London, 1880).

————. *Narrative of the Voyages of P.S. de G.* (London, 1895).

[Moll, Herman]. *A View of the Coasts, Countrys, & Islands within the Limits of the South-Sea Company* (2nd edn, London, 1711).

————. *Atlas Geographicus* (London, 1711–17).

Nuttall, Z., ed. *New Light on Drake* (London, 1914).

Ogilby, John. *America* (London, 1671).

Penzer, N.M., ed. *The World Encompassed . . . Carefully Collected Out of the Notes of Master Francis Fletcher* [1626] (London, 1926).

[Petavius, et al.]. *A Geographicall Description of the World* (London, 1682).

Pullen, John. *Memoirs of the Maritime Affairs of Great-Britain* (London, 1732).

Purchas, Samuel. *Hakluytus Posthumus or Purchas his Pilgrimes* (London, 1625, reprinted Glasgow, 1905–7).

Purry, J.P. *A Method for Determining the Best Climate of the Earth* (London, 1744).

Quinn, D.B., ed. *The Voyages and Colonising Enterprises of Sir Humphrey Gilbert* (London, 1940).

———. *The Last Voyage of Thomas Cavendish 1591–1592* (Chicago, 1975).

Quiros, Pedro Fernando de. *'Terra Australis Incognita', or A New Southerne Discoverie, Containing a Fifth Part of the World* (London, 1617).

[Ringrose, Basil]. *Bucaniers of America. The Second Volume Containing the Dangerous Voyage and Bold Attempts of Captain Bartholomew Sharp and Others; Performed upon the Coasts of the South Sea* (London, 1685).

Rogers, Woodes. *A Cruising Voyage Round the World* (London, 1712). Also: ed. G.E. Manwaring (1928), reprinted with a new Introduction by Percy G. Adams (New York, 1970).

Sanz, Carlos, ed. *Australia: Su Descubrimiento y Denominación* (Madrid, 1973).

Sharp, Andrew, ed. *The Voyages of Abel Janszoon Tasman* (Oxford, 1968).

Shelvocke, George. *A Voyage Round the World by Way of the Great South Sea* (London, 1726). Also: ed. W.G. Perrin (London, 1928).

Sprat, Thomas. *History of the Royal Society* (London, 1667).

Swift, Jonathan. *Gulliver's Travels* (London, 1726). Also: ed. Peter Dixon and John Chalker (Harmondsworth, 1967).

———. *A Tale of a Tub* (London, 1704). Also: ed. A.C. Guthketch and D. Nichol Smith (2nd edn, Oxford, 1958).

Taylor, E.G.R., ed. *A Brief Summe of Geographie* [by Roger Barlow] (London, 1932).

———. *The Original Writings and Correspondence of the Two Richard Hakluyts* (London, 1935).

———. *The Troublesome Voyage of Captain Edward Fenton 1582–83* (Cambridge, 1959).

Thomas, Pascoe. *A True and Impartial Journal of a Voyage to the South Seas* (London, 1745).

Thrower, Norman J.W., ed. *The Three Voyages of Edmond Halley* (London, 1981).

Trumbull, William. *Downshire Manuscripts*, VI, *Papers of William Trumbull the Elder 1616–1618* (London, Historical Manuscripts Commission, 1995).

[Varens, Bernard]. *Cosmography and Geography in Two Parts* (London, 1683).

Wallis, Helen, ed. *Carteret's Voyage Round the World 1766–1769* (Cambridge, 1965).

———. *The Maps and Text of the Boke of Idrography Presented by Jean Rotz to Henry VIII* (Oxford, 1981).

[Walter, Richard, and Robins, Benjamin]. *A Voyage Round the World in the Years MDCCXL, I, II, III, IV by George Anson* (London, 1748).

Welbe, John. *An Answer to Captain Dampier's Vindication* (London, [1708]).

[Whatley, Stephen]. *A Complete System of Geography* (London, 1747).

Williams, Glyndwr, ed. *Documents Relating to Anson's Voyage Round the World 1740–1744* (London, Navy Records Society, 1967).

Williamson, J.A., ed. *The Observations of Sir Richard Hawkins* (London, 1933).

Wilson, James, ed. *Mathematical Tracts of the Late Benjamin Robins, Esq: Fellow of the Royal Society and Engineer-General to the Honourable the East India Company* (London, 1761).

Wright, I.A., ed. *Documents Concerning English Voyages to the Spanish Main, 1569–1580* (London, 1932).

[Young, John]. *An Affecting Narrative of the Unfortunate Voyage and Catastrophe of His Majesty's Ship Wager* (London, 1751).

iii) Newspapers and Periodicals

The following newspapers in the Burney Collection, British Library, were found useful:

1711: *Daily Courant*; *Post Boy*; *London Gazette*; also Daniel Defoe's *Review of the State of the British Nation*

1744: *London Daily Advertiser*; *General Advertiser*; *London Evening Post*; *Daily Post*; *Penny London Morning Advertiser*; *The Universal Spectator*

1748–9: *London Daily Advertiser*; *General Advertiser*; *London Evening Post*

Of the periodicals of the period, *The Gentleman's Magazine* contained much of relevance, especially vols 12 (1742), 13 (1743), 19 (1749).

Secondary Works

Adams, Percy G. *Travelers and Travel Liars 1660–1800* (Berkeley and Los Angeles, 1962).

Alsop, J.D. 'A Darien Epilogue: Robert Allen in Spanish America, 1698–1707', *The Americas*, 43 (1986), pp. 197–201.

Andrews, Kenneth R. *Drake's Voyages* (London, 1967).

————. 'The Aims of Drake's Expedition of 1577–1580', *American Historical Review*, 73 (1968), pp. 724–41.

————. 'Beyond the Equinoctial: England and South America in the Sixteenth Century', *Journal of Imperial and Commonwealth History*, 10 (1981), pp. 4–24.

————. *Trade, Plunder and Settlement: Maritime Enterprise and the Genesis of the British Empire, 1480–1630* (Cambridge, 1984).

Baer, Joel H. 'William Dampier at the Crossroads: New Light on the "Missing Years", 1691–1697', *International Journal of Maritime History*, 8 (1996), pp. 97–117.

Batten, Charles L., Jr. 'Literary Responses to the Eighteenth-Century Voyages', in Howse, *Background to Discovery*, pp. 128–59.

Baugh, Daniel. *British Naval Administration in the Age of Walpole* (Princeton, 1965).

————. 'Seapower and Science: The Motives for Pacific Exploration', in Howse, *Background to Discovery*, pp. 1–55.

Bradley, Peter T. *The Lure of Peru: Maritime Intrusions into the South Sea, 1598–1710* (London, 1989).

————. 'Narborough's Don Carlos', *Mariner's Mirror*, 72 (1986), pp. 465–75.

Broc, Numa. *La Géographie des Philosophes: Géographies et Voyageurs Français au XVIIIe-Siècle* (Paris, 1974).

Bromley, J.S. 'Outlaws at Sea, 1660–1720: Liberty, Equality and Fraternity among the Caribbean Freebooters', in Frederick Krantz, *History from Below: Studies in Popular Protest and Popular Ideology in Honour of George Rudé* (Berkeley and Los Angeles, 1992).

Burg, B.R. *Sodomy and the Pirate Tradition* (New York, 1984).

Burney, John. *A Chronological History of the Voyages and Discoveries in the South Sea or Pacific Ocean* (London, 1803–17).

Carpenter, Kenneth J. *The History of Scurvy and Vitamin C* (Cambridge, 1986).

Carswell, John. *The South Sea Bubble* (2nd edn, Stroud, Glos., 1993).

Case, Arthur E. *Four Essays on Gulliver's Travels* (Princeton, 1995).

Chope, R. Pearse. 'New Light on Sir Richard Grenville', *Trans. of the Devonshire Association*, 49 (1917), pp. 210–82.

Collingridge, George. *The Discovery of Australia* (Sydney, 1895).

Cook, Warren L. *Flood Tide of Empire: Spain and the Pacific Northwest, 1543–1819* (New Haven, 1973).

Cummins, John. *Francis Drake: The Lives of a Hero* (London, 1995).

Dahlgren, E.W. *Les Relations commerciales et maritimes entre la France et les côtes de l'Océan Pacifique au commencement du XVIIIe siècle*, I (Paris, 1909).

Dening, Greg. *Mr Bligh's Bad Language: Passion, Power and Theatre on the Bounty* (Cambridge, 1992).

Dermigny, Louis. *La Chine et l'Occident: Le Commerce à Canton au XVIIIe Siècle 1719–1833* (Paris, 1964).

Dunmore, John. *French Explorers in the Pacific*, I, *The Eighteenth Century* (Oxford, 1965).

Earle, Peter. *The World of Defoe* (London, 1976).

———. *The Sack of Panama* (London, 1981).

Edwards, Philip. *The Story of the Voyage: Sea-Narratives in Eighteenth-Century England* (Cambridge, 1994).

Eisler, William. *The Furthest Shore: Images of Terra Australis from the Middle Ages to Captain Cook* (Cambridge, 1995).

Elliott-Drake, Lady. *The Family and Heirs of Sir Francis Drake* (London, 1911).

Fausett, David. *Writing the New World: Imaginary Voyages and Utopias of the Great Southern Land* (Syracuse, NY, 1993).

———. *The Strange Surprizing Sources of Robinson Crusoe* (Amsterdam and Atlanta, GA, 1994).

———. *Images of the Antipodes in the Eighteenth Century: A Study in Stereotyping* (Amsterdam, 1994).

Fishman, Burton J. 'Defoe, Herman Moll and the Geography of South America', *Huntington Library Quarterly*, 36 (1973), pp. 227–38.

Frantz, R.W. *The English Traveller and the Movement of Ideas 1600–1732* (New York, 1968).

Furbank, P.N., and Owens, W.R. *Defoe De-Attributions: A Critique of J.R. Moore's Checklist* (London, 1994).

Geiger, John, and Beattie, Owen. *Dead Silence: The Greatest Mystery in Arctic Discovery* (London, 1993).

Gibson, Ross. *The Diminishing Paradise: Changing Literary Perceptions of Australia* (Sydney, 1984).

Green, J.N., ed. *Australia's Oldest Wreck*, British Archaeological Reports, Supplementary Series 27 (Oxford, 1977).

Greenblatt, Stephen. *Marvelous Possessions: The Wonder of the New World* (Chicago, 1991).

Hanna, Warren. *Lost Harbor* (Berkeley and Los Angeles, 1979).

Helgerson, Richard. *Forms of Nationhood: The Elizabethan Writing of England* (Chicago, 1992).

Helm, June. 'Matonabbee's Map', *Arctic Anthropology*, 26 (1989), pp. 29–30.

Holmes, M.G. *From New Spain by Land to the Californias 1519–1668* (Glendale, CA, 1963).

Howse, Derek, ed. *Background to Discovery: The Motives for Pacific Exploration from Dampier to Cook* (Berkeley and Los Angeles, 1990).

Jack, Jane H. 'A New Voyage Round the World: Defoe's *Roman à Thèse*', *Huntington Library Quarterly*, 24 (1960–1), pp. 323–36.

Jack-Hinton, Colin. *The Search for the Islands of Solomon 1567–1838* (Oxford, 1969).

James, W.T. 'Nostalgia for Paradise: *Terra Australis* in the Seveenth Century', in Ian Donaldson, ed., *Australia and the European Imagination* (Canberra, 1982).

Kenny, John. *Before the First Fleet: Europeans in Australia 1606–1777* (Kenthurst, NSW, 1995).

Lagarde, Lucie. 'Le Passage du Nord-Ouest et la Mer de l'Ouest dans la Cartographie Française du 18e Siècle, Contribution à l'Etude de l'Œuvre des Delisle et Buache', *Imago Mundi*, 41 (1989), pp. 19–43.

Lawrence, Christopher. 'Disciplining Disease: Scurvy, the Navy, and Imperial Expansion, 1750–1825', in David P. Miller and Peter H. Reill, eds., *Visions of Empire: Voyages, Botany and Representations of Nature* (Cambridge, 1996).

Lee, C.D. 'Alexander Selkirk and the Last Voyage of the *Cinque Ports* Galley', *Mariner's Mirror*, 73 (1987), pp. 387–9.

Legge, L.G. Wickham, 'Torcy's Account of Matthew Prior's Negotiations . . . in July 1711', *English Historical Review*, 29 (1914), pp. 525–32.

Lessa, William A. *Drake's Island of Thieves: Ethnological Sleuthing* (Honolulu, 1975).

Little, Bryan. *Crusoe's Captain: Being the Life of Woodes Rogers, Seaman, Trader, Colonial Governor* (London, 1960).

Lloyd, Christopher. 'Bartholomew Sharp, Buccaneer', *Mariner's Mirror*, 42 (1956), pp. 291–301.

Lloyd, Christopher, and Coulter, J.L.S. *Medicine and the Navy*, III, *1714–1815* (Edinburgh, 1961).

Lynam, Edward. *The Mapmaker's Art* (London, 1953).

Marchant, Leslie R. *France Australe* (Perth, 1982).

Markley, Robert. '"So Inexhaustible a Treasure of Gold": Defoe, Capitalism, and the Romance of the South Sea', in Jonathan Lamb, Robert P. Maccubin and David F. Morrill, eds, *The South Pacific in the Eighteenth Century: Narratives and Myths* (Baltimore, 1995).

Marner, Serena K. 'William Dampier and his Botanical Collections', in Howard Morphy and Elizabeth Edwards, eds, *Australia in Oxford* (Hertford, 1988).

Mathes, W. Michael, ed. *The Capture of the Santa Ana* (Los Angeles, 1969).

McLachlan, Jean O. *Trade and Peace with Old Spain 1667–1750* (Cambridge, 1940).

Moore, J.R. 'Defoe and the South Sea Company', *Boston Public Library Quarterly*, 5 (1953), pp. 175–88.

Morison, Samuel Eliot. *The Great Explorers: The European Discovery of America* (New York, 1978).

Nowell, C.E. 'The Discovery of the Pacific: A Suggested Change of Approach', *Pacific Historical Review*, 17 (1947), pp. 1–10.

Pack, S.W.C. *The Wager Mutiny* (London, 1964).

Palmeri, Frank, ed. *Critical Essays on Jonathan Swift* (New York, 1993).

Parker, John. *Books to Build an Empire* (Amsterdam, 1965).

Parry, J.H., ed., *The European Reconnaissance* (New York, 1968).

———. *The Discovery of South America* (London, 1979).

Polk, Dora Beale. *The Island of California: A History of the Myth* (Lincoln, NB, and London, 1995).

Prebble, John. *The Darien Disaster* (Harmondsworth, 1970).

Quinn, D.B., ed. *The Hakluyt Handbook* (London, 1974).

———. *Drake's Circumnavigation of the Globe: A Review* (Exeter, 1981).

Rawson, Claude. *Order from Confusion Sprung* (London, 1985).

———. ed. *The Character of Swift's Satire: A Revised Focus* (Cranbury, NJ, 1983).

Reinhartz, Dennis. 'Shared Vision: Herman Moll and his Intellectual Circle and the Great South Sea', *Terrae Incognitae*, 19 (1988), pp. 1–10.

Rich, E.E. *The History of the Hudson's Bay Company 1670–1870*, I (London, 1958).

Ritchie, Robert C. *Captain Kidd and the War against the Pirates* (Cambridge, MA, 1986).

Rogers, B.M.H. 'Dampier's Debts', *Mariner's Mirror*, 15 (1924), pp. 322–4.

———. 'Dampier's Voyage of 1703', *Mariner's Mirror*, 15 (1924), pp. 367–8.

———. 'Woodes Rogers's Privateering Voyage of 1708–11', *Mariner's Mirror*, 19 (1928), pp. 196–211.

Rogers, Pat. *Robinson Crusoe* (London, 1979).

Schilder, Günter. *Australia Unveiled. The Share of the Dutch Navigators in the Discovery of Australia* (Amsterdam, 1976).

———. 'New Holland: The Dutch Discoveries', in Williams and Frost, *Terra Australis to Australia*, pp. 83–116.

———. *Monumenta Cartographica Neerlandica*, III (Alphen aan den Rijn, Netherlands, 1990).

Schurz, W.L. *The Manila Galleon* (New York, 1939).

Secord, A.W. *Studies in the Narrative Method of Defoe* (Urbana, IL, 1924; repr. New York, 1963).

Seed, Patricia. *Ceremonies of Possession in Europe's Conquest of the New World, 1492–1640* (Cambridge, 1995).

Seeler, Oliver. 'Drake's Lost Harbour Found Again!', *The Map Collector*, 54 (Spring, 1991), pp. 32–4.

Seidel, Michael. *Robinson Crusoe: Island Myths and the Novel* (Boston, 1991).

Sharp, Andrew. *The Discovery of the Pacific Islands* (Oxford, 1960).

Shell, Richard. 'The Chamorro Flying Proa', *Mariner's Mirror*, 72 (1986), pp. 135–43.

Sherman, William H. *John Dee: The Politics of Reading and Writing in the English Renaissance* (Amherst, MA, 1995).

Shipman, Joseph C. *William Dampier: Seaman-Scientist* (Lawrence, KS, 1962).

Shirley, Rodney. *The Mapping of the World: Early Printed World Maps 1472–1700* (London, 1993).

Somerville, Boyle. *Commodore Anson's Voyage into the South Seas and Around the World* (London, 1934).

Spate, O.K.H. *The Pacific since Magellan*: I, *The Spanish Lake* (Canberra, 1979); II, *Monopolists and Freebooters* (London and Canberra, 1983).

———. ' "South Sea" to "Pacific Ocean" ', *Journal of Pacific History*, 12 (1977), pp. 205–11.

Sperling, J.G. *The South Sea Company: An Historical Essay and Bibliographical Finding List* (Boston, MA, 1962).

Starkey, David. *British Privateering Enterprise in the Eighteenth Century* (Exeter, 1990).

Steele, Colin. *English Interpreters of the Iberian New World from Purchas to Stevens. A Bibliographical Study 1603–1726* (Oxford, 1975).

Sugden, John. *Sir Francis Drake* (New York, 1990).

Taylor, E.G.R. *Tudor Geography 1485–1583* (London, 1930).

———. 'Master John Dee, Drake and the Straits of Anian', *Mariner's Mirror*, 15 (1929), pp. 125–30.

———. 'More Light on Drake', *Mariner's Mirror*, 16 (1930), pp. 134–51.

———. 'The Missing Draft Project of Drake's Voyage of 1577–80', *Geographical Journal*, 75 (1930), pp. 44–7.

Thrower, Norman, J.W., ed. *Sir Francis Drake and the Famous Voyage, 1577–1580* (Berkeley and Los Angeles, 1984).

Tooley, R.V. *California as an Island* (London, 1964).

Verner, Coolie. 'John Seller and the English Chart Trade in Seventeenth-Century England', in Norman J.W. Thrower, ed., *The Compleat Plattmaker* (Berkeley and Los Angeles, 1978), pp. 127–57.

Wagner, H.R. *Spanish Voyages to the Northwest Coast* (San Francisco, 1929).

———. 'Apocryphal Voyages to the Northwest Coast of America', *Proceedings of the American Antiquarian Society*, 41 (1931), pp. 179–234.

Wallis, Helen. 'The Cartography of Drake's Voyage', in Thrower, *Drake and the Famous Voyage*, pp. 121–63.

———. 'Edward Wright and the 1599 World Map', in Quinn, *Hakluyt Handbook* (London, 1974), pp. 69–73.

———. 'Java la Grande: The Enigma of the Dieppe Maps', in Williams and Frost, *Terra Australis to Australia*, pp. 39–82.

———. 'Further Comments on the "Lost Harbour" ', *The Map Collector*, 49 (Winter, 1989), pp. 34–47.

———. 'English Enterprise in the Region of the Strait of Magellan', in John Parker, ed., *Merchants and Scholars: Essays in the History of Exploration and Trade* (Minneapolis, 1965).

Ward, Christopher. *Imperial Panama: Commerce and Conflict in Isthmian America, 1550–1800* (Albuquerque, 1993).

Ward, Robert (Bob). 'Lost Harbour Found! The Truth about Drake and the Pacific', *The Map Collector*, 45 (Winter, 1988), pp. 2–9.

Watt, James. 'Commodore Anson's Circumnavigation (1740–1744): The Bequests of Disaster at Sea', *Transactions and Studies of the College of Physicians of Philadelphia*, Ser. 5, Vol. 7 (1985), pp. 223–38.

Williams, Glyndwr. *The British Search for the Northwest Passage in the Eighteenth Century* (London, 1962).

———. ' "The Inexhaustible Fountain of Gold": English Projects and Ventures in the South Sea, 1670–1750', in John E. Flint and Glyndwr Williams, *Perspectives of Empire* (London, 1973), pp. 27–53.

———. '"Far More Happier than We Europeans": Reactions to the Australian Aborigines on Cook's Voyage', *Australian Studies*, 19 (1981), pp. 499–512.

———. 'New Holland to New South Wales: The English Approaches', in Williams and Frost, *Terra Australis to Australia*, pp. 117–60.

———. 'Anson at Canton, 1743: "A Little Secret History"', in Cecil H. Clough and P.E.H. Hair, eds, *The European Outthrust and Encounter* (Liverpool, 1994), pp. 270–90.

———, and Frost, Alan, eds. *Terra Australis to Australia* (Melbourne, 1988).

Williamson, J.A. *The Age of Drake* (London, 1938).

Wilson, Kathleen. *The Sense of the People: Politics, Culture and Imperialism in England, 1715–1785* (Cambridge, 1995).

Woodward, R.L. *Robinson Crusoe's Island: A History of the Juan Fernández Islands* (Chapel Hill, NC, 1969).

Wroth, Lawrence C. *The Way of a Ship: An Essay on the Literature of Navigation* (Portland, ME, 1937).

Zahediah, Nuala. '"A Frugal, Prudential and Hopeful Trade": Privateering in Jamaica, 1655–89', *Journal of Imperial and Commonwealth History*, 18 (1990), pp. 145–68.

Index